GOD'S WORD
TO ISRAEL

GOD'S WORD
TO ISRAEL

JOSEPH JENSEN, O.S.B.

 Michael Glazier, Inc.
Wilmington, Delaware

ABOUT THE AUTHOR

Joseph Jensen, O.S.B., studied theology at Collegio Sant' Anselmo, Rome. He did his graduate Scripture work at the Pontifical Biblical Institute and at Catholic University where he is currently teaching. He is Executive Secretary of the Catholic Biblical Association, Managing Editor of *Old Testament Abstracts*. His publications include *Isaiah 1-39*, #8 of the OLD TESTAMENT MESSAGE series.

Third printing with revised Bibliographies, 1986.

This revised edition first published in 1982 by Michael Glazier, Inc., 1935 West Fourth Street, Wilmington Delaware 19805.

Library of Congress Catalog Card Number 68-14348.
International Standard Book Number 0-89453-289-8.
Cover art by Lillian Brulc.
Printed in the United States of America.

TO THE MEMORY

OF

MY FATHER

PREFACE

MANY WHO RECOGNIZE the abiding value of the Old Testament as God's word neglect its study because it seems such a difficult and forbidding field to enter. A difficult field it is, but one that is also fascinating and rewarding. The effort put into this challenging study is effort well-spent; even a modest degree of proficiency brings rich rewards. The aim of the present text is to set forth the central message of the Old Testament, as that is seen through Christian faith and in the light of modern research, and to help the beginner read it with profit. To this end, and to give as unified a treatment as possible, a combination of the historical, literary, and thematic approaches has been utilized.

No attempt has been made to cover every aspect of the Old Testament. To do this within a text of limited size would result in fragmentation and superficiality. Instead, the most important matters have been chosen and given the space and emphasis they deserve. While the text was prepared with the introductory Old Testament college course principally in mind, and this largely determined the depth and complexity of treatment, the first edition was sometimes employed with profit in more advanced courses; the chapter-end reading suggestions of the present edition have, therefore, been selected with an eye to meeting the needs of various levels.

The primary purpose of this second edition is the updating of the text and the bibliographies in the light of more recent biblical studies and archeological and historical findings, but there have been considerable changes in the overall structure, as well. The introductory materials that formed Chapters 3 and 4 of the first edition (revelation, inspiration, inerrancy, Canon of Scripture, and interpretation) have now been dealt with in appendices at the close of the book, sometimes with extensive alterations. I continue to believe that it is important to treat these matters in the introductory course, but the present arrangement makes for greater flexibility in the time and manner of treatment, as well as being less intrusive for those who wish to omit them. My own procedure is to give these materials as preassigned reading early in the course and then to spend one class period discussing them.

I wish to thank Michael Glazier, Inc., and, in particular, Mr. Glazier himself for allowing me to present this revision, and for the good help I have had in its preparation. Thanks are also expressed to St. Meinrad's Abbey for permission to quote from *Rome and the Study of Scripture* (7th ed., 1964).

Joseph Jensen, O.S.B.

CONTENTS

INTRODUCTION

Any book which has undergone five printings and now reappears in a new, revised edition must have a great deal going for it. Joseph Jensen has refined and perfected what was already an excellent tool for studying the Old Testament as *God's Word to Israel*.

First of all, as GOD's Word, the Old Testament is not only treated with reverence but is also accepted as a message, binding upon our conscience. We will be a different type of person, much better or unfortunately much worse, depending upon whether we accept and interact positively with God's word, or whether we deliberately ignore, playfully put it aside, or openly repudiate it. We must know, however, that "If we sin willfully after receiving the truth, there remains for us... a fearful expectation of judgment" (Heb 10:26).

Yet this same word, a "two-edged sword that penetrates and divides soul and spirit, joints and marrow and judges the reflections and thoughts of the heart" (Heb 4:12) can also be a source of new life and sweeter joy. We are told in Psalm 19 that the law or the word of the Lord acts in such a way as to be "refreshing the soul... giving wisdom to the simple... rejoicing the heart... sweeter also than syrup" (Ps 19:8-11).

In *God's Word to Israel* we are dealing with the Old Testament as God's WORD. This fact means at once that it is also a human dialogue. "Word" is communication, not monologue, and how it is heard becomes an important ingredient in what it means for later generations, namely, ourselves. Jensen has wisely allocated the speculative study of inspiration, inerrancy, and canonicity to appendices, and he deals with this word of communication between God and Israel realistically. He introduces the reader to the different styles of "listening" and communication in Israel's history—as priests and levites, as prophets and seers, as "schools" or disciples, transmitting earlier traditions. In one sense, the purpose of this book is to attune our ears to the human accents of God's WORD.

Throughout the Old Testament we live with ISRAEL, one single people through whom God's word reaches us. Israel was chosen "from all the nations on the face of the earth"; this was not because it was the largest of all nations, for, as the Scriptures bluntly confess, "you are really the smallest of all the nations"; rather "it was because the Lord loved you and because of his fidelity to the oath he had sworn to your ancestors" (Deut 7:7-8). We cannot ignore Israel and still expect to hear God's word. In fact, we cannot overlook Israel or the Jewish people today. Even in a context that speaks of the call of the gentiles and the division of Christianity from Israel, St. Paul declared that "God's gifts and his call of Israel are irrevocable" (Rom 11:29). Earlier he had written, "to them still belong the sonship, the glory, the covenants, and giving of the law, the worship and the promises" (Rom 9:4, RSV).

For many reasons we need the entire history of *God's Word to Israel.* What transpired during Israel's history in the tiny land of Palestine continues to exist even now across the wide extent of planet earth. To be a universal person today, to be prepared for God's word in the passage of our individual lives from youth to old age and death, the Old Testament prepares us well.

Let me add that Jensen's book, *God's Word to Israel,* is an enabling force that God's Word to Israel shall impact our lives with strength, joy and direction. With wise experience as a teacher, with the sure touch of a careful scholar, and with a clear mind and steady hand, he introduces us, challenges us, and most of all makes us a friend of God who speaks his word to Israel—to us—in the Old Testament. I am privileged to endorse this fine book, prepared principally for college courses yet well adapted to a variety of others, as well as for private study.

Carroll Stuhlmueller, C.P.
Professor of Old Testament Studies
Catholic Theological Union at Chicago

REFERENCES
AND ABBREVIATIONS

GENERAL

ANET: Pritchard, J., ed., *Ancient Near Eastern Texts Relating to the Old Testament*, 3rd ed.; Princeton, N.J.: Princeton University Press, 1975.

ATI: Anderson, G. W., ed., *Tradition & Interpretation: Essays by Members of the Society for Old Testament Studies.* Oxford: Clarendon Press, 1979.

AUOT: Anderson, B. W., *Understanding the Old Testament.* 3rd ed.; Englewood Cliffs, N.J.: Prentice-Hall, Inc., 1975.

BA: *The Biblical Archeologist.* The American Schools of Oriental Research. Cambridge, Mass., 1938—.

BAR: Wright, G. E., and D. N. Freedman, eds., *The Biblical Archeologist Reader.* Garden City, N.Y.: Doubleday & Company, Inc., 1961.

BAR 2:   Freedman, D. N., and E. F. Campbell, eds., *The Biblical Archeologist Reader, Vol. II.* Garden City, N.Y.: Doubleday & Company, Inc., 1964.

BAR 3:   Campbell, E. F., and D. N. Freedman, eds., *The Biblical Archeologist Reader, Vol. III.* Garden City, N.Y.: Doubleday & Company, Inc. 1970.

BARev: *Biblical Archaeology Review:* Washington, D.C.: Biblical Archaeological Society, 1975—.

BHI: Bright, J., *A History of Israel.* 3rd ed., Philadelphia: Westminster Press, 1981.

BTB: *Biblical Theology Bulletin.* Jamaica, N. Y.: St. John's University, 1971—.

CBQ: *The Catholic Biblical Quarterly.* The Catholic Biblical Association of America, Washington, D.C., 1939—.

DAS: The encyclical, *Divino Afflante Spiritu.*

Int: *Interpretation.* A journal of Bible and theology. Richmond, Va., 1947—.

JBC: Brown, R.E., J. A. Fitzmyer, and R. E. Murphy, eds., *The Jerome Biblical Commentary.* 2 vols. Englewood Cliffs, N.J.: Prentice-Hall, Inc., 1968.

JBL: *Journal of Biblical Literature.* Society of Biblical Literature. Decatur, Ga., 1881—.

MTES: McKenzie, J. L., *The Two-Edged Sword.* Milwaukee: Bruce Publishing Company, 1956.

NAB: The New American Bible translation.

NCE: *The New Catholic Encyclopedia.* 15 vols. New York: McGraw-Hill Book Company, Inc., 1967.

OTA: *Old Testament Abstracts.* Washington, D.C.: The Catholic Biblical Association of America, 1978—.

OTM: *Old Testament Message.* Wilmington, Del.: Michael Glazier, Inc., 1981—.

OTRG: *Old Testament Reading Guide.* Collegeville, Minn.: The Liturgical Press, 1965—.

PBS: *Pamphlet Bible Series.* New York: The Paulist Press, 1960—.

RSS: *Rome and the Study of Scripture.* 7th ed., St. Meinrad, Ind.: Abbey Press, 1964.

RSV: The Revised Standard Version.

TBT: *The Bible Today.* Collegeville, Minn.: The Liturgical Press, 1962—.

TD: Theology Digest. St. Louis: St. Louis University, 1953—.

VAI: de Vaux, R., *Ancient Israel,* tr. J. McHugh. New York: McGraw-Hill Book Company, Inc., 1961.

WBAK: Wright, G. E., *Biblical Archeology.* Rev. ed.; Philadelphia: Westminster Press, 1962.

WITOT: Weiser, A., *Introduction to the Old Testament,* D. M. Barton, London: Darton, Longman & Todd, 1961.

Books of the Bible[1]

Old Testament (OT)

Amos	Amos	Jonah	Jonah
Bar	Baruch	Josh	Joshua
1-2 Chr	1-2 Chronicles	1-2 Kgs	1-2 Kings
Cant	Canticle of Canticles	Lam	Lamentations
	(Song of Solomon)	Lev	Leviticus
Dan	Daniel	Mal	Malachi
Deut	Deuteronomy	1-2 Macc	1-2 Maccabees
Eccl	Ecclesiastes	Mic	Micah
Esth	Esther	Nah	Nahum
Exod	Exodus	Neh	Nehemiah
Ezek	Ezekiel	Num	Numbers
Ezra	Ezra	Obad	Obadiah
Gen	Genesis	Prov	Proverbs
Hab	Habakkuk	Ps(s)[2]	Psalm(s)
Hag	Haggai	Ruth	Ruth
Hos	Hosea	Sir	Sirach
Isa	Isaiah		(Ecclesiasticus)
Job	Job	1-2 Sam	1-2 Samuel
Jdt	Judith	Tob	Tobit
Jer	Jeremiah	Wis	Wisdom
Judg	Judges	Zeph	Zephaniah
Joel	Joel	Zech	Zechariah

New Testament (NT)

Acts	Acts of the Apostles	Mark	Mark
Col	Colossians	Matt	Matthew
1-2 Cor	1-2 Corinthians	Phil	Philippians
Eph	Ephesians	Phlm	Philemon
Gal	Galatians	1-2 Pet	1-2 Peter
Heb	Hebrews	Rev	Revelation
Jas	James		(Apocalypse)
1-3 John	1-3 John	Rom	Romans
John	John	1-2 Thess	1-2 Thessalonians
Jude	Jude	Titus	Titus
Luke	Luke	1-2 Tim	1-2 Timothy

[1]In scriptural references a semi-colon separates passages in different books or in different chapters of the same book; a colon separates verse from chapter; and a comma separates individual verses or groups of verses in the same chapter. Thus, Exod 12:3-10; 14:2-4, 7-8 would mean: Exodus, chapter 12, verses 3 to 10; Exodus, chapter 14, verses 2 to 4 and 7 to 8.

[2]The numbering of the psalms follows the *NAB*, which follows the Hebrew text. (Some Bible translations give the numbering according to the Septuagint [the Greek OT] as well. Where two numbers are given for a psalm, the larger is according to the Hebrew, the smaller according to the Greek.) *NAB* verse numbers also follow the Hebrew text; the verse numbers of the *RSV* will differ by one or two in many psalms.

1

Word of God
and People of God

ALTHOUGH WE TEND TO THINK of the Bible as the primary source of our instruction and faith, in point of fact the believing community and its liturgy comes first, both logically and chronologically. There is no room here for a "chicken or the egg" dispute: without the believing community there would never have been a Bible. Even our initial and ongoing instruction in the faith rests primarily on the community and its liturgy. Because the mystery of Christian redemption is a present, vital reality, the principal approach to it can never be through books or academic study. The modern renewal has helped us to appreciate better the role of the liturgy in making the mystery of redemption present to us and in making us sharers in it. But through the liturgical rites we not only worship God and actively share in the mystery of Christ; we are also instructed in the truths of salvation.

Baptism teaches us that the passage through the Red Sea is the beginning of redemption; through the Eucharist we learn that the death and resurrection of Christ is its climax. Thus the living Church brings us into contact with the truths of redemption and will continue to do so until the end of time. In this manner we would have been assured of knowledge of and participation in God's redemptive plan even if no word of the Bible had been written.

The mysteries we celebrate in the liturgy rest upon a succession of concrete events which occurred in time and place. In the Bible we have an inspired account of the manner of God's intervention so that we may be more fully and surely instructed in these things than we could be by the liturgy alone. Liturgy and Bible, of course, cannot be separated. Many parts of the Bible are drawn from the proclamation of the early liturgy, and the later liturgy draws heavily on the Bible.

God's redemptive work, the Christian believes, reached its climax in Jesus Christ, but it had its beginning long before His coming. Jesus

1

was not born into a vacuum, nor did He undertake a work for which there had been no preparation. The author of the Epistle to the Hebrews could sum up the relationship of the work of Christ to all that had preceded with the words: "In times past God spoke in fragmentary and varied ways to our fathers through the prophets; in this, the final age, he has spoken to us through his Son, whom he had made heir of all things and through whom he first created the universe" (Heb 1:1-2). God's revelation finds its perfect expression in one divine Word, but this Word was not spoken in isolation; it was preceded by the "fragmentary and varied" utterances that prepared the way for it. God's word is never barren nor does it return to Him empty, but, as a dynamic force, accomplishes all the things for which He sent it (Isa 55:10-11). So it is that the process of revelation through His Word does not issue in a series of static formulas, but in redemption, a people, a liturgy.

The central message of the *NT* is that the redemption which Israel had long expected has at last been accomplished. The events by which God called Israel, formed its expectation, and brought this expectation to fulfillment, make up the message contained in the Bible—not a list of dry propositions, not a compilation of abstract truths, but a series of events which take place in human history. The events by which God is believed to have revealed Himself and His plan for the redemption of fallen mankind is often called "salvation history" (*Heilsgeschichte*). The term supposes a God who is truly the Lord of history and whose will is to save.

Israel was unique among ancient peoples in many ways. One example of this uniqueness was that she looked for a golden age in the time to come rather than looking back with nostalgia to the times of the past. The explanation of this hope is to be found in her experience of God in the course of her history. The Israelites as a people first came to know their God in the events of the exodus, events which revealed Him as a God of deliverance, as a redeemer. The first impression was never to be effaced; later interventions simply confirmed it. The elation which followed the realization that they were a chosen people was tempered by further experience: He was a demanding God who would have Israel's total allegiance; He could punish by humiliation, defeat, even near-destruction, the tendency to presume upon the privilege of election.

This manner of treatment is instructive in showing that Israel was chosen not so much for privilege as for service. God's intention to save extended to all the earth and Israel was the instrument chosen for the realization of this plan. Israel sometimes considered herself alone the object of God's concern, and often the salvation hoped for was too closely identified with prosperity, untroubled possession of the land, and victory over enemies. The realization of the malice of sin, of the extent of man's helplessness in the face of it, and of his need for reconciliation with God—this was something which was acquired but slowly. Only at the close of the biblical revelation are we fully instructed in what total redemption means. But the essentials are already found in the *OT*: the call of Abraham takes on profound significance placed, as it is, after the pitiful accounts of man's early generations on earth (p. 62); the Book of Jonah and other parts of the *OT* indicate an awareness of Israel's mission to all men; and Deutero-Isaiah sees this mission to consist in reconciling mankind to God (p. 198).

Yet is was to Israel's credit that she was not too quickly stampeded into an overly spiritualized concept of redemption. She was too keenly aware (as many moderns are not) of the positive values of mankind's *human* nature, and of its involvement with the rest of creation and with society, to think of a redemption which consisted simply in the "salvation of the soul" but did not affect the whole person and its relation to these other things. No profound understanding of the redemption preached in the *NT* is possible without a grasp of the *OT* view of man and the human situation, for it is the background presupposed in the ministry of Jesus and in the teachings of Paul, John, and the other *NT* writers.

The same is true of many other aspects of *NT* teaching. Jesus came proclaiming the advent of the Kingdom of God, referred to Himself as Son of Man, was hailed as Son of David, and established a New Covenant in His blood. These and the many other concepts which we find on every page of the *NT* are intelligible only against their *OT* background. For this reason it must be stated flatly that there is no substitute for the study of the *OT* if we would understand the *NT*.

There is, of course, a discontinuity between the two Testaments. The reason for this is found in the manner in which God's plan was fulfilled. The terminus of the movement inaugurated and sustained by God's interventions was redemption—a redemption which was to be at once the supreme gift of God and Israel's accomplishment of her mission. Israel's mission was accomplished in the perfect response of obedience of Jesus Christ, Son of Abraham, Son of David, whom God sent as His ultimate gift and as the perfect revelation of His love for mankind. Thus expectation finds fulfillment and a new People of God is formed of those who, united to Christ in a new covenant, make His response their own. Yet there is also continuity with the past. The coming of Christ and the formation of His Church are, after all, the final acts of a drama of redemption begun when God called Abraham and promised to make of him a mighty nation and when He revealed Himself as a God of deliverance in leading Israel out of Egypt.

The *NT* is related to the *OT* as fulfillment to promise. This does not mean that we seek in every line of the *OT* a prophecy or a promise of the events recounted in the *NT*. Rather, we see in the *OT* numerous themes of the revelation of God's purpose and of the manner in which He is to fulfill it that ultimately find a satisfactory explanation only in the work of Christ. More important than prophecy, typology, or foreshadowing (although these *are* found) are the beginnings: trickles which appear as it were spontaneously, grow into streams, and finally converge into a river of mighty proportions. This origin, growth, and convergence of themes of redemption finds its term in the redemptive work of Christ, and something of the process is described in the "Redemptive Themes" of later chapters.

The Bible is salvation history and it is primarily from this point of view that it should be studied. None of the other possible approaches put us into contact so well with the central message of the Bible. The men who wrote it saw in the events they narrated the acts of God in history, and whoever would understand their teachings should approach the Bible with this in mind.

The qualification, *salvation* history, reminds us that the biblical authors were not interested in writing history for its own sake, but rather for the sake of recounting the activity of God in the events of Israel's history. For this reason the study of Israel's past as salvation history does not simply coincide with the study of Israel's past as scientific history. The scientific historian concerns himself with records of observable phenomena and from these he attempts to reconstruct the past. The activity of God, since it cannot be directly observed or measured, is outside the proper sphere of his discipline; if he affirms such activity, it is as an act of faith rather than as a scientific conclusion. (So, too, the unbelieving historian who denies the activity of God in Israel's history is not expressing a *scientific* conclusion but a judgment he has made on some other basis.) Even as historian, however, he may conclude that the political, military, and economic factors operative in Israel do not adequately explain the course of Israel's history and that an imponderable factor has been at work. Where are the Ammonites, the Moabites, the Edomites, the Philistines today? Who wins conquests for Marduk or offers sacrifice to Bel now? The nations near Israel and similar to her in many ways have disappeared, while Israel has not. The sons of Abraham are like the sands of the sea for number; and the faith of Israel has continued and developed and has profoundly affected the history of the world. The historian has the right to seek an answer, but he may well feel that only faith can supply it.

The men who wrote the Bible shared the conviction that Israel was unique. They recounted Israel's history in order to proclaim the wonders that God had worked within her. The events are not narrated coldly and objectively but are set within an interpretative framework that lets their significance, as understood by the biblical authors, shine through. While earlier generations accepted without question the very details of the biblical accounts in the belief that inspiration guaranteed their accuracy, this is no longer possible. In our day it is neither possible nor desirable to dispense with the critical investigation needed to learn what, in fact, happened. By bringing us closer to an objective account of the facts, scientific historical study helps us to see where event ends and interpretation begins, and thus helps us to understand the message of the Bible more fully.

Since the events and their interpretation come to us in a body of literature, it is necessary to employ all the means of literary investigation to seek out the Bible's teaching. The proper end of Scripture study should be not to learn something *about* the Bible, but to become as conversant as possible with the Bible itself—to become familiar with the texts and to understand them. To this end there is no alternative to studying the individual books. It will usually be helpful to know not only something of the historical circumstances in which a particular biblical book was written, but also something of the stages it passed through as it reached its present form, as these have been reconstructed by literary criticism, and the end for which the author wrote.

The order in which the books are studied is of some importance. In general the order adopted in this text traces the history of Israel without breaking up important literary complexes. Thus, because the deuteronomic history (p. 100) has a certain unity and carries us to the exile, no prophetic books are introduced before this group has been discussed, even though some of the prophetic books have their background in the monarchic period. The wisdom books are treated as a unit to simplify the overall presentation. This order of teatment corresponds in good measure to the traditional Jewish three-part division of the Canon of Scripture:

The Law (or Pentateuch or Five Books of Moses)
The Prophets
    Former Prophets (Joshua, Judges, Samuel, Kings)
    Latter Prophets (Isaiah, Jeremiah, Ezekiel, and "the twelve")
The Writings

This is a useful division to which we will have occasion to refer later (see also pp. 148, 270).

In studying the Bible we are not dealing with events remote from us, but with things which form the very fabric of our faith and our lives. St. Paul tells us that Abraham is the father of all who believe (Rom 4:12,16). That it is through faith rather than physical generation that we are grafted onto the holy stock of Israel in no way weakens our position. Israel's history has become our history, just as Israel's God has become our God. If today the pious Jew can say, "*I* came out of Egypt," so also can the Christian who believes that in Christ redemptive history reached its term.

The following chapter deals with matters introductory to the *OT* and useful for its study; the same is true of the materials found in the appendices at the end of the text, which could well be reviewed at this point. But the reader eager for the content of the *OT* itself has the option of proceeding at once to Chapter 3, with its brief geographical and historical survey, and to Chapter 4, on the composition of the Pentateuch.

READING SUGGESTIONS

Anderson, B. W., ed., *The Old Testament and Christian Faith.* New York: Herder and Herder, 1969.

Barton, J., *Reading the Old Testament. Method in Biblical Study.* Philadelphia: Westminster Press, 1984.

Harrington, D., *Interpreting the Old Testament. OTM*, Vol. 1.

Pannenberg, W., *Theology and the Kingdom of God.* Philadelphia: Westminster Press, 1969.

Rogerson, J., ed., *Beginning Old Testament Study.* Philadelphia: Westminster Press, 1982.

Westermann, C., ed., *Essays on Old Testament Hermeneutics.* tr. J. L. Mays. Richmond: John Knox Press, 1963.

Wolff, H. W., *The Old Testament: A Guide to Its Writings*, tr. K. R. Crim. Philadelphia: Fortress Press, 1973.

Fretheim, T. E., "The Old Testament in Christian Proclamation," *Word & World* 3 (1983) 223-230.

Murphy, R. E., "History, Eschatology, and the Old Testament," *Continuum* 7 (1970) 583-93.

_____, "Christian Understanding of the Old Testament," *TD* 18 (1970) 320-32.

_____, and C. Peter, "The Role of the Bible in Roman Catholic Theology," *Int* 25 (1971) 78-94.

Stevenson, W. T., "History as Myth: Some Implications for History and Theology," *Cross Currents* 20 (1970) 15-28.

For an excellent annotated survey of the most useful tools for Bible study, see J. A. Fitzmyer, *An Introductory Bibliography for the Study of Scripture* (Rev. ed.; Subsidia biblica 3; Rome: Biblical Institute, 1981).

Highly to be recommended is the practice of consulting a reliable Bible dictionary on key *OT* terms; note especially the following:

Achtemeier, Paul J., ed., *Harper's Bible Dictionary.* San Francisco: Harper & Row, 1985.

Bauer, J. B., ed., *Sacramentum verbi; an Encyclopedia of Biblical Theology,* New York: Herder & Herder, 1970.

Botterweck, G. J., *Theological Dictionary of the Old Testament.* Grand Rapids: Eerdmans, 1974—.

Buttrick, G. A., ed., *The Interpreter's Dictionary of the Bible*, 4 vols. New York: Abingdon Press, 1962. (See following.)

Crim, K., ed., *The Interpreter's Dictionary of the Bible: Supplementary Volume.* Nashville: Abingdon, 1976.

Hartman, L. F., tr. and rev., *Encyclopedic Dictionary of the Bible.* New York: McGraw-Hill Book Company, Inc., 1963.

McKenzie, J. L., *Dictionary of the Bible.* Milwaukee: The Bruce Publishing Company, 1965.

2

Modern Study of the Bible

PERHAPS THE ONE ASPECT of modern Bible study that sets it off from that of earlier ages is the deeper recognition and appreciation of the human element of the Bible. As long as the Bible was *in practice* regarded almost solely from the viewpoint of its divine origin, not enough attention was paid to its human origin and the light this sheds on its meaning. One recalls, for instance, the words of St. Gregory: "Most superfluous it is to inquire who wrote these things—we loyally believe the Holy Spirit to be the author of the book. He wrote it who dictated it; He wrote it who inspired its execution."[1] But while the believer affirms the divine origin of the Scriptures, he or she also recognizes the incarnational aspect of all phases of God's redemptive plan. The Christian sees the supreme revelation of God's love and nature in one who was truly man, who in very fact shared our human nature, whom St. John could describe as "what we have seen with our eyes, what we have looked upon and our hands have handled" (1 John 1:1).

More to the point then, are the words of Pius XII: "For as the substantial Word of God became like to men in all things, 'except sin,' so the words of God, expressed in human language, are made like to human speech in every respect, except error."[2] In order to understand what God intends to say to us in the words of the Bible, therefore, it is necessary to understand what its human authors intended to say to their contemporaries. To read their words "in context" is to see them in the human condition in which they were produced.

Many lines of modern investigation have conspired to underline the human element of the Bible. Chief among these have been literary

[1] *Praefatio in Job,* n. 2; *RSS* 25.
[2] *Divino Aflante Spiritu,* par. 37; *RSS* 98.

7

criticism, archeology, and studies in ancient literature, languages, and cultures. It will be necessary to say a few words about each of these.[3]

LITERARY CRITICISM

By literary criticism is meant the scientific investigation of the vocabulary, style, content, historical allusions, etc., of a literary piece in order to determine its place of origin, the time of its composition, its author, the sources he used, and the stages by which it reached its present state. A famous example of literary criticism was its use in 1439 by Lorenzo Valla, priest and later member of the Papal Curia. Valla proved that the Donation of Constantine was a forgery contrived some four centuries after the time of Constantine. Literary criticism did not begin with Valla, for it is indeed an ancient art. Yet the Renaissance, combining an emerging scientific objectivity with a keen interest in the study of the ancient classics, was a propitious time for its development.

The intensive use of literary criticism in biblical studies did not follow at once. The Bible, regarded primarily as a divine composition, was considered to be above such human investigation. However, the 18th-century Enlightenment put an end to such scruples on the part of many; characterized as it was by rationalism, it tended to look upon the Bible as a purely human document and to investigate it as such. The results of such investigations were often tinged with rationalistic prejudices. For a long time orthodox faith, both Catholic and Protestant, continued to resist such human incursion into what it considered the sphere of the divine, but the movement was irreversible. Today, however, literary criticism as a tool for understanding the Bible, is seen for the blessing it is, and no modern Scripture study is possible without it. We can now learn much about the human situation in which the books of the Bible were written and understand better what the men who wrote them wanted to say. For example, it is now possible to establish that the Book of Daniel is apocalyptic rather than prophetic, that it was written during the 2nd century B.C. rather than during the Babylonian Exile, and that it was intended to strengthen and console Jews suffering religious persecution around the time of the Maccabean uprising (p. 252). This both makes the book more intelligible and enables us to solve difficulties that inevitably accompanied the earlier (incorrect) understanding of its nature, origin, and purpose.

Literary investigation is often carried a step further in the approach called Form Criticism (*Formgeschichte, Gattungsgeschichte*). Few

---

[3]Other branches of science have exercised *indirect* influence on Bible study. For example, geology, anthropology, and paleontology, by establishing a different version of the origin of the earth, of life, and of mankind than that derived from the early chapters of Genesis, have forced believers to reexamine these texts. The net result has been a deeper understanding of the Bible.

books of the Bible were composed at one time, in one place, by one author; most of them are the result of a combination of earlier oral traditions or literary pieces which had independent existences prior to their incorporation into the final composition. Form Criticism attempts to isolate these pieces, to classify them according to literary form (p. 284), to determine the life situation (*Sitz im Leben*) in which they arose, and to reconstruct the process by which they came from their original state to that in which they are now found. This method was first used by Hermann Gunkel and applied especially to the Pentateuch and the Psalms. The approach has revolutionized the study of the Psalms (p. 223). Form Criticism has also been employed to good effect on poetic passages in the historical books, on genealogies, name lists, and short narratives. In some biblical materials the use of Form Criticism may build upon the previous employment of Source Criticism (*Quellengeschichte*), which attempts to determine from what traditions, written or oral, longer compositions are drawn. This is of special importance in the study of the Pentateuch (see Chapter 4) and the synoptic gospels. And Form Criticism often leads to the use of Redaction Criticism (*Redaktionsgeschichte*), the attempt to view the smaller unity within the larger source in which it is found; this helps reveal the purpose, characteristic ideas, and theology of the editor (redactor) in weaving these smaller unities into a longer, more or less unified composition—a process which may have been highly creative and made him more an author than an editor. (Again, see Chapter 4 and the relevance this has for the four source-traditions discussed there.)

Finally, it is important not to lose sight of the woods for the trees; that is, our investigation of the individual books of the Bible and their parts ought always to be carried out with an awareness of the whole Canon of Scripture. While the prehistory of the parts that make it up can be very instructive, the meaning it should have for us here and now will best emerge when we view it in the context of the whole Bible. The Spirit-guided believing community is responsible for what has been included in the Canon and for the arrangement of its parts, and this final stage ought to yield its deepest meaning to our study and meditation.

ARCHEOLOGY

Archeological investigations have also contributed to Bible study by supplying information about the ancient Near East, the historical context in which the Bible was written. The net result has been to make the human dimension of the Bible more intelligible. The modern, scientific method of archeology is usually dated from Sir Flinders Petrie's six-week dig at Tell el-Hesi (probably the biblical Eglon) in 1890. Many valuable finds had been made before that, but more could have been learned and errors avoided if a truly scientific method had been employed. An illustration of this was Heinrich Schliemann's celebrated investigation at ancient Troy. He did indeed prove that Hissarlik was the site of the city immortalized in Homer's *Iliad*, and he recovered a fabulous treasure. We know now, however, that in digging down to the lowest level of the mound, he was, in fact, investigating a settlement far more ancient than Homer's Troy and that the treasure he recovered had been buried long before the King Priam of the *Iliad* was born. More regrettably, in digging to the lowest level of the mound, Schliemann destroyed the levels above without adequate examination or record, thus obliterating the traces of the city he sought to investigate.

THE SCIENTIFIC TECHNIQUE OF ARCHEOLOGY. Sir Flinders Petrie brought to Palestine ten years of experience in Egyptian archeology and a respect for pottery as a means of establishing chronology. At the outset he recognized that the strata to be seen along the side of the mound represented successive settlements on the spot, and the technique of stratigraphy was born. Petrie carefully noted the pottery characteristic of each level and used it as a means of dating the various levels. The progression of forms of pottery made it possible to establish a relative chronology (i.e., the time relationship of the levels to one another); whenever it was possible to date a particular level, there was a basis for absolute chronology (i.e., the date to be assigned to each level). The techniques of stratigraphy and pottery dating are essential for modern scientific excavation.

In order to understand the significance of these techniques, one should recall the manner in which the ancient mounds were formed. The site of a city is usually chosen because of its favorable situation: defensible position, water supply, proximity to commercial routes and arable land, etc. These advantages usually remain constant, and so the same site may be used again and again even after previous populations have been destroyed or forced to evacuate. In ancient times the debris of an earlier population would not be cleared away in order to build again, but simply flattened enough to form the foundation for new buildings. Sometimes nature did most of the leveling by eroding the soft building materials usually employed (mud, mud brick, or baked brick). Each successive occupation would form a new layer above the preceding one; but preserved beneath it were remains of the earlier city.

The artificial mound which results from successive layers of occupation is called a *tell*, and it contains within itself a veritable history of the site. The tell retains not only traces of the structures of each level, but also some of the artifacts produced or imported by the men who lived there. One of the most important of these artifacts is pottery. In an age before the blessings of glass bottles, tin cans, cardboard boxes, and plastic bags, vessels of baked clay were used to hold just about every-

Figure 1. *In the dry climate of Egypt even papyrus sometimes survived for thousands of years. This picture of an Egyptian woman applying make-up is preserved on a papyrus sheet from the 2nd millennium B.C. Courtesy of the Soprintendenza Egittologia, Turin, Italy.*

thing. Such vessels were easily broken and the resultant pieces (potsherds) now litter every level of occupation after the time of the invention of pottery. New forms of pottery, new methods of production, and new ways of decoration constantly replaced the old. Since certain types of pottery can be recognized as characteristic of a given period and of no other, the sequence of occupation can be determined even when no clear stratification is observable.

Sometimes the same type of pottery is found in widely separated localities (especially when it is of sufficient quality for export), and so the levels of various sites can be correlated. Once a particular type of pottery has been dated (usually by its association with something which has already been dated on other grounds), it can be used as an index to the age of a level wherever it is found. Needless to say, almost any item uncovered will be helpful in reconstructing the daily lives of the people who dwelt at a given place and time. Fishhooks, arrow heads, sickles, needles, and so forth, indicate the various occupations that were carried on, while objects that have obviously been produced elsewhere are an index to commercial relations.

Modern excavation is carried out with exactitude and care. Great quantities of earth are sifted so that all objects, even the tiniest, may be recovered, and care must be taken to separate mud walls from accumu-

lated dirt—obviously a tricky business. When a fragile item is uncovered, the last stages of digging may be done with knife blade and
brush. In order to learn about diet, archeologists have hunted for
charred cereal grains on ancient hearths. Robert Braidwood, in fact,
seeking information on the transition from food gathering to food
production, has utilized *impressions* of cereal grains on a clay floor of
about 10,000 years ago; microphotography of the finds for comparison
with modern domesticated and wild grains was part of the technique.

From such careful investigation of the material remains of the past a
great deal has been learned about the ancient Near East. It is now known
at what period there was a settled population in Transjordan, when
major cities in Canaan were destroyed and resettled, what pagan
temples in Canaan and Mesopotamia were like, and how the houses
of the poor compared with those of the rich in the days of Amos. The
broad histories of such important Palestinian cities as Jericho, Bethel,
Shechem, Gibeon, Hazor, Taanach, and Lachish can now be traced.
While these investigations often do strikingly confirm the accounts
found in the Bible (and occasionally raise problems), their purpose is
not primarily "to prove the Bible true." Archeology has shown the
historical reliability of many biblical narratives and thus helps establish
a basis for faith; but to demonstrate that in these events God has
revealed Himself or has acted, which is primarily what the Bible is
asserting and where we find the most essential "truth" of the Bible, lies
not in the province of scientific investigation.

LITERARY FINDS. The archeological finds discussed so far are classified
as non-literary. In addition, archeology has brought to light much of
the significant literature of the ancient Near East, and specialists in
the ancient Oriental languages have made it possible to decipher most
of the finds. Some texts of these dead civilizations had long been preserved among museum displays and on monuments of the past, but little
was known of their interpretation. It was only in 1822 that Champollion,
who had devoted his life to solving the mystery of Egyptian hiero-
glyphics, made significant progress in unlocking these ancient secrets.
The ancient languages of Mesopotamia have also yielded before the
determined efforts of scholars.

And these texts are being recovered in such abundance that many
of them have yet to be published and interpreted. At Mari alone more
than 20,000 tablets were unearthed. This city on the Euphrates was
already ancient when Abraham passed it on his way from Ur to Haran.
Letters from the mighty Hammurabi and other kings of antiquity
were found in its archives, as well as business documents and other
records. At Nuzi, a city in what is now Iraq, were unearthed thousands
of tablets which inform us about social customs of the world in which
Abraham moved. The palace of Ashurbanipal near Nineveh yielded
tens of thousands of tablets—a royal library in which were found the

Babylonian Epic of Creation (the *Enuma Elish*), the Gilgamesh Epic (which includes a Babylonian account of the great flood), and other mythological and religious texts. Still relatively new are the significant finds at Ebla (Tell Mardikh) in northern Syria, an important culture which flourished ca. 2400-2250 B.C. The thousands of tablets found there will take years to decipher, publish, and evaluate, but what has already emerged suggests exciting possibilities. About 20% of the texts are in the early Semitic idiom spoken at Ebla; they will shed much light on the development of Hebrew and other Semitic languages. And although the texts are from a period several centuries before Abraham, it is intriguing to note the frequent attestation of biblical names such as Eber, Ishmael, and Michael, and possibly even a shortened form of the divine name Yahweh. Sodom seems to be mentioned as a city then in existence. (For location of the archeological sites mentioned, see Figure 3, p. 23).

Inscriptions and tablets found in Asia Minor (especially at Bogazköy) tell the history, laws, customs, and myths of the Hittites whose mighty empire (ca. 1500-1200) was largely unknown until recent times. A chance find by a peasant at Ras Shamra in northern Syria led archeologists to the discovery of the ruins of Ugarit, an important city whose history stretched from the 5th or possibly 6th millennium B.C. to its final abandonment ca. 1200 B.C. On the basis of texts found there it is now clear that many poetic forms, images, and concepts from this Canaanite culture were adapted by *OT* writers to express their own beliefs. At Tell el-Amarna in Egypt have been found part of the archives of Amenophis III and Amenophis IV (Akhenaten). These "Amarna letters," mainly from Canaanite princes of the 14th century B.C., give information concerning conditions in Palestine at that time.

Texts from the period of Israel's monarchy have also been found in Palestine. One of the most interesting is the victory stele of Mesha, king of Moab, giving the Moabite version of the battle described in 2 Kings 3. At Samaria were found ostraca (inscribed potsherds) recording transactions from the days of Jeroboam II. A most exciting find were the "Lachish letters," ostraca written ca. 588 B.C. during the Babylonian siege which reduced Lachish, Jerusalem, and the rest of Judah. In Jerusalem itself has been found the inscription marking the completion of the 1,749 foot tunnel carved through solid rock in the days of King Hezekiah to bring water into the city (2 Kgs 20:20; 2 Chr 32:30).

This is but a brief summary of some of the better known finds.[4] These texts are important for the information they give concerning historical matters in the *OT* world, and for the light they bring to its literary background. They tell what the men of those times believed, how they worshiped, and how they expressed themselves. The net

---

[4]The interested reader can be directed to the rich literature on this subject as it appears in the "Archeology" section of the successive issues of *OTA*.

Figure 2.
*Ostraca might
be inscribed
with pictures as
well as texts. This
12th century ostracon
depicts Ramses III
smiting the foes of Egypt.
Courtesy of the Koninklijke
Musea voor Kunst en
Geschiedenis,
Brussels, Belgium.*

result has been, again, to illumine the human dimension of the Bible. Now we can see how the children of Israel fit into the world of their own times, how they used or adopted the literary procedures, and how they depended upon or reacted against the mores and customs of the peoples around them.

This greater understanding of the human element of the Bible has led to a deeper appreciation of the uniqueness of Israel's faith. From material remains we now know that the Temple of Jerusalem resembled both in floor plan and ornamentation others that have been excavated in neighboring regions. Yet while the pagan temple contained in its "holy of holies" a statue of the god to which the temple was dedicated, in Israel this most sacred room contained only the Ark of the Covenant to represent the throne of the invisible God, the Lord who is so transcendent that no image can represent Him. The same sort of contrast is verified in the literary findings. One scholar, speaking of Ugaritic writings, says: "To put it tritely, their ideas about men are distinctly more edifying than those about gods."[5] Examples from other places would not be hard to find; one thinks of Ishtar's attempt to seduce Gilgamesh, or the bickering among the gods after the great Deluge in the Epic of Gilgamesh (*ANET*, 83-84, 95). Nowhere in these tales does one find a sustained resemblance to the moral, stern, and demanding, yet compassionate, merciful, and saving God who appears on every page of the Bible. So much was Israel a part of its world that they used the same literary forms and even told the same stories; yet their conception of God is so much a stranger in this same world as to lend credence to the claim of special revelation.

DEAD SEA SCROLLS—TEXTUAL CRITICISM. This brief account of the recovery of the past would not be complete without reference to the Dead Sea Scrolls. In 1947 manuscripts stored away by the community of Qumran began coming to light. These men were Jewish Essene monks who lived in caves among the mountains near the northwestern shore of the Dead Sea and met for meals and worship in the buildings at Qumran. The Qumran community endured from the 2nd century B.C. to 68 A.D.; their beliefs and writings, therefore, are valuable background for understanding the Palestine of Jesus' day and the milieu from which the *NT* emerged.[6] Since the Qumran writings pertain to the background of the *NT* rather than of the *OT*, no extended treatment of them will be given here; however, a word about the importance of the Qumran finds for the *OT* is in order.

First of all, they form part of the historical background for the last period of the *OT*. Historically the Qumran group emerged partly as a protest against the degenerate policies of the Maccabean warriors who freed the Jews from Syrian persecution in the 2nd century B.C. Secondly, Qumran writings, such as their commentaries and testimonia,[7] show how certain *OT* texts were being interpreted by some at the end of the *OT* period. Thirdly, the distribution of texts and fragments of *OT* books provides data on the formation of the Jewish Canon of Scripture. Finally, and most important, is the use of *OT* manuscripts found at Qumran for textual criticism.

Textual criticism is the scientific endeavor to recover the primitive, original reading of a literary passage or book by the comparison and evaluation of early manuscripts and translations. The need for textual

---

[5]H. L. Ginsberg, "Ugaritic Studies and the Bible," *BAR 2* 42.

[6]The recurrent suggestion that the scrolls substantially alter our understanding of Christian origins has no basis in fact. For a reply by an expert in the Qumran material, see P. W. Skehan, "Capriccio Allegro or How Not to Learn in Ten Years," *The Christian Century* 83,40 (Oct. 5, 1966), 1211-13.

[7]Strings of *OT* quotations, mainly prophetic texts, to which they attributed special significance.

criticism springs from the fact that the original autograph manuscripts of the *OT* books disappeared long before the end of the *OT* period; the texts were preserved only in the numerous copies made from the original, some more exact than others. Manuscripts often vary from one another and so it is necessary to compare them in order to establish the best, that is the original, reading. This problem is not peculiar to the *OT* but exists for the *NT*, the Greek and Latin classics, and for other ancient writings as well.

The problem is especially acute for the *OT*, however. Early in the Christian era, Jewish scholars standardized the *OT* texts and systematically eliminated most of the variant readings. There was also the Jewish custom, born of respect for the sacred text, of burying manuscripts that were worn out and no longer usable. The result was that very few *OT* Hebrew manuscripts remained from before the 10th century A.D. and that even these represented the standardized (Masoretic) tradition. As a consequence, textual criticism had little to work with other than ancient translations—mainly the Greek, Syriac, and Aramaic versions. Since the discovery of the Qumran scrolls, however, we have substantial parts of the *OT* in Hebrew manuscripts far older than any others known to scholars; some of them can be dated as early as the 2nd century B.C. That these manuscripts are ancient does not automatically make them better witnesses to the original than the Masoretic text, but at least they make it possible to go back to an earlier stage than the official fixation of the text.

Literary criticism began to exercise a decisive influence in Scripture studies before archeology, and the latter came along as a welcome corrective. Exercising their discipline with no outside control and rejecting the reliability of the biblical traditions, extremists among literary critics sometimes produced ingenious but arbitrary reconstructions of Israel's early faith and development. Their extreme positions repelled many who revere the Bible as the word of God, with the result that the latter rejected even the valid insights of the critics.

The advent of more precise information about the ancient Near East has helped these divergent positions move closer together. Objective evidence has both curtailed the speculations of the extreme critics and forced the more conservative to see the human element of the Bible, to recognize the fact of development in Israel's faith, and to read each text against its historical background. The Bible is no longer viewed as a flat surface on which every statement may be read as objectively exact from the point of view of history, science, theology, and ethics. It is seen, rather, as the progressive record of the work of God, incarnate in the history of a people.

BIBLICAL THEOLOGY

The view just described is not born of scientific studies alone, but rather of the happy marriage of faith and science. This brings us to another aspect of modern Bible studies, Biblical theology. An approach to Scripture which contents itself with archeological, historical, linguistic, and literary analysis alone is incomplete, sterile, and, to the believer, almost irrelevant. Studies which do not ultimately contribute to our understanding of the work of God have lost sight of the Bible as the word of God. Fortunately, there is today an abundance of excellent works which combine the valid insights of earlier ages with modern advances to produce syntheses that place before us more clearly than ever before the riches of Scripture.

Three special tendencies characterize such studies: respect for the unity of the biblical revelation; presentation of the message of the Bible in the categories of thought found in Scripture itself; and recognition of the dialogue aspect of scriptural revelation. A few words about each of these follow.

UNITY. The conviction that there is a unity to the biblical message is not new, of course; it is already apparent in the passage of Heb 1:1-2, quoted in Chapter 1, and in many other *NT* passages which see the *OT* fulfilled in the Christian dispensation. It is also found in the typological interpretation of the *OT* by the early Church Fathers, and in many other Christian studies. The sense of the unity of the biblical message has often been neglected, however, especially when Scripture texts were employed mainly for apologetic purposes, without regard for their relation to the total context ("proof text" method), or when study proceded almost exclusively by way of dissection and literary analysis. A complete approach will be more holistic, regarding both the development of each area throughout the Bible, from its beginning to its completion (diachronic), and the complex of related ideas or concepts at any given time (synchronic). As pointed out earlier, proper emphasis needs also to be given to the Canon of Scripture as a whole and to individual parts as they relate to the whole Canon. (See references to Childs in chapter-end bibliography.)

BIBLICAL THOUGHT PATTERNS. Systematic speculative theology will always, must always, attempt to transpose the contents of revelation into abstract philosophical terms and categories in order to carry out the functions proper to that discipline. Yet there are disadvantages in this. There is the danger that the new mode of expression will be simply equated with the old, that the rich biblical thought will be reduced to abstractions, and that, in presenting the contents of the Bible to the faithful, philosophical terms will be used which convey little or nothing to them. All of these things have, in fact, occurred, at one time or another. A better approach is to present the biblical message in a manner closer to its original formulation in Scripture.

R. A. F. MacKenzie defines biblical theology as "the science which studies divine revelation as it is recorded in the inspired Word of God and combines it into an intelligible body of doctrine according to the concepts and patterns of the inspired writers."[8] There is no doubt that the concepts and thought patterns of the men of the ancient Near East differ from those of modern western men, and that this causes a difficulty in understanding the biblical authors. One solution is to try to transpose their thoughts into our manner of expression; the other is to try to understand their thought patterns and their manner of expression "from within," as it were. An analogy from the field of languages may be helpful. If we wish to know the content of a composition written in a foreign language, we may consult a translation, or we may learn the language in which it is written. The first course may be simpler, but the second is far more satisfactory.

Any attempt to explain in a few lines, the difference between ancient Semitic thought patterns and modern western thought will necessarily involve some oversimplification. We may begin, however, by saying that modern western thought owes much to the Greek philosophers and love for precision and logic. Thus our thought tends to be discursive, abstract, and linear, attempts to arrive at universal conclusions by abstraction, and expresses its conclusions with mathematical precision by exact definition. Semitic thought, on the other hand, is concrete, existential, and intuitive, expresses itself in parallelism, antithesis, and paradox, and attempts to evoke a picture, a mood, a response. Another approach would be to contrast the syllogism (e.g., "all men are rational animals; Peter is a man; therefore Peter is a rational animal") with the parable ("The kingdom of heaven is like a king who made a wedding feast for his son . . ."). The syllogism arrives at a conclusion which is stated clearly and unambiguously so that it can be grasped. The parable, by refusing to classify and define, leaves reality in all the richness of its complexity so that the implications may be contemplated. It is structured so as to say something to one's innermost self and to lead to a decision, a choice.

The refusal of Semitic thought to deal in abstractions is not necessarily a fault. St. Thomas tells us that abstraction is necessary because of the weakness of the created human intellect; it cannot know all of reality in its complexity and individuation and so it forms universal concepts with which to work. But other approaches to reality are possible. The Semite deals with the concrete and particular because it embodies a certain portion of total reality and can be used to evoke far more than it actually is, without the weakening implied in abstraction or mere symbolism. The concrete reality does serve as a symbol, but it puts us in touch with total reality in a way that abstraction or mere symbolism cannot. Concrete reality thus has a sacramental aspect.

Biblical theology also builds on an awareness of the content of specific biblical terms and concepts. The Hebrew words which are translated

---

[8]R. A. F. MacKenzie, "The Concept of Biblical Theology," *Studies in Salvation History*, ed. L. Salm (Englewood Cliffs, N.J.: Prentice-Hall, Inc., 1964), p. 36.

as "soul," "body," "spirit," "peace," "justice," "mercy," "love," and "salvation" have such different notions behind them than the English words used to render them that we can easily be misled. Again, some words, e.g., "blood," had for the biblical authors a special force and significance that they do not have for us; yet to be aware of this significance is often essential for understanding the Bible. The same is true of concepts (as distinct from specific words) that we hold partly in common with them, such as "life," "death," "covenant," and "kingship." An awareness of the meaning of terms and concepts[9] like these is necessary to a deep understanding of the message of Scripture.

DIALOGUE. Finally, biblical theology necessarily tends to engage the individual and to draw him into the drama of the Bible. The progressive unfolding of revelation through redemptive history is not a one-sided monologue but a dialogue: God speaks and man responds.

The response demanded is not simply believing what God has revealed, but rather a faith which consists in a total commitment of oneself to God's will and to God's plan. The purpose of God's plan is to call each person into the sphere of His saving work, to bring all into the People of God, and so to continue the effects of redemptive history in them until its consummation. This can only be done if men of every age make their own the "Amen" of Abraham, Moses, Isaiah, Jeremiah, as well as the "Amen" of Jesus. To enable us to say this "Amen" with full awareness of what it means can be one effect of biblical theology.

ECUMENISM

No discussion of modern biblical study would be complete without some reference to its ecumenical dimension. Indeed, it may be said that today's ecumenical movement owes more to biblical study than to any other cause. This is not the place to recount the steps by which Catholic and Protestant Scripture scholars moved from the suspicious, hostile, polemical post-Reformation attitude to the present irenic situation. But we may at least point out that the objectivity which necessarily resulted from the application of the scientific method to the study of Scripture eliminated much of the narrow, *a priori*, sectarian interpretation which had characterized Scripture studies in earlier centuries.

The cautious admonitions of the Church's teaching authority (the Magisterium) around the turn of the century during the modernist crisis helped preserve the purity of the Catholic faith; but they also had the effect of slowing the progress of the biblical investigations of Catholic scholars so that in many areas they became dependent upon

---

[9]Many of these will be discussed in the course of the following chapters. The habit of consulting good Bible encyclopedias on such terms is a rewarding and enriching one.

the studies of Protestants. A great advantage resulted from this, however, for in reading these works Catholic scholars came to esteem their authors as never before for their scholarly integrity and religious sincerity. Good will is infectious, and soon Protestants and Catholics became aware that the areas of agreement between them were far more extensive than the areas of disagreement, and that this fact deserved to be emphasized. There has been a comparable amelioration of relations between Christians and Jews in the area of Scripture study. Protestants, Catholics, and Jews use each other's works with far more regard to their quality and objective value than the religion of the author. Active collaboration on joint projects is now the norm.

READING SUGGESTIONS

JBC §70; 74. *MTES* 295-312. *WBA* 17-28.

Aharoni, Y., *The Archaeology of the Land of Israel.* Philadelphia: Westminster Press, 1982.

Boadt, L., *Reading the Old Testament: An Introduction.* New York: Paulist Press, 1984.

Caird, G. B., *The Language and Imagery of the Bible.* Philadelphia: Westminster Press, 1980.

Childs, B. S., *Biblical Theology in Crisis.* Philadelphia: Westminster Press, 1970.

_____, *Introduction to the Old Testament as Scripture.* Philadelpia: Fortress Press, 1979.

Cross, F. M., *Canaanite Myth and Hebrew Epic.* Cambridge: Harvard University Press, 1973.

Fischer, J. A., *How to Read the Bible.* Englewood Cliffs, N. J.: Prentice-Hall, 1981.

Freedman, D. N., and J. C. Greenfield, eds., *New Directions in Biblical Archeology.* Garden City, N.Y.: Doubleday & Company, Inc., 1971.

Habel, N., *Literary Criticism of the Old Testament.* Philadelphia: Fortress Press, 1971.

Hoppe, L. J., *What Are They Saying About Biblical Archaeology?* New York: Paulist Press, 1984.

Kenyon, K. M., *Archaeology in the Holy Land.* 5th ed.; Nashville: Nelson, 1985 (c1979).

Lance, H. D., *The Old Testament and the Archaeologist.* Philadelphia: Fortress Press, 1981.

Lohfink, G., *The Bible: NOW I Get It.* Garden City: Doubleday & Company, Inc., 1979.

Montet, P., *Egypt and the Bible*, tr. L. R. Keylock. Philadelphia: Fortress Press, 1968.

Teeple, H. M., *The Historical Approach to the Bible*. Evanston: Religion and Ethics Institute, 1982.

Birch, B. C., "Old Testament Theology: Its Task and Future," *Horizons in Biblical Theology* 6 (1984) iii-viii (and see rest of issue, given largely to biblical theology).

Collins, J. J., "The 'Historical' Character of the Old Testament in Recent Biblical Theology," *CBQ* 41 (1979) 185-204.

Craigie, P. C., "The Tablets from Ugarit and Their Importance for Biblical Studies," *BA Rev* 9 (5, 1983) 62-73.

Ginsberg, H. I., "Ugaritic Studies and the Bible," *BAR* 2 34-50.

Gray, J., "Recent Archaeological Discoveries and Their Bearing on the Old Testament," *ATI* 65-95.

Knierim, R., "Old Testament Form Criticism Reconsidered," *Int* 27 (1973) 435-68.

Lemaire, A., "Mari, the Bible, and the Northwest Semitic World," *BA* 47 (1984) 101-108.

Matthiae, P., "New Discoveries at Ebla. The Excavation of the Western Palace and the Royal Necropolis of the Amorite Period," *BA* 47 (1984) 18-32.

Millard, A. R., "The Practice of Writing in Ancient Israel," *BA* 35 (1972) 98-111.

Myers, E. M., "The Bible and Archaeology," *BA* 47 (1984) 36-40.

Pettinato, G., "Ebla and the Bible," *BA* 43 (1980) 203-216.

Skehan, P. W., "The Biblical Scrolls from Qumran and the Text of the Old Testament," *BAR* 3 240-53.

3

Panorama

IN THE CHAPTERS that follow, as we examine the various stages in the formation of the people and its book, the principal facts of Israel's history will be discussed in detail. Here, however, it seems good to give a bird's-eye view of the action as a whole, seen in its geographical setting. This will provide a frame of reference to unify later discussions. This presentation will be brief and simple and will avoid the critical problems that must be introduced later; basically it will be the uncomplicated story that leaps to the eye from the Bible itself.

Figure 3 shows the "Fertile Crescent," the region stretching from the Nile, along the Mediterranean coast, across Syria to Mesopotamia, and down to the Persian Gulf. Irrigation in the river valleys and rainfall on coastal and mountain regions account for the productivity of the crescent-shaped sweep of land. This is the scene of the *OT* drama. Palestine appears as hardly more than a postage stamp on the surface of our earth, yet its position is unique in many ways. It is at the juncture of three continents—Asia, Africa, and Europe; that this location was providential became clear when, from this little land, the gospel message went forth "even to the ends of the earth."

Palestine is located between Egypt and Mesopotamia, cradles of great world powers during much of *OT* history. The map alone, perhaps, does not indicate the extent to which Palestine was "between" these two regions; the Arabian Desert was virtually uncrossable, so that overland travel from Egypt and Arabia to Mesopotamia and Asia Minor or vice versa had to pass through Palestine. This was a mixed blessing. One result was that heavy commercial traffic brought possibilities of great profit (which a wise man such as Solomon could capitalize on), but another was a militarily strategic importance that was not matched by Israel's power as a nation. There were no great natural boundaries to give security to the powers in Egypt, Mesopo-

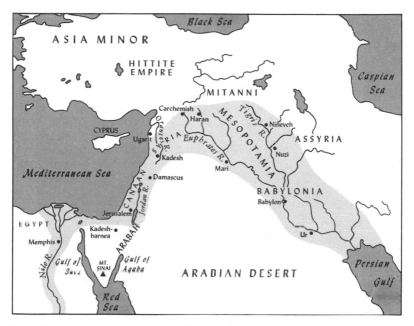

Figure 3. *The Fertile Crescent ca. 1500 B.C. Light shading indicates the areas made fertile by rainfall or irrigation.*

tamia, and Asia Minor, and so effective control of Palestine was necessary both for safety and as the key to expansion. The power struggle went on through the centuries. Now Assyria, now Babylonia, now the Hittites, now Egypt held the upper hand; warring armies crossed and recrossed the little land, and Palestine was often made a pawn of imperialistic policies. If Assyria or Babylonia dreamed of a world empire, the way to Egypt, often their most serious rival, lay through Palestine. Decisive battles between Egyptian armies and those of her northern foes took place, as often as not, at Megiddo, near Mt. Carmel (see Figure 4). At no time in her history, then, did Israel live in isolation, and much of the time she had a role to play in world politics.

The north-south orientation of Palestine is imposed not only by the desert on the east, but also by its terrain, as you can see in Figure 4. The Jordan Valley, running roughly north and south, is very deep—the surface of the Sea of Galilee is about 700 ft. below sea level and that of the Dead Sea about 1,290 ft. below sea level. This depression continues to the north in the rift between the Lebanon and Anti-Lebanon Mountains, and to the south in the Wadi Arabah, the valley which coaxes the Red Sea to extend the arm called the Gulf of Aqaba. Roughly parallel to the Jordan Valley are the Eastern Highlands, a string of hills that slope off to the east into the desert, and the Western Highlands, a string of hills that slope down to the Coastal Plain. East to west traffic is difficult, but important roads run north and south along the Eastern Highlands, the Western Highlands, and the Coastal Plain. The coastal road begins to cross to the east near Mt. Carmel, where the string of hills is broken between central and northern Palestine by the Plain of Mediggo (also called Plain of Esdraelon). The strategic importance of this passage accounts for the many decisive battles fought there;

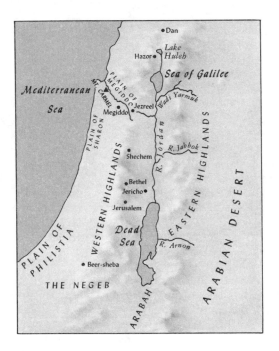

Figure 4.   *Palestine (Canaan).*

it is even named as the location of the great final struggle in the apocalyptic tradition.[1]

The first stage of salvation history is the Patriarchal Age, which begins with the call of Abraham. The biblical tradition tells us that his family came originally from "Ur of the Chaldees," but had migrated to Haran when Abraham responded to the invitation: "Go forth from the land of your kinsfolk and from your father's house to a land that I will show you" (Gen 12:1). This event probably should be dated in the 19th century B.C., though it may have been as much as two centuries later. He and his wife Sarah were childless and without human hope

---

[1]The Armageddon of Rev 16:16 means "hill of Megiddo."

of offspring, but, in fulfillment of promise, Isaac was born to them in their old age. To Isaac is born Jacob, and to Jacob the twelve sons from whom spring the twelve tribes of Israel. The promises made to Abraham are renewed to Isaac and Jacob in turn. Joseph, one of the twelve, is betrayed by his brothers and winds up a slave in Egypt; but because God is with him, he eventually becomes Pharaoh's right-hand man. In time of famine Jacob sends his sons to Egypt to buy food; Joseph recognizes them and, after testing their good will, arranges for Jacob and his offspring to settle in Egypt (Genesis 12-50).

For the next period, the Sojourn in Egypt, the Israelites preserved but few recollections. Even the length is variously reported as 400, 430, and 215 years. When the account in Exodus opens, the Israelites are being harshly treated and subjected to forced labor. At this juncture God raises up Moses, who, aided by afflictions sent to terrify the Egyptians, leads the Israelites out of Egypt. The exodus may be dated with some confidence in the first half of the 13th century. The Israelites journey first to Mt. Sinai where they enter into covenant with Yahweh, the God who delivered them, and receive from Him the laws by which they are to live (Exod 1:1-Num 10:10). They next move on to Kadesh-barnea from which they are to invade Palestine. An attack from the south is attempted unsuccessfully, and that generation is condemned, for disobedience and rebellion, to wander in the wilderness until all those who were adults when they left Egypt had perished. Most of the traditional forty years of this "Wilderness Generation" were spent in the vicinity of Kadesh (Num 10:11-20:13; Deut 1:6-46).

Near the end of the life of Moses we find the Israelites again on the move. After bypassing the little kingdoms of Edom and Moab, they join battle with the Amorites dwelling north of Moab and conquer extensive territory in Transjordan. Moses ascends Mt. Nebo, sees the Promised Land that he will never enter, and dies (Num 20:14-36:13; Deut 2:1-3:29; 34:1-12).

Under Joshua, Moses' successor, the Israelites cross the Jordan near Jericho and subjugate a great part of Palestine through military conquest. The invasion, described in Joshua 1-12, can be dated with confidence to the second half of the 13th century. In the following Period of the Judges (ca. 1200-1050 B.C.), the Israelites attempt to increase their holdings, meet counterattacks from the Canaanites, and beat back incursions of other peoples (Judges 1-16). The most serious threat is posed by the Philistines, one element of the "Sea Peoples" that attacked extensively along the Mediterranean coastline. The Philistines established themselves in Palestine at the beginning of the 12th century and by the end of the Period of the Judges were in virtual control (Judges 14:4).

It was because of the Philistine menace that the Israelites took their next momentous step. When their forces were swept from the field by the Philistines at the battle of Aphek, ca. 1050 B.C., it was clear that a reorganization was called for. Samuel acceded to their request and anointed Saul king over them ca. 1020 B.C.[2] Saul had a measure of success at first, but came to grief when he met the Philistines in a pitched battle at Mt. Gilboa on the edge of the Plain of Megiddo; he was slain and Israel's army was scattered (1 Samuel 1-31). David, a popular young hero, was quickly accepted as king by his own tribe of Judah and somewhat later by the northern tribes. Under him the Israelite forces were regrouped; the Philistines were handed a series of stunning defeats and never again were a menace to Israel. David reduced the last pockets of Canaanite resistance, captured Jerusalem, and then turned his attention to the surrounding territories. Under his leadership Israel extended her boundaries and possessions to limits never surpassed in her later history (2 Samuel 1-24).

Solomon, David's son, succeeding to the throne in 961 B.C., inherited a peaceful and prosperous kingdom. He exploited the commercial possibilities of Israel's position, resources, and products, and so brought much wealth into the country. Solomon's reign is proverbial for its opulence. Even such wealth, however, could not keep pace with his love for luxury and ambitious building projects, and he eventually resorted to the unpopular measures of taxation and forced labor (1 Kings 1-11). Cracks in the foundation began to appear in Solomon's day, but the house came crashing down about the ears of Rehoboam, his successor. Rehoboam's unsympathetic rejection of a reasoned plea from the northern tribes for an easing of the burden provoked a rebellion, and from this moment (922 B.C.) dates the schism that was never healed. The northern tribes proclaimed Jeroboam their king, and so begins the period of the Divided Monarchy. The sister kingdoms generally regarded each other with hostility; occasionally they warred against each other, occasionally they were allies. This situation lasted for about two centuries, until, in 721 B.C., the Northern Kingdom was submerged in the tide of an expanding Assyria (1 Kings 12-2 Kings 17). Judah managed to outlast Assyria, although it was forced to become a vassal as the Northern Kingdom had earlier done. Late in the 7th century Assyria collapsed before the onslaught of a resurgent Babylonia, but the relief afforded Judah was only temporary; soon it was paying tribute to this new overlord. The tragedy of the Northern Kingdom was repeated: Judah joined with a number of smaller states to throw off subjection to the Neo-Babylonians and was soundly defeated. Jerusalem was besieged, taken, and destroyed (587 B.C.), and much of the population was deported to Babylonia (2 Kings 18-25).

Humanly speaking this should have been the end of the Chosen People; they might have been expected to mingle with other deported peoples and with the Babylonians, and to have lost their national

---

[2]Ancient chronology presents many unsolved problems and the experts often differ widely in proposing dates. The chronology followed in this book is generally that of W. F. Albright as refined by D. N. Freedman and E. F. Campbell, Jr., in "The Chronology of Israel and the Ancient Near East," *The Bible and the Ancient Near East*, ed. G. E. Wright (Garden City, N.Y.: Doubleday & Company, Inc., 1961), pp. 203-28.

identity. There was also the temptation to despair and to lose faith. That this did not happen is to be credited to the prophets sent by God, both before and during the exile. They interpreted the fall of the kingdom (which the preexilic prophets had foretold) as a punishment for Israel's forsaking the covenant, and they promised a restoration to their land and a new relationship with God. The Exilic Period is not covered by any of the *OT* historical books, but its conditions are reflected in the oracles of Ezekiel and of the anonymous prophet we call Deutero-Isaiah (Isaiah 40-55). Through the work of these two great men (and probably of others), the spirit, faith, hope of the people were strengthened and restored. The power of Babylon was brought to an end by the Persian army under Cyrus. When Cyrus gave permission for the captive people to return to their land in 538 B.C., they were in far better shape, religiously speaking, than they had been in 587 B.C. Their monotheism was unquestioned, and they had found a new devotion to the Law and to those institutions which now set them apart from their neighbors, the Sabbath observance and circumcision. From this moment they may properly be called Jews.

Those who returned to Palestine faced difficulties in this Period of the Restoration for which the glowing promises of the prophets had not prepared them. Encouraged by the prophets Haggai and Zechariah they built a new Temple and dedicated it in 515 B.C. Later Ezra and Nehemiah brought a greater measure of stability (Ezra; Nehemiah; Haggai; Zechariah 1-9).

Although Alexander's conquest of the Near East (334-323 B.C.) did not involve military action in Palestine, the Hellenization of this part of the world that resulted did have profound effects on the Jews. When Alexander died childless in 323 B.C., his empire was divided up among his generals. Palestine eventually came under the control of the Seleucid kings of Syria. Antiochus IV (175-163 B.C.) tried to impose Hellenistic ways upon the Jews, even in matters where they conflicted with traditional Jewish faith and practice. When persuasion failed, bloody persecution followed; Jerusalem was occupied and the Temple profaned. The Jewish reaction was a revolt under the leadership of the Maccabees which eventually resulted in the expulsion of the Syrian forces and brought freedom of religion (1 Maccabees; 2 Maccabees). Meanwhile, however, Roman power had been carrying all before it, and in 63 B.C. Syria and Palestine became a province of the Roman Empire, thus ending Jewish independence. It is under the domination of Rome that we find Palestine when the *NT* opens.

Reading Suggestions

JBC §73; 75. "Israel 3. History" in *NCE*.
Aharoni, Y., and M. Avi-Yonah, *The Macmillan Bible Atlas*. Rev. ed.; New York: Macmillan Publishing Co., Inc., 1977.

Aharoni, Y., *The Land of the Bible. A Historical Geography.* Philadelphia: Westminster Press, 1980.

Bright, J., *A History of Israel.* 3rd ed.; Philadelphia: Westminster
Press, 1981.

Herrmann, S., *A History of Israel in Old Testament Times.* Rev. ed.;
Philadelphia: Fortress Press, 1981.

May, H. G., *Oxford Bible Atlas.* 3rd ed.; New York: Oxford University
Press, 1984.

Fleming, J., "Putting the Bible on the Map," *BA Rev* 9 (6, 1983) 32-46.

Har-El, M., "The Pride of the Jordan — The Jungle of the Jordan,"
BA 41 (1978) 65-75.

BRIEF CHRONOLOGICAL CHART*

Period	Date	Historical Books	Prophetic Books
Patriarchal	1850?-1700?	Gen 12-50	
Sojourn in Egypt	1700?-1280?	Gen 46-Exod 12	
Exodus	1280?	Exod 1-15	
Wilderness Generation	1280-1240?	Exod 16-Num 36; Deut 1-3	
Invasion	1240?	Joshua	
Judges	1200-1050	Judges	
Samuel	1050-1020	1 Sam 1-10	
Monarchy			
United Kingdom	1020-922	1 Sam 11- 1 Kgs 11 1 Chr 10- 2 Chr 11	
Divided Kingdom	922-721	1 Kgs 12- 2 Kgs 17; 2 Chr 29-36	Amos; Hosea; Isaiah; Micah
Judah alone	721-587	2 Kgs 18-25 2 Chr 29-36	Isaiah; Jeremiah; Nahum; Zephaniah; Habakkuk
Exile	587-538		Ezekiel; Isa 40-55
Persian Domination	539-336		
Restoration	538—	Ezra; Nehemiah	Haggai; Zech 1-8 Joel; Malachi; Isa 56-66
Greek Domination	334-63	1 Macc; 2 Macc	Zech 9-14
Maccabean Uprising	began 166		
Roman Domination	63—		
Birth of Christ	ca. 6 B.C.		

*For further detail, see the chronological chart, pp. 289-293.

4

The Composition
of the Pentateuch

THE CORNERSTONE of Christianity and the heart of Judaism is the Pentateuch—known also as the Torah, the Law, and the five books of Moses. The reason for its importance is not hard to find. The vehicle and unifying factor of redemptive history is a people—more specifically, the people chosen by God and made the object of His promises. The Pentateuch answers the questions: Who is this people? Where did they come from? Why were they called? Not only is the formation and call described, but these events are placed against a broader background that makes clear their ultimate meaning.

The term "Pentateuch" signifies a composition in five volumes or scrolls. It is not a collection of five books but a single work, later divided into five parts for convenience—though the divisions do correspond well to the subject matter. We call them Genesis, Exodus, Leviticus, Numbers, and Deuteronomy. The designation "the five books of Moses" reflects an ancient belief that Moses authored the Pentateuch. The designation has value in underlining the profound influence of Moses as God's agent for the exodus, mediator of the covenant, first legislator, and founder of Israelite faith and worship. Modern studies have shown, however, that the Pentateuch is the result of several centuries of growth, centuries in which the foundation laid by Moses was strengthened, deepened, and perfected; it represents both primitive and advanced stages of Israelite faith, and contains laws that reflect the practice of many different periods. The whole is permeated by the spirit and authority of Moses.

THE "THEORY OF DOCUMENTS"

Difficulties with Mosaic literary authorship of certain parts of the Pentateuch have long been felt. For example, it is difficult to explain how Moses wrote of his own death and burial (Deut 34:1-8). Jewish tradition had an answer in the legend which told how God revealed to Moses the details of his death and how he wrote them with the tears streaming down his cheeks! The critics may have been amused, but they were not convinced. Other anachronisms were pointed out: the remark "The Canaanites were then in the land" (Gen 12:6) obviously belongs to a time after Moses, when the Canaanites had been replaced by Israelites. And Moses could hardly be responsible for the anachronistic references to the Philistines (Gen 21:32,34; 26:1,8).

Certain discrepancies also suggest that not all could have been the work of one hand. For example, the description of Sarah as so beautiful that she could turn Pharaoh's head (Gen 12:11-15) doesn't seem to be in agreement with chronological notices that would place her age at 65 at this time. There seem to be duplicate and triplicate accounts of the same event; for example, the case of a Patriarch who passes his wife off as his sister (Gen 12:10-20; 20; 26:6-11), the gift of manna and quail (Exodus 16; Numbers 11), and the naming of Bethel (Gen 28:19; 35:15). In Genesis 1 man is created after the animals, while in Genesis 2 he is created before them. Certain laws in the Pentateuch, for example those concerning agriculture and the monarchy, can hardly stem from the time of Sinai. The provisions of some laws are at variance with one another; for example, Exod 20:24-25 permits a number of altars, while Deuteronomy 12 insists there should be only one. In fact the historical books indicate that even responsible Israelite leaders like Samuel and Elijah knew no law that restricted sacrifice to a single place (1 Sam 7:5-9; 9:11-14; 10:8; 1 Kings 18); Elijah even complains to the Lord of altars being town down (1 Kgs 19:10). Some narratives are so full of repetitions and discordant statements that they seem to be composed of two divergent accounts, e.g., the story of the flood (Genesis 6-8).

The use of divine names provided a clue. In addition to the common Hebrew word for God, *elohim*, used to designate also pagan deities, the Israelites had a proper name for the God they worshiped, Yahweh (rendered as "LORD" in most translations). Israelite tradition had two conflicting versions of the origin of this name: Exod 3:13-15 implies and Exod 6:2-3 states that the name Yahweh came to the Israelites only in the time of Moses, while Gen 4:26 supposes that men knew and used it from earliest antiquity. The Patriarchal narratives also suppose that it was known to Abraham, Isaac, and Jacob (Gen 12:8; 14:22; 15:2,7; etc.). The pattern of the use of the names in Genesis and Exodus seems significant: from the beginning of Genesis until the revelation of the name Yahweh to Moses in Exod 3:15, Elohim is used much more frequently than Yahweh, while from this point on the use of Yahweh becomes greatly preponderant. This made it possible to theorize that two documents had been utilized, one using Yahweh from beginning to end, the other reserving the use of Yahweh until Exod 3:15, consistent with the tradition that the name was first revealed to Moses. Many passages in Genesis seemed to mix the two names indiscriminately, but those which adhered exclusively to one name could be isolated and assigned to one document or the other. These hypothetical documents were designated as the Yahwist and the Elohist for obvious reasons. This was the first stage in the theory of documents.

Closer study of the so-called Elohist, however, revealed two distinct series of texts: one was simple in diction, legalistic and liturgical in tone and interest; the other was folksy and anecdotal. Thus a further distinction was made; one series was designated as the Priestly Code (P), while the other continued to be called the Elohist (E). These two, along with the Yahwist (J),[1] so the theory ran, were the sources from which Genesis-Numbers were composed. Once sections of the documents had been isolated in Genesis on the basis of the divine names, it was possible to identify other constants (characteristic vocabulary, ideas, and preoccupations) and so to extend the separation of documents beyond Genesis. It was soon recognized that Deuteronomy formed a source distinct from anything found in Genesis-Numbers, and this source was designated simply Deuteronomist (D). These four sources are the "documents" of the classical "theory of documents."

Once this stage of the theory had been reached, impressive results were possible. For example, a first creation account (Gen 1:1-2:4a) could be distinguished from a second creation account (Gen 2:4b-24). In the first (from P), Elohim (God) is used throughout; the style is dry and terse; order and harmony is apparent; and the concept of God is quite transcendent, almost abstract, as He creates all things by His word. In the second (from J), Yahweh Elohim (Lord God)[2] is used throughout; the order of creation is different, and the orderliness of the first account is not in evidence; God is presented anthropomorphically as He fashions man from clay, plants a garden, and forms woman from the man's rib.

Another example may be taken from the flood narrative. The repetitious and contradictory details of the story could now be sorted out between J and P to produce two fairly complete and self-consistent accounts. The following lines reproduce only some of the verses as an illustration:

J	P
6:5. When the Lord saw how great was man's wickedness on earth, and how no desire that his heart con-	6:11. In the eyes of God the earth was corrupt and full of lawlessness. (12) When God saw how corrupt the earth

---

[1]The Yahwist is designated J rather than Y because the European scholars who developed the theory spelled the divine name with a "J."

[2]It is probable that Yahweh alone originally stood in Genesis 3 and that Elohim was added by an early editor. Yahweh alone is used in the continuation of the story in Genesis 4.

ceived was ever anything but evil, (6) he regretted that he had made man on the earth, and his heart was grieved. (7) So the Lord said: "I will wipe out from the earth the men whom I have created, and not only the men, but also the beasts and the creeping things and the birds of the air, for I am sorry that I made them." (8) But Noah found favor with the Lord.

7:1. Then the Lord said to Noah: "Go into the ark, you and all your household, for you alone in this age have I found to be truly just. (2) Of every clean animal, take with you seven pairs, a male and its mate; and of the unclean animals, one pair, a male and its mate; (3) likewise, of every clean bird of the air, seven pairs, a male and a female. Thus you will keep their issue alive over all the earth. (4) Seven days from now I will bring rain down on the earth for forty days and forty nights, and so I will wipe out from the surface of the earth every moving creature that I have made." (5) Noah did just as the Lord had commanded him.

7:7. Together with his sons, his wife, and his sons' wives, Noah went into the ark because of the waters of the flood. . . . (10) As soon as the seven days were over, the waters of the flood came upon the earth. (12) For forty days and forty nights heavy rain poured down on the earth. (16b) Then the Lord shut him in. (17) The flood continued upon the earth for forty days. As the waters increased, they lifted the ark, so that it rose above the earth.

had become, since all mortals led depraved lives on earth, (13) he said to Noah: "I have decided to put an end to all mortals on earth; the earth is full of lawlessness because of them. So I will destroy them and all life on earth."

6:17. "I, on my part, am about to bring the flood on the earth, to destroy everywhere all creatures in which there is the breath of life; everything on earth shall perish. (18) But with you I will establish my covenant; you and your sons, your wife and your sons' wives, shall go into the ark. (19) Of all other living creatures you shall bring two into the ark, one male and one female, that you may keep them alive with you. (20) Of all kinds of birds, of all kinds of creeping things, two of each shall come into the ark with you, to stay alive. (21) Moreover, you are to provide yourself with all the food that is to be eaten, and store it away, that it may serve as provisions for you and for them." (22) This Noah did; he carried out all the commands that God gave him.

7:6. Noah was six hundred years old when the flood waters came upon the earth. . . . (11) In the six hundredth year of Noah's life, in the second month, on the seventeenth day of the month: it was on that day that all the fountains of the great abyss burst forth, and the floodgates of the sky were opened. (13) On the precise day named, Noah and his sons Shem, Ham and Japheth, and Noah's wife, and the three wives of Noah's sons had entered the ark, (14) together with every kind of wild beast, every kind of domestic animal, every kind of creeping thing of the earth, and every kind of bird. . . . (18) The swelling waters increased greatly, but the ark floated on the surface of the waters.

(19) Higher and higher above the earth rose the waters, until all the highest mountains were submerged. (20) the crest rising fifteen cubits higher than the submerged mountains.

7:22. Everything on dry land with the faintest breath of life in its nostrils died out. (23) The Lord wiped out every living thing on earth: man and cattle, the creeping things and the birds of the air; all were wiped out from the earth.

Only Noah and those with him in the ark were left.
8:2b. The downpour from the sky was held back. (3a) Gradually the waters receded from the earth. (6) At the end of forty days Noah opened the hatch he had made in the ark, . . .

7:21. All creatures that stirred on earth perished: birds, cattle, wild animals, and all that swarmed on the earth, as well as all mankind. (24) The waters maintained their crest over the earth for one hundred and fifty days.

8:1. Then God remembered Noah and all the animals, wild and tame, that were with him in the ark. So God made a wind sweep over the earth, and the waters began to subside. (2a) The fountains of the abyss and the floodgates of the sky were closed. (3b) At the end of one hundred and fifty days, the waters had so diminished (4) that, in the seventh month, on the seventeenth day of the month, the ark came to rest on the mountains of Ararat.

While the discordant details (e.g., the number of animals, the source of water, the length of the flood) are unintelligible in the composite narrative, they are seen simply to represent variant accounts when the traditions have been separated. Notice that the J account is anthropomorphic (God's heart is grieved, He shuts the door of the ark) like the second creation account, and that P's enumeration of living creatures corresponds to the first creation account.

WORK OF WELLHAUSEN. The name of Julius Wellhausen (+1918) is closely connected with the theory of documents because he defended it with brilliant argumentation and convincingly defended the relative chronology of the documents now accepted by all. The identification and separation of the documents were tasks already accomplished when Wellhausen entered the lists, but the order of the documents (relative chronology) and the dates to be assigned to each (absolute chronology) were still being debated.

Wellhausen saw that Deuteronomy held the key to the chronological problem. He showed that the author of D was familiar with the historical material in J and E (which D found already combined—JE), but not that in P; P, therefore, was the most recent of the sources, and JE were anterior to D. The same conclusion was reached by an analysis of the laws contained in the Pentateuch. D contained many provisions from the Code of the Covenant (from E—Exod 20:22-23:33), but contacts with the laws of P were few. Further, the "one altar" legislation of Deuteronomy 12 had the appearance of a polemic against the multiplicity of altars permitted in Exod 20:24-25; P, on the other hand, knew of only one altar and therefore supposes a situation in which Deuteronomy 12 had been fully accepted. Wellhausen also saw that there had been an evolution in the priestly institution. In JE there is no restriction on who may offer sacrifice; in D priestly functions are committed to the tribe of Levi without distinction between priest and Levite (Deut 18:1-8); but in P, only the descendants of Aaron function as priests while the other Levites are their ministers (Num 3:5-10). J had already been shown to be slightly more primitive than E, so the order stood: J, E, D, P.

To establish the dates of the documents, Wellhausen turned to the historical books. The law book found in the 18th year of King Josiah (2 Kings 22—see p. 102) had long been identified with Deuteronomy. Wellhausen believed that it had been composed shortly before its discovery in 622 B.C. and so dated D in the late 7th century. He placed the composition of J and E in the early monarchy, in the 9th and 8th centuries respectively. He argued that Kings showed no knowledge of the special laws found in P, but that the influence of P was manifest in Chronicles, a postexilic book (see especially the difference in the account of David's transfer of the Ark to Jerusalem in 1 Chronicles 13 and 15, as compared with 2 Samuel 6). P was also seen to be an advance on the provisions found in Ezekiel 40-48 (Ezekiel was an exilic prophet). P therefore dated from the 5th century, after the return from the exile.

Yet there were defects in Wellhausen's work, quite aside from the present persuasion that some of his dates were too low. (For revised dates, see the discussion of the individual sources below.) Wellhausen had too little esteem for the historical value of the contents of the documents; he thought that they reflected not the events of which they purported to tell, but merely the conditions of the century to which he dated their composition. Little knowing how accurately oral tradition can preserve memories of the past and little knowing how widely spread was the use of writing in the ancient Near East, he did not believe that an 8th century author in Israel could know anything of substance about the Patriarchs, the exodus, or Moses. Concerning the Patriarchs he says: "It is true, we attain to no historical knowledge of the patriarchs, but only of the time when the stories about them arose in the Israelite people; this later age is here unconsciously projected, in its inner and outward features, into hoar antiquity, and is reflected there like a glorified mirage."[3] Or again: "Abraham alone is certainly not the name of a people like Isaac and Lot: he is somewhat hard to interpret. That

---

[3]*Prolegomena to the History of Ancient Israel*, tr. A. Menzies and J. S. Black (Edinburgh: A. & C. Black, 1885), pp. 318-19.

is not to say in such a connection as this we may regard him as a historical person; he might with more likelihood be regarded as a free creation of unconscious art."[4] Wellhausen also thought that he saw in the succession of documents, as did some others of his time, a substantial evolution in Israel's faith during the *OT* period: an evolution from polydaemonism to national henotheism to ethical monotheism—the last stage due to the work of the prophets and arrived at only in the exilic and postexilic periods.

AFTER WELLHAUSEN. Wellhausen's skepticism of Israel's historical and religious traditions dates to an age which knew little about the ancient Near East. As scientific advances fill in our knowledge of the biblical background (p. 12), skepticism of this sort becomes less and less possible.[5]

Wellhausen thought of the documents as "composed" at definite, ascertainable times; this is another misapprehension that further study has removed. Rather than thinking of the "documents" as written compositions, it might be better to think of them as receptacles of earlier traditions. Form Criticism (see p. 8) has shown that each of the documents can be broken down into many smaller unities; these unities had very diverse origins, and some of them are extremely old. The date assigned to a document must not be thought to mark the origin of the material in it but rather to designate the term of a long development—the period at which the material "crystallized" or became relatively fixed. Even P, the most recent of the documents, contains much ancient material.

How, then, it may be asked, is it possible to rank the documents chronologically? How could such diverse material have received the characteristic stamps that makes it possible to distinguish J from E? How is it even possible to speak of "documents"? The answer is that characteristic features were imparted to the materials by the traditionary circles (or, in some cases, even by individuals) that preserved, shaped, and transmitted them. Examples of what is meant by the term "traditionary circle" are hard to find in our modern culture, but for *OT* times we might think of Israel's priestly groups, bands of prophets (see p. 149), and wisdom schools (see p. 232)—relatively well defined groups that preserved and shaped traditions, impressing upon them their own peculiar ethos and, to some extent, their own specialized vocabulary. As for "documents," many now regard the term as misleading and substitute another (traditions, sources, strata) for it. Some authors have even gone so far as to deny that the four sources can be ranked

---

[4]*Ibid.*, p. 320.

[5]See J. Bright, "Modern Study of Old Testament Literature," in *The Bible and the Ancient Near East*, ed. G. E. Wright (Garden City, N. Y.: Doubleday and Company, Inc., 1961), p. 16.

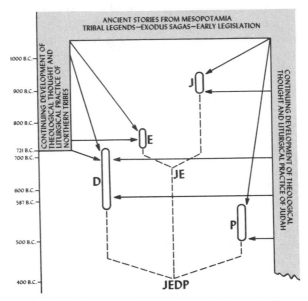

Figure 5. *The Formation of the Pentateuch. Arrows indicate the origin and time span of the materials incorporated into the pentateuchal documents; dotted lines indicate transmission of documents in relatively fixed form.*

chronologically at all, regarding them rather as parallel developments. They point out that the different practices reflected in the sources need not come from different periods; in some cases they could have existed at the same time in different circles.

Nevertheless, the chronological ranking is not without meaning. Almost all the material in J and E is early and received a fairly fixed form during the early monarchy—something that could not be said of P; D's formulation of the same laws found in E represents an advance and therefore a later period; the cultic practices of P are largely post-exilic, while those of the other sources are not. Yet it is true that the age of any given passage must be determined on its own merits, not simply on the basis of the source it is preserved in.

The documentary hypothesis has always been rejected by some and continues to come under attack from one quarter or another. Nevertheless, no better explanation has as yet been found of the complexities of composition of the Pentateuch, and it continues to command a good consensus among scholars.[6]

---

[6]See the comments of B. Vawter, *On Genesis: A New Reading* (Garden City, N.Y.: Doubleday & Company, Inc., 1977), pp. 15-17.

Theology and Characteristics
of the Source-Traditions

Merely to have learned something of the composition of the Pentateuch is a help in understanding it; conflicts and complexities formerly inexplicable now become intelligible. Yet this study can render a more positive service in making the structure of the Pentateuch as a whole more meaningful and in illuminating individual passages. In the following pages we will look at some of the salient features of the source-traditions.

Source-Tradition J. The Yahwist source provides the outline and much of the content of the Pentateuch (or, more accurately, of the Tetrateuch; J, E, and P run only through Genesis-Numbers). The pattern of creation, fall, vocation of Abraham and the promises to him, oppression in Egypt, exodus, Sinai covenant, and the initial stages of the conquest (Transjordan) are all found in J; the other sources have supplemented the contents of J without adding anything essentially new. The Yahwist presents the events subsequent to the Patriarchal Period as the fulfillment of the promises made to the Fathers and thus as redemptive history; and by prefixing Primeval History to the call of Abraham, he sets the whole of Israel's history in the context of God's redemptive will for all men.

While the content of J is not wholly uniform, it would seem to be in the main the work of an individual. Although working for the most part with traditional materials, he left upon the completed work the distinctive stamp of his own creative ability. He has been termed one of the greatest religious geniuses of all time, one of the world's greatest literary figures, etc. His utilization of traditions from southern cult centers and his interest in the Patriarch Judah place him in the territory of Judah. Modern scholars date him around the mid-tenth century B.C., about a century earlier than Wellhausen did. The tenth century, the heyday of the great kingdom of David and Solomon, was a time of profound transformation of many of Israel's religious forms and institutions. The tribal league had dissolved and with it had gone Israel's tradition of charismatic leaders; the monarchy with its hereditary succession seemed to some a rejection of Israel's religious tradition. Saul had resisted Samuel; secular power stood independent of religious control. Yet even in this process of secularization the Yahwist saw that Israel had not slipped from Yahweh's provident hand, that redemptive history continued, for, in fact, the kingdom of David represented the fulfillment of promises made to the Fathers. This insight into the workings of God, not only through religious forms and institutions, but also in the political and secular—we might even call it the religious meaning of the profane—is characteristic of the Yahwist's account throughout and is indicative of the depths of his thought.

It is indicative also of the Yahwist's deep sympathy for mankind in its actual situation and of his awareness of God's constant concern. Human life in the concrete is the center of attention, for it is here that people meet God and either respond to Him or turn from Him. The human tragedy stems from sin: mankind, through self-assertiveness, turns from God instead of seeking Him. With profound psychological insight the Yahwist portrays the ravages of sin in human life; with equal sensitivity he reveals the heart of God who wills to liberate His creature from the grasp of sin, but who cherishes no illusions concerning the fragile nature of the clay into which He has infused the breath of life.

The drama of sin and redemption is not set forth in a series of reflections on the meaning of life, but in the vivid description of events. With a word or a phrase the actors are characterized, their sentiments revealed in their words and deeds. These word pictures which go to the heart of the human situation in its religious dimension are among the best known narratives in world literature; they explain and justify the Yahwist's reputation as story-teller and theologian.

J does not clearly distinguish (as does P) various stages of religious dispensation (primeval, Patriarchal, Mosaic), but projects elements of later Israelite religion into the earliest ages. Not only do men "call upon the name of Yahweh" from the earliest generations, but Noah offers sacrifice (as do Cain and Abel) and distinguishes between clean and unclean animals. In this can be seen the universalistic spirit of the Yahwist, who knew that in no age or culture was God without His witnesses. Another characteristic of J is its anthropomorphic presentation of God: He fashions man from clay like a potter, walks in the garden in the cool of day, is grieved to the heart, regrets He made man, shuts the door of the ark from the outside, etc. Yet there is nothing crude or naive in J's conception of the God who abhors and punishes sin but never forgets justice and mercy; the anthropomorphisms serve to underline His nearness to man.

Some of the important J passages are the following: Gen 2:4b-4:26; 11:1-9; 12:1-4a, 6-20; 18:1-19:38; 24:1-25:6; 26:1-27, 45; 38:1-39:23; 43:1-44:34; Exod 4:1-16, 22-31; 5:5-23; 34:1-5, 10-28.[7]

SOURCE-TRADITION E. This strand is often difficult to separate from J, to which it is similar in many ways. Both are early and primitive, both employ the prose style and vocabulary of the early monarchy. According to some authors, these two sources came to be woven together into a single narrative. Many passages of the Pentateuch must be

---

[7]In this list and in those which will be given for E and P, no attempt is made at completeness or absolute precision. Only longer passages which are relatively unmixed with other sources are given so that by consulting them you may become familiar with the tone and contents of the individual source-traditions. If greater detail is required, consult commentaries on the passages in question. Authors will not agree on all particulars.

designated simply JE without further precision. E must originally have been a continuous record from the Patriarchal Period to the wilderness generation (some would extend it to the conquest), but because it closely paralleled J, many parts of it were omitted in the final combination in the interests of a unified narrative. The parts of E which were preserved, then, were those which either had no counterpart in J or were so dissimilar that they were not clearly doublets. What can be reconstructed of E is therefore incomplete and episodic.

This tradition reached relatively fixed form a century or more after J did. The special concerns it manifests place it in the north; very possibly it took shape in prophetic circles there (cf. Num 11:16-17, 24-30; 12:6-8). E is much less anthropomorphic than J in its presentation of God; in place of the familiar encounters of J, God usually addresses man in a dream or through His angel (Gen 20:3; 31:10-13, 24; 46:2). E has a greater concern for the morality of the Patriarchs. In J no excuse is given for Abraham saying that Sarah was his sister (Gen 12:18-19), but in E the deception is mitigated by the notice that she was his half-sister (Gen 20:12); the heartless dismissal of Hagar, unexcused in the J account (Gen 16:4-6), is justified by divine revelation in the parallel incident in E (Gen 21:10-14).

E has no Primeval History and apparently began with the call of Abraham. God is known to the Patriarchs as Elohim and by other titles, while the name Yahweh is reserved until its disclosure to Moses in Exod 3:14-15. As in J, the Patriarchs build altars in various places; such notices are absent in P, which knows only one legitimate place of worship. While J provides no legislation except the Ritual Decalogue (Exod 34:14-26), E contains the extensive Code of the Covenant (Exod 20:22-23:33); some authors also see the Ten Commandments (Exod 20:2-17) originally imbedded in E, though this is a disputed point. As in J, the providence of God in forming and guiding the people Israel is strongly underlined. The narratives of E generally lack the force and depth of those of J, though there are occasional passages of rare quality, as the story of the testing of Abraham (Genesis 22). The mountain of the covenant is called Horeb in E, Sinai in J and P.

Some of the important passages of E are the following: Genesis 20; 21:6-21; 22; 31; 40:1-42:37; Exod 1:15-2:14; 3:1-6, 9-15; 17:3-18:27; 20:22-23:33.

Source-Tradition D. This (to oversimplify a bit) is coextensive with Deuteronomy, which will be treated in Chapter 9.

Source-Tradition P. The title Priestly Code suits this stratum very well, for it is characterized by concern for cultic matters and religious legislation. Leviticus, composed almost wholly of legislation and priestly rubrics, is P from beginning to end. Narratives are usually brief and unadorned and are often given for the sake of the religious institutions or legislation they introduce, e.g., circumcision (Genesis 17) and the Passover ritual (Exod 12:1-20, 40-51). P is fond of genealogies with exact ages (cf. Genesis 5); other chronological indications are often given to the year, month, and day (cf. P section of flood narrative, p. 32). The style is usually precise, detailed, and monotonous (cf. the first creation account; the description of the Tabernacle and its furnishings, Exodus 35-40). P is not afraid to be repetitious; each tribal prince presented the same offerings for the dedication of the Tabernacle, but the long list is gone through twelve times (Numbers 7). These characteristics are so pronounced that it is often possible to identify P even in translation.

Although P did not reach its final form until after the exile, much of its material, as pointed out above, is quite ancient. P's highly systematized presentation is the result of centuries of clarifying and distilling doctrine within the same priestly school. One result of this is that P's conception of God is exalted and transcendent. It would be untrue to say there are no anthropomorphisms in P, for it is hardly possible to speak of God at all without them; we can say, however, that in P they are of the most refined sort. When God creates, He simply says, "Let there be . . ."; when He communicates with man, it is often by His word alone, without vision or dream. P reserves the use of the name Yahweh until Exod 6:2, and here it is introduced without even the theophany of the burning bush, simply with the words, "God also said to Moses . . ." We are a long way from the picture of the God who fashioned man from clay and walked in the garden with him; God's transcendence is exalted, but His nearness hardly appears.

In P human personalities and problems fall out of focus and its approach is overwhelmingly God-centered; yet P *is* concerned with relations between God and mankind, whom God calls to approach Him through a series of covenants: with Noah and his descendants, with Abraham and his descendants, and with all of Israel under Moses at Mt. Sinai. The field of attention is progressively narrowed until, in the last of these covenants, the People of God is formed; this covenant constitutes them as God's worshiping community. The laws given are to make them holy as the People of God ought to be, and the cult is given that they may approach Him in awe and reverence. Of course it is in large measure the life and worship of the postexilic community that P has projected back into the days of Moses, but there is theological justification for this. The community of the restoration was just as much the People of God, the true Israel, the covenant partner, as the generation of the exodus had been; their up-dated liturgy was just as much a means of approach to God as that of earlier ages, just as divinely sanctioned, and just as legitimately placed in the context of Mt. Sinai. Thus P's theology, too, is one of salvation history and progressive revelation.

Although some (e.g., M. Noth) claim that those responsible for P were also the final editors of the Pentateuch, this is rather to be denied (see, most recently, Vawter, *On Genesis*, pp. 22-23).

Some of the important passages from P are the following: Gen 1:1-2:4a; 5:1-28, 30-32; 11:10-27; 17; 23; 36; Exod 6:2-7:13; 12:1-20, 40-51; 16; 25-31; 35-40; Leviticus 1-27; Num 1:1-10:28; 15; 17-19; 25-31; 33-36.

LATER ADVANCES IN
PENTATEUCHAL STUDY

The documentary theory is not the final word in pentateuchal criticism by any means. Later studies have gone in three directions that we can mention. Form Criticism (p. 8) attempts to carry the investigation back a stage earlier than the four sources. It identifies the smaller units within a source and asks when, where, and why each one arose and how it had developed before becoming part of J, E, D, or P. One result has been to emphasize the importance of cult centers in formulating and preserving the ancient traditions.

The approach of tradition-history recognizes that certain themes in the Pentateuch (e.g., the promise to the Patriarchs, deliverance from Egypt, and the wilderness wanderings), being found in all the documents, rest on traditions anterior to the documents themselves, and attempts to determine their origin and development. Martin Noth has pioneered in this work, though because of certain of his methodological principles, many scholars disagree with his conclusions. (See Noth and Bright in chapter-end bibliography.)

Other studies attempt to clarify the structure of the Pentateuch as a whole. The outline of the Pentateuch, as pointed out above, is provided by J; but J did not simply invent the scheme. Gerhard von Rad isolated certain passages (Deut 6:20-24; 26:5-9; and Josh 24:2-13), ancient liturgical formulas, which he calls "cultic credos." These ancient pieces already tell of God's gracious acts for Israel: the Patriarchs, deliverance from oppression in Egypt, and the gift of Palestine are the elements they contain. Von Rad argued that the Yahwist structured his narrative by expanding this outline to include a primeval history, the Sinai tradition (covenant and law), and greater emphasis on the Patriarchs.

That the basic pattern is older than the Yahwist and found its clearest expression in the liturgy may be taken as certain; that the Yahwist was the first to work a primeval history into the scheme as a prologue to redemptive history is also most probable. Yet a comparison of J and E[8] points to a common source (to be dated no later than the Period of the Judges) that already contained patriarchal traditions, oppression, exodus, Sinai, and conquest. The common source was Israel's liturgical celebration of these historical events. The role of the liturgy is to make

[8]The parallel character of the narratives of J and E indicate a specific relationship. Since there is no evidence of direct dependence of one on the other, they must both depend on an earlier common tradition.

the saving event present each day or each year to each new generation. The rite includes the proclamation of the saving event and the response of gratitude and obedience by the worshipers. Exodus, Covenant, and Law are a natural triad in this context, and it would seem that the structure of the Pentateuch stems ultimately from Israel's ancient liturgy.

READING SUGGESTIONS

JBC §1. *OTRG* #1. *PBS* #1. "Pentateuch," "Elohist," "Priestly Writers, Pentateuchal," "Yahwist," "Wellhausen, Julius," in *NCE. AUOT* 23-26, 203-16, 267-70, 421-36. *BHI* 67-73. *WITOT:* 69-125, 135-42.

Bailey, L. R., *The Pentateuch.* Nashville: Abingdon, 1981.

Clines, D. J. A., *The Theme of the Pentateuch.* Sheffield: The University, 1978.

Noth, M., *A History of Pentateuchal Traditions*, tr. B. W. Anderson. Englewood Cliffs, N.J.: Prentice-Hall, Inc., 1972.

Speiser, E. A., *Genesis. AB* 1; Garden City, N.Y.: Doubleday & Company, Inc., 1964, pp. XX-XLIII.

von Rad. G., *Genesis*, tr. J. H. Marks. Philadelphia: Westminster Press, 1961, pp. 13-30.

Vawter, B., *On Genesis: A New Reading.* Garden City, N.Y.: Doubleday & Company, Inc., 1977, pp. 15-33.

Blenkinsopp, J., "The Structure of P," *CBQ*, 38 (1976) 275-92.

Clements, R. E., "Pentateuchal Problems," *ATI* 96-124.

Ellis, P., "The Priestly Theologian's Anthropology," *TBT* #83 (Feb. 1976) 657-62.

Hunt, I., "The Yahwist," *TBT* #29 (Mar. 1967) 2043-47.

LaVerdiere, E., "The Elohist 'E'," *TBT* #55 (Oct. 1971) 427-33.

Lohfink, N., "Primal sins in the priestly history," *TD* 20 (1972) 23-25.

Wolff, H. W., "The Elohistic Fragments in the Pentateuch," *Int* 26 (1972) 158-73.

5

Primeval History

(Scripture Reading: Genesis 1-11)

A GOOD CASE could be made for beginning our Scripture study with the exodus rather than with Primeval History. The exodus is, after all, the point at which Israel began to be a people, the point at which their history begins. It was at the exodus that Yahweh revealed Himself to them as a God of salvation, and it was in the light of the exodus that both their subsequent history and their earlier traditions took on meaning. In particular, God's dealings with the Patriarchs became intelligible only because of what happened to Israel in the exodus and later. Clearly, only the experience of the exodus made the writing of Genesis possible. But this does not prejudice the rightful place of Genesis at the beginning of salvation history. God's redemptive plan was revealed gradually, through a series of insights into the meaning of His acts in human history; only gradually could the various pieces be fitted into place. Once the picture began to emerge, it was clear that God had been at work in the days of Abraham, Isaac, and Jacob, through revelation, covenant, and promise. God's dealings with the Patriarchs had the nature of a preparation for the exodus and deserve to rank as the first chapter of redemptive history.

Granted, then, that Patriarchal History presents steps preparatory to the call of Israel, a further question remains: what was God's motive in forming a people in the first place? It is Primeval History that answers this question. Before attention begins to center on one family at the call of Abraham, we are given a glimpse of the universal human situation: mankind created good, but going from bad to worse as the ravages of sin result in the estrangement of man from God and man from man. This glimpse of mankind from the garden to the Tower of Babel lets us see his radical need for redemption; only then are we prepared to understand the call of Abraham and the promises made to him. In this sense, Primeval History is the prologue to redemptive history.

SOURCES, LITERARY FORM,

AND HISTORICITY

The question of sources poses itself acutely as soon as we begin to investigate Primeval History. Those inspired writers who told of Israel's monarchy could occasionally, at least, consult the royal archives, contemporary written documents, and even living witnesses; those who told of the exodus could draw on the cultic recitals of the saving deeds of Yahweh; even those who told of the Patriarchs drew on tribal and clan history. But what if we go one step further back, to the generations before Abraham? What if we go all the way back to creation? Clearly the question of sources is now quite a different one.

The answers that satisfied earlier generations will not do for us. When it was thought that the time of the human race on earth had been only a few thousand years it was possible to believe that the story of Eden had been passed on from generation to generation; about 25 generations from Adam to Moses was all that was required. In fact, tens of thousands of generations would be involved if even a conservative estimate of 1,000,000 years for mankind's time on earth is accepted. When we reflect, further, that the monotheism of the Bible narratives could not have survived even a few generations of oral transmission in a pagan milieu, the solution of oral tradition is seen to be wholly untenable.

The suggestion that the *stories* of Genesis 1-11 (as distinct from teachings they contain) represent a direct revelation to the biblical author of what happened "in the beginning" must also be ruled out, for we would expect an account that came directly from God to be free from factual error. To give one example: Genesis 4 presents the second generation of men (Cain and Abel) as food-producers (farmer and shepherd, respectively), while anthropology finds that men passed from the food-gathering to the food-producing stage only fairly recently—probably no more than 10,000 years ago. To look to science for scientific truth is not to set it above the Bible but to give it a role in interpretation.

If tradition and revelation are ruled out as the source of the tableaux of Genesis 1-11, we must suppose that the authors made use of stories current in their culture—stories which they selected and adapted for what they wanted to teach about the early history of man. As G . E. Wright observes:

> It must be admitted that the Bible, while dealing with the facts of history in its own particular way, continually pushes beyond what is factually known because the knowledge of God leads both backward to creation and forward to the eschaton. Consequently, the farther back the Bible pushes, the more it is forced to use traditional material, rewritten to bring it into harmony with the author's purpose.[1]

[1]*God Who Acts* (London: SCM Press Ltd., 1952), p. 127. (Distributed in the U.S.A. by Alec R. Allenson, Naperville, Ill.)

That the authors did utilize earlier tales and did not compose "from whole cloth" is clear from literary analysis and from parallels existing between the Bible and other ancient Eastern literature. Careful study shows that some of these stories originated in Mesopotamia and dated (in their original form) to long before the call of Abraham. But as they were retold in Israel, they were adapted and changed to eliminate the polytheistic elements of the original and to better express Israel's conception of God and His providence.

The biblical accounts can be of no help for a scientific reconstruction of cosmic or human origins; they were never intended for this. They *are* intended as statements of faith concerning cosmic and human origins, the relation of God to creation in general and to man in particular, the relationship between human sin and man's present situation, and so on. The method employed, a pointed retelling of stories which already enjoyed wide currency and a certain authority, is far more compatible with Semitic thought patterns than abstract expositions would be.

Obviously such narratives are not historical in the same sense that 2 Samuel and 1 Maccabees are. Not that the narratives of Genesis 1-11 are to be considered simply as parables (concrete, lifelike stories used to illustrate religious truths). Some of them speak of unique, unrepeatable events (creation, the Fall), and therefore are factual in content, however wanting in historical detail the narratives may be. It is at this point that appeal to revelation may be made, for the authors are not presenting *simply* human insights into the human situation, however keen and valid they may be; their teachings rest ultimately on the nature and will of God as these were known by the People to whom God had spoken.

These reflections raise the question of the literary form of these chapters. In recent years the tendency has been to classify these stories as "myth"; when the term is properly understood it is unexceptionable, instructive, and probably more accurate than any of the other terms suggested. I am not referring to the popular conception of myth, nor even to the standard dictionary definitions; that is to say, myth here is not taken as synonymous with falsehood or as necessarily connected with polytheism. Modern studies by specialists in ancient literatures and cultures show that the essence of myth is something quite other than is popularly supposed. Every culture attempts to understand and to explain the realities that lie at the heart of human existence; the "explanations" may be expressed in various forms, one of which, common especially in primitive cultures, is myth. Myth, in this sense, may be defined as an imaginative, concrete way of presenting insights acquired into the realities that closely affect man's life. The teaching of a myth may be either true or false, depending upon whether the insights presented are valid or not. It is not to be supposed that the mythmaker reasons abstractly to his conclusions and then presents the results in the form of a concrete story for the sake of the benighted people he was addressing. On the contrary, the story itself reflects the manner in which his thought proceeded, though this is not to say that the story is simply identical with his vision of reality.

The myth will naturally reflect the view of divinity and the cosmos held by the myth-maker. If the myths of Egypt and Mesopotamia, of Greece and Rome are polytheistic in nature, that is because they reflect the religious thought of their creators; if the gods and goddesses portrayed in these myths are often virtually identified with the forces of nature, that is because their authors had no conception of transcendent divinity; and if these myths are now of interest almost exclusively for the history of literature and religious thought, it is because the explanations they offered have been found to be inadequate. The stories of Genesis 1-11 exhibit the same patterns of thought and the same sort of expressions, but the God portrayed in them is one, holy, and transcendent; what they tell us of mankind's relation to God and to nature is as meaningful and as pertinent today as it was when they were first composed. Books and commentaries have been written on these chapters, but their content has never been exhausted.

It is doubtful that the matters they deal with could have been treated as successfully in any other way. Indeed, since myth attempts to deal with realities that affect the human situation but which lie outside human experience, realities which can only be approximated but not grasped by even the most advanced discursive thought, it can be said that religious thought can never wholly dispense with myth. The statement of the creed "He ascended into heaven, sits at the right hand of God the Father almighty" is couched in mythological terms, but it is doubtful that the language of abstraction could more effectively describe the mystery of the exaltation of Christ.

CREATION AND FALL

FIRST CREATION ACCOUNT: Gen 1:1-2:4a (P). Although for obvious reasons the creation narrative stands at the beginning of the Bible, it should be pointed out again that Israel thought of the Lord primarily as the Savior of the exodus, only secondarily as Creator. An Israelite might well have summed it up by saying: "Yahweh is the God who led us out of Egypt; He also, of course, created heaven and earth." Whatever mighty deed, whatever feat of divine power had been done they attributed to their God. The exodus they had experienced; creation was something they arrived at through reflection. "Reflection" is, in fact, a good characterization of the procedure of this narrative. Von Rad describes it as follows:

> In essence it is . . . Priestly doctrine, i.e., ancient, sacred knowledge, preserved and handed on by many generations of priests, repeatedly pondered, taught, and reformed and expanded most carefully and compactly by new reflections and experiences of

faith. To write out these thirty-five verses, Israel's faith required centuries of carefully collected reflection. . . . The final form of the material as we have it may date from the exile, but its roots and beginnings certainly lie hidden in the bosom of the oldest Yahweh community.[2]

The apparent conflicts between Genesis 1 and the theories of science pose no problem; it is not a question of reconciling the two, but of recognizing that they are speaking of different matters. Genesis 1 speaks of the activity of God in bringing the world into being, concerning which science has nothing to say; the circumstantial account is not intended to instruct us precisely in scientific matters, but is part of the literary technique employed to describe in human terms the unsearchable mystery of creation.

The production of something out of nothing is not clearly expressed in the text. The emphasis is rather on the formation of cosmos out of chaos. The starting point (v 2) is a formless waste; the terms "waste and void" (*tohu wa-bohu*) and "abyss" describe the formlessness and disorder that prevail until God begins His creative activity. The transition from the disorder of the primeval chaos to the order of the cosmos is perhaps the closest the ancient Hebrews could come to creation *ex nihilo*. If the earth again becomes *tohu wa-bohu*, it means that God is undoing the work of creation (cf. Jer 4:23); this conception lies behind P's account of the flood, in which the earth is returned to the embrace of the chaotic abyss when the fountains of the abyss burst forth and the floodgates of heaven are opened (Gen 7:11).

The cosmos which is produced is, naturally enough, the one familiar to ancient Semites (Figure 6); the firmament, a sort of inverted bowl, serves to hold back the waters above the disk of the earth and so make permanent the division "in the midst of the waters" made on the second day (v 6).

The creation of light at the very beginning, independently of the sun, which is created only on the fourth day, strikes us as grandly illogical. In fact, it was precisely the logic of the account that demanded this. The author wished to give order to his account by incorporating it into a scheme of a week, a sevenfold succession of day and night; for this the creation of light needed to be the first work. Darkness already existed as a chaotic force, but with the creation of light it is incorporated into cosmic order—a wonderful transformation wrought by the creative power of God. A fringe benefit, so to speak, of separating light from the sun, moon, and stars, was that it enabled the heavenly bodies to be relegated to the fourth day. Surrounding cultures worshiped them as divinities, but in Genesis they are given a secondary place and are assigned their tasks of designating times and seasons.

The "days" of the scheme of creation are to be understood as days of 24 hours. This, the normal meaning of the Hebrew word employed

[2]Gerhard von Rad, *Genesis*, tr. by John H. Marks (The Westminster Press, N.Y., and SCM Press, London. Copyright © 1961, by W. L. Jenkins), pp. 61-62. Used by permission.

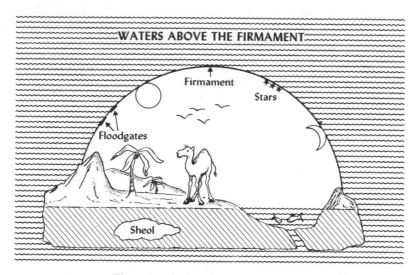

Figure 6.   *Ancient Semitic Cosmology.*

(*yom*), is further required by the references to "evening and morning" and the clear intention that the seven days add up to a week. Since the seven-day scheme is a literary artifice intended to give order and structure to the account, it does not suggest that the author believed the cosmos was formed in this period. He constructed two series of three days and four works each, so arranged that the elements of the second series would correspond to those of the first, as the following table shows:

FIRST SERIES			SECOND SERIES		
Day	*Work*	*Description*	*Day*	*Work*	*Description*
1st	1	creation of light; separation of light from darkness	4th	5	creation of heavenly bodies ("lights")
2nd	2	creation of firmament; separation of waters above from waters below	5th	6	production of water animals and birds
3rd	3	separation of land from waters below	6th	7	production of land animals
	4	production of vegetation		8	creation of mankind

Note that each series has one work on each of the first two days and two works on the third. The relationship of each work of the second series to the corresponding one of the first series is obvious except in the case of the last one; the link becomes apparent in v 29, where vegetation is given to mankind as food. The scheme, whose contrived and artificial nature is apparent, was constructed for the sake of its order and balance; the author was not insisting that things happened in just that way.

Thus, the account tells us, all that is has been made by God and is characterized by order and harmony. Another quality of creation is its goodness; seven times is expressed the divine satisfaction: "God saw that it was (very) good." In these words lies the basis of all true humanism, for the positive values we recognize in the human situation go back directly or indirectly to the goodness of creation. No Manicheism, no contempt for matter is possible for one rooted in the biblical concept of creation.

The creation of mankind is given special emphasis. It comes as the final work and is preceded by the deliberation: "Let us make man in our image and likeness" (v 26). The event is described in a hymn of wonder:

> God created man in his image.
> In the image of God he created him;
> male and female he created them.

The distinction of the sexes at creation and the blessing of fertility bestowed upon the first couple attributes the institution of marriage to God Himself. Mankind is placed in charge of creation and commanded to fill the earth and subdue it.

The creation of mankind in God's "image and likeness" has often been understood too abstractly. The phrase does indicate that mankind is set above the rest of creation through a special kinship with God; but the author was not thinking in terms of a spiritual soul (of which he had no conception) or of intellect and free will. In his thought the human person somehow resembled God even in a physical sense. This in turn suggests the practice by which a king sets up a statue of himself in a part of his domain where he does not personally appear, as an indication of his claim to sovereignty there. Just so, mankind is a representation of God and exercises dominion over the rest of creation in God's name. Through mankind creation receives its ordination to God; mankind, in virtue of being made in God's image, exercises the role of high priest of creation.

The note on diet—that both man and beast eat only food from plants—is a modest suggestion of paradisiac peace and harmony; only after the flood and the sin that caused it will P alter this dispensation (9:3).

In spite of the peaceful tone of this account, it contains a stern polemic against a false view of the world, of its relation to God, and of the very nature of the deity. This aspect appears, however, only when the account is viewed against its relevant background, the pagan myths of creation current in the cultures surrounding Israel. The *Enuma Elish*,[3] the Akkadian creation epic, is the fullest of these and is typical of the others. In the beginning exist only Apsu and Ti'amat, the primordial waters personified as the divine male and female principles; through the mingling of their bodies are begotten the other gods, who appear on the scene in bewildering profusion. A disagreement arises among the gods and Apsu is slain; the others divide into two camps and battle lines are drawn. On one side is Ti'amat with her allies; the prolific Ti'amat brings forth fearful monsters "sharp of tooth, unsparing of fang, with venom for blood" to aid her. Opposing her are the other gods. All fear to enter into battle with the dread Ti'amat until Marduk, "the wisest of gods," offers himself as champion on the condition that he be named the chief of the gods. Marduk is duly enthroned, goes forth to do battle, and overcomes and slays Ti'amat. Thereupon he proceeds to the work of creation, for which Ti'amat's body is the starting point. The Mesopotamian cosmology was that common in the ancient Near East, that held by the Israelites and illustrated above. Marduk splits Ti'amat's body into two parts and sets half of it up as the sky, in which the heavenly bodies (with the deities connected with them) are then placed to order years and seasons; from the lower half of the monster the earth is fashioned. Then the instigator of the rebellion, the god Kingu, is slain, and from his blood mankind is fashioned; the motive:

> He shall be charged with the service of the gods
> That they might be at ease!

The struggle between Marduk and Ti'amat reveals the basically dualistic conception of reality in the *Enuma Elish*. The primordial struggle between the gods was the mythic counterpart of what Mesopotamian man saw in nature each year as the land seemed about to be returned to the power of chaos in the spring rains and floods. The monster of chaos had been overcome "in the beginning," but the struggle was renewed annually. The *Enuma Elish* was more than simply a story to be listened to; it was a drama to be reenacted in the cult each year so as to assure the triumph of the forces of order.

What relationship does all this bear to Genesis 1? The similarities of the Akkadian creation epic to P's account are greater than they may appear to be at first glance. In each case there is preexisting chaos[4] which is divided into two parts for the creative work; in each, attention is given to the fashioning of the firmament and the dry land, to the

[3]*ANET* 60-72. The extant texts date from the 1st millennium B.C., but the composition of the epic probably goes back to the first half of the 2nd millennium. The quotations given are from *ANET*.

[4]The Hebrew word in Gen 1:2 for "abyss," *tehom* (root: *t-h-m*), is etymologically connected with the name Ti'amat (root: *t-'-m*; the -at is the feminine termination).

heavenly luminaries and their assigned tasks, and to the formation of mankind.

The differences, however, are instructive and justify the assertion that P's narrative is a counterstatement to the pagan myth. The differences concern especially the nature of the deity and the relationship between the deity and the world. In the pagan myth it is difficult to distinguish between the gods and the material universe, so closely are the gods connected or identified with the parts and forces of nature. Polytheistic and dualistic, the pagan myth must pass through theogony (begetting of the gods) and theomachy (battle of the gods) before creation itself. In Genesis, on the other hand, God is no part of the world He creates; He is wholly transcendent and calls the various elements of the world into being by His word. The abyss may have been conceived of as present from the beginning, but in Genesis it is not the monster of chaos threatening to devour the creating God. Here the abyss is inert and passive before Him.[5]

Against the background of the Mesopotamian version of origins, the emphasis on order in P's account takes on new meaning; the world created by Israel's God is not in danger each year of falling back into chaos. The scheme of a week for the creative work not only contributes to the sense of order but also dissociates creation from the annual cycle. God creates in six days and rests on the seventh. The repose of the seventh day undoubtedly is connected with the Sabbath observance, but it also has the effect of underlining the completion of the creative work; it is not a cycle to be repeated each year, not a work in danger of being undone—God finishes and He rests. The difference between the *Enuma Elish* and Genesis 1 on the creation of mankind is obvious: in one case it is an afterthought, in the other the culmination and crown; in one case man is the lackey of the gods, in the other the high-priest of creation, the link between it and God. Wherever the biblical writers obtained their lofty conception of creation, it wasn't from the cultures around them.

SECOND CREATION ACCOUNT AND THE FALL: **2:4b-3:24 (J)**. Although J's creation account was originally independent of P's version, there are certain advantages in its present position. For one thing, J concentrates so exclusively on the human situation,[6] bringing in other

---

[5]This is not universally true of the *OT*, however. In many poetic passages the struggle with the chaos monster (called Rahab, Leviathan, etc., names found also in pagan literature) does figure; e.g., Ps 74:12-14. The intention in such texts is to vindicate for Yahweh every mighty deed of salvation, whether strictly historical or not, rather than to affirm the reality of such a struggle or the dualistic conception it implies. In some places there has been an obvious reinterpretation, as when Rahab is identified with Egypt (Isa 30:6-7). Isa 51:9-11 connects the primordial victory with the conquest of the sea at the exodus and makes this a type of later deeds of deliverance.

[6]It has been said that in P's account man is the apex of a pyramid, in J's he is the center of a circle.

details only to the extent that they affect this, that it does not give a full account of origins. For another, P's statement that "God saw that all He had made was very good" now provides a backdrop for the story of the Fall that the Yahwistic author could only have approved of.

The anthropomorphisms that characterize this story from one end to the other are not to be attributed simply to naiveté; the author was aware of them and willed them as a means of portraying vividly God's personal concern for His human creature. The God who fashions man from the soil, who plants a garden for him, who forms a mate to share his life, who encounters the guilty couple while walking in the garden, and who makes clothes for them is a God who is very near and involved.

The description of man's formation from the soil and his animation by the breath of God gives a precious insight into the ancient Semitic anthropology, i.e., their conception of man's composition and nature. Western thought, in spite of its predominantly Christian and biblical faith, has tended to follow the system of Plato and other Greek philosophers[7] in which human nature is viewed as an uneasy union of two opposed elements, one material (mortal body), the other spiritual (immortal soul). A thinly disguised contempt for matter leads this system to view death as a liberation and the state in which the soul is free of the body as the ideal; paradoxically, the human person attains perfection only when it ceases to be complete and begins to be a separated soul. Gen 2:7 has too often been understood to say that God formed man's *body* from the ground and breathed a *soul* into it. In fact, the text says that God formed the *man* from the ground and breathed into his nostrils the breath (*neshamah*) of life, so that man became a living being (*nephesh*). *Man is man: connected to the earth*

The human being, according to Hebrew thought, was a unity, a living, animated body, whose life was supplied by the breath of God. When the individual died, life was simply extinguished as this breath departed. Until near the end of the *OT* period there was no belief in a satisfactory form of survival after death; their descriptions of conscious existence in the abode of the dead (Sheol), were hardly more than imaginative ways of conceiving the grave. Our English translations of the *OT* often use the word "soul" (usually a rendering of the Hebrew *nephesh*), but we would be misled if we took it to mean, like our word "soul," a spiritual element that survives the body. *Nephesh* can mean breath, self, person, etc.; Hebrew can even speak of a dead *nephesh* (Lev 21:11). To the extent that this conception of the human person seemed (in the early period) to exclude the possibility of survival beyond the grave,

---

[7] "The Hellenic conception of man has been described as that of an angel in a slot machine, a soul (the invisible, spiritual, essential ego) incarcerated in a frame of matter, from which it trusts eventually to be liberated." In Hebrew thought, however: "Man does not *have* a body, he *is* a body. He is flesh-animated-by-soul, the whole conceived as a psychophysical unity." J. A. T. Robinson, *The Body: A Study in Pauline Theology* (London: SCM Press Ltd., 1952), p. 14. (Distributed in the U.S.A. by Alec R. Allenson, Naperville, Ill.)

it was imperfect and incomplete. Yet it did have the advantage of preserving the human person in its concrete, existential situation, as a part of material creation—something the overly spiritualized Platonic view did not do. Only by seeing mankind in its existential situation (as God does!) will we understand what the Bible means by redemption.

The man is placed in a garden of delights. He has access to the many trees "pleasant to the sight and good for food" which were planted there, including, apparently, the tree of life. By this the author tells us that man, in spite of his frail nature, was destined not for death but for continued life. Only one thing is lacking to him: companionship. The sequence in which God forms the animals from the earth (as man had been) and leads each to the man to receive a name demonstrates man's dominion over the animals, something P asserts in a different way. But none of them are a suitable companion for him—a special creation is called for. The climax of what may be called Act I comes as God forms woman from a rib of the man and gives her to him as his wife. No more charming way could be found to say that man and woman are equal and of the same nature and are meant for each other in marriage by divine ordination.[8] Without sin there is no sense of guilt, and so the idyllic scene ends with the note that the couple are naked but unashamed.

One sequence in Disney's unique film *Fantasia* shows primitive forms of animal creation living in peaceful harmony, amiably sharing the vegetation and shouldering one another at the watering holes. Suddenly there bursts upon this scene the terror and fury of the first great carnivore, pictured (by a minor anachronism) as *Tyrannosaurus rex* of demonic mien. The peace vanishes, replaced now by fear, flight, and destruction. In some such manner the Yahwistic author pictured the intrusion of sin into creation. Although rooted in free human acts, it had an almost objectively independent existence, consuming, destroying, growing . . .

The author has depicted the man and woman in an idyllic state: established by God in a delightful garden, they were under His providential care and enjoyed a certain fellowship with Him; they were free from want, not subject to death, and in harmony with one another and with creation. The single prohibition ("from the tree of knowledge of good and evil you must not eat") must be viewed in the light of the other indications of God's loving concern, but it is laid down on the authority of the Lord of the garden: "the day you eat of it you shall surely die." There were many trees in the garden "pleasant to the sight and good for food," and so it is nothing but rebellious self-

---

[8]Cf. the comment of St. Bernardino: "God did not make a woman out of a bone of Adam's foot, so that he should tread her underground, nor out of a bone of his head, so that she should dominate him; but he made her out of his rib, which is close to his heart, to teach him to love her truly, as his companion." From Iris Origo, *The World of San Bernardino* (New York: Harcourt, Brace & World, Inc., 1962), p. 57.

assertiveness that leads the couple to decide that it is precisely *this* tree that they must eat of. It is the serpent who teaches them to question the commandment, to suspect God's motives, to doubt the punishment; above all, he holds out the promise "you will be like God." The deed is done and retribution follows: the guilty pair are ejected from the garden and lose all its blessings; now they will know privation, toil, and pain, and, because access to the tree of life is now denied them, death will ultimately overtake them. The tragedy of the Fall is the tragedy of man's rejection of his state as creature and of his attempt to seize divine prerogatives by vindicating for himself complete autonomy; by so doing he loses the benefits of knowing what he is and of knowing his true relationship to his Creator.

The account leaves us with many questions and problems. Is the author trying to tell us anything about the nature of the first sin? What does he assert about the primitive state of mankind? Can sin, in fact, be linked to the woes of mankind's present state? Do the things he teaches conflict with the findings of science? An attempt must be made to answer these questions.

It is unlikely that the author knew anything about the circumstances or nature of the first sin except that it was—like every sin—an act of disobedience and pride. It seems, however, that he was willing to tell the story in terms that would condemn by implication an evil practice of his own day, the pagan fertility rites. Because the religious cultures of the Fertile Crescent thought a very close relationship existed between gods and nature, they believed that acts of the gods had an automatic effect in nature. Thus they believed that fertility in flocks, field, and family was produced by the sexual union of these deities specially associated with fertility; in Canaan these were Baal and Anath. The cycle of the seasons necessarily reflected the adventures of Baal. The death of vegetation in the fall meant he had died; in the spring he revived and mated with his consort to renew the earth's fertility. To insure that the cycle would not fail, the myth was acted out in the cult. Ritual prostitution was part of the cult, for it was believed that by such imitative or "sympathetic" magic the divine pair would be brought together.

Certain elements of Genesis 2-3 suggest direct or indirect reference to sex and fertility, e.g., nakedness (the fertility goddess was frequently represented nude in art), the serpent (a symbol often associated with the fertility goddess), knowledge of good and evil, becoming like gods,[9] and the punishments in child-bearing and in tilling the ground. Thus by introducing the serpent with his specious promises immediately after the woman had been given to the man as his wife but before they had

[9]This interpretation is supported by the connection between sexual relations and wisdom and godlikeness in the *Epic of Gilgamesh* (*ANET* 72-99). Enkidu, a naked savage who roams the steppe and enjoys the friendship of the animals, is seduced by a harlot; he finds that the animals now flee from him, but is consoled by the words: "Thou art wise, Enkidu, art become like a god!" (*ANET* 74-75).

come together, the author may be hinting that they placed their marriage under the auspices of the fertility deities; expecting in this way communion with the divine forces of nature, they discover only that they have been degraded and have lost the very privileges they hoped to secure. The fertility cult was abominable by the standards of Yahwism not only because of the sexual aberrations involved, but also because it introduced the sexual principle (and therefore distinction and division) into deity, led people to seek a blessedness which could never transcend nature, and sought to control deity and to compel, through magical influence, the bestowal of blessings. Yet it was a temptation to which Israelites often yielded, either by turning to pagan gods or by introducing pagan practices into the cult of Yahweh. By telling the story of the Fall as he did, the author may be suggesting indirectly that man's attempt to find blessedness in nature and the nature deities was the root cause of the evils that afflict him.

Does the author seriously teach that the first couple enjoyed a privileged state before their sin? There is a sense in which his story has a universal application. The term used for the man, *adam*, is not a proper name (though it is used as one beginning at Gen 4:25) and commonly designates mankind in general, not an individual. The experience of *adam* is the experience of each individual—rejection of God, rebellion, sense of guilt and shame, and punishment. This is partly because all the descendants of the first couple find themselves in the state they chose, and partly because all have known personal sin and its consequences. Yet the story is far more a sort of morality play whose elements are all verified in us. The author thinks of the first couple as knowing a world in which there was no sin. The author asserts, furthermore, that mankind was not subject to death in that blessed state, for that is the obvious meaning of the tree of life. We know that the author did not have explicit knowledge of what the life of the first human creatures was like and that he worked largely with traditional materials. Yet the story of the garden and the fall has no real parallel in the known extrabiblical literature, even though certain elements of it do; it is the author's own construction, therefore, and he must have intended its teaching to be taken seriously.

But a problem immediately presents itself: nothing that science teaches would lead us to suspect that the first couple would find themselves in an ideal situation; quite the contrary. Scientific evidence suggests that mankind evolved from lower animals, and we are inclined to judge that the earliest human beings would find themselves in about the same relationship to their environment as their non-human progenitors were and in the same condition of mortality. They would be subject to the same needs and diseases, preyed upon by the same enemies. As for harmony in nature before sin, important species of carnivores came and went before mankind appeared; their teeth were not designed for chewing grass.

Figure 7.
*The fertility goddess
was imported into
Egypt under Canaanite
influence. In this
Egyptian relief she is
seen holding a lotus and
serpents. Courtesy of
the Trustees of the
British Museum.*

To take the last point first, we must beware of making the Bible say
more about the original state than it actually says; theological construction and pious imagination have described the original state in
terms that go far beyond anything found in Genesis 1-3, and there is no
obligation to defend all of it. As for human mortality, it can be pointed
out that science, if it stays within its own competence, can tell us only
what would be natural for early mankind in the environment into
which it emerged; it can tell us nothing of any special dispensation God
might have willed to make. It can be said that Genesis 2-3 suggests that
the primal state of man was not simply natural to him. The garden is
not the whole earth but a place specially provided; the sentence of death
does no violence to the nature of one drawn from the earth: "dust you
are and unto dust you shall return."

Having said this, however, I can add that it is not the only possible
answer nor necessarily the best. Every assertion must be understood
against the background from which it is made; in the case at hand the
background is the biblical author's conception of death—a conception
in many ways different than ours. Professional undertaking with its
cosmetics and satin-lined coffins, air-conditioning and flowers, deep
graves and concrete vaults, has isolated us from much of the stark
reality that death was to the ancient; to him it meant rigor mortis,

putrefaction, and worms. For us death may mean passing from this vale of tears to the presence of God, but for the ancient Hebrew it meant leaving the land of the only blessings he knew for a shadowy, hardly conscious existence in Sheol.

Far worse, death meant leaving the land of the living, the only place where God's power, mercy, and regard were known, for He was the living God and the God of the living; His influence was hardly considered to extend to Sheol. Death for the ancient Hebrew was not simply the end of physical life but the end of all that was worthwhile and the final separation from God—an unmitigated evil in which no consoling aspect could be found. The author knew that the God who had revealed Himself to Israel as all-good had created mankind not for this sort of ultimate death but for life and for fellowship with Him; if death is now the lot of man, it can only be because he rejected the gift of God through sin. This is what is taught in the story of the garden, the tree of life,[10] and the tree of knowledge. "Death" in this story is not a metaphor for "the state of sin," but stands for the ultimate fate of mankind estranged from God; it is intimately bound up with the fact of sin, and lesser afflictions are anticipations of it. This is an insight that later advances in religious thought cannot reject.

The story contains other great insights regarding mankind's present state and the fact of sin. If we can imagine a world without sin—without hatred, strife, injustice, pride, selfishness, and all the evils which flow from these—then we can imagine what the state of mankind

---

[10]Using the almost identical symbolism of "the plant of life," the *Epic of Gilgamesh* teaches a very different attitude of the gods concerning mankind, life, and death. Gilgamesh, a mighty hero of legend, suddenly warned of his own mortality by the death of his boon-companion, Enkidu, sets out in quest of immortality. He finally obtains the plant of life, only to have it stolen by a serpent. Gilgamesh is thus left with no remedy for his mortality, and the moral of the story seems to revolve back to the advice given by the goddess Siduri somewhat earlier:

> Gilgamesh, whither rovest thou?
> The life thou pursuest thou shalt not find.
> When the gods created mankind,
> Death for mankind they set aside,
> Life in their own hands retaining.
> Thou, Gilgamesh, let full be thy belly,
> Make thou merry by day and by night.
> Of each day make thou a feast of rejoicing,
> Day and night dance thou and play!
> Let thy garments be sparkling fresh,
> Thy head be washed; bathe thou in water.
> Pay heed to the little one that holds on to thy hand.
> Let thy spouse delight in thy bosom!
> For this is the task of mankind! (*ANET* 90).

The gods who created mankind for death will never offer the gift of life; the God who offered life only to have it rejected can offer it again.

would have been before sin. Sin drives a wedge into the human
community ("The woman whom you put here with me—she gave me
the fruit from the tree, and so I ate it") and introduced division into
the individual himself. The author, seeing that this is the state of all
mankind, tells us that sin was introduced by the first parents of all.
Do we feel inclined to contradict him?

The words of God, "Cursed be the ground because of you . . . thorns
and thistles shall it bring forth to you," suggest that mankind's relation
to the rest of creation has been altered by the fact of sin. Here, too, is a
profound insight. In each of the accounts of origins, mankind is the
highpoint of God's creative activity; the rest of material creation is
subjected to him and therefore can attain its end of serving God only
through him. When man rebels, all of creation falls with him. When
man, the rational creature, the only means by which dumb creation can
be directed and consecrated to God, seeks autonomy and rejects his
place before God, the order of the cosmos is destroyed. Material
creation, because of mankind's solidarity with it, is turned from its
proper end when man turns from his proper end. But a further result is
that its relationship to man is altered. Before, nature was a gift of God,
now it is a hostile environment; whatever hardships it might have in-
flicted on the human creature before through caprice or intractability
could not have been conceived as punishments, but now they fall upon
one who knows himself to be a rebel. Although such statements may
have no meaning in the realm of empirical science, as theological
affirmations their validity remains. Any redemption to come must be
cosmic in scope, for "creation was made subject to futility" and "all
creation groans and is in agony even until now" (Rom 8:20,22).

FROM THE FALL TO ABRAHAM

The account of the Fall serves as an introduction to the stories of
Genesis 4-11 in which the progressive corruption of mankind is chron-
icled. This theme is found mainly in the J cycle, into which the final
editor has inserted P's traditions of primeval history.

CAIN AND ABEL: **4:1-6 (J).** The tale of the shepherd whose sacrifice is
accepted and the farmer who commits murder reflects the rivalry of two
ways of life. The Israelites, recalling their nomadic ancestors and the
days of the exodus, regarded the shepherd life as more suited for seeking
God, and they recognized the temptations that came with settling down
in Canaan as farmers.

There is some evidence that the story of Cain and Abel originally
belonged in a later context. For one thing, the story supposes a greater
population than its present position allows; for another, it seems that
Cain (Heb.: *qyn*) is to be identified with the Kenan (*qynn*) of P's ge-

nealogy (5:9-14) and traditionally belonged to the fourth generation rather than to the second. The author's purpose in placing this account immediately after the Fall was to underline the connection between the primal rebellion and the continuing, advancing evil in Adam's children. Already a pair of brothers were pursuing two different walks of life and offering their sacrifices at separate altars; hostility erupts and ends in murder. Cain does not evoke our sympathy as Adam did; his crime is prompted by envy and jealousy, and he rejects the warning which is offered him. Cain does not flee in shame and fright as the Lord draws near as Adam had done, but answers brazenly, "Am I my brother's keeper?" More forcefully than by a sermon of thousands of words does J instruct us by putting this cynical question in the mouth of the man who had just murdered his brother! Cain's line (4:17-24—J) advances in the technology of civilization but also in wickedness; compared to the casual slaughter of Lamech, Cain's murder seems a feeble crime.

GENEALOGY: 5 (P). The genealogy has always been of considerable importance in the Near East. In Scripture it is used not only to record successive generations, but also as a vehicle of teaching. For example, St. Luke is reminding us of the universal nature of Jesus' redemptive mission when he traces His origin back to Adam (Luke 3:23-38). The genealogy can also be a sort of "instant history" for covering long periods in a minimum of space,[11] and that is the main function of P's list of patriarchs in Genesis 5. Except for the story of Noah and the flood, in fact, P has little but genealogy to link creation and the call of Abraham; the line is traced from Adam to Noah in Genesis 5 and carried on to Abraham in 10:1, 21-31; 11:10-27.

The longevity of the patriarchs of Genesis 5 no longer troubles us as it did earlier ages, for it is now apparent that P was following an artificial convention rather than making an historical assertion. Similar lists (for one, see *ANET* 265) found in Mesopotamia likewise span the period from creation to the flood in nine or ten generations of extraordinary length. Compared to them, P's ages are quite restrained; the Sumerian king list records reigns ranging from an extreme 43,200 years to a brief 18,600 years—a poor unfortunate cut off in his youth, no doubt! The advanced ages reflect an ancient belief in a remarkable vitality in the first generations. P contains no Fall narrative, but the steady decline in the age spans in successive genealogies[12] may reflect the ravages of sin from the time of the flood on.

[11]Cf. 1 Chronicles 1-9 where the period from Adam to David is spanned almost solely through genealogies.

[12]From Adam to Noah the ages range between 1000 and 700 years; from Shem to Terah between 600 to 200 years; from Abraham to Jacob between 200 to 100 years.

THE FLOOD: 6:1-9:17 (J AND P). The biblical account of the flood[13] is a
classic example of the retelling of an ancient pagan story in the light
of Israelite faith. Of the many versions of the flood story that have
come down to us, the most complete is that preserved in the *Epic of
Gilgamesh*. In the course of Gilgamesh's quest for immortality he finds
Utnapishtim, the hero of the flood, the Akkadian counterpart of Noah.
Utnapishtim, who resides with his wife far away "at the mouth of the
rivers," launches into a very detailed report of his adventures. The gods
had determined to destroy mankind by a flood, but one of them warns
Utnapishtim and orders him to build a huge ship. He constructs and
provisions it according to specification and takes aboard "the seed of
all living things." He and his family are saved in the ship from the
fearful storm that flattens and submerges all else, terrifying the gods
by its fury. The storm abates on the seventh day. The ship comes to a
halt on a mountain top and remains there for seven days, during which
Utnapishtim sends forth a dove, a swallow, and a raven. He leaves the
ship and offers sacrifice; the gods, delighted by the sweet smell, come
to the sacrifice and, after resolving their own quarrels, admit Utnapishtim and his wife to the ranks of the immortals.

The many resemblances to the biblical flood story are obvious; the
story, in one form or another, was common property in the ancient Near
East. That some recollection of an actual cataclysm stands behind the
account is quite likely, even though we cannot be sure when and where
it was; the suggestion that it was geographically and anthropologically
universal, however, is part of the exaggeration of the story. The men of
those days, in any case, considered it an epochal event, and what
interests us particularly is how they told of it. In accord with the mentality of the times, little account was taken of secondary causes, but it
was simply attributed to the activity of God or the gods. In the Mesopotamian version the picture of the gods is not an edifying one and reveals
scant reverence for them. They are said to cower like dogs before the
fearful force of the storm and to cluster like flies about Utnapishtim
as he offers sacrifice to them. No reason is given for the decision of the
gods to destroy mankind, although at one point Ishtar reproaches
herself with the question:

> How could I bespeak evil in the Assembly of the gods,
> Ordering battle for the destruction of my people?

Later she wishes Enlil excluded from a share in Utnapishtim's sacrifice:

> For he, unreasoning, brought on the deluge
> And my people consigned to destruction.

[13]For the separation of the sources, see p. 31. Gen 6:1-4 probably comes from an ancient
pagan piece which attempted to explain the origin of giants from carnal union between
gods and mortal women—a common theme in folklore. In J's use the "sons of God" are
angels and the piece has the function of describing the cosmic corruption which preceded
the flood.

Enlil is, in fact, considerably irritated when he learns that someone has been spared from the destruction.

How differently the story is told in Genesis! There is no suggestion that events could escape the control of God; no thought that He could act unreasonably. Human sin is the sufficient explanation for sending the calamity, and Noah's blamelessness is the reason that he is spared. In J's primeval history, then, the flood story becomes another example of the advance of wickedness in the world (6:1-8) and its disastrous results. Yet the aftermath (8:20-22) is not without significance: God will henceforth renounce this way of dealing with sin, and even alleges the evil bent of the human heart as an excusing factor—the very reason given for the flood in 6:5. Yet J would not suggest that the all holy God could simply abide or condone sin; it might not be far-fetched to suspect, then, that a plan of redemption is in the offing.

P's sequel to the flood (9:1-17) is more complex. The advent of sin has dissipated the paradisiac aspects of the first generations and mankind ceases to be vegetarian; the relationship of humans to other creatures is thus worsened. God's merciful promise, parallel to that in J, is here expressed in the form of a covenant, with the rainbow as its sign. Since Noah is the new father of the human race, the covenant made with him is universal in scope; God's concern is thus seen to be with mankind as such in this first of P's covenants. The two later ones (Abrahamitic and Sinaitic) will progressively narrow the attention to Israel.

Utnapishtim had been elevated to the ranks of the immortals after the flood. No such glorification awaits Noah; the next scene (9:20-27—J) finds him drunk and naked. There are no human heroes in Scripture! The story as it now stands is confusing with its transition from the sin of Ham to the cursing of Canaan and possibly is the result of the fusion of two traditions. Since the people in the piece stand for the nations which will spring from them, the story contains a comment on the sexual aberrations of the Canaanites and the punishments they deserve.

THE TOWER OF BABEL: **11:1-9 (J)**. Skipping the Table of the Nations (Genesis 10), we come to the story of the Tower of Babel. Although it presents difficulties of interpretation, this final episode in Primeval History has great importance. Originally it was an etiology (p. 285, n. 12) of the diversity of languages, but in the Yahwist's complex it takes on a profounder meaning. The story is Mesopotamian in origin and most scholars hold that the tower it speaks of is a ziggurat, a temple-tower built of many, progressively smaller levels; such structures were well-known in Mesopotamia. The story may originally have told of men who wished to scale the heavens and storm the abode of the gods, but nothing of that remains in J's adaptation; rather, with fine irony, the Lord is said to "come down" from His lofty height to see the work. As the story now stands the specific sin of the builders is not clearly expressed; it seems to be contained in the boast that they would "make a name for themselves" (v 4)—attain to power and greatness quite apart from God—coupled with the observation that "nothing will later stop them from doing whatever they presume to do" (v 6). The confusing of languages was, then, a preventive rather than a punitive measure; but the effect, in any case, was that mankind moved another long stride from the ideal conditions at the beginning: "From there the Lord scattered them all over the earth."

What is the import of this story for the Yahwist? He was interested in far more than a popular (and thoroughly unscientific) explanation of the diversification of languages. He looked at the world of men and women about him and saw division and separation at every level of existence—brother from brother and nation from nation—so that strife of every kind was possible and actual; mankind was "scattered." Ultimately, he knew, this situation was the result of sin in the world, and in the story of the tower he found a ready-made vehicle for expressing this truth.

But if the story of the Tower of Babel is the last in Primeval History, it thereby forms the crucial link which, in J's plan, joins salvation history, beginning with the call of Abraham, to these opening narratives. Von Rad points out that each act of sin and punishment in the preceding chapters is accompanied by an act of grace and mercy on the part of God, mitigating the penalty and supporting mankind: Adam and Eve were expelled from the garden but did not immediately experience the death threatened (2:17); Cain was cursed for his murder and driven from the presence of God but was preserved from the death penalty he deserved (4:11-15); even after the sin-provoked disaster of the flood, God allows mankind a new start and promises His preservation. Von Rad continues:

> This consoling preservation, that revelation of God's hidden gracious will, is missing, however, at one place, namely, at the end of the primeval history. The story about the Tower of Babel concludes with God's judgment on mankind; there is no word

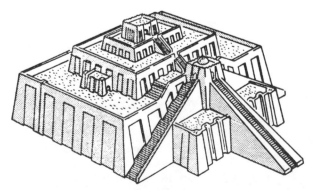

Figure 8.   *Reconstruction of the ancient ziggurat at Ur.*

of grace. The whole of primeval history, therefore, seems to break off in shrill dissonance, and the question formulated above arises even more urgently: Is God's relationship to the nations now finally broken; is God's gracious forbearance now exhausted; has God rejected the nations in wrath forever? That is the burdensome question which no thoughtful reader of ch. 11 can avoid; indeed, one can say that our narrator intended by means of the whole plan of his primeval history to raise precisely this question and to pose it in all its severity. Only then is the reader properly prepared to take up the strangely new thing that now follows the comfortless story about the building of the tower: the election and blessing of Abraham. We stand, therefore, at the point where primeval history and sacred history dovetail, and thus at one of the most important places in the entire Old Testament. Primeval history had shown an increasing disturbance in the relationship between humanity and God and had culminated in God's judgment on the nations. The question about God's salvation for all nations remains open and unanswerable in *primeval* history. But our narrator *does* give an answer, namely, at the point where sacred history begins. Here in the promise that is given Abraham something is again said about God's saving will and indeed about a salvation extending far beyond the limits of the covenant people to "all the families of the earth" (ch. 12.3). . . . Thus that difficult question about God's relationship to the nations is answered. . . . It is therefore misleading to find in ch. 11 that conclusion to the primeval history, as is usually done. . . . Rather, its conclusion, indeed its key, is ch. 12:1-3, for only from there does the theological significance of this universal preface to saving history become understandable.[14]

Thus the stories of Primeval History, with their deep insight into the meaning of sin and its consequences, are intended to show man's need for redemption and so prepare for the opening chapter of God's plan of redemption in the call of Abraham.

[14]*Genesis*, pp. 149-150.

Reading Suggestions

JBC §2. *PBS* #2, 7-25. *AUOT* 210-16. *MTES* 72-108.

Anderson, B. W., ed., *Creation in the Old Testament*. Philadelphia: Fortress Press, 1984.

Coats, G. W., *Genesis with an Introduction to Narrative Literature*. Grand Rapids: Eerdmans, 1984.

Heidel, A., *The Gilgamesh Epic and Old Testament Parallels*. Chicago: University of Chicago Press, 1946.

L'Heureux, C. E., *In and Out of Paradise*. New York: Paulist Press, 1983.

Maher, M., *Genesis*. *OTM*, Vol. 2.

Miller, P. D., Jr., *Genesis 1-11: Studies in Structure and Theme*. Sheffield: The University, 1978.

Speiser, E. A., *Genesis*, pp. 3-81.

Teeple, H. M., *The Noah's Ark Nonsense*. Evanston, Ill.: Religion and Ethics Institute, 1978.

von Rad, G., *Genesis*, pp. 43-158.

Vawter, B., *On Genesis*, pp. 37-163.

Westermann, C., *Genesis 1-11*. Minneapolis: Augsburg Publishing House, 1984.

Wolff, H. W., *Anthropology of the Old Testament*. Philadelphia: Fortress Press, 1981.

Bailey, L., "Wood from 'Mount Ararat': Noah's Ark?" *BA* 40 (1977) 137-46.

Brueggemann, W., "Of the Same Flesh and Bone (Gn 2,23a)," *CBQ* 32 (1970) 532-42.

Clines, D. J. A., "Theme in Genesis 1-11," *CBQ* 38 (1976) 483-507.

Coats, G. W., "The God of Death (*Power and Obedience in the Primeval History*)," *Int* 29 (1975) 227-39.

Coogan, M. D., "The Storm God and the Sea," *TBT* #79 (Oct, 1975) 457-64.

Fukita, S., "Theology of Hope in Genesis 1-11," *TBT* #80 (Nov. 1975) 519-27.

McKenzie, J. L., "God and Nature in the Old Testament," *Myths and Realities*. Milwaukee: The Bruce Publishing Company, 1963, pp. 85-132; "Myth and the Old Testament," *ibid.*, pp. 182-200; "Literary Characteristics of Genesis 2-3," *ibid.*, pp. 146-81.

Maly, E. H., "The Book of Genesis," *TBT* #85 (Oct. 1976) 878-84.

Marrs, R., "The Sons of God (Genesis 6:1-4)," *Restoration Quarterly* 23 (1980) 218-24.

Murtagh, J., "The Creation Accounts in the Old Testament and in Ancient Egypt," *TBT* #55 (Oct. 1971) 447-57.

Oden, R. A., Jr., "Transformation in Near Eastern Myths: Genesis 1-11 and the old Babylonian Epic of Atrahasis," *Religion* 11 (1981) 21-37.

Olbricht, T. H., "The Theology of Genesis," *Restoration Quarterly* 23 (1980) 201-217.

Schoonenberg, P., "Genesis and Evolution," *Listening: Journal of Religion and Culture* 15 (1980) 150-158.

Watson, P., "The Tree of Life," *Restoration Quarterly* 23 (1980) 232-38.

Williams, J. G., "Genesis 3," 35 (1981) 274-79.

Wilson, R. R., "The Old Testament Genealogies in Recent Research," *JBL* 94 (1975) 169-89.

6

A Wandering Aramean

(Scripture Reading: Genesis 12-50)

I HE LORD SAID to Abram: "Go forth from the land of your kinsfolk and from your father's house to a land that I will show you. I will make of you a great nation, and I will bless you; I will make your name great, so that you will be a blessing. I will bless those who bless you and curse those who curse you. All the communities of the earth shall find blessing in you" (Gen 12:1-3).

God's saving grace to mankind begins at that point where human forces are powerless to effect deliverance. Nowhere is this principle verified more strikingly than at the beginning of redemptive history. After the story in which the nations are scattered, the Yahwist recounts the call of Abraham and God's promises to him; God intervenes to begin a long chain of events which is to issue in salvation for the nations.[1]

The story of Abraham, Isaac, and Jacob is composed of many separate units of diverse origin which the Yahwist has skillfully and dramatically woven around the theme of the promise; later tradition has enriched the story with material from E and P without disturbing the basic pattern. God's summons to Abraham is introduced abruptly, with only a genealogy and some family history as background (11:10-32). Abraham's family is said to have migrated from "Ur of the Chaldees" to Haran, where God's call comes to him. From there he goes to Canaan (Palestine) in response to God's command. Canaan already had a settled population; much of it was Semitic, like Abraham himself.

Although only Sarah and Lot are named as companions of his migration, he was the head of a sizable clan (14:14), with extensive flocks of sheep and goats. Abraham, like Isaac and Jacob after him,

---

[1]For the sense of the "blessing formula" in Gen 12:3, see 48:20. On the supposition that Abraham's call is intended to dovetail with the Tower of Babel narrative, the Yahwist was thinking of a more positive share for the nations in Abraham's blessing than is literally stated in this traditional formula.

was a nomad or, more accurately, a seminomad. Modern Bedouins, examples of true nomads, are able to survive in the desert with relatively little dependence on civilization and enjoy unrestricted movement; this is possible because their economy is largely built on the camel.[2] But sheep and goats cannot penetrate far into the desert and must have water daily. Thus the needs of Abraham's flock kept him wandering in search of new pastures, but restricted him to the belt of moderate rainfall between the desert and the settled, cultivated land. The tendency was towards sedentarization, especially after larger cattle, like oxen, were added to the flocks; Isaac and Jacob seem even to have done some farming (26:12; 37:6-7). Had this process gone full term, as it had with so many before them, the Patriarchs and their descendants would simply have been swallowed up in the Canaanite population to which they were so closely related. The descent into Egypt, recounted in the closing chapters of Genesis, provides an explanation of why this did not happen.

When the Israelites went forth from Egypt, after many generations there, they had become a numerous people and were on their way to take possession of Canaan. In these events the biblical authors saw the fulfillment of the promises made by God to the Fathers, and they recounted the stories of Abraham, Isaac, and Jacob as a prologue to the exodus. Later we will ask whether they will bear the interpretation placed upon them. First the impact of the stories as they now stand should be appreciated.

SUMMONS AND PROMISE

The opening account of Abraham's call and his response (12:1-9) contain several themes I can mention only briefly. First, there is the gratuity of election. "Why Abraham?" we might ask. Scripture answers only that God chose him; God's freedom is not circumscribed by the qualities or even the merits of His creatures. Humanly speaking we would say that Abraham was a poor choice to become a great nation; according to the biblical tradition he was already advanced in years (12:4b—P) and was wed to a barren wife (11:30—J). On the individual level, too, God's saving grace begins where human forces fail! Secondly, there is the sublime obedience of Abraham and the faith which prompted it. Because of God's command and promise he left behind country and kinsfolk for a land that is not even named. The "faith" manifested here is not simply believing something, but a concrete commitment of himself to One who is able to fulfill His promises. The dialogue of salvation history gets off to an encouraging start as Abra-

---

[2]According to Albright, camels were domesticated in large numbers only around the 12th century and the references to them in Genesis are anachronistic "modernizing" touches.

ham answers a resounding "Amen!" Abraham weakens from time to time in his commitment, but in the final test showed himself willing to offer up in obedience even the child of promise (Genesis 22).

But it is especially the promises which occupy the center of attention in this account and in the rest of patriarchal history—the promises of progeny, land, and blessing. The childless man is to have offspring and become a great nation (12:2; "the father of a multitude of nations" according to P—17:5). The wanderer is to possess a land. Was the land promised to Abraham or to his descendants? The promise is found in many forms, and it is legitimate to suspect that the texts which speak only of Abraham's descendants possessing the land (e.g., 12:7) reflect the historical event rather than the earliest tradition. Semitic thought so closely identified patriarch and clan that the difference would have appeared slight. A certain poignant fulfillment is seen in the purchase of the burial plot (Genesis 23) into which each of the Fathers passes at death (25:9-10; 35:29; 50:13). The long deferment of fulfillment of the promise creates the tension which provides the drama of Genesis 12-50.

The bulk of the material of Genesis 12-50 is connected directly or indirectly with the promise—its frequent renewal, its confirmation by covenant, obstacles in the way of its fulfillment, human attempts to grasp it, human failure to trust it. It is repeated to Abraham (13:13-17; 15:5-7; 17:4-8; etc.) and renewed for Isaac (26:2-5) and Jacob (28:13-14). In two important passages the promise is confirmed by covenant (15:1-21; 17:1-14). A covenant is a solemn agreement ratified by some external rite. In the ancient Near East it had a deeper significance than a mere agreement, however, for it inaugurated a degree of fellowship and sharing of goods and supposed a certain community of interests. "For the stronger," observes Johannes Pedersen, "it is a question of making covenants in order to carry through one's aims; for the weaker to make a covenant with the strong in order to enjoy his strength."[3]

In the difficult, composite, but ancient narrative of 15:1-21 (JE), the Lord Himself, in fiery display, performs a covenant rite whose antiquity is attested by non-biblical texts. The Hebrew idiom, to *cut* a covenant, arose from the ancient practice of slaughtering an animal as a sacrifice and as a dramatized curse (see Jer 34:18). Although it is difficult to imagine what concrete experience lies behind this vivid description of God's covenant with Abraham, the passage is remarkable for the sense of religious awe that pervades it. This is no simple retrojection of the Sinai covenant, for there are notable differences; this one rests on a promise of future blessings and imposes no obligations, while that of Sinai will rest on God's gracious acts of the exodus and will impose specific commandments.

[3]*Israel, Its Life and Culture* I-II (London: Oxford University Press, 1926), p. 286.

The other covenant passage, 17:1-14 (P), is neither so picturesque nor so ancient. P's concern for religious institutions is seen in the giving of circumcision as sign of the covenant with Abraham. Circumcision was a custom already ancient and widely practiced in the world of the Patriarchs and did not, in fact, set them off from their neighbors. Among other peoples it was administered as a purificatory puberty or pre-marriage rite (cf. 17:25; 34:13-17), but in Israel it was done on the eighth day and, so, aptly symbolized entrance into the covenant community. It does not seem, however, that Israel attributed this significance to the rite before the exile, and our passage, therefore, reflects a late period.

The accounts of Sarah's posing as Abraham's sister (12:10-20; 20) receive their significance from the promise: Sarah in Pharaoh's or Abimelech's harem means the promise in jeopardy! But God watches over His word and intervenes to restore Sarah to her husband. Later there is an attempt to force the promise, as the still barren Sarah tries to become a mother vicariously, so to speak, by giving Hagar, her slave girl, to Abraham's embrace (Genesis 16). But the son born of this union, Ishmael, was not to be the child of promise (17:15-22).

The drama is sustained even after the birth of Isaac. Sarah, always able to master her lord, demands and obtains the expulsion of Hagar and Ishmael to safeguard Isaac's heritage (21:9-21). Later Isaac's life hangs in the balance as God leads Abraham to recognize that the promise comes from Him and remains in His keeping (Genesis 22). When it is a question of a suitable wife for Isaac, God's continued providence is palpably demonstrated (Genesis 24). The promise advances another generation with the birth of Jacob (25:19-26), but there is a complication in the form of a senior twin brother—to whom the first share of the family blessing, strength, and goods should go. Jacob, however, by astute bargaining and unscrupulous trickery, obtains the birthright and his father's blessing (25:27-34; 27). God's plan does not need human wickedness to succeed, but just as darkness had been integrated at creation into an ordered cosmos, so Jacob's deceit is utilized in God's plan.

The promise is again significantly advanced as Jacob, fleeing to Haran to escape Esau's anger, obtains from Laban, his uncle, the two wives who, with their slave girls, bear him the twelve sons who become the patriarchs of the twelve tribes of Israel. At the very outset, however, Jacob's trickery receives its reward when Laban substitutes dull-eyed Leah for lovely Rachel; moreover most of his latter years, after his return with his family to Canaan, are weighed down with grief because his sons deceived him concerning the fate of Joseph.

The Joseph cycle (Genesis 37-50) is not dominated by the theme of the promise to the same extent, but even here are emphasized God's providence, His power to bring good out of evil, and His preservation of Abraham's offspring. Joseph's words to his brothers sum it up: "Even though you meant harm to me, God meant it for good, to achieve his present end, the survival of many people" (50:20; cf. 45:5).

SOURCES AND HISTORICITY

Traditional tales from diverse sources have been utilized in telling the story of the Fathers, and the fact that there is any discernible unity in the presentation is a great tribute to the authors and editors of Genesis. In some of these tales the theme of the promise was not original but was imposed on them by the individuals or schools responsible for J, E, and P. To admit this is not to deny the truth of what they teach: the God who delivered Israel from Egypt and made her His people by covenant was already at work in the days of the Fathers, revealing Himself and inaugurating His plan of salvation. A closer study of the sources will provide a basis for evaluating this teaching.

Much of the material in Genesis 12-50 can be classified as tribal legends, i.e., stories preserved in Israel about her tribes and their founders. Many of them are very old, but in the retelling they have been adapted to the situation of the historical Israel and have been "refracted" by its more fully formed faith. One example, mentioned above, is P's account of God's covenant with Abraham; another is the use of the name Yahweh by the Patriarchs.[4] Still another is the device that makes all twelve tribal founders the sons of one man, Jacob. Historical Israel was constituted by the confederation of twelve tribes, some of them closely related, others less so (p. 112); in time these tribes came to regard themselves as related through the brotherhood of their founders, and this artificial picture is projected back into Genesis. The various components of Israel all had legends concerning their origins and their ancestors; after the tribes reached their normative state these legends were integrated into one prehistory of "all Israel." For this reason, although Abraham, Isaac, and Jacob were undoubtedly ancestors of various elements of Israel, we cannot assert that the father-son-grandson relationship is historical.

Some of these legends tell of the adventures of tribes and peoples through stories of individuals. The rivalry between Jacob and Esau (reckoned as father of the Edomites) reflects Israel's struggle with Edom and eventual ascendancy; the destruction of Shechem was accomplished by the *tribes* of Simeon and Levi, not the brothers (34:13-29); the account of the covenant between Jacob and Laban (31:44-54) probably originated in the settlement of a border dispute between Israel and an Aramean tribe.

---

[4]The tradition of E and P, that the name Yahweh was known in Israel only from the time of Moses, is correct; none of the theophoric names used by Israelites and their ancestors are compounded with Yahweh before the time of Moses.

Yet the stories are genuinely ancient and, in spite of such concessions, contain valuable information about the individual Patriarchs. Wellhausen, as we have seen, suggested that Abraham was "a free creation of unconscious art," and there are scholars of note today who would hold that the patriarchal stories reflect a period late in Israel's history rather than the Middle Bronze Age; Thomas L. Thompson and John Van Seters in particular have thus argued with subtlety and erudition.[5] Nevertheless, most scholars are convinced that the stories about the Fathers, on the whole, reflect the conditions and customs of the period in which the Bible places them, the first half of the 2nd millennium, and that the picture of their migrations, manner of life, and worship is a trustworthy one.

That the ancestors of Israel came from Upper Mesopotamia is supported both by the names of Abraham's forefathers and relatives (Peleg, Serug, Nahor, Terah, and Haran—cf. 11:16–26—are identical with place names in Upper Mesopotamia) and by traditions incorporated into Genesis 1–11. Many of these stories or elements of them (e.g., the description of Eden, the flood, and the Tower of Babel) have close parallels in the literature of Mesopotamia but bear almost no relation to that of Canaan or Egypt; if the traditional dating of the documents is followed, Israelite contacts with Mesopotamia during the monarchy would be too late to explain the presence of such material in J.

Many of the patriarchal practices and customs do not correspond at all to those of later Israel but fit nicely into the 2nd millennium, especially as it is now known to us from Mesopotamian sources. The most easily defensible explanation is that these stories have been handed on from that period with great fidelity. For example, Abraham's expectation that, without children of his own, his servant would be his heir (15:2–3) does not reflect biblical custom, but it is a custom reflected in the Nuzi tablets[6] (p. 12). Other documents from the same place tell of the sale of a birthright (for three sheep— somewhat more than Esau received) and of the binding force of a will made orally on one's deathbed; they provide background for the Jacob-Esau stories. Whether the Nuzi tablets give satisfactory background for some of the other customs illustrated in the patriarchal stories, e.g., the provision of a slave-girl to bear children to the man if the wife does not, Rachel's theft of her father's household idols (to provide inheritance rights for Jacob?), and the wife-sister motif, is now less certain. With reference to the last example, however, we can

---

[5] A good idea of the discussion raging in this area can be obtained by perusing the articles summarized in OTA 1 (1978) #120–123, 448, 450, 456, 464, 723.

[6] The Nuzi Tablets are from the 15th century, composed by Hurrians (the biblical Horites), a non-Semitic people who entered Upper Mesopotamia from the mountains of Armenia; it is probable, however, that customs witnessed by the tablets were taken over from the older, Semitic culture of the area.

point out that it is difficult to see why Israelites would invent stories that picture Abraham's wife as his half-sister (20:12) or Jacob as marrying a pair of sisters (29:15-30), unions which the later Israelite mores considered abominable (Lev 18:9, 18, 29).

While our clearest records of some of these customs are from the 15th century, the customs themselves are undoubtedly much older. When evidence from nomenclature, migrations, and the political situation is taken into account the patriarchal stories fit best into the earlier centuries of the 2nd millennium. Unfortunately it is difficult to be more precise than this, for no person or event of Genesis 12-50 can be surely identified with anything recorded by profane history. The battle of the kings described in Genesis 14 supposes a settled population in Transjordan, however, and archeological investigations indicate that after the 20th or 19th centuries the towns and cities were abandoned until the 13th century. Thus, Albright, Vawter, and others date the events of Genesis 14 (and Abraham) in the 19th century. The settlement of Abraham's family at Haran and the subsequent migration of Abraham to Palestine would then fit well into the movements of the Amorites (a Semitic people with whom the Israelites acknowledged kinship) which began ca. 2000 and continued for some time. Amorites took over Haran about this time and later penetrated into Palestine.

Religious Significance
of the Patriarchs

The Israelites knew that their ancestors before Abraham "dwelt beyond the River and served other gods" (Josh 24:2); but they believed that knowledge of the true God began with Abraham, so that when Yahweh commissioned Moses to lead them from Egypt, He could identify Himself as the God of the Fathers, "the God of Abraham, the God of Isaac, the God of Jacob" (Exod 3:6, 15-16; cf. 6:2). How valid is this belief? Moses led a group of Semitic clans from Egypt to Canaan in the name of Yahweh, the God who had revealed Himself to him; there is no reason to doubt the tradition that Moses identified Yahweh with the God of their ancestors who promised them the land of Canaan. In this sense, at least, the religion of the Patriarchs was a real beginning of and preparation for Israelite faith. But more can be said. Although the patriarchal stories have been overlaid by later theology, certain unique aspects of Israel's faith are already present in parts which are undeniably ancient; among these are personal call, promise, covenant, and historical plan. There is little in what we know of the religions of the Fertile Crescent to explain the emergence of these elements.

Genesis shows the Patriarchs as, in many ways, children of their own times. They lived like other seminomads, visited the same cities, and observed the same customs. They erected altars and sacred pillars; they even designated the God they worshiped as El, the name of the head of the Amorite and Canaanite pantheons, although they commonly qualified the term by some word or phrase: El-Shaddai ("Mighty God"? "God of the Mountain"?—17:1; 28:3); El-Olam ("Eternal God"—21:33); El-Bethel (31:13); El, the God of Israel (33:20); El, the God of your father (46:3); etc. The last two names relate God to individuals (Israel in 33:20 is another name for Jacob), like some other titles for God used by the Patriarchs: the Kinsman of Isaac (31:42), the Mighty One of Jacob (49:24), etc. Even this conception of an individual relationship between the divinity worshiped and the head of the tribe seems to have been widespread among nomadic groups. Yet when we add to this the call to Abraham, the promise, and the confirmation of the promise by covenant, we have a combination that suggests a personal concern on the part of God that has no parallel. Although the theme of the promise has been extended to episodes in which it did not originally appear, it is nevertheless part of the original tradition and the primary reason for the preservation of the tradition. Remove the promise and the story isn't worth telling.

It is the promise, primarily, that gives the historical dimension to patriarchal history, and even, since it is capable of ever more profound reinterpretation and always needs a deeper fulfillment, to all of biblical history. The God who promises to give Abraham the land, to make him into a great nation, to bless all nations through him, is the God who controls history and can work His plan in all the earth, among all peoples. In Abraham, God renews His friendship with mankind, and they share it who become partakers of Abraham's heritage.

Whether we call the faith of the Patriarchs "monotheistic" or not will depend largely on how we define that term. A covenant would seem to involve exclusive adherence to one God from whom all good things are hoped. The power of the God of the Fathers extends to all places, all ages, and all peoples: Abraham hears His call in Haran and experiences His help in Egypt; He disposes of the land at His will and works out His plan in history. We find here no repudiation of the existence of other gods, but that is hardly to be expected at this point. On the other hand, there is no later moment at which Israel's developing faith switched from many gods to one God; that point has already been passed. It is reasonable to postulate revelation as the beginning of Israel's unique faith. Israel's tradition names the Patriarchs as the first recipients, and critical investigation finds no grounds for rejecting that tradition.

READING SUGGESTIONS

PBS #2, 25-33; #3. *OTRG* #4. *AUOT* 26-30, 216-25. *BHI* 74-103.
MTES 112-15. *VAI* 289-94, 309-311. *WBA* 40-52.

Coats, G. W., *From Canaan to Egypt: Structural and Theological
    Context for the Joseph Story.* Washington, D.C.: The Catholic
    Biblical Association, 1976.
Davidson, R., *Genesis 12-50.* New York: Cambridge University Press,
    1979.
Gibson, J. C. L., *Genesis, Volume 2.* Philadelphia: Westminster Press,
    1982.
Hunt, I., *The World of the Patriarchs.* Englewood Cliffs, N.J.:
    Prentice-Hall, Inc., 1967.
Millard, A. R., and Wiseman, D. J., eds., *Essays on the Patriarchal
    Narratives.* Winona Lake, Ind.: Eisenbrauns, 1983.
von Rad, G., *Genesis,* pp. 159-434.
Speiser, E. A., *Genesis,* pp. 85-378.
Vawter, B., *On Genesis,* pp. 167-476.
Westermann, C., *The Promises to the Fathers. Studies on the Patri-
    archal Narratives.* Philadelphia: Fortress Press, 1980.

Cazelles, H., "The History of Israel in the Pre-exilic Period," *ATI*
    274-81.
Coats, G. W., "The Joseph Story and Ancient Wisdom: A Reappraisal,"
    CBQ 35 (1973) 285-97.
_____, "Abraham's Sacrifice of Faith (*A Form-Critical Study of
    Genesis 22*)," *Int* 27 (1973) 389-400.
Fretheim, T., "The Jacob Traditions: Theology and Hermeneutic,"
    Int 26 (1972) 419-36.
Gordon, C. H., "Biblical Customs and the Nuzu Tablets," *BAR 2*
    21-33.
Harland, J. P., "The Destruction of the Cities of the Plain," *BAR*
    59-75.
Myers, J. M., "The Way of the Fathers," *Int* 29 (1975) 121-40.
Sarna, N. M., "Abraham in History," *Biblical Archeology Review* 3
    (1977) 5-9.
Sena, P. J., "Abraham—First Step Toward Reconciliation," *TBT*
    #85 (Oct. 1976) 872-77.
Thompson, T. L., "A New Attempt to Date the Patriarchal Narra-
    tives," *Journal of the American Oriental Society* 98 (1978)
    76-84.
Wcela, E. A., "The Abraham Stories, History and Faith," *BTB*
    10 (1980) 176-81.

7

"Out of Egypt
I Called My Son"

(Recommended Scripture Reading: Exodus 1–4; 11–12; 14–16;
19–24; 32–34; Numbers 13–14; 20–25; Deuteronomy 34)

IN THE LAST chapter we saw that the normative "twelve sons,
twelve tribes" scheme is an oversimplification of a more complex
reality. Many ethnic elements went into the composition of Israel,
some of which were acquired only in the process of conquering the
land. The complexity dates even to the time of the exodus; biblical
tradition itself records the fact that "a crowd of mixed ancestry also
went up with them" (Exod 12:38).

What was it, then, that welded separate groups and individuals into
a unity that could be called (and henceforth would be, from that day
to this) a people? The answer: the common experience of the
deliverance from Egypt and the covenant at Mt. Sinai. The importance of these two closely linked events can hardly be exaggerated, for
by them the people Israel was formed. The exodus from Egypt and the
events at Mt. Sinai, filled out with stories of Israel's experiences in the
desert, make up the remainder of the narrative portions of the Pentateuch. Before we return to the biblical traditions, however, we must
say something of the background against which these events took
place.

LAND OF BONDAGE

The closing chapters of Genesis report that the descendants of Jacob
migrated to Egypt because of famine in Palestine. The land of their
sojourn had already known a long history when they arrived; the
Great Sphinx was already ancient. The succession of thirty dynasties
that ruled there stretch from early in the 3rd millennium to 332 B.C.,
but the beginnings of Egyptian government go back to the 4th millennium. Early in her history the two parts of the land, Upper Egypt (the

Figure 9. *Slaves making bricks in Egypt. In this scene from a 15th century B.C. tomb painting, clay is mixed with water, pressed into moulds, and set out to dry. The oversized figure at the right of the top panel is an Egyptian overseer. From C. R. Lepsius,* Denkmäler aus Aegypten und Aethiopien, II *(Berlin, 1849-1859).*

southern part, stretched out along the Nile) and lower Egypt (the northern part, mainly the Nile Delta area) were united. She called herself "the land of two kingdoms," and one pharaoh ruled both except in times of weakness and division. As early as the Old Kingdom (29th to 23rd centuries), Egypt, a virtually treeless land, imported cedar from Phoenicia; and Byblos, on the Phoenician coast, was practically an Egyptian colony. During the Middle Kingdom (21st to 18th centuries), campaigns to the north brought Palestine and part of Phoenicia under Egyptian control for a while. The disruption of that control toward the end of the period resulted partly from the Amorite incursions mentioned above, partly from internal weakness.

Because this feebleness continued under the succeeding dynasties, no effective resistance could be offered to the waves of foreign invaders who now took over control of Egypt, establishing themselves first on the Delta (ca. 1720) and then extending their power to the rest of the land. These invaders, the Hyksos ("foreign chieftains"), provided the pharaohs of the 15th and 16th dynasties. They seem to have come mainly from Palestine and Syria and were of predominantly Semitic stock. They may have been set on the move by pressure from the Hurrian invasion (p. 70, n. 6). The Hyksos established their capital at Avaris on the Delta and from there maintained control not only of Egypt, but also of extensive holdings in Palestine and Syria. It is likely, as we will see, that it was under the Hyksos that the Israelite clans came to Egypt.

The traditional Egyptian nobility at Thebes in Upper Egypt eventually rallied to seize independence and then to attack the hated foreigners. Under Amòsis (ca. 1552-1527), founder of the 18th dynasty (ca. 1552–1306), the Hyksos were driven from Egypt, and the Palestinian fortress (at Sharuhen) in which they took refuge destroyed. The vigorous pharaohs of the new dynasty led armies to the north year after year to bring Palestine and beyond under their control, and so to insure themselves against another invasion. They succeeded in extending their empire to the Euphrates. It was Egypt's finest hour. Further progress was blocked by Mitanni, a kingdom founded by Hurrians and Indo-Aryans in Upper Mesopotamia. After an initial clash, an agreement was reached; accord was mutually advantageous, for the rising power of the Hittites in Asia Minor was a threat to both.

The Amarna letters (p. 13), ca. 1376–1350, indicate a period of Egyptian weakness. These communications, mainly from kings of Canaanite and Syrian city-states subject to Egypt, reflect a breakdown in Egypt's Asian empire. They tell of disloyalty on the part of many of Egypt's vassals and of the incursions of bands of Habiru.[1] The appeals for help to deal with these troubles were ignored and the Hittites, now on the march, profited from the confusion and anarchy to take over much of Egypt's Asian territory. Mitanni, too, appealed in vain for help and soon became a Hittite vassal. The Egyptian general Haremhab and the pharaohs of the 19th dynasty (ca. 1306–1200) set about restoring the empire, and under Ramses II (1290–1224) the inevitable conflict with the Hittites took place. Neither side could win a conclusive victory, however, and eventually peace was reached through treaty (ca. 1270). Ramses II then undertook an intensive building campaign at home. He restored Avaris (a work begun by Seti I, his father), renamed it Raamses and made it his capital in place of Thebes, the capital since the expulsion of the Hyksos. The Egyptian texts speak of Apiru (here: state slaves) working on these projects.

The successor of Ramses II was Merneptah (1224–1211); he is important to us because after one of his campaigns in Asia he erected a triumphal stele which names Israel among his victims ("Israel is laid waste, his seed is not." *ANET* 378). This is the earliest non-biblical reference to the Israelites; it indicates, as usually interpreted, that they were in Palestine by Merneptah's fifth year (ca. 1220). They were not yet fully settled, for they are designated as a people rather than a land. Almost at once this pharaoh had to face the first of a series of attacks

---

[1]References to the Habiru are found in texts from the 20th to the 12th centuries, in various places from Ur to Egypt ("Apiru" in Egyptian texts). They appear in diverse roles—as free-booters, mercenaries, prisoners of war, state slaves, etc. The term is not ethnic but seems to designate groups on the fringes of society, without property, and without normal legal rights. "Hebrew" is probably etymologically equivalent to Habiru, but it is not simply identical in meaning; in the Bible, "Hebrew" is applied only to Israelites and their ancestors, while the Habiru were more widely scattered in space and time. Yet the biblical term does fit into the broader picture in that it is used to designate Abraham and his descendants only in situations where, socially or politically, they were "Habiru." While the Habiru of the Amarna letters are not the Israelites invading under Joshua, a possible connection will be pointed out in Chapter 10.

by the so-called Sea Peoples, invaders from the Aegean Islands. The Hittite Empire fell before them, and although Egypt (under Ramses III) finally drove them off, except for the Philistines who settled on the southern coast of Palestine, the effort cost so much that she was never a mighty power again.

Deliverance from Egypt

My father was a wandering Aramean who went down to Egypt with a small household and lived there as an alien. But there he became a nation great, strong and numerous. When the Egyptians maltreated and oppressed us, imposing hard labor upon us, we cried to the Lord, the God of our fathers, and he heard our cry and saw our affliction, our toil and our oppression. He brought us out of Egypt with his strong hand and outstretched arm, with terrifying power, with signs and wonders (Deut 26:5-8).

No Egyptian text gives an account of the exodus;[2] the escape of a group of state slaves was not a matter of great importance to them. We know of the exodus only through the traditions preserved in the Bible, such as the admirable summary contained in the liturgical prayer given above. There can be no doubting the fact, however, for it is too firmly embedded in every layer of Israelite tradition. The nature of the traditions—liturgical, confessional, poetical—rules out the possibility of a reconstruction that is wholly satisfactory from an historical point of view, but the general picture and many details are consistent with what we know from other sources.

Israel's accounts of the exodus were preserved and transmitted in compositions intended to recall Yahweh's mighty works and evoke Israel's grateful response, such as the "cultic credos" (Deut 26:5-9; 6:20-24; Josh 24:2-13), or poetic compositions like Exodus 15; Ps 77:14-21; 78; 105; 106; 114; 135; 136. Covenant renewal ceremonies at the great sanctuaries, too, would have been occasions for reciting the saving acts of God which had made Israel a people.

The annual Passover celebration deserves special mention in this regard. Exodus 12 reports that Moses prescribed the Passover ritual on the eve of the exodus: each family was to sacrifice a lamb, smear its blood on the doorposts, and celebrate a sacred meal at night on the flesh of the lamb. He further commanded them to repeat this rite each year in commemoration of their deliverance and to explain the meaning of it to their children. This chapter really reflects how the Passover was celebrated at a later time (vv 1-20, 40-51 are from P, vv 24-27

---

[2]Unless the reference to Israel on the Merneptah stele be taken, with some scholars, to be an attempt to make the exodus an Egyptian triumph: Israel has been driven into the desert to perish. Indeed, to believe Egyptian records, no pharaoh ever lost a battle! On any view, the stele text contains the first in a long line of premature obituaries on God's people.

from D), rather than its institution. But the practice of reciting the events of the exodus on this annual feast, a custom observed in Jewish families to this day, must have arisen early. The Passover feast itself was an ancient one; its ritual indicates that it arose among nomad shepherds. It was probably celebrated by the Israelites even before the Egyptian sojourn. But because the remarkable deliverance occurred at about the same time of year, possibly in close conjunction with it (cf. 5:1), this old nomadic feast came to be celebrated as a commemoration of it.[3] The connection is already present in J (12:21-23, 29-39) and undoubtedly is much older. The Passover celebration was, then, one context in which exodus traditions were handed on.

The Pentateuchal authors, therefore, had a variety of sources, some of them quite ancient,[4] from which to tell the story of the exodus. For a strictly scientific history they would have been inadequate, but they do contain much that is historical.

SOJOURN, EXODUS, AND HISTORY. We have seen how difficult it is to date the events of patriarchal history; taking the biblical accounts alone this would be true also of the descent into Egypt, the exodus, and the conquest. Fortunately, however, the lines can be drawn more finely for these events. Evidence that will be mentioned in Ch. 10 points to the second half of the 13th century for the conquest, and an exodus about 40 years earlier fits well most of the available data. A probable time can also be given for the descent into Egypt. The latter chapters of Genesis tell of Joseph's rise to high office in Egypt and of the settlement of Jacob's family in "the land of Goshen" (46:28-47:6). After a long time (430 years, according to Exod 12:40), "a new king, who knew nothing of Joseph, came to power in Egypt" (Exod 1:8). The Israelites were enslaved, forced to build the cities of Pithom and Raamses (1:11), and to undertake other labors. If we date the Israelite migration to Egypt during the Hyksos period, Joseph's rise to power and the lordly treatment of Jacob's family become intelligible; most of the Hyksos were Semites themselves and would have been more likely to grant such favors than would native Egyptians.

The name Goshen has not been found outside the Bible, but scholarly opinion locates it in the Wadi Tumilat region, northeast of the Delta. The easy transit from Goshen to the pharaoh's presence

---

[3] In a similar fashion the Feast of Unleavened Bread, originally an agricultural feast adopted only after the settlement in Canaan, possibly from the Canaanites, was later combined with the Passover so that it, too, came to commemorate the exodus. Such "historicization" of ancient feasts in no way weakens the historical character of the events commemorated, but rather points up the difference between the Israelite and pagan religions: whereas the latter are tied to nature and the cycle of the seasons, the former exalts the action of God in history; even celebrations which began as seasonal feasts were transformed into commemorations of God's saving acts.

[4] According to Albright, Exodus 15 is the oldest Hebrew poem of any length that we have.

(Gen 47:1–11) supposes the court was nearby, and that would suit Hyksos times, when the capital was at Avaris on the Delta. If we suppose that Jacob's family entered Egypt during the 17th century, while the Hyksos were in power, possibly as a peaceful phase of that movement, we won't be far wrong. After the expulsion of the Hyksos, Egyptian oppression of the foreign elements which had entered with them could be expected; the biblical traditions reflect just such a situation.

The early part of the reign of Ramses II (1290–1224) is the probable time of the exodus. Exod 1:11 says that the Israelites built Pithom and Raamses, and we know that this work was begun under Seti I (ca. 1305–1290) and completed under Ramses.[5] The Egyptian texts attribute the labor to Apiru, and in this instance the term must include the biblical Hebrews (p. 76, no. 1). The accounts of Moses' frequent interviews with the pharaoh (Exodus 5–12) suppose that the royal court is near Goshen, and this detail too points to the time of Ramses II. Avaris was destroyed when the Hyksos were expelled, and the capital was moved to Thebes; it was not until Ramses rebuilt Avaris and renamed it for himself that there was again a Delta capital. The evidence of Merneptah's stele also suits an exodus under Ramses.

CALL OF MOSES. It has been said often enough that if the Bible did not λ tell us of Moses, we should have to invent him. However much we may exalt the divine initiative in the formation of Israel, some great human genius must also have played a part. Fortunately, we have no need to invent Moses, for the Bible tells us much about him. Though not an eloquent speaker (4:10), he was nevertheless a great religious leader. His attempt to resist God's call (3:11–4:17) suggests that he foresaw what great suffering it would involve—a constant tug of war between the absolute demands of a God he would not disobey and a recalcitrant people he would not abandon; yet once having submitted to the will of God, he carried out his mission with heroic fidelity. Science can add little to what the Bible tells of Moses, nor should we expect it to. We do know, however, that his name is authentically Egyptian; it is a theophoric name on the order of Tuth-mosis, but abbreviated by omission of the god's name.

It is on the occasion of Moses' call that E and P record the revelation of the name Yahweh. Some authors suggest that the name was χ mediated to Moses in Midian by Jethro, his father-in-law, priest of an unnamed god (3:1). The theory is proposed very attractively by H. H. Rowley[6] but cannot be considered proven. Exod 3:14 purports to explain the meaning of the name, but the passage was composed when

[5]If Exod 2:23 and 4:19 are understood to require separate rulers for the oppression and exodus, then Seti I is the pharaoh of the oppression, Ramses II the pharaoh of the exodus.

[6]*From Joseph to Joshua* (London: Oxford University Press, 1950), pp. 149-61. Rowley's dating of the exodus is somewhat different than that followed here.

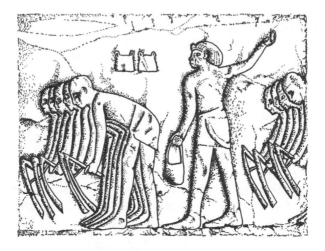

Figure 10. *"I have witnessed the affliction of my people in Egypt and have heard their cry of complaint against their slave drivers"* (Exod 3:7). *From an Egyptian relief.*

the name was already ancient and its meaning forgotten. Probably the name is a causative[7] form of the verb "to be" and meant "He causes (or makes) to be," and so expresses creative power. Exod 3:14 does, indeed, derive the name from the verb "to be," but in a somewhat different sense. The phrase "I am who I am" seems to indicate a refusal to give a name (even though the phrase is immediately taken as supplying the name) and suggests that God's nature is too mysterious and profound to be expressed in any name. In Semitic thought a name is not simply an arbitrary sound to designate a person, but an expression of his or her inmost being.

However the name is explained and however it came to Moses, it was he who mediated it to Israel and in the context of the exodus. For this reason its primary association for them was salvation; Yahweh would always be for them first and foremost the God of the exodus, the God of deliverance and salvation. "It is I, I Yahweh; there is no savior but me," wrote Deutero-Isaiah (Isa 43:11) during the exile, echoing the thought of Israel through all the ages.

SIGNS AND WONDERS. It makes a difference what you call a thing. The person who scoffs at "the Loch Ness monster" might display scientific curiosity about the possibility of "a prehistoric survival at Loch Ness." Now, it is legitimate to define "miracle" as an effect surpass-

---

[7] English usually expresses causation by a combination of verbs, but there are a few words in which causation is expressed by a variation in the root of the simple verb: to fell, to set, to lay, and to drench, are causatives of to fall, to sit, to lie, and to drink.

ing the powers of nature or contrary to the laws of nature, as theologians often do; but we must beware of trying to satisfy this definition every time the Bible speaks of God's intervention.

The biblical authors did not have our conception of the "laws of nature" and so could not have precisely the concept of miracle explained above. They spoke rather of mighty deeds, of signs and wonders performed by God in working out His plan in history. For them God is the Creator and Ruler of nature and was well able to rally its forces to accomplish His will; there was no syllogizing about what nature could do and what it could not do. Creation is moved at the presence of its Maker: He touches the mountains and they smoke (Ps 104:32); "The sea beheld and fled; Jordan turned back. The mountains skipped like rams. . . . Before the face of the Lord, tremble, O earth . . ." (Ps 114:3–4, 7). To ask "How, then, can we *prove* (to ourselves or others) that God has acted?" betrays an apologetic concern that they did not have. The accounts which report God's mighty deeds are confessional documents, intended to glorify God for what He has done, and are written from a deep and simple faith. But there is nothing naive in the recognition that the Creator of the forces of nature is responsible for their effects whether for weal or woe; such effects must play a role in God's providential design.

The "proof" that God has acted is found not in the naturally impossible character of the events but in the meaning they have within the drama. Moses experiences the call of God and is commissioned to lead the Israelites from Egypt; this he does and, when he has brought them to Mt. Sinai, mediates a covenant between them and the God who called them forth. The People of God is formed, and an essential step in redemptive history has been taken. It is within this context that the meaning of the plagues of Egypt as God's mighty deeds must be viewed. Frogs, gnats, cattle pestilence, hail, and locusts can surely be regarded as natural phenomena. The putrefaction of the Nile and the darkness, too, can be explained as natural events.[8] We cannot argue that, since they appeared and disappeared at the word of Moses, they must be supernatural; the nature of our sources does not permit us to insist on such details. Yet the succession of events which made Israel's escape possible must have been truly extraordinary, for the signs and wonders of the exodus deeply impressed themselves upon Israel's national consciousness for all time to come.

To hold that God acts *through* nature as often as not is no denial that miracles, in the strict sense, are related in the Bible; each case must be judged on its own merits. It would, accordingly, be false to

---

[8]The tenth plague, the death of the first-born, is not so easily susceptible of a natural explanation. It is possible, as many hold, that the account grew out of the Passover celebration. The blood ritual in the original nomadic feast was intended as a protection from danger; when the Passover began to be celebrated as a commemoration of the exodus (p. 77), the blood ritual was reinterpreted as a protection from a plague which had fallen on each Egyptian household—the death of the first-born.

the minds of the biblical authors to try to rationalize every wonder they report; attempts to do this soon betray the prejudices that prompt them.

No element of the exodus epic was more keenly remembered than the intervention which allowed Israel to escape the Egyptian chariotry by crossing the sea[9] just when all seemed lost (Exod 14:10-22). The event is so overlaid with various stages of tradition that it is impossible to recover the original event. The important point is that in the moment of direst need a way of salvation was given.

EVENTS AT SINAI

The Hebrew slaves who arrived at Mt. Sinai under Moses (Exodus 19) had already acquired a certain unity through their common experience of the exodus and the march through the wilderness. At Mt. Sinai a new experience awaited them, for there they were awed by a fearful theophany; Yahweh makes His presence known to all the people, while Moses continues as mediator.

COVENANT. To the experience of the exodus is added a new basis of unity, one which could be extended also to later generations. As God had once entered into covenant with Abraham, so He now does with the people acquired by His mighty deeds. There is no reason to doubt that Israel's covenant dates back to the desert generation. Only covenant or something very like it could explain the character of Israel as she first emerges into the light of history, a people based on loyalty to one God.

The importance of the covenant for Israel can hardly be exaggerated. No other basis for peoplehood could have served the Israel we know from the OT. Race or geography would not do, for they cannot confer a religious character; Israel was always racially mixed, in fact, and at times (as at Sinai) had no land of her own. And no other basis of peoplehood could serve so well for a plan of redemption that is ultimately universal in scope.

The covenant is a consequence of election. Yahweh had chosen Israel to be His People; through the covenant this relationship is given

---

[9]It is not possible to identify the body of water in question with any certainty. The Hebrew name, *yam suph,* means Reed Sea (perhaps a description rather than a proper name). No body of water by that name is known, though a 13th century Egyptian document refers to a Papyrus Marsh near Raamses. Other possibilities are the Bitter Lakes, Lake Timsah, and Lake Balah. It is not impossible, however, that ancient tradition thought the crossing had been at some part of the Red Sea, such as the northern tip of the Gulf of Suez, for wherever *yam suph* occurs in other contexts, it refers to the Red Sea, or at least to the Gulf of Aqaba (e.g., 1 Kgs 9:26). The route of the exodus remains unclear and even the location of Mt. Sinai is not certain.

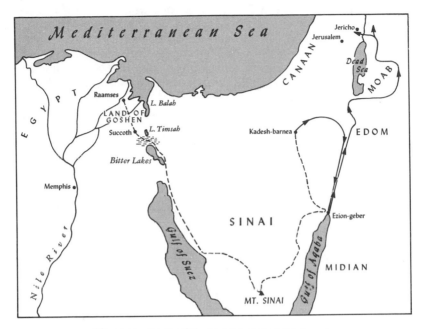

Figure 11. *Route of the Exodus and of the Invasion.*
---- probable Exodus route.
-► probable Invasion route.

form and permanence. Israel becomes Yahweh's covenant partner in
response to His elective love; the dialogue of redemptive history continues. The covenant becomes the basis of Israel's relationship to God
through historical events and sets her faith worlds apart from the
religions around her, tied as they were to the cycle of nature, fertility
cults, magical practices, and capricious divinities. Faithfulness was expected of a covenant partner. In the years and centuries ahead Israel
would often be wanting in covenant loyalty (*hesed*), but was never
abandoned by the God who called her. Israel's most frequent song of
praise would be *ki le'olam hasdo*—"For his *hesed* is everlasting."

We should be aware that the use of the covenant concept to describe
divine-human relations is an analogy. Analogy is, in fact, the expe-
dient to which we are constantly driven in any attempt to talk about
God. We can speak meaningfully about the "Fatherhood of God,"
for example, only because of our knowledge of human fatherhood. So
also Israel could speak of covenant with God only because they were
already familiar with covenant as a human institution. Covenant, as
practiced in the life of Israel, was understood to inaugurate a new relationship, one often similar to blood kinship, and to involve a sharing
of *shalom* and blessing; the weaker partner shares in the strength of

the stronger, and between the two only one will should exist (see J. Pedersen, *Israel, Its Life and Culture,* pp. 263-310). It is instructive to remember that Israel can be spoken of as "partner" because the multitude can be thought of as a single entity, in fact a covenant community. An important consequence, which shines through in much of Israel's legislation and underlies much prophetic teaching, is that between the members of the covenant community, too, should exist a real sense of kinship, a sharing of *shalom* and blessing, and that true justice (*sedaqah*) which goes beyond mere legal obligation. Thus at the very heart of Israel's religion are found the vertical and horizontal dimensions of the covenant—religious obligation to God and right behavior within the covenant community—which will later be summed up in the two-fold commandment of love.

This approach to covenant seems a more valid and fruitful one than the frequent tendency to compare it with international treaty forms, though this is a matter we cannot neglect to discuss. Many scholars[10] think that the closest parallels to the Sinai covenant are found in documents of the Hittities, an empire which flourished ca. 1450–1200, within which period the events at Mt. Sinai must be dated. The Hittite treaties are of two types: the parity treaty, in which two kings of equal rank undertook mutual obligations; and the suzerainty or vassal treaty, in which an overlord imposed obligations upon a vassal. It has been said that the Sinai covenant is cast in the form of a suzerainty treaty. This is, indeed, in accord with the spirit of Sinai: whereas in the patriarchal covenants Yahweh had bound Himself through promises, at Sinai He appears as Israel's sovereign, calling her to bind herself to Him as His people and to accept His commandments. He does not bind Himself to any specific obligation, though it is understood that He intends to further the welfare and salvation of His people. The following paragraphs give the usual provisions of the suzerainty treaty and the OT parallels which have been adduced:

1) *Preamble.* The sovereign who is making the covenant identifies himself by his name and titles. Exod 20:2 begins: "I am Yahweh your God."

2) *Historical prologue.* The great king describes the past benefits bestowed upon the vassal king. Exod 20:2 continues: "who brought you out of the land of Egypt, that place of slavery."

3) *Stipulations.* These are the obligations imposed upon the vassal. They are interesting from point of view both of form and of content. Many of them are cast in the imperative (apodictic—p. 88) form, which is that of the Decalogue and many other OT laws. The vassal may be commanded not to render service to any other king, to support the great king with troops in case of war, to trust the king, to report disloyal talk, to return fugitives, not to covet land that belongs to the

---

[10]See especially G. E. Mendenhall, "Ancient Oriental Law and Biblical Law" and "Covenant Forms in Israelite Tradition," *BAR 3,* 3-24, 25-33.

king, to appear once a year before the king, etc. In Exodus the Decalogue and other legislation would stand as the stipulations. The OT legislation is a mixture of imperative and conditional statements, just as the Hittite stipulations are. Some of Israel's laws are also similar in content; cf. especially the prohibition against other loyalties ("You shall not have other gods besides me"— Exod 20:3), the prohibition against coveting a neighbor's property (20:17), and the command to appear regularly to offer tribute and renew loyalty (23:17).

4) *Preservation of treaty and periodic reading.* This provision is not found in Exodus, though Deut 10:5 reports that the tablets of the Decalogue were deposited in the Ark.

5) *List of gods as witnesses.* Since a treaty is an agreement confirmed by oath, the gods are called upon to witness it; they are the ones who will punish infractions of the oath taken in their name. Since the OT acknowledges no divinity but Yahweh, this element is not to be expected there; in Deut 4:26; 30:19; and 31:28, however, Moses calls heaven and earth (included with the gods in the Hittite lists) as witnesses against the Israelites.

6) *Curses and blessings.* These are the punishments and rewards which the gods are asked to visit on those who break or keep the treaty—the divine sanctions. Exod 23:20-33 speaks of blessings God is to bestow on the Israelites, though it doesn't resemble the Hittite lists; much closer parallels are found in Deuteronomy 28 and Leviticus 26.

There is not doubt that the treaty form lies behind some covenant formulations in the *OT*. The exhortation and covenant renewal in Joshua 24 contain many elements of the treaty form: identification and historical prologue (vv 2-13); stipulations (vv 14, 23; cf. v 25); the people themselves called as witnesses (v 22; cf. vv 26-27); and a threat which is the equivalent of a curse (v 20). Since the provisions of Deuteronomy 27 and their implementation in Joshua 8:30-35 probably refer to the same ceremony as Joshua 24 (p. 116), an extended list of curses (and blessings?) was provided; if the Covenant Code (Exod 20:22-23:33) originally went with this ceremony (p. 89), there were stipulations in abundance. Many sections of Deuteronomy, too, suggest the treaty form. The central section, 5-28, exhibits the following elements: historical and hortatory prologue (5-11); laws (12-26); blessings and curses (28). Since Joshua 24 and Deuteronomy both go back ultimately to northern traditions, it would seem that the use of the treaty form was well established among the northern tribes.

It may be doubted, however, whether the Sinai covenant was enacted in the treaty form. Dennis J. McCarthy points out[11] that even as Exodus 19-24 now stands, it bears only a remote resemblance to the treaty form: 20:2 is rather inadequate as an historical prologue, and the blessings of 23:20-33 do not resemble those of the treaties. Since the Covenant Code (with which 23:20-33 belong) probably does not per-

---

[11] *Treaty and Covenant* (2nd ed.; Rome: Pontifical Biblical Institute, 1978), 241-76.

tain historically to Sinai, one of the essential elements, the curse-blessing formula, is entirely missing. Thus, once literary criticism has had its say, very little is left of the treaty form in the Sinai account.

We are still in a position to assert much about the Sinai covenant, for we can retain: a) the theophany; b) at least the early items of the Decalogue, in particular, the commands to worship Yahweh alone and to make no images; and c) two separate traditions of the covenant ceremony (24:3-8 and 24:1-2, 9-11). In addition, Exodus 34, though its present context presents it as a renewal of the covenant after the affair of the golden calf (32), seems to be J's account of the Sinai covenant itself. The awe-inspiring theophany, coupled with the gracious deeds of the exodus, dispose the people to submit themselves to Yahweh as their God; the central provision of the Decalogue, "you shall not have other gods besides me," supplies the fundamental framework for living as His people; and the concluding ceremonies ratify the covenant, inaugurate the cult, and signify (and effect) the fellowship which will henceforth exist between Yahweh and His People. In 24:3-8 the people explicitly accept the covenant with its provisions; then the blood of sacrificed animals is sprinkled upon them and upon the altar (representing God) to signify community of life. A communion meal, not recounted in this source, would then have followed.

LAW. It is impossible to separate the discussion of *OT* law from the covenant. The covenant establishes a new relationship between God and His People. The laws that go with the covenant can be said to define that relationship; they explain how Israelites are to behave towards their God and towards one another; less often, they speak of relations with others outside the covenant community. Because law had this nature, it was not regarded as an intolerable burden but, like the covenant, as a sign of God's elective love.

Because of the connection between covenant and law, all of Israel's legislation, from whatever age, is located in the context of Mt. Sinai. The tradition that makes Moses the great lawgiver of Israel is undoubtedly an accurate one. He presided at the birth of Israel as a people through exodus and covenant, and lawgiving was an essential part of this function—laws were needed to govern covenant relations and to transform a mixed multitude into a society. As the People of God, the very laws which governed their society were considered expressions of the covenant and therefore holy. In the decades and centuries that followed, Israel's society developed through various stages, nomadic, agricultural, and commercial; new laws were needed to regulate new situations, but they always retained the same relationship to the covenant. For this reason laws from even much later periods are placed in the context of Mt. Sinai, introduced by: "And the Lord said to Moses: Thus shall you say to the children of Israel . . ." No deception is intended by this formula; it is a theological affirmation of highest worth. In other societies the king would sometimes codify existing laws and publish the collection in his name (e.g., the Code of Hammurabi, *ANET* 164-80). In Israel, law existed before kingship, and even the laws which were enacted under the monarchy were attributed to Moses. It was not the authority of the king they represented, but the authority of the covenant.

If the relationship between law and covenant is properly understood, we will not regard the covenant as a sort of commercial contract by which Israel kept God's law, and He, as a reward, bestowed blessings upon them—a *do ut des, quid pro quo* arrangement. Many blessings were to come to the Israelites through the covenant (Exod 19:5-6; 23:20-33; 34:10-11), but these were the result of having become God's People, not rewards for obeying laws. The blessings of the covenant were conditional only in the sense that the covenant itself was conditional. To disregard the provisions of the covenant, especially the central one of loyalty to Yahweh, would cancel all blessings and bring dire consequences, because this constituted a breach of the covenant itself. At a later period Jeremiah believed this had happened (Jer 31:32).

Since the sins of individuals could involve the whole community in X disaster, sanctions were enacted against those who should transgress the commandments. The punishment for many such sins (e.g., worshiping other gods, cursing mother or father, murder, adultery) was death (cf. Exod 22:19; 21:12, 17; Lev 20:10). Sanctions had to extend to much broader areas than those covered by the Decalogue in order to include all phases of community life. Not only religious, but social, civil, and criminal law were necessary.

Usually the laws providing sanctions were formulated in conditional form: "If a man . . . (description of crime), then . . . (specification of penalty)." This form, called casuistic because it involves cases of conduct (cf. Latin *casus*), is found in all the law codes of the ancient Near East. The best known of these is the Code of Hammurabi (ca. 1725), but a half dozen others, distributed in time from the end of the 3rd millennium to the 7th century, have been found. Many of Israel's laws are similar to those of these codes not only in grammatical form, but also in content.

For example, Exod 21:28-32 prescribes the penalty for the owner of an ox which has gored someone, taking into account whether or not the ox was in the habit of doing this and the social status of the one killed. In the Code of Hammurabi the same case is considered, with identical distinctions and similar penalties (*ANET* 176). The Israelite levirate marriage law (Deut 25:5-10) provides that if a man dies without a son, his brother shall marry the widow in order to provide an heir for the deceased; compare this with the following Middle Assyrian law: "If, while a woman is still living in her father's house, her husband died. . . . If she has no son, her father-in-law shall marry her to the son of his choice . . .'' (*ANET* 182). Deut 22:23-27 provides that if a man has sexual intercourse with a betrothed[12] virgin in the city, they are both to be put to death; if it occurred in the country, however, the girl is not punished, for it is assumed that she cried for help but there was no one to hear her. Compare this with the following Hittite law: "If a man seizes a woman in the mountains, it is the man's crime and he will be killed. But if he seizes her in (her) house, it is the woman's crime and the woman shall be killed" (*ANET* 196). Such similarities do not indicate direct borrowing; each code is reflecting, in its own way, a widely diffused customary law.

That Israel knew and used laws common to other cultures should occasion no surprise. She met the same civil and social situations her ancestors and neighbors had been meeting for ages, and often applied the same remedies. Nor is it surprising that Israel took over from her earlier background certain superstitious notions—taboos, ideas of "clean" and "unclean," etc.—that came to be expressed in her cultic laws (e.g., Leviticus 11-15; Numbers 19; Deut 14:3-21). Holiness and uncleanness were sometimes conceived very concretely as something that could be transferred by physical contact. The progressive nature of revelation supposes that there is advance from less perfect to more perfect stages; such primitive notions often served as the starting point for deep insights into the nature of God and His moral demands.

The laws that Israel had in common with other cultures are habitually cast in the casuistic form and concern civil and criminal matters. Many other laws, especially moral, religious, and cultic ones, were cast in the apodictic (imperative) form ("do [not] . . ."; "thou shalt [not] . . ."). The second person imperative is found in the treaty stipulations, as we have seen, and in the wisdom tradition, but as a *law* form it would seem to be unique in Israel. The question of how it came to be a law form in Israel is debated, and many have urged the treaty form as the source. However, apodictic law in Israel appears to antedate her use of the treaty form for covenant formulations. More recently the origin of apodictic law in Israel has been related to clan ethic—the precepts laid down by a father or clan chieftain (cf. Jer. 35:6-10). Close parallels can be found in the father-to-son advice in wisdom literature (p. 233). This may well come to be accepted as the best explanation of the apodictic form.

The Israelite conception of law as the revelation of God's will is unique. The connection between religion and law in Israel assured a concept of morality and moral obligation which was unknown elsewhere. The nature cults, in fact, virtually assured a separation between religion and morality, at least in the sphere of sexuality. Mendenhall comments: "The Canaanite . . . cities have the reputa-

---

[12]Betrothal established a legal right similar to marriage and so the punishment is that for adultery.

tion for possessing a very low standard of morality, from which charge we could defend them only by assuming that they did not take their religion very seriously."[13]

The *OT* legislation is very extensive and accounts for most of the material from Exodus 20 to the end of the Pentateuch. Much of the material is not systematically arranged, although laws of the same sort are sometimes grouped together. Some order can be brought to the subject by distinguishing the separate collections of laws which have been combined in our present Pentateuch.

a) *The Decalogue* (Ten Commandments): Exod 20:2-17; Deut 5:6-21. This collection sets forth the Lord's most basic demands as Israel understood them. Whether the whole Decalogue dates to the time of Moses is disputed; many competent scholars insist that it does, though some indications suggest it is a somewhat later summary. The obligation of loyalty to one God and the prohibition of representing Him in images, basic provisions of this code, are characteristics of Israelite faith. In their present form some of the laws have been expanded with explanations and motives (cf. Exod 20:22-23 with Deut 5:12-15).

b) *Covenant Code* (E): Exod 20:22-23:33. Although closely tied to the Sinai covenant and taking its name from Exod 24:7, this collection comes from a later time. Its provisions indicate a society of shepherds and farmers without commercial activities and therefore point to a time before the monarchy. Many scholars hold that it belongs to the covenant ceremony at Shechem of Joshua 24 (see p. 116).

c) *Ritual Decalogue* (J): Exod 34:14-26. This collection is inserted, surprisingly, where a repetition of the Ten Commandments would be expected; it is given as the text written on the stone tablets which replaced the ones Moses had broken. It contains thirteen laws, probably by expansion of an original ten. It is an ancient code, but its origins are obscure.

d) *Deuteronomic Code:* Deuteronomy 12-26. See Chapter 9.

e) *Law of Holiness:* Leviticus 17-26. Although contained in the P source, this collection forms a unity by itself, with a concluding section of blessings and punishments, perhaps dating from the late monarchy. The title comes from the subject matter and from the refrain, repeated in various forms: "Be holy, for I, the Lord, your God, am holy." ·

f) *Priestly Code.* This is not a single collection but a series of them scattered throughout the Pentateuch. Like the Holiness Code, it deals mainly with religious and cultic matters; cf. Leviticus 1-7, on sacrifice; 8-10, on priests; 11-16, on ritual; Numbers 28-29, on festivals. Many of the rites described are those of the postexilic community.

[13]"Ancient Oriental and Biblical Law," *BAR 3*, 15.

WILDERNESS GENERATION

Scattered from Exodus 16 to the end of Numbers are stories of the events in the desert from the crossing of the sea to the conquest of Transjordan. Running throughout are the themes of God's providential care of His people in the barren land and of their grumblings and backslidings; but we read also of their establishment as a cultic community and of their first battles.

The most important of these items is the establishment of Israel as a cultic community. For this reason the preparations for the Tabernacle (Exodus 25–31) are placed just after the ratification of the covenant, and its construction (35–40) after the renewal of the covenant necessitated by the affair of the golden calf. Although some elements of P's description are taken from David's tent shrine and Solomon's Temple, the basic picture of a portable tent-shrine of a wooden frame covered with animal skins is ancient and authentic. When the Tabernacle is completed Yahweh makes His abode among His people (40:34–38).

Animal sacrifice played an important role in Israel's worship from the days of the desert, though P's description (Leviticus 1–7) comes from a later period. As an expression of religious dispositions, animal sacrifice was of great value; if the prophets later seemed to condemn Israel's rites without distinction, it was because sacrifice was offered in place of religious dispositions instead of with them—an abuse to which ritual is open today and always. In sacrifice the end was not destruction of the victim but the offering of life; the worshiper made this a means of offering himself to God in total surrender. The priestly act was not the slaying of the victim but the offering of the blood, which stood for life and was believed to blot out the obstacles to fellowship with God caused by sin. The rite itself was accompanied by the singing of psalms and the recital of God's gracious deeds. In most cases part of the rite was a communion banquet on the flesh of the victim which, holy through divine acceptance, now was a means of fellowship with God.

The Sinai Peninsula provides few means for supporting a multitude such as that which Moses led (even granting that Exod 12:37 greatly exaggerates). Their sustenance must have come mainly from the milk and meat of their flocks, but Israel preserved the recollection of those unexpected blessings, manna, quail, water from the rock (Exod 16:4–17:7; Numbers 11; 20:2–13). They remembered especially the manna[14] as a sign of God's care. The stories about it have heightened the marvelous aspect, but they have also transformed it into a means of divine pedagogy—that Israel might learn to observe the Sabbath

---

[14]Manna, a sweet substance produced by insects which suck the tamarisk tree, is known today on the Sinai Peninsula and elsewhere in the East.

(Exod 16:25-30) and to know "that not by bread alone does man live, but by every word that comes forth from the mouth of the Lord" (Deut 8:3).

Later generations would look back on the desert years as an idyllic time, a honeymoon after the covenant union, when Israel was alone with her God, before she was seduced by Canaanite ways: "I remember the devotion of your youth, how you loved me as a bride, following me in the desert, in a land unsown" (Jer 2:2). Hosea would call for a return to the spirit of the desert: "She shall respond there as in the days of her youth, when she came up from the land of Egypt" (Hos 2:17).

Yet Israel's response in the Pentateuchal traditions is far from ideal. The Israelites long for the fleshpots of Egypt and ask sarcastically whether there were no burial places in Egypt (the land of the pyramids!) that they should be brought into the desert to die (Exod 15:11; 16:3; Num 11:4-6). Time and again they murmur and try the patience of the Lord; they even threaten to stone Moses and return to Egypt. More serious is their idolatry at the very foot of Mt. Sinai (Exodus 32) and again on the threshold of the Promised Land (Numbers 25). The recalcitrance of Israel, later mercilessly condemned by the prophets, began in the desert. Yet Israel's preservation of these memories demonstrates the realization that her history was not to glorify her but the God who led her. Beneath the burden of her sins Israel learned contrition and came to experience the mercy of Yahweh.

The events recorded in Numbers 13-20 are centered around Kadesh-Barnea, an oasis in the Negeb, to which the Israelites journeyed from Mt. Sinai. An abortive attempt at invasion of Palestine from the south was followed by a stay at Kadesh of 38 years (Deut 2:14). The failure of the invasion was attributed to a disobedience so flagrant that that generation was condemned to perish in the desert, excluded from the Promised Land (Numbers 13-14). The rise of a new generation sees a resumption of the march. Edom and Moab, strong and hostile, are bypassed, and Israel defeats the Amorite tribes north of Moab to gain territory and a base of operations in Transjordan. Moses ascends Mt. Nebo for a pathetic glimpse of the Promised Land before his death, excluded from entering by a sin recorded only obscurely by tradition (Num 20:2-13; Deuteronomy 34).

The reliability of some of these traditions is attested by what is now known of the places mentioned. In particular, it is probable that Edom and Moab were established in the 13th century and could have forbidden passage to the Israelites. It may be uncritical, however, to combine the Kadesh traditions with those of the exodus and of Sinai as the Pentateuch has done. The "all Israel" concept may have operated here to combine traditions from originally distinct groups and so produce a unified picture. This complex problem will be further discussed in Chap. 10.

READING SUGGESTIONS

JBC §3-5. *PBS* #4-8. *OTRG* #3; #10, 114-22. *AUOT* 38-97. *BHI* 105-26. *MTES* 115-31. *VAI* 143-63, 415-56. *WBA* 53-68.

Burns, R., *Exodus, Leviticus, Numbers, Excursus on Feasts, Ritual, Typology. OTM*, Vol. 3.

Childs, B. S., *The Book of Exodus*. Philadelphia: Westminster Press, 1974.

Hillers, D., *Covenant: The History of a Biblical Idea*. Baltimore: Johns Hopkins, 1969.

Hyatt, J. P., *Exodus*. Grand Rapids: Eerdmans, 1981.

McCarthy, D. J., *Old Testament Covenant: A Survey of Current Opinion*. Richmond: John Knox Press, 1972.

Noth, M., *Exodus*, tr. J. S. Bowden. Philadelphia: Westminster Press, 1962.

Riggans, W., *Numbers*. Philadelphia: Westminster Press, 1983.

Agus, J. B., "The Covenant Concept — Particularistic, Pluralistic, or Futuristic?" *Journal of Ecumenical Studies* 18 (1981) 217-30.

Andreasen, N. E., "Festival and Freedom (*A Study of an Old Testament Theme*)," *Int* 28 (1974) 281-97.

Batto, B. F., "Red Sea or Reed Sea?" *BARev* 10 (4, 1984) 56-63.

Beit-Arieh, I., "Fifteen Years in Sinai," *BARev* 10 (4, 1984) 26-54.

Bellefontaine, E., "The First Commandment Revisited," *TBT* #81 (Dec. 1975) 602-609.

Bodenheimer, F. S., "The Manna of Sinai," *BAR* 76-80.

Campbell, E. F., "Moses and the Foundations of Israel," *Int* 29 (1975) 141-54.

Cazelles, H., "The History of Israel in the Pre-exilic Period," *ATI* 281-84.

Cross, F. M., "The Priestly Tabernacle," *BAR* 201-28.

Grindel, J. A., "The Book of Numbers," *TBT* #89 (Mar. 1977) 1142-50.

Harrelson, W., "Guidance in the Wilderness: The Theology of Numbers," *Int* 13 (1959) 24-36.

Jensen, J., "The Book of Exodus," *TBT* #86 (Nov. 1976) 938-44.

McCarthy, D. J., "Exod 3:14: History, Philology and Theology," *CBQ* 40 (1978) 311-22.

Mendenhall, G. E., "Ancient Oriental Law and Biblical Law," *BAR* 3 3-24.

_____. "Covenant Forms in Israelite Tradition," ibid., 25-33.

Nielsen, E., "Moses and the Law," *Vetus Testamentum* 32 (1982) 87-98.

Pierce, J., "The Exodus Miracle," *TBT* #90 (Apr. 1977) 1194-98.

Sakenfeld, K., "The Promise of Divine Forgiveness in Numbers 14," *CBQ* 37 (1975) 317-330.

Sklba, R. J., "The Redeemer of Israel," *CBQ* 34 (1972) 1-18.

Stuhlmueller, C., "Leviticus—The Teeth of the Divine Will," *TBT* #88 (Feb. 1977) 1082-88.

von Waldow, H. E., "Social Responsibility and Social Structure in Early Israel," *CBQ* 32 (1970) 182-204.

Wilson, R. R., "The Hardening of Pharaoh's Heart," *CBQ* 41 (1979) 18-36.

8

Redemptive Themes
in the Pentateuch

THERE ARE many ways in which the *OT* and the *NT* are bound together. *OT* prophecies are fulfilled in *NT* events; *OT* types find their antitypes in the *NT* (p. 280); *OT* images are continued in the *NT* (e.g., the tree of life used to show that in Christ man regains what he lost in the Fall—Rev 22:2). More important than these, however, are the *OT* beginnings of the actual working out of God's plan of salvation: the election of a family, the formation of a people, the initiation of a covenant, and so forth. These beginnings undergo organic growth in the *OT* but reach maturity only in the work of Christ. Salvation history demands such beginnings for, by its very nature, it must have a starting point, development in time, and a climax that is truly redemptive. The complex of developments that relate to future salvation is called messianism; although the term is derived from the expectation of an ideal king of the future (the Messiah—p. 147), the concept is both anterior to and broader than this expectation.

In this and other "Redemptive Themes" chapters, then, we are investigating *OT* beginnings and developments that find their culmination in *NT* redemption. Instead of using the term "redemptive themes," we could speak of "the mystery of Christ," in the sense it often has in the *NT,* especially in St. Paul, of the eternal plan of God to save all people, Jews and Gentiles together, through Christ—a plan formerly hidden but now revealed (Rom 16:25–26; Eph 1:9–10; 3:4–9). Granted that the ways of God are too deep ever to be adequately plumbed by our thought, "mystery" here emphasizes what has been made known rather than what is still hidden. In this sense, then, the "mystery of Christ" is the whole of God's plan of salvation for all mankind in Christ. Once the completion is seen, it should be possible to relate the beginning to it, and that is what we hope to do with various aspects of the Pentateuch.

PROLOGUE

Genesis 1-11 is called the prologue to salvation history because these chapters graphically portray mankind's need for redemption by describing the Fall and our progressively worsening situation. Transgression of God's commandment establishes man as a rebel whose end can only be total death; his relationship to the rest of creation is disturbed, and multiple divisions are introduced into the human situation. The acts of grace found in this section, such as the covenant with Noah, do not properly begin a history of salvation but rather demonstrate God's patience and sustaining help, perhaps hinting at a plan to be initiated later.

Many would see in Gen 3:15, the so called proto-evangelium, a hint or even a promise of a redeemer to come. This interpretation can be sustained only by making some rather doubtful assumptions: that the serpent stands for Satan; that the woman's seed or offspring is to be understood as an individual; and that the verse promises victory to the woman's offspring. It is natural for us to identify the instigator of the first sin with Satan, but it doesn't follow that J did so, and this would even seem to be excluded. The concept of a diabolical adversary comes quite late in *OT* thought; even as late as the Book of Job (ca. 500), Satan appears as a member of God's court who has the function of scrutinizing and testing mankind (p. 242), but not yet as an enemy of God's plan. Once the concept of a diabolical adversary did emerge, it was natural to identify the serpent of Genesis 3 with him; this did, in fact, happen (Wis 2:24; Rev 12:9). But we can't read this back into Genesis; the original author seems to have introduced the serpent in order to relate the primal sin to the fertility rites (p. 54).

The statement that there will be enmity between the woman's offspring and the serpent's offspring sounds like a promise of warfare for successive generations; the Hebrew word for "seed" or "offspring" (*zera*) is normally collective in sense. The final statement ("he will strike at your head, while you strike at his heel") also suggests a continued state of strife. The same Hebrew verb (*shuph*) is used in both clauses. This word occurs but rarely and its meaning isn't certain, but probably is "to wound," "to bruise," or "to attack"; the serpent strikes at the man's heel, the man kicks or stamps at the serpent's head. If the author intended a promise of salvation, he phrased it very obscurely. Since much of the rest of Primeval History concerns mankind's surrender to the seductions of rebellion, the verse points programmatically to later events. No outcome is foretold for this struggle, but God's concern for mankind and His support is revealed; after the fiasco of the Tower of Babel, God takes action with the call of Abraham.

PATRIARCHAL HISTORY

The call of Abraham constitutes the beginning of beginnings in redemptive history. The promises made to him (immortality through numerous progeny, land to possess, a name that would live in blessing) amounted to a perfect blessedness, a salvation that he could understand and appreciate. But if the call of Abraham has any relation to Primeval History and what it tells of mankind's state and his needs, then God intended more than Abraham could have comprehended. Liberation from sin and restoration of the order disturbed by sin is God's gift to us in Christ and is what He intended when He first invited Abraham to respond. St. Matthew is at pains to present Jesus as "son of Abraham" (Matt 1:1–17) because he, as a witness of Christian faith, sees in Him the one in whom not only Abraham and Israel find their final blessing, but also the nations.

EXODUS, COVENANT, AND LAW

The promise to Abraham of a people to spring from him is realized in the constitution of Israel as People of God through the exodus event and covenant. It is a beginning of the people in a new way. The exodus also stands at the beginning of redemption. The literal meaning of redemption is a buying back, a ransoming of one from the power of another. It can be applied to God's activity only analogously, of course, for God pays no price to a captor. The exodus is redemptive in that Yahweh rescues Israel from slavery and oppression, not by paying a price but through His might (Exod 6:6); by so delivering Israel He acquires them as His special people.

In a later age, when Israel had been sent into exile, the prophets would promise a new deliverance in words that recalled the exodus. But because she had been exiled as punishment for sin, the promised restoration was to include forgiveness of sin and a new heart. In this and other ways Israel's understanding of what redemption entails was deepened in the course of her history.

We have already spoken of the importance of covenant as the basis of the new people, dispensing as it does with race, geography, and political institutions as a basis of peoplehood. The centrality of the concept is indicated by the fact that the two parts of the Bible are called the Old and New Testaments—another way of saying old and new covenants. In spite of the discontinuity implied in the "old" and "new," growth and continuity are present. The very moment at which Jesus established His new covenant was the solemn commemoration of the exodus, and His words "This is my blood of the covenant" (Mark 14:24) take up the words of Moses in Exod 24:8, "This is the blood of the covenant which the Lord has made with you." The connection is not simply one of literary reflection; the new covenant grows out of the old, presupposes it, and would not have been possible without it.

Although in Christ a new law succeeds the old, the two are bound together organically. Each occupies the same place in regard to its respective covenant, i.e., each defines the relations of the people to God and of its members to one another, and each is the means of grateful response for God's redemptive act. Furthermore, the law of the *NT* is based upon that of the *OT*; Jesus' moral teaching is unique in that it cuts through non-essentials, distills the essence, and penetrates to the inner spirit, but His starting point was the *OT* legislation. The *OT* already contained the commands, central to Jesus' teaching, of love of God and love of neighbor (Deut 6:5; Lev 19:18); doubtless Jesus broadened the concept of "neighbor" and gave the law a new power by His own example of love. While Christians are not bound by the old law as such, they recognize that many of its precepts need to be observed. The law of love may be said to subsume rather than to abolish the old law; many of its provisions are now seen to be otiose, but others are reimposed with a new, firmer obligation by love itself (Rom 13:8-10). No one who lives according to the Sermon on the Mount violates the spirit of the Decalogue.

WILDERNESS GENERATION

Israel at the foot of Mt. Sinai was established as covenant partner and cultic community to respond to God in obedience and worship. We have seen that Israel's far from perfect obedience in the desert was programmatic for the rest of her history. While her response remained unsatisfactory, there could be no thought of an accomplishment of the mission for which God had chosen her. Jesus came to render to God the perfect response of obedience and worship; he came not as a substitute for Israel, but to embody Israel as the one in whom Israel should fulfill her mission. It is because Jesus is the embodiment of Israel that St. Matthew applies to Him the words of Hos 11:1, "Out of Egypt I have called my son" (cf. Exod 4:23), and that the Gospel narratives portray Jesus in the desert overcoming temptations like the ones Israel in the desert succumbed to (Mark 4:1-11; Luke 4:1-13).

The perfect conformity of Jesus to His and Israel's mission brought Him to the death which He accepted in obedience to His Father. Because the offering of His life to the Father was made willingly and freely, as an act of submission and worship, it constituted a sacrifice far more perfect than those of the official cult; Jesus' words "my blood of the new covenant" identify His death as a sacrifice like the one which inaugurated the old covenant. The sacrificial death of Christ presents the perfect response to God that it was Israel's mission to give. His death as a sacrifice is the vehicle by which He offered Himself to the Father and so accomplished perfectly what the animal sacrifices of the cult were intended to do. Henceforth men were to make the sacrifice of Christ their own and to offer it to God as the vehicle of their own obedience and self-oblation. That it was Christ's intention that men share His sacrifice in this way is implied in the invitation: "Take and eat . . . take and drink. . . ." Animal sacrifices for this end henceforth became pointless and would play no part in Christian worship.

With the establishment of Israel as God's people by covenant, the one true God takes up His abode in their midst in the Tabernacle built at His command. The fiery cloud that settled upon the Tabernacle (Exod 40:34-38), the Tabernacle itself, and the Ark were all signs of this presence of God among His people. Later Solomon's Temple would be the chosen place, and when that was rejected Ezekiel saw in vision a chariot that bore the glory of Yahweh into the midst of the exiles in Babylon (Ezekiel 1)! Later Jewish theologians would coin the term *shekinah* to designate the tabernacling of God among men. Of course no structure made with hands can contain the Lord of the universe, and yet these material things were means of mediating His special presence. The *NT* sees the final and most perfect manifestation of the *shekinah* in the presence of God among men through the humanity of Jesus. In the Priestly Code the term for the Tabernacle is *mishkan* (dwelling). St. John had this in mind when, describing the Incarnation, he said: "And the Word became flesh and made his dwelling among us" (John 1:14).

READING SUGGESTIONS

Cochrane, C. C., *The Gospel According to Genesis.* Grand Rapids: Eerdmans, 1984.

Gage, W. A., *The Gospel of Genesis. Studies in Protology and Eschatology.* Winona Lake, Ind.: Carpenter Books, 1984.

von Rad., G., *God at Work in Israel.* Nashville: Abingdon Press, 1980.

Coogan, M. D., "The Storm God and the Sea," *TBT* #79 (Oct. 1975) 457-64.

Fujita, S., "Theology of Hope in Genesis 1-11," *TBT* #80 (Nov. 1975) 519-27.

Miller, C. H., "Salvation History: An Interpretation Tool," *TBT* #100 (Feb. 1979) 1873-78.

Myers, J. "The Way of the Fathers," *Int* 29 (1975) 121-40.

Sena, P. J., "Abraham — First Step Toward Reconciliation," *TBT* #85 (Oct. 1976) 872-77.

Snell, P., "The Bible and Ecology," *TBT* #104 (Nov. 1979) 2180-85.

Tolhurst, J. F., "In the beginning . . . it was so," *TBT* #102 (Apr. 1979) 2042-53.

Vawter, B., "History and Kerygma in the Old Testament," in *A Light unto my Path: Old Testament Studies in Honor of Jacob M. Myers,* H. N. Bream *et al.,* eds. Philadelphia: Temple University Press, 1974. Pp. 475-91.

9

Deuteronomy and
the Deuteronomic School

(Recommended Scripture reading: 2 Kings 22–23;
Deuteronomy 4–13; 20; 29–30)

THE PRECEDING discussion has treated Deuteronomy as part of
the Pentateuch, but has put off any extended discussion of it until
now. The truth is that the relation of Deuteronomy to the books that
precede it and follow it is somewhat ambiguous, or, more accurately,
ambivalent. On the one hand, Deuteronomy is certainly part of the
Pentateuch as it now stands. It has been provided with a setting that
dovetails it with the ending of Numbers, and the career of Moses,
begun in Exodus and continued in Leviticus and Numbers, is completed with his death in Deuteronomy 34. Moreover, Deuteronomy is
concerned with election, covenant, legislation, and some of the other
themes important in Genesis-Numbers.

On the other hand, it seems fairly clear that Deuteronomy originally
existed independent of Genesis-Numbers and that it has close connec-
tions with the books that follow. Although the source-traditions J, E,
and P are found mingled in Genesis-Numbers, the source-tradition D
(to oversimplify slightly) is restricted to Deuteronomy. This may be
represented schematically as follows:

Gen   Exod   Lev   Num   Deut

JEP   D

Thus, from a compositional point of view, Deuteronomy seems to be
distinct from the rest of the Pentateuch.

A similar conclusion is reached by a glance at the historical narratives contained in the Pentateuch. The action of Genesis-Numbers
progresses from creation to the formation of Israel by exodus and
covenant, to the conquest of Transjordan; only the death of Moses is

lacking to complete the drama of pre-Palestinian Israel. Deuteronomy, however, does not really carry on from here; its action begins with the departure from Mt. Horeb (Mt. Sinai), so that there is a great overlap. But while Deuteronomy's starting point does not mesh well with what has preceded, it forms a splendid introduction for the books that follow (Joshua, Judges, 1-2 Samuel, 1-2 Kings), and there is a steady progression in the action narratives in the complex Deuteronomy-2 Kings. This may be presented schematically as follows:

Patriarchs-Exodus-Sinai-Transjordan

Gen	Exod	Lev	Num	Deut	Josh	Judg	1-2 Sam	1-2 Kgs

Sinai-Transjordan-Invasion-Consolidation-Monarchy

But Deuteronomy's connection with the following books is deeper than simply progressive action, for the same themes, theological thought, and characteristic expressions are found throughout. Not only are passages which must be labeled "deuteronomic" found in Joshua-2 Kings,[1] but it is precisely such passages that provide the theological framework of these books and cause them to reflect the spirit of Deuteronomy. It is quite likely that at one time Deuteronomy stood at the head of these books but was later detached from them to be added to the Pentateuch.

For these reasons it seems best to consider Deuteronomy primarily in relation to the books that follow and to speak of a "deuteronomic corpus," i.e., Deuteronomy-2 Kings. These historical books reflect the spirit of Deuteronomy because the circle or group responsible for Deuteronomy, or one deeply imbued with its spirit, played an important part in either composing or editing them. All admit that ancient traditions were utilized in the composition of these books, but scholars do not agree whether the deuteronomic school itself produced the books from ancient sources or rather reworked books which already existed. More will be said of this in discussing the individual books. At present we must turn our attention to Deuteronomy itself.

THE ORIGIN OF DEUTERONOMY

Deuteronomy may be described as a sustained exhortation to faithfulness to the covenant, a demand for sincere response

---

[1] E.g., Joshua 1; 23; Judg 2:6-3:6; 1 Kgs 8:14-61; 2 Kgs 17:7-18; 21:4-16. In addition, see the comments on the four-point plan in which the story of each Major Judge is told (p. 120) in Judges and the manner of judging each king in 1-2 Kings.

manifested in loyal obedience to the Law. A literary artifice presents most of the book as a discourse (or rather a series of discourses) in the mouth of Moses; the setting is Transjordan, shortly before the death of Moses. The outline which follows gives an indication of the contents:

A. *First Address*
   1. Historical summary of the events from the departure from Sinai to the conquest of Transjordan: 1–3
   2. Exhortation: 4:1–43
B. *Second Address*
   1. Exhortation: 4:44–11:32
   2. Deuteronomic Law Code: 12–26; 28
C. *Third Address:* 29–30
D. *Supplements* (covenant ceremony; Song of Moses; Blessing of Moses; death of Moses): 27; 31–34

The literary device of placing this material in the mouth of Moses is justified by the fact that the laws and exhortations therein are wholly in the spirit of Moses, the great mediator of the covenant. The true origin of the book, however, must be sought elsewhere, with the help of information provided by the historical books and an analysis of Deuteronomy itself. In discussing the composition of the Pentateuch we had occasion to refer to the finding of a law book in 622, in the days of King Josiah, a law book which must almost certainly be identified with at least a major portion of Deuteronomy² (see 2 Kings 22–23). The distress which led Josiah to rend his garments at the reading of the book (2 Kgs 22:11–13, 19) is easy to understand if we think of the curses contained in Deuteronomy, especially those in ch. 28. The religious reform carried out by Josiah corresponds well with the provisions of Deuteronomy; in particular, the celebration of the Passover at Jerusalem instead of locally (2 Kgs 23:21–23) points to the innovation of Deut 16:5-7.

The identification of Deuteronomy with the "book of the law" discovered under Josiah tells when in Israelite history the book first became known, but it doesn't immediately indicate its origin. For this we must turn to an analysis of the book itself.

An investigation of Deuteronomy shows that much of the material found in it stems from the traditions of the Northern Kingdom. This is indicated in part by terminology which it has in common with the northern source-tradition E (e.g., Horeb for Sinai, Amorites for Canaanites), and in part by the fact that many of its laws come from the Covenant Code (Exod 20:22—23:33; see p. 89), which is also from E and represents northern usage. The laws in Deuteronomy, however, are not simply announced, as in the Covenant Code, but are preached with fervor and warmth; the speaker insists that they must be ob-

²Most probably Deuteronomy, at this stage, consisted simply of Moses' second address (see outline).

served, and he gives motives. Such preaching of the law seems to have been done by Levites and to have had its *Sitz im Leben* in covenant renewal ceremonies in the north, especially at the great cult center of Shechem.

With the collapse of the Northern Kingdom in 721, many of the Israelites fled to the south; among these, it is theorized, were Levites with traditions,[3] partly oral and partly written, which were later incorporated into Deuteronomy. It is impossible to say with certainty whether or not the demand for unity of sanctuary (i.e., that there be but a single shrine for sacrifice and pilgrimage), one of the important provisions of Deuteronomy in the form in which it was found in 622, was contained in this stage of the deuteronomic tradition. At the time of the discovery of the book, and ever afterwards, there was no doubt that the unique shrine therein referred to was the Temple of Jerusalem. Some scholars hold, however, that there had already been an attempt to centralize worship at some northern shrine (Shechem, for example), and that the passages which impose this find their origin here. This is possible, but it seems more likely that the provision for centralization was incorporated in the south, at a later stage, and that it applied from the very beginning to Jerusalem.

There is reason to believe that by the time of King Hezekiah (715–687) there was a deuteronomic circle in Judah strong enough to make its influence felt at the capital. Long before the appearance of a deuteronomic code, Hezekiah initiated a reform that was an anticipation of the one later undertaken by Josiah. This reform, like Josiah's, included the destruction of pagan cult objects and even of the Yahweh shrines other than the Temple (2 Kings 18:14; cf. v 22) and the observance of Passover in Jerusalem for all (2 Chronicles 30).

Von Rad traces the emergence of the group behind this reform back to the events of 701 and thereafter. Since the Assyrian invasion of that year stripped Judah of its standing army, it was necessary to resort to a more ancient practice—the Holy War waged with a militia raised from the free peasant population (see Deuteronomy 20). In this group many ancient traditions, mainly from the north, and a more conservative brand of Yahwism had been preserved. Their spokesmen were the country Levites who, with their new importance, were able to exert a salutary influence toward reform. The movement begun under Hezekiah, however, was undone by his son, the ill-famed King Manasseh (687–642). He, subservient to his Assyrian overlords, reintroduced syncretistic, pagan practices and persecuted loyal Yahwists (2 Kgs 21:1–9, 16).

---

[3] An alternative theory would see prophetic groups of the north as the traditionary circle which brought the deuteronomic traditions south after the fall of Israel and from which Deuteronomy had its origin. See esp. E. W. Nicholson, *Deuteronomy and Tradition* (Philadelphia: Fortress Press, 1967). It is to be noted that Moses is depicted as a prophet in Deut 18:15–19; 34:10–12 and that in the deuteronomic history the prophet can be presented as a proclaimer of Yahweh's Law (2 Kgs 17:13).

Under such circumstances, we may suppose, the reform group was driven underground. Their work had been brought to an end for the present, but they incorporated their ancient traditions and the lessons learned in their attempt to apply them to the present into a book. This was the "book of the law" found in the days of Josiah. Those who composed it probably hoped to see its provisions implemented in better days, but Manasseh's long reign of 55 years dashed such illusions for that generation. Before the "better days" could come, they would all be dead and the book forgotten. Eventually, however, it was brought to light and did indeed serve as a blueprint for reform.

The Levitical circles that produced Deuteronomy did not simply disappear, of course; their work and spirit were continued by their successors. It was probably the latter who were responsible for the deuteronomic history, a task which continued into exilic times. The first edition of the deuteronomic history was produced towards the end of the monarchy, perhaps in the days of Josiah; its end was to ward off disaster by calling the people back to faithfulness. During the exile these books were reworked again, and it was probably at this time that most of the chapters of Deuteronomy that were not part of the original core were added. The end of many of the new passages was to show that God's threats had been carried out, that He was just in destroying the nation which had rejected His covenant, but that mercy and restoration were to be hoped for from the Lord who regarded the heart-felt repentance of His people.[4]

The Spirit of Deuteronomy

The characteristics of Deuteronomy are so pronounced and its diction so distinctive that they are easy to recognize even in translation. They stem largely from Deuteronomy's warmth, fervor, and sense of urgency, along with its emphasis on God's love for Israel, His election of her, and the need for a faithful response. Most of the laws contained in Deuteronomy do not differ notably from other legislation; many of them are taken over from the Covenant Code, as mentioned above. Deuteronomy, however, does not simply enumerate them, but eloquently commends their observance. The speaker urges the need to obey them and therefore heaps up motives, adding constant reminders of the penalty for disobedience.

The reason for the sense of urgency in Deuteronomy is not far to seek. During the time that the earliest deuteronomic traditions were taking shape, the northern kingdom was facing a series of crises. The threat to Israel's very existence must have been apparent to clear heads from the moment a resurgent and aggressive Assyria began her expan-

[4]Cf. Deut 4:25–31; 28:45–68; 32:19–43; 1 Kgs 8:46–53; 2 Kgs 21:10–15; 25:1–26, 27–30.

sion; long before the catastrophe of 721, the ten northern tribes faced extinction on several occasions. But the real source of danger lay at a level different than that of Assyria's militaristic ambitions. As God's covenant people, Israel's only *raison d'être*, and therefore its only ground of hope, was faithfulness to the God who had called her into being—and this was precisely what was lacking. Their sins, as we learn from the historical and prophetical books, ranged from the oppression of the poor and perversion of justice to out-and-out idolatry.

In such circumstances the prophets foresaw the danger that Yahweh would punish by destruction. Already in the prosperous and apparently secure days of Jeroboam II, men such as Amos and Hosea could read the signs and foretell the end; Amos even then lamented "the collapse of Joseph" (Amos 6:6). The only hope of salvation, they warned, lay in radical conversion and return to obedience. The deuteronomists, strongly influenced by the prophets, echoed these warnings. What the deuteronomists have added is an explicit insistence on covenant and on the observance of the Law as the expression of faithfulness.

In spite of such warnings the Northern Kingdom did fall. The deuteronomic passage which reports the destruction (2 Kgs 17:7-18) ends with the ominous note: "Only the tribe of Judah was left." It was to Judah that the deuteronomic traditions migrated, but there was no reason here to lessen the note of urgency. With Israel gone, Judah lay in the path of Assyria's advance—and Judah was no better than Israel had been! The destruction of Assyria by the Neo-Babylonian Empire towards the end of the 7th century did not materially alter the situation, but simply substituted one overlord for another. Judah had not learned the lesson of Israel's fall. It was this lesson that the deuteronomists strove urgently to drive home.

YAHWEH ALONE. The most essential element in the faithfulness demanded of Israel was adherance to and worship of Yahweh alone. Yahweh's love and election forms the basis of a one-to-one relationship: "He has chosen you from all the nations on the face of the earth to be a people peculiarly his own" (7:6; cf. 14:2). This choice was not based on Israel's greatness or fidelity, for Israel was the smallest of all nations and stiff-necked, to boot; it was based simply upon the love which led God to make the promises to the Patriarchs (7:7-8; 9:4-6). The formula so dear to Jeremiah, "I will be your God and you shall be my people,"[5] does not occur in Deuteronomy, but it expresses well Deuteronomy's conception of the covenant.

For this reason the first commandment is of central importance and receives extended commentary in Deuteronomy; see 4:15-24; 5:6-10; 6:4-9. Well-known are the words which Jesus called the "greatest

---

[5] Jer 7:23; cf. also 11:4; 24:7; 31:33. Jeremiah seems to have supported Josiah's reform and was probably influenced by deuteronomic thought.

commandment":[6] "Hear, O Israel! The Lord is our God, the Lord alone! Therefore, you shall love the Lord, your God, with all your heart, and with all your soul, and with all your strength" (6:4–5).

The exhortations and laws of Deuteronomy, therefore, are directed towards encouraging a greater faithfulness to Israel's Lord and towards eliminating occasions of apostasy. To eliminate temptations to idolatry, Deuteronomy insists on the destruction of pagans and their shrines (7:1–5, 12–26; 12:1–3; 20:10–18). Since the true historical background of the promulgation of the book was the late monarchy rather than the eve of the invasion, the destruction of Canaanites and their cities could not have been seriously contemplated. But such prescriptions did serve as a vivid warning against contamination, and the provisions for the destruction of pagan shrines were, in fact, to be put into effect. Extreme measures are urged also against fellow Israelites if they should try to lead others "to follow other gods, whom you have not known, and to serve them," whether it be a prophet ("even though the sign or wonder he has foretold you comes to pass") or a near relative ("your own full brother, or your son or daughter, or your beloved wife, or your intimate friend"); the Israelite city that allows itself to be seduced shall be put under the ban (13:2–19).

UNITY OF SANCTUARY. A more positive means of promoting loyalty was the attempt to establish perfect unity of sanctuary. The idea of a single shrine for all Israel was by no means a new one. Although a plurality of altars is explicitly permitted in early legislation (Exod 20:24) and is implied in the patriarchal narratives,[7] a central shrine was an important element of the tribal league from the very start of the settlement in Palestine. It was located successively at different places, wherever the Ark of the Covenant was. Experience now taught that a multiplicity of shrines could be a source of evil; they were often established at old centers of Baal worship, and ancient heathen practices were sometimes imported into the worship of Yahweh. For this reason the prophets at times inveighed against such shrines and against the multiplication of cult centers (Hos 8:11; Jer 11:13). What, then, could be a more effective way of inculcating loyalty to one God than by restricting official worship to a single place? "One God, one altar" is the motto that lies behind the demand for centralization in Deuteronomy 12. This law would have worked particular hardship on

---

[6] Mark 12:29–30. These words form the opening lines of the *Shema* (composed of Deut 6:4–9; 11:13–21; and Num 15:37–41, the great prayer of Judaism, recited daily by every devout Jew.

[7] The accounts of the Patriarchs building altars (Gen 12:7, 8; 22:9; 26:25; 33:20; 35:1–7) in various places (Shechem, Bethel, Beer-sheba) were, in all likelihood, preserved at these places and had the effect of legitimizing them as cult centers. Such accounts are found only in J and E; P, which knew of only one altar, did not preserve records of others.

those Levites who earned their keep by presiding at local shrines, and so Deuteronomy constantly commends them to the charity of the people, along with widows and orphans (12:12, 18, 19; 14:28-29). Deuteronomy did, indeed, provide that they be permitted to function at Jerusalem on the same terms as the Temple clergy already there (18:6-8), but the priests of the Temple seem to have successfully resisted this provision (2 Kings 23:9).

Even while insisting on unity of sanctuary, Deuteronomy avoids any crude or materialistic idea of the localization of God and of His dwelling in an edifice made with hands—ideas not wholly absent in David's pious wish to build a house for Yahweh (2 Sam 7:2, 5). For Deuteronomy and the deuteronomic sections in the later books, the central shrine is a dwelling for Yahweh's "name."[8] The presence of Yahweh's power, blessing, majesty, and every other quality is suggested by the expression, but crude misconceptions are ruled out.

REWARD AND PUNISHMENT. Deuteronomy not only stresses the goodness and love of God and His past favors as motives for faithfulness, but also insists with a particular emphasis on the rewards for obedience and the punishments for disobedience.[9] Specifically, the reward for obedience will be the peaceful and untroubled possession of the land, abundant fertility, and all the other blessings which make life happy and prosperous. The punishment for disobedience is the reverse of these things, with emphasis on the loss of the land:

> Should you then degrade yourself by fashioning an idol, . . . I call heaven and earth this day to witness against you, that you shall all quickly perish from the land which you will occupy when you cross the Jordan. You shall not live in it for any length of time but shall be promptly wiped out. The Lord will scatter you among the nations, and there shall remain but a handful of you among the nations to which the Lord will lead you (4:26-27).

This theme of rewards and punishments is sometimes set forth in a "blessing or curse" formula, in conformity with covenant usage. This is done thoroughly and in great detail in ch. 28, more succinctly in 11:26-28:

> I set before you here, this day, a blessing and a curse: a blessing for obeying the commandments of the Lord, your God, which I enjoin on you today; a curse if you do not obey the commandments of the Lord, your God, but turn aside from the way I ordain for you today, to follow other gods, whom you have not known.

CHOOSE LIFE TODAY! The final purpose of the fervent exhortations of Deuteronomy is to confront the individual with an unavoidable decision: between the alternatives of faithful adherence to Yahweh and re-

---

[8]Deut 12:11, 21; 14:23; 16:2, 11; 1 Kgs 3:2; 8:29; 2 Kgs 21:4, 7; 23:27.
[9]4:25-31; 7:12-15; 11:10-32; 28; 29:15—30:20.

jection of Him in favor of other gods there is no middle ground; nor does the possibility of avoiding a decision exist. The choice is not presented on a "take it or leave it" basis; it is precisely to induce the hearer to make the right choice that all of Deuteronomy's eloquent preaching is directed. "I have set before you life and death, the blessing and the curse. Choose life, then, that you and your descendants may live . . ." (30:19-20).

The literary device of placing these exhortations in the mouth of Moses as he addresses the Israelites before their entrance into the Promised Land does not have the effect of making them remote for the reader. Quite the contrary! The veil of this fiction falls away almost immediately; precisely because the hearer is addressed directly ("you!"), he finds himself transported to the foot of Mt. Sinai to gaze into the fiery theophany and to hear the awesome voice of God, and then whisked back to the Plains of Moab to hear the stern warnings of Moses. The repetition of words and phrases like "today" and "this day" serve to heighten the impression; e.g., *"This day* the Lord, your God, commands you to observe these statutes and decrees. . . . *Today* you are making this agreement with the Lord" (26:16-17). Sometimes the contemporary reference becomes quite explicit: "The Lord, our God, made a covenant with us at Horeb; not with our fathers did he make this covenant, but with us, all of us who are alive here this day" (5:2-3; cf. 29:9-14). The intent is not to frighten but to encourage; six centuries of infidelity can be wiped out at a stroke if only Israel will choose Yahweh *today!*

Since the end of Deuteronomy was to lead the people to choose Yahweh *this day* and to adhere to Him in covenant faithfulness, it is no accident that the structure of Deuteronomy closely reflects the structure of a ceremony for covenant renewal. We have already seen, in studying the covenant, that Deuteronomy is one of the best *OT* examples of the treaty form (p. 85). Even in its early form the book provided the proper setting for the liturgical renewal of the covenant, with its historical and hortatory introduction (5-11), laws (12-26), and blessings and curses (28). The addition of the historical prologue of 1-3 and the ceremony of ch. 27 were further steps in the same direction.

The teachings and themes of Deuteronomy have been presented at some length because of their intrinsic importance, because they must always remain relevant for the individual Christian who realizes how fully he or she has entered into Israel's sacred heritage, and because they form the theological framework of the deuteronomic history. Doubtless there were disadvantages in some of the deuteronomic emphases. The virtual identification of covenant faithfulness with obedience to commandment which is found in some texts could and did lead to externalism where inner conversion was needed. The insistence on rewards and punishments, when read outside the framework of Deuteronomy's deeply religious spirit, could and did foster a "salvation through merit" mentality, and created other theological problems. But these were perversions of the deuteronomic spirit—human weakness seeking "bread alone" instead of "every word that comes forth from the mouth of the Lord" (8:3).

READING SUGGESTIONS

JBC §6. *OTRG* #10. *PBS* #9–10. *A UOT* 348–64. *VAI* 331–44. *WITOT* 125–35.

Clifford, R., *Deuteronomy, Excursus on Covenant & Law. OTM*, Vol. 4.

Fretheim, T. E., *Deuteronomic History*. Nashville: Abingdon Press, 1983.

Nicholson, E., *Deuteronomy and Tradition*. Philadelphia: Fortress Press, 1967.

Noth, M., *The Deuteronomistic History*. Sheffield: The University, 1981.

von Rad, G., *Deuteronomy*. Philadelphia: Westminster Press, 1966.

Braulik, G., "Law as Gospel: Justification and Pardon According to the Deuteronomic Torah," *Int* 38 (1984) 5–14.

Callaway, P. R., "Deut 21:18–21: Proverbial Wisdom and Law," *JBL* 103 (1984) 341–52.

Gammie, J. G., "The Theology of Retribution in the Book of Deuteronomy," *CBQ* 32 (1970) 1–12.

Hoppe, L. J., "The Meaning of Deuteronomy," *BTB* 10 (1980) 111–17.

McBride, S. D., Jr., "The Yoke of the Kingdom (*An Exposition of Deuteronomy 6:4–5*)," *Int* 27 (1973) 273–306.

Myers, J. M., "The Requisites for Response," *Int* 15 (1961) 14–31.

Peifer, C., "The Book of Deuteronomy," *TBT* #90 (Apr. 1977) 1213–19.

Toombs, L. E., "Love and Justice in Deuteronomy," *Int* 19 (1965) 399–411.

Walsh, M. F., "Shema Yisrael: Reflections on Deuteronomy 6:4–9," *TBT* #90 (Apr. 1977) 1220–25.

Wenham, G. J., "The Deuteronomic Theology of the Book of Joshua," *JBL* 90 (1971) 140–48.

Wifall, W. R., Jr., "Israel's Origins: Beyond Noth and Gottwald," *BTB* 12 (1982) 8–10.

10

"He Gave Them
the Lands of the Nations"

(Recommended Scripture reading: Joshua 1–12; 23–24;
Judges 1; 2:6–8:3; 13–18)

"THE JEW who lives outside Palestine is without a God in this world." Thus did one Jewish theologian express the importance of Yahweh's land in Israel's thought. Indeed, its importance should not be minimized. To Israel it was "the land he promised on oath to our fathers" (Deut 6:28), and possession of it showed that Yahweh was faithful to His promises and able to lead Israel to the goal He intended. History involves events in time and place; most of the events of salvation history have happened on this little strip of land.

HISTORICAL PROBLEMS

Exactly how Israel came to possess this land is a very complex problem. The Book of Joshua, it is true, gives a lucid account: a united Israel attacked across the Jordan, laying waste Jericho and Ai to establish a base in the central hill country; rapid campaigns in the south and the north brought most of the rest of the land under their control, which was then divided among the twelve tribes. This simple and unified account answered well the ends of the author of Joshua (p. 116), but it is at odds with the traditions in Judges 1, which describe a piecemeal occupation by individual tribes of much of the same territory, and it raises historical difficulties. For example, archeologists find that both Jericho and Ai were in ruins at the time we must date the onslaught under Joshua. As in the case of the exodus, any discussion of the events must proceed from a critical use of the biblical traditions and the findings of archeology.

The biblical traditions of the conquest, however, hardly compare with those of the exodus. The exodus was more significant theologically and Israel's recollection of it was keener. Then too the possession of the land was a present and obvious fact, while the exodus remained alive only to the extent that it was recalled and celebrated. By the time Israel's writers attempted to piece together a picture of the occupation, the sources could not have been very abundant; they consisted of recollections about individual campaigns, stories of tribal heroes, and poetic pieces like the Song of Deborah (Judges 5).

Fortunately, now that we are dealing with specific sites, archeology can be used to check biblical traditions and supply additional information. For example, archeology shows that the biblical traditions of the invasion fit best into the second half of the 13th century. The account of the occupation of Transjordan in Numbers 20-22 suits that time because Israel could not have encountered a settled and fortified Moab and Edom before then, and the Merneptah stele probably indicates that Israel had penetrated the area no later than ca. 1220 (p. 76). In addition, excavations reveal that many Palestinian cities, including Bethel, Lachish, Hazor, and Debir, some of them mentioned in Joshua, were destroyed in this period. By the time the tribes had settled down, before the end of the period of the Judges, pressure from the Philistines, who attacked Palestine ca. 1200, was felt (Judges 13–16).

The Canaanite political pattern of independent city-states, most of them small, did not provide the type of organization that could easily resist a determined onslaught. They sometimes formed coalitions when danger threatened, but it was not possible to rally and unify any large part of the population. On the other hand, semi-nomadic invaders such as the Israelites had little technique or equipment for reducing fortified cities, and they found the Canaanite chariotry formidable.

It was not, however, the local Canaanite forces that would normally be the greatest obstacle to invaders from the outside, but the imperial powers of the Fertile Crescent. Because of its strategic importance, Palestine was kept firmly under the control of whatever power was able to assert its claim at a given period. At the time of Joshua's penetration, Egypt was the nominal overlord of Palestine; but from the time Ramses II secured his frontier by treaty with the Hittites (ca. 1270) little effective control was exercised there. By the middle of the 13th century the Hittites were already engaged with the Sea Peoples in the struggle which ended their empire and were in no position to police Palestine. And no Mesopotamian power was then strong enough to exercise control that far west. At the time of the Israelite invasion and for some time afterwards, Palestine was in a political power vacuum. Humanly speaking, this was one factor that made Israel's occupation possible. This is another way of saying, from a theological point of view, that providence embraces all aspects of human history.

No wholly satisfactory reconstruction of the conquest has yet been given. It is not that information is lacking; in spite of obscurities in some key areas, there are facts enough to confuse the clearest head. None of the theories so far proposed, however, satisfies all the data. The invasion was more complex than Joshua suggests. It involved different groups attacking in different places at different times. Once the various groups coalesced, their originally distinct traditions, containing much that is genuinely historical, were united to give a unified account of a concerted invasion by "all Israel"; this is the picture we find in Joshua. The theological supposition is clear: by virtue of their incorporation into the covenant community, the new elements become sharers of Israel's goods and its history, including the promises and the experience of Yahweh's saving deeds in the exodus. If our passion for objective history is not satisfied by this procedure, we have the greater consolation of learning the practical effects of incorporation into Israel.

Some of the indications of the complexity of the process by which Israel took over Palestine are found in the Bible itself, while others come from outside sources. From non-biblical sources there is evidence that Asher and possibly Zebulun were already occupying their territory before the time of Ramses II and the exodus. The biblical account of a great covenant ceremony held at Shechem (Joshua 24) surprises us, for nothing is said in Joshua of its capture or of the cities of central Palestine in general; excavation confirms that there was no break in occupation or culture at Shechem during this period.

The recognition that tribal rather than family relationships lie beneath the stories of Jacob's twelve sons opens another source of information, difficult though it is to interpret. The "battle of the births" between Rachel (with Bilhah, her maid) and Leah (with Zilphah, her maid) in Genesis 29–30 results in the following scheme:

Leah	Zilphah	Rachel	Bilhah
Reuben	Gad	Joseph	Dan
Simeon	Asher	(Ephraim	Naphtali
Levi		Manasseh)	
Judah		Benjamin	
Issachar			
Zebulun			

This plan suggests various degrees of kinship and dignity (full brothers and half brothers, sons of wives and sons of concubines) which presumably reflect tribal conditions; sometimes these can be squared with the situation of the tribes in Palestine, sometimes not.

For example, Reuben's place as first-born suggests a position of power and preeminence among the tribes, though this is not borne out in the traditions of the conquest and settlement. The tribe's decline, reflected in Gen 49:3–4 and Deut 33:6, was complete before the time

Figure 12.
*Palestine during
the period of the
Tribal League.*

of the monarchy. Joseph receives the first-born's privilege of a double
portion when his sons, Ephraim and Manasseh, are adopted by Jacob
(Genesis 48). The statement that Jacob placed his right hand upon the
younger son, Ephraim, indicates an unexpected ascendancy of that
tribe, well attested from the period of Judges on, over the brother
tribe. The groupings in the above scheme do not consistently reflect
geographical dispositions, as a glance at Figure 12 will show, nor do
they accord with the evidence of Judah's basic separateness from the
northern tribes (see below).

The account of the raid on Shechem by Levi and Simeon (Genesis
34) must be connected with some phase of the invasion, but just how it
fits in is obscure; that Jacob could will Shechem to Joseph (Gen 48:22)
suggests that it was in Israelite hands even during the sojourn in
Egypt! Levi, which finally ends up as a group dedicated to the service
of the altar, certainly began as a secular tribe. The malediction of Levi
in Gen 49:5–7 reflects the loss of territory once held and probably attributes it to the treachery at Shechem. Simeon shared this venture
with Levi in central Palestine, but ends up in the territory of Judah,
without land of its own.

These are some of the indications of the complexity of Israel's settlement in Palestine. While the conquest cannot be reconstructed in

detail, some things can be asserted with a degree of probability. First, it can be said that not all of those who became members of the tribal federation left Egypt under Moses or entered Palestine under Joshua. "Israel," as it finally came to be, included some groups that had invaded in earlier waves and others that had been in Palestine all along. The Habiru whose incursions are described in the Amarna letters (ca. 1376–1350—p. 76) took over territory which was later incorporated into Israel. The letters indicate that the Habiru seized control of the Shechem area and other territories in the fourteenth century; if such groups made common cause with Joshua and his men, invading in the thirteenth century, the failure of the Book of Joshua to mention a battle for Shechem is intelligible.

G. E. Mendenhall, building on the work of E. F. Campbell, maintains that the Amarna Age Habiru were not outside invaders at all, but Canaanite peasants revolting against the religious, economic, and political obligations of the city-state feudal organization. They left the city-states and migrated in great numbers to the fringe areas, banding together as Habiru, people outside the framework of society. Once organized, they were able to take over some of the territories they had left by overthrowing the kings and their supporters. Mendenhall thinks the political situation in Palestine was similar in the 13th century and that the arrival of the Hebrews from Egypt, with their news of liberation from oppression in the name of their God Yahweh, provided a rallying point for the elements already in revolt. This hypothesis seems a likely answer to one aspect of the problem, namely, the relations of the invading Israelites to large segments of the Canaanite population, most of which was assimilated rather than destroyed. The union was not a military alliance, but a true conversion to Yahwism as the very antithesis of what was hated in the Canaanite power structure. Albright and others, too, have emphasized the missionary appeal of the new religion. Yet there seems no reason to reduce the Hebrews of the exodus to numerical insignificance, as Mendenhall does, or to see here a virtually complete explanation of the invasion.

Secondly, it is likely that Judah occupied its territory independently of the other tribes and had a separate history for a considerable period; this is possibly reflected in the tradition of Judah separating from his brothers in Genesis 38. The Song of Deborah (Judges 5) praises the tribes which did battle against Sisera and blames others which did not respond to the call, but Judah is not mentioned. After the death of Saul, David is accepted as king by Judah at once, but not until some years later by the northern tribes. Rehoboam, Solomon's successor, accepted at once in Judah, goes to Shechem as a matter of course to be accepted by the northern tribes. But even before his rejection, which spelled permanent separation of north and south, the phrase "Israel and Judah" occurs often enough to show that they were looked upon as separate entities (1 Sam 18:16; 2 Sam 11:11; 1

Kgs 4:20; etc.). Judg 1:2–20 speaks of Judah with Simeon alone conquering the territory they were to occupy, and this seems a more accurate account than the united action depicted in Joshua. Judah's entrance may well have been from the south; the invasion from Kadesh may have been more successful than Num 14:39–45 indicates. If Judah had entered and campaigned with the other tribes, it would be difficult to explain the origin of the sharp cleavage between "Judah" and "Israel."

It is hard to say when Judah joined the Israelite confederacy. The belt of Canaanite territory between Judah and central Palestine made communications difficult, but not impossible; the principle strongholds, Jerusalem and Gezer, were not taken until the days of David and Solomon, respectively, and union was an accomplished fact before that. The fact that the Abraham and Isaac traditions (related mainly to Judahite territory) and the Jacob traditions (related mainly to northern territory) have been integrated under the "all Israel" concept in both J and E indicates that they were already integrated in the common source that lies behind them, and this must be dated in the period of the Judges.

Thirdly, the invasion of the tribes which came out of Egypt with Moses was across the Jordan into central Palestine, as Joshua indicates. The Rachel tribes, i.e., the "house of Joseph" (Ephraim and Manasseh) and Benjamin, at least, made up this group. The Egyptian sojourn traditions are attached more closely to Joseph than to any other element of Israel, and those reckoned as his descendants must have been among the exodus tribes. The traditional leader of the campaign, Joshua, was an Ephraimite; and the center of the tribal confederation was established in the territory of the Joseph tribes and long remained there. Most of the action described in Joshua 2–9 took place in land that became Benjaminite territory; so did the action of the ancient poetic fragment in Josh 10:12–13.

The early phases of this occupation may not have been too violent; the central hill country was thinly populated and could have been taken over fairly easily. Some of this land, as we have seen, was already in friendly hands; Shechem apparently did not need to be conquered, and Joshua 9 tells of the willing submission of the Gibeonite cities. Nevertheless, this was not simply a peaceful infiltration. Although the accounts of the capture of Jericho and Ai present difficulties, the destruction of Bethel, attributed to the "house of Joseph" in Judg 1:22–25, is attested by archeology. The poetic fragment in Josh 10:12–13 shows that Joshua's military reputation goes back to earliest times, even though the book has exaggerated his role in the invasion. While it is safe to associate him with the conquest of the central area, his campaign in the south is probably part of the idealizing process of the book (see below). The overthrow of the five cities in the south (Josh 10:28–39), confirmed by archeology for Lachish, Eglon, and Debir, must have been part of Judah's campaign;

Judg 1:11–20 attributes their fall to Judah and allied clans. We may
suspect that the same idealizing process is at work in the account of
Joshua's northern campaign (Joshua 14), though solid arguments are
lacking; the evidence for a 13th century destruction of Hazor,
however, the only city attributed to him there, is sufficiently clear. In
the following century the Israelite tribes were victorious over a Canaanite coalition at the Plain of Megiddo, thus removing a great
threat and easing communication between north and central Palestine.

Fourthly, the event which formally constituted "Israel" from the
diverse elements that had occupied Palestine was the great covenant
ceremony at Shechem described in Joshua 24. It amounted to an extension of the Sinai covenant to all of the others willing to accept it
and its terms. Joshua exhorts them to put away other gods, declaring
that he and his house (the "house of Joseph"?) would serve Yahweh
(24:14–15). The people accept the terms and the covenant is concluded
(vv 24–25). Thus was constituted the tribal league, the federation of
tribes bound by covenant to their God and to one another, that Israel
was to be until the days of the monarchy. For many this was to remain
the ideal for Israel which no other type of organization should ever
replace.

THE BOOK OF JOSHUA

It should already be clear that Joshua presents an idealized account of
the invasion: all Israel, united under one leader and aided by a succession of miracles, sweeps from victory to victory until virtually all the
land is in her power; all Canaanites in sight are slaughtered, their cities
burned to the ground; after the land has been divided among the tribes
and the covenant renewed, Joshua dies at a ripe old age. A simplified
outline shows the movement of the book:

  A. *Conquest of Palestine:* 1–12
  B. *Division of the Land:* 13–21
  C. *Concluding Events:* 22–24
      1. The disputed altar: 22
      2. Joshua's farewell speech: 23
      3. Covenant ceremony; Joshua's death: 24

The book may be classified as epic history: it speaks of real events,
but with the unity of theme, elevation of style, grandeur of sweep, and
intervention of the divine characteristic of the epic.[1] An author's end
determines the literary form he uses; in the case at hand, the end was
to show that Yahweh had been faithful to His promise to give the land
to Israel. This could be best achieved by the author's making an epic

---

[1]This description is appropriate for much of the exodus narrative, too, but not for
biblical history in general, as a glance at Judges or Samuel will show.

of the conquest. No deceit was intended by this. By the time the author of Joshua wrote, the land had long been Israel's possession; his telescoped version of the conquest underlines the link between promise and fulfillment (cf. 1:3 with 23:14).

Taking possession of Yahweh's land was a sacred act, and the author describes the process with all the ceremony of a solemn religious rite. We might almost call it a liturgical invasion. Before setting out, the people sanctify themselves (3:5); the clergy, bearing the Ark of Covenant, lead the way and the people follow in procession (3:6); when the procession reaches the Jordan, the waters cease flowing and all pass over dry-shod (3:14–4:18). To open hostilities the procession winds its way seven times around Jericho; trumpets sound, the people shout, and the walls come tumbling down (6:1–20). No spoil is taken, for this is Yahweh's victory. The cleansing of the land begins as Jericho, with its idols and those who worshiped them, goes up in flames (6:21, 24).

Artificial though the account may be, the author has woven together a tapestry from ancient sources and ancient practices with remarkable effect. To call the account artificial is not to deny it all historical value. Ritual sanctification was part of Israel's holy war discipline (1 Sam 21:5), as was the use of the Ark in battle (1 Samuel 4). The description of the stoppage of the Jordan (3:16) resembles stoppages occurring within modern memory when the Jordan valley has been blocked by landslides. When the forces of nature fought for her, Israel saw there the hand of her God.

We have seen, furthermore, that archeology confirms the destruction of many of the cities listed in Joshua as destroyed; this is no coincidence, but indicates that Joshua frequently utilized historically reliable traditions. The difficulty with the account of Jericho, however, has received no satisfactory solution. Jericho's founding goes back to the 8th millennium, before the invention of pottery. Its massive walls were built and destroyed a number of times, the last destruction being ca. 1580—long before Joshua. A subsequent occupation, from ca. 1400 to ca. 1325, after which the site was abandoned for several centuries, hardly provides the occasion for Joshua 6, in which the walls figure so prominently.

New discoveries may be made which will dramatically vindicate the biblical account, but until then it seems best to explain Joshua 6 some other way. If Jericho had been standing at the time of Joshua's invasion, it would have been a formidable obstacle to their advance, for it guarded the best route to the central highlands. In fact they found it already in ruins, without their having to lift a finger. Its destruction, so necessary for their success ("look at those walls!"), could be attributed, by means of a story, to providential intervention. The story may incorporate historical details of the actual destruction, preserved in the family of the pagan harlot Rahab (6:23)—which would explain the inclusion of a not very edifying element in an otherwise edifying story.

The case of Ai, in ruins from ca. 2400 to ca. 1000, is somewhat simpler. It is probable that the account of the destruction of Bethel was transferred to Ai, partly because its name (which means "ruin") invited an explanation (8:28), partly because Bethel was immediately rebuilt by the Israelites and left no sign of its fall. This would also explain the otherwise surprising fact that Bethel's destruction is not mentioned in Joshua.

The compilation of Joshua was the work of the deuteronomists, to whom are due its basic framework and spirit. The central section, consisting mainly of tribal boundaries and lists, was added later by priestly authors. It fits in well with the original scheme and purpose of the book. How great the faith that saw in dry lists such as these the documentation of God's goodness to Israel!

The intention of the deuteronomists in demonstrating God's faithfulness to His promises was to invite Israel to respond in fidelity; this is seen especially in Joshua's exhortation (23), a deuteronomic composition. The book is also a demonstration of what a faithful Israel can accomplish and how a faithful Israel ought to behave; only in the affair of Achan is there a serious failure (7). Joshua epitomizes this faithfulness and is a living example of what can be accomplished by an undivided heart. His own personality hardly appears, for he is presented as a second Moses (1:5-7); before him the Jordan parts as the sea had for Moses, and he delivers a final exhortation (23) like that of Moses in Deuteronomy.

It was their zeal for religion, paradoxically, that led the deuteronomists to portray the invasion as far more cruel than it actually was. To them it seemed that if Israel had exterminated the Canaanites, she would have been spared many temptations to apostasy; Joshua, therefore, describes an ideal Israel as mercilessly clearing the land of its former inhabitants. Israel did practice the ban as did the peoples around her; but it is no accident that we find the ban applied most rigorously in the most artificial part of the narrative (10:28-40). On the other hand, the actual breadth of spirit of Israel is concealed. It is said that only through trickery did the Gibeonites become allied to Israel; and the heterogeneous character of the covenanting groups in Joshua 24, an ancient and genuine tradition in spite of some deuteronomic touches, is hidden.

Israel may be idealized, but Yahweh alone is exalted. The land is His gift, not the reward of merit; the effect of the many marvelous interventions is to bestow the credit of victory where Israel knew it belonged. Enemies fall by hailstones rained down by Him, and when time is needed, the sun stands still (10:11-13):[2] "for the Lord fought for Israel" (10:14)!

---

[2] It is impossible to say what concrete event stands behind this ancient poetic fragment. For one explanation, see Rowley, *The Growth of the Old Testament* (New York: Harper & Row, Publishers, 1963 [c1950]), pp. 55-56.

THE BOOK OF JUDGES

The character of Judges contrasts strongly with that of Joshua. The action in Judges is episodic rather than unified, as Israel succumbs repeatedly to temptation and falls into the hands of her enemies. Although this contrast emerges from the literary procedures of the two books, it reflects in part the historical reality. Once the invading tribes had gained space in which to settle down, the elan and organization of their attack were dissipated. They were now subjected to the counterattacks of unconquered Canaanites (Judges 4–5), to raids by marauding tribes like the Midianites (6–8), to encroachment by neighboring Moabites (3:12–30) and Ammonites (10–11) and finally by the invading Philistines (13–16).

A more subtle but deadlier danger came from the Canaanites with whom they were at peace and from their lore. The Israelites were now on the way to becoming farmers and had much to learn from those experienced in agriculture. "Agriculture" suggests to us things like fertilizers, contour plowing, and crop rotation; but in Israel's day successful farming seemed rather to depend on the fertility cult (p. 54). How could anyone hope to till the soil successfully without activating the forces of fertility? In the exodus and the conquest Yahweh had proved Himself a warrior God (Exod 15:3), but could He give corn and wine and oil? Was this not rather the province of Baal and Asherah? Many former Baal worshipers had joined Israel, and we may wonder how thorough their conversion was. The assertion of Judges that Israel fell repeatedly into Baal worship can hardly be questioned. Such falling away might take the form of open apostasy, as the *OT* always labels it, or it might tend toward identifying Yahweh and Baal. "Baal," although applied as a proper name, was basically a common noun which meant "lord"; the number of Israelite names compounded with Baal (including those of two of Saul's sons) indicate how far the ambiguity could be carried.

The main sources for Judges were stories about tribal heroes. Individually composed and transmitted, these ancient tales authentically reflect the religious, social, and political situation of the period (roughly, from 1200 to 1050). They were passed on orally until, perhaps in the early monarchy, they were written down. Some of them existed in variant forms, as the parallel accounts of Deborah (4 and 5) and the composite accounts of Gideon, Jephthah, and Abimelech indicate. Most of them concern northern heroes and must have migrated to Judah around the time of the fall of the Northern Kingdom. The stories, which had probably already been gathered into a collection before their utilization by the deuteronomists, exhibit a common religious theme, the deliverance of Israel from enemies by charismatic leaders raised up by Yahweh.

These leaders are called "Judges," some hold, not because they rendered judicial decisions, but because they restored justice by delivering the afflicted. This is the meaning "to judge" often has in the *OT* (cf. Ps 43:1; Isa 1:17). Others believe that the term was originally applied to the Minor Judges (see outline below), men who are named but concerning whom we are told little; it is suggested that they were officials whose role it was to arbitrate justice under the law of the Tribal League (cf. what is said of Samuel in 1 Sam 7:15-8:3). This period of Israel's history would thus have been named primarily for them and the terminology later applied to the military leaders we call "Major Judges." In any case, these latter were "charismatic leaders" because they were called to their task and given the power to carry it out by the advent of the "Spirit of Yahweh" upon them (3:10; 6:34; 11:29; etc.). These stories originally dealt with the affairs of single tribes or, occasionally, with a group of them. In their present form the "all Israel" concept has operated to give them a broader setting.

The deuteronomists took over this collection of stories, revised and supplemented it, and made it part of their great historical work. The final form exhibits the following outline (names of Judges are in italics; Major Judges are indicated by asterisks):

A. *Fragmentary Records of the Conquest:* 1:1-2:5
B. *Main Body:* 2:6-16:31
    1. Moralizing introduction: 2:6-3:6
    2. The Judges:
        **Othniel:* 3:7-11
        **Ehud:* 3:12-30
        Shamgar: 3:31
        **Deborah and Barak:* 4:1-5:31
        **Gideon:* 6-8
        Abimelech: 9
        Tola, Jair: 10:1-2, 3-5
        **Jephthah:* 10:6-12:7
        Ibzan, Elon, Abdon: 12:8-10, 11-12, 13-15
        **Samson:* 13-16
C. *Appendices:* 17-21
    1. Migration of the Danites: 17-18
    2. Crime and punishment of the Benjaminites: 19-21.

The deuteronomists left the ancient stories intact, but set them in a framework that made them examples of the deuteronomic theology of history, according to which Israel's national fortunes reflect her faithfulness to the covenant. The story of each Major Judge is prefaced with the notice that the Israelites had sinned against Yahweh (by serving the Baals, when specified), who gave them over to _____ (name of enemy), who oppressed them for _____ years; when the Israelites cried to Yahweh, He raised up _____ (name of Judge) to deliver them. The story of the Judge is then recounted and is closed with the note that the land enjoyed peace for _____ years. So that this 4-point framework (sin, punishment, repentance, deliverance) could not be missed, the deuteronomists supplied a sample of it in

2:11-19, without any names. Then it is repeated with the blanks filled in, so to speak, in the story of Othniel. Apparently little was known of him, and the story consists of hardly anything more than the framework.

The stories of Judges tell us much of early Israel and the tribal league. The Song of Deborah (5), judged by all to be nearly contemporary with the events it describes, supplemented by the variant prose account (4), tells of the overthrow of a powerful Canaanite coalition centered around the Plain of Megiddo. A war of the tribal league was a holy war, just as the invasion had been, and the duty to respond to the call was a grave one. Poorly armed as they were (5:8), the Israelites would have been no match for the Canaanite chariotry, but "from heaven the stars, too, fought" (5:20); through rainstorm and flood the enemy's chariots were bogged down and Israel won a smashing victory.[3] Even on this occasion not all the tribes answered the call; the Song chides Reuben, Gilead (Gad), Dan, and Asher for their absence.

The fact that the Moabites could cross the Jordan and exact tribute in Benjaminite territory (3:12-30) suggests there was no firm union of tribes to oppose them. Even intertribal conflicts occur, as when the Ephraimites attempt to vindicate their claim to preeminence (8:1-3; 12:1-6). The Samson cycle, in spite of its folkloristic character, is no doubt accurate in the impression it gives of a virtually unopposed Philistine take-over of southwestern Palestine. The tales of the charismatic leaders and their successes exalt the tribal league ideal, and the Abimelech story has antimonarchic tendencies. Yet from the book as a whole it appears that the tribal league did not always meet the military challenge.

The first of the two appendices, with its implicit condemnation of the shrine at Dan, accords well with the deuteronomic concern for unity of sanctuary. The second, however, appears to be a late, partly fictional composition, and must have been added to the deuteronomic work. Both of them were later edited by one who saw in the disorders of the times an indication that a strong leader was needed and commented: "In those days there was no king in Israel; everyone did what he thought best" (17:6; 21:25; cf. 18:1; 19:1).

---

[3]The inadequacy of human means is regularly underlined so that the victory may be seen to be Yahweh's. Cf., e.g., the reduction of Gideon's force to 300 men. Even the candid reports of the questionable character of some of the Judges (Ehud, Jephthah, Samson) is intended to show that Yahweh alone is to be exalted.

READING SUGGESTIONS

JBC §7-8. *PBS* #11-12. *OTRG* #5. *AUOT* 110-55. *BHI* 126-75. *VAI* 258-65. *WBA* 69-120. *WITOT* 143-57.

Hamlin, E. J., *Inheriting the Land. A Commentary on the Book of Joshua.* Grand Rapids: Eerdmans, 1984.
Hoppe, Leslie, OFM, *Joshua, Judges, Charismatic Leadership in Israel. OTM*, Vol. 5.
McKenzie, J. L., *The World of the Judges.* Englewood Cliffs, N.J.: Prentice-Hall, Inc., 1966.

Anderson, B. W., "The Place of Shechem in the Bible," *BAR 2* 265-75.
Borowski, O., "Five Ways to Defend an Ancient City," *BARev* 9 (2, 1983) 73-76.
Campbell, E. F., "The Amarna Letters and the Amarna Period," *BAR 3* 54-75; "The Excavation of Shechem and the Biblical Tradition," *BAR 2* 275-300.
Dion, P.-E., "The 'Fear Not' Formula and the Holy War," *CBQ* 32 (1970) 565-70.
Exum, J. C., "The Theological Dimension of the Samson Saga," *Vetus Testamentum* 33 (1983) 30-45.
Griffin, P., "The Epic of Joshua," *Scripture* 14 (1962) 75-81.
Halpern, B., "Gibeon: Israelite Diplomacy in the Conquest Era," *CBQ* 37 (1975) 303-16.
Hauser, A. J., "The 'Minor Judges' — A Re-examination," *JBL* 94 (1975) 190-200.
Isserlin, B. S. J., "The Israelite Conquest of Canaan: A Comparative Review of the Arguments Applicable," *Palestine Exploration Quarterly* 111 (1983) 85-94.
Kearney, P. J., "The Role of the Gibeonites in the Deuteronomic History," *CBQ* 35 (1973) 1-19.
Lindars, B., "Deborah's Song: Women in the Old Testament," *Bulletin of John Rylands Library* 65 (1983) 158-75.
Mendenhall, G. E., "The Hebrew Conquest of Palestine," *BAR 3* 100-20.
Niditch, S., "The 'Sodomite' Theme in Judges 19-20: Family, Community, and Social Disintegration, *CBQ* 44 (1982) 365-78.
Thompson, J. A., "The Israelite Village," *Buried History* 19 (1983) 51-58.
—————, "The 'Town' in Old Testament Times," *Ibid.*, 35-42.
Yadin, Y., "Excavations at Hazor," *BAR 2* 191-224.

11

Of Kings and Judgment

(Recommended Scripture reading: 1 Samuel 1-20; 27-31; 2 Samuel
1-8; 11-12; 15-20; 24; 1 Kings 1-5; 9-13; 18-22; 2 Kings 9-11; 17-25)

THE MOST important period of *OT* Israel is that of the monarchy—the time of David and Solomon, the time in which prophecy
developed and flourished. Fortunately, our sources for this period are
more abundant and reliable than for any other. There is a wealth of
information in Samuel and Kings (supplemented in some particulars
by Chronicles and the prophetic books), and some of the records now
recovered from surrounding nations contain instructive references to
Israel.[1] The story of the rise of the monarchy, its division, the fall of
Israel and then of Judah can be reconstructed with a great deal of confidence. The period is a long (ca. 1050-587) and turbulent one, so we
will be able to cover only the high points.

History of the Monarchy

Beginnings. The tribal league, as we have seen, was in many ways the
ideal organization for Israel. It was religious in nature as well as
political, and its loose organization permitted maximum freedom, imposing little more than the maintenance of the central shrine and the
obligation of tribal levies for the holy war. Yet it proved incapable of
meeting the challenge of an organized, well-equipped force like the
Philistines. As they spread westward and northward from their beach-
head on the Mediterranean coast, the Philistines began by crowding

[1]Such records may contain information not found in the Bible, may supplement and
provide background for understanding the biblical records, or may independently support the biblical narratives. Examples of the last case are the Assyrian account of Sennacherib's siege of Jerusalem (*ANET* 287) and Babylonian records of the allowance
provided for King Jehoiachin in exile (*ANET* 308).

Israelites from their territory (cf. the migration of Dan in Judges 18), and ended by subjugating most of the land. They had a monopoly on iron (1 Sam 13:19-22), which was just beginning to make its appearance in Palestine, and were able to use their chariots to good effect on the plains.

The death-knell of the tribal league was sounded at a battle near Aphek (ca. 1050), near the edge of the coastal plain. The Israelites brought the Ark from the central shrine, then at Shiloh, in the hope that it would bring them victory. Instead, the Israelites were defeated and the Ark captured (1 Samuel 4), and the Philistines went on to destroy Shiloh. Although the Ark was returned by the Philistines, terrified by the plagues which fell upon them, the fact that it lay neglected until David brought it to Jerusalem showed that the old order was dead.

Yet Israel was not at once ready to accept a new order. Saul came to the throne only by the path of charismatic leadership. When he heard of the cruel terms offered by the Ammonites besieging Jabesh-gilead, "the Spirit of God rushed upon Saul" (11:6); he rallied men from the tribes and raised the siege. Thereupon, under the direction of Samuel, the most influential religious leader of the time, Saul was acclaimed king at Gilgal (ca. 1020).[2] In her time of need, it seemed, God had again provided Israel with a leader. Saul turned his attention to the Philistines, who by this time had established control over the central hill country and maintained garrisons there. An initial success, sparked by the daring of Saul's son Jonathan, encouraged more and more men to flock to Saul's banner, and the Philistines were driven from the hill country. It was an encouraging start, but no more; it was one thing to drive occupation troops from home territory and quite another to meet Philistine chariotry on the plains.

But Saul's problems were complicated by his relations with Samuel and his own insecurity. Samuel, who had not been eager for a king, now turned against Saul for his failure to subordinate his mission to religious authority. According to one source, Saul was guilty of exercising religious functions contrary to Samuel's wishes (13:8-15), according to another, he was guilty of violating the ban (15). Saul's success had already been such that Samuel's rejection of him did not bring his downfall, but the matter preyed on his mind. When Saul later saw the success and popularity of the young warrior David, he feared he was being eclipsed and that his own authority was endangered (18:6-16). Saul began to exhibit signs of derangement; he attempted to kill David and, when David had fled, massacred the 85 priests of the sanctuary at Nob who had unwittingly helped him (22:6-19). David took up a wandering life in the south, now head of a

---

[2]Three separate traditions tell of Saul's elevation (9:15-10:8; 10:17-27; 11); while they cannot be wholly reconciled with one another, they all tell of divine designation of Saul and of Samuel's intervention.

Figure 13.
*Prisoners of Ramses III.
The one on the left
is one of the Sea Peoples,
possibly a Philistine;
the other is a Syrian.
Courtesy of the Oriental
Institute, University
of Chicago.*

band of several hundred discontents who had rallied to him, living by banditry and the protection racket. When Saul, neglecting the war with the Philistines, led his troops into the wilderness of Judah in pursuit of him, David fled with his tough little army to the Philistines and became their vassal.

Saul resumed the Philistine war but was not able to repeat his earlier successes. When the Philistines marched north along the coast to the Plain of Megiddo, Saul marched up to meet them. His forces suffered a terrible defeat, and he and three of his sons were killed. The remnant of Israel's army fled to Transjordan, where Ishbaal, Saul's remaining son, set up a shaky government. Israel had no tradition of dynastic succession, however, and Ishbaal's claim rested mainly on the support of Abner, Saul's general.

THE KINGDOM OF DAVID AND SOLOMON. Shortly after Saul's death, David was proclaimed king in Judah (ca. 1000), the favor of whose clan leaders he had never ceased to court. He established his capital at Hebron. A clash between the men of David and those of Ishbaal, in which Abner killed a brother of Joab, David's general, led to a civil war in which the balance of power gradually passed to David (2 Sam 2:12–3:1). The weak and ineffectual Ishbaal soon alienated Abner, who offered to throw his considerable influence in the north to David. This golden opportunity was lost when Joab treacherously slew Abner in revenge for his brother. Shortly later Ishbaal was murdered by two of his own men who hoped to win David's favor; he, however, had them executed.

The people of the north then chose David as their king. Even in the days of Saul he had exhibited such courage, might, and leadership that he had overshadowed Saul; the maidens had sung: "Saul has slain his thousands, and David his ten thousands" (1 Sam 18:7). They were aware, too, of a priestly or prophetic oracle that designated David as the future ruler (2 Sam 5:2). The giving of this oracle is not recorded, but there are additional references to it (1 Sam 25:30; 2 Sam 3:9–10, 18).

The Philistines had permitted David to accept rule in Judah because it was advantageous to have their vassal on the throne there. But as king of a united Israel, David was a threat to their plans of empire, and they took the offensive at once. The battle, fought near Jerusalem (still in Canaanite hands), ended in a rout for the Philistines; a second battle in the same place ended Philistine activity in the hill country for good. Few details are recorded of later engagements, but the results are clear enough: Philistine power was broken, and they were restricted to a small strip of coastland. David continued his military successes by taking Jerusalem and all other Palestinian land still in the hands of Canaanites. Then he subjugated Ammon, Moab, and Edom. During his siege of the Ammonite capital, Aramean forces from the north attacked his army, only to be defeated; after the siege David carried the war to them, routing the kings who ruled at Zobah and Damascus. All these territories became part of a very respectable empire, and all paid tribute to David.

Israel was now a far cry from what she had been during the days of the Judges. Instead of a league of twelve struggling tribes, she was a monarchy and mistress of a sizable empire. Yet David wanted to build on the old order and to incorporate its spirit into the new. Indeed, given Israel's consciousness of her nature and origins, this was the only path to stability and strength; later kings would neglect it to their sorrow. After David took Jerusalem, he made it his capital and brought there the Ark of the Covenant, neglected since its return by the Philistines. Jerusalem was centrally located and had never belonged to any of the tribes, so its new rank as capital would not raise tribal jealousies. By bringing the Ark there, David made Jerusalem the religious center of the nation. He installed Abiathar, the sole survivor of the amphictyonic priesthood after Saul's massacre (1 Sam 22:16–23), as priest of the shrine along with Zadok, a priest previously unmentioned.[3] Local shrines continued to exist, but this became the shrine of the Ark and therefore the shrine of all Israel and a special place of pilgrimage. In this way David bound the new order to the old as closely as possible.

---

[3]Rowley has suggested that Zadok, who appears so abruptly at this point, was the Canaanite priest at Jerusalem until its conquest and his conversion. 1 Chr 6:1–8 supplies Zadok with Levitical ancestry, but this may be dictated by theological considerations. Others believe he was originally a priest at Hebron (where David was anointed king); in taking both Abiathar (originally at the shrine at Shiloh) and Zadok as his priests, David would be including two rival priestly factions which traced their origins to Moses and Aaron, respectively. See F. M. Cross, *Canaanite Myth and Hebrew Epic* (Cambridge: Harvard University Press, 1973), pp. 195–215.

David's empire was now secure, but his latter days were troubled by internal problems, mainly within his own family. The question of who would succeed him to the throne had not been settled, for there was no tradition of hereditary monarchy in Israel and David had not named a successor. In these circumstances David's sons began maneuvering for position. One of them, Absalom, had himself proclaimed king at Hebron (David's old capital) and marched on Jerusalem. Incredible as it may seem, Absalom had won sufficient support to cause David and his group of professional soldiers to flee. David regrouped his forces in Transjordan and there Absalom's army was defeated; Absalom was killed by Joab, contrary to David's orders.

The throne was secured for Solomon only at the very end of David's life. Adonijah, another of David's sons, supported by Abiathar and Joab, proclaimed himself king. Only then, at the urging of Bathsheba and the prophet Nathan, did David crown Solomon as his co-regent and successor; the support of the military, under Benaiah, undoubtedly helped. Solomon thus inherited an empire reasonably secure from without. He strengthened its defenses by fortifying cities[4] and developing a chariot corps (something David had never done). Although there were ominous losses in the north and south, he kept his territory fairly well intact. Under Solomon, Israel reached a height

Figure 14. *Kingdom of David and Solomon.*
----limits of kingdom.

[4]Archeology confirms Solomonic fortification of Megiddo, Hazor, Gezer, and other sites. The Megiddo stables formerly attributed to Solomon, however, are now dated later and were probably built by Ahab.

Figure 15. *Solomon's Temple. Copy of drawing made by C. F. Stevens from specifications provided by W. F. Albright and G. E. Wright.* [See BA 18(1955)41–44.].

of prosperity never rivaled before or after. Palestine's strategic position made it possible for him to exploit the caravan trade. He built the port of Ezion-geber (Elath), on the Gulf of Aqaba, and a fleet of ships to tap the lucrative trade in the territories around the Red Sea. Solomon's copper mines in the Arabah[5] were also an important source of wealth.

One of Solomon's most memorable accomplishments, of course, was the construction of the Temple. Small by Egyptian and Mesopotamian standards, it must have seemed impressive to the Israelites, with its 45 foot ceiling, its decoration, and its lavish use of gold leaf; it was a fitting edifice to house the Ark of Yahweh of Hosts. Yet it could not have won the favor of all. Its builder was an architect from Tyre, and in its floor plan, decorations, and conception it was typically Canaanite. At an earlier date, when David had thought of building a "house for Yahweh," Nathan had discouraged him from breaking with the ancient tradition of a tent shrine (2 Sam 7:5–7). A time would come when the Temple would play a role in prophetic theology, but at this stage it may have provoked prophetic hostility to Solomon.

Solomon was a lavish spender. The Temple and his other building projects were a drain on the treasury. And there were other expenses. While the thousand wives attributed to him in 1 Kgs 11:3 may be something of an exaggeration, he did have a large harem (marriage to daughters of other rulers was, in those days, a matter of foreign policy). This, along with the officials and servants of a burgeoning bureaucracy, and his other projects, so outran income that he resorted to taxing his people and to pawning territory to Hiram, king of Tyre (1 Kgs 9:10–14). For his building projects he even resorted to forced

[5]There is ample archeological evidence of Solomon's mining and smelting operations, even though the building at Ezion-geber, formerly thought to be a smelter, has now been identified as a storehouse. See *BA* 28(1965)70–87.

labor (1 Kgs 5:13-14)—the very thing Israel had left Egypt to escape! For these and other reasons, Solomon's reign had its dark side. A wise successor would be needed to avert disaster.

THE DIVIDED MONARCHY. Unfortunately a wise successor was not forthcoming. While Solomon still lived, the prophet Ahijah had encouraged Jeroboam, an Ephraimite whom Solomon had made overseer of the forced labor, to set himself over the northern tribes. When Solomon got wind of it, Jeroboam had had to flee to Egypt (1 Kgs 11:26-40); but when Solomon died (922), he returned to demand a more lenient policy. Rehoboam, Solomon's son, harshly rejected the demand, and the northern tribes separated from Judah, acclaiming Jeroboam their king (12:1-20). Jeroboam made his capital at Shechem but later moved it to Tirzah.

One of Jeroboam's first acts was to neutralize the attraction of the Jerusalem Temple by establishing Dan and Bethel, both cult centers from ancient times, as national sanctuaries, and by setting up golden bulls there. These bulls were not intended as idols but as pedestals upon which the invisible Yahweh was conceived to be enthroned, just as He was over the Ark. The ignorant may have worshiped them, and, in any case, the bull symbol was a danger because of its connection with the fertility cults.

While a united Israel had been a power to reckon with, the split resulted in two second-rate states. Within a short time, most of the border territories conquered by David were lost, and Pharaoh Shishak launched a raid that devasted Palestine from one end to the other. Trouble from Egypt was not frequent, however, and Judah, the smaller of the two states, though closer to Egypt, was more remote from Mesopotamia, whence danger would come in years ahead. Judah was also blessed with greater stability, for the Davidic dynasty continued to rule throughout the remaining 335 years of her existence. Israel had nine ruling families in the two centuries she survived, and only two of these continued for more than two generations.

Omri (876-869), whose family provided four successive kings for Israel, built Samaria and made it his capital. Because of the danger from the new independent Aramean state of Damascus, he cultivated close relations with Judah and with Tyre; as part of this effort he married his son Ahab to Jezebel, a Tyrian princess. Jezebel bent all her efforts to propagate the cult of the Tyrian Baal in the Northern Kingdom. The strenuous opposition of Elijah (1 Kings 17-19) did not wholly neutralize her paganizing influence, but reaction against such policies eventually brought Omri's dynasty to an end.

The rising power of Assyria, now trying to take over Syria and Palestine, forced Israel (under Ahab—869-850) and Damascus to forget their differences and form a defensive coalition with other threatened states. In 853 the coalition fought Assyria to a standstill and so won a respite.

Figure 16. *The storm-god Hadad standing on a bull. From an 8th century Assyrian relief. Photo by James B. Pritchard.*

Omri's dynasty came to an end in a blood bath. Widespread hostilities to the religious policies fostered by Jezebel led to an uprising (with prophetic instigation—2 Kings 9) under Jehu that terminated in a bloody purge that swept away Jezebel and all baalizing elements. King Ahaziah of Judah, who happened to be in Israel then, was wantonly slain. Jehu thus became king (842–815) and founder of a dynasty that lasted five generations, but he alienated two valuable allies, Tyre and Judah. Thus weakened he soon had to pay tribute to Shalmaneser III, king of Assyria; after Assyria withdrew, he lost much of his territory to Damascus. Jehu's dynasty did, however, lead Israel to a resurgence in the 8th century. Under Jehoash (801–786) and Jeroboam II (786–746), one of the north's most capable kings, Israel recovered all the land she had lost and entered a period of unrivaled prosperity. The oracles of Amos and Hosea, however, reveal a state of religious corruption and social disintegration—an Israel on the verge of collapse.

The period of Assyria's now deadly earnest expansion under Tiglath-pileser III (745-727) was a time of political anarchy in Israel. In the 25 years from the death of Jeroboam II until the fall of Samaria, six kings sat upon the throne of Israel; four times the ruling king was felled by the hand of his successor. The fifth of the six kings, Pekah (737-732), became leader of the anti-Assyrian coalition. When Judah, under Ahaz (735-715), refused to join the coalition, the forces of Israel and Damascus invaded Judah (the Syro-Ephraimitic War). Ahaz sent tribute to Assyria and begged for help. Tiglath-pileser defeated the coalition, destroyed Damascus (732), and made Israel his vassal, reducing her territory to a fraction of her former holdings. Several years later Pekah's successor, Hoshea, foolishly hoping for help from Egypt, refused tribute; Assyria invaded, took Samaria (721), and deported its population. The Northern Kingdom had come to an end.

The deported population (not all the people by any means—Assyrian records give the number at 27,290) did not maintain its identity in Assyria and was lost to history. Many others migrated to Judah either before or after the fall of Samaria, bringing with them the religious traditions of the north. Although there must have been many sincere and religious people among those who remained, the Yahwistic spirit in the north had been badly diluted even before the end; the settlement in their midst of pagan populations from other lands, part of Assyria's policy of deportation, could only have worsened matters. Hezekiah, Josiah, and Jeremiah addressed invitations to the northern territories without any enduring results. The descendants of this population were the Samaritans, whom the Jews returning from the Babylonian Exile would not permit to share in the rebuilding of the Temple.

THEN THERE WAS ONE. Judah was now a vassal of Assyria, a condition which not only robbed her of independence and forced her to pay tribute, but also involved official recognition of Assyria's gods, with attendant evils for Judah's religious life. Ahaz seems to have willingly submitted to all this, but his son Hezekiah (715-687) was of a different stamp. Religious and nationalistic zeal both seemed to dictate revolt against the Assyrian overlord, and Hezekiah laid his plans carefully. They included a thoroughgoing religious reform, an attempt to bring the territory of the northern tribes under his control (unsuccessful), and a strengthening of Jerusalem's defenses. At this time he dug a 1,749 foot tunnel through solid rock to bring water from the spring Gihon into the city. At the death of Sargon II, against the advice of Isaiah, he revolted in concert with other vassals, including Babylon, Tyre, and some of the Philistine cities, and with promise of help from Egypt. Sargon's successor, Sennacherib (704-681), settled first with Babylon and then swooped down on Palestine (701); he captured 46 fortified cities (including Lachish, whose fall he depicted in a sculptured relief) and besieged Jerusalem. Hezekiah was forced to submit and to pay a heavy tribute. Jerusalem, however, was not taken, as even the Assyrian records indicate; its deliverance was attributed to divine intervention and did much to foster a belief in its inviolability.[6]

Towards the middle of the 7th century Assyria reached the peak of her power; even Egypt was conquered. Although Manasseh (687-642), Hezekiah's son and successor, had little choice but to remain a loyal vassal, the degree of his subservience in religious matters enraged loyal Yahwists; Hezekiah's reform was undone, pagan cult objects and practices were given place in the very precincts of the Temple, and opposition to the king's policies was murderously suppressed (2 Kings 21; cf. Jer 15:1-4). But after the brief reign of Manasseh's son, Amon, came Josiah (640-609), a king ready to strike for independence.

Moreover, the Assyrian empire was beginning to collapse; troubled by a rebellious Babylonia in the south and by incursions of barbarians

[6] 2 Kgs 18:13-19:36 may contain accounts of two separate campaigns of Sennacherib: one in 701 (18:13-16) which ended with Hezekiah's submission; the other (18:17-19:36), perhaps ca. 688, in which confident resistance encouraged by Isaiah was crowned by a marvelous deliverance. See *BHI* 296-308.

Figure 17. *Jehu does obeisance before Shalmaneser III while Assyrian soldiers stand behind him in one of the twenty panels of the famous Black Obelisk. Three other panels complete this scene, showing Israelite servants loaded with tribute for Shalmaneser. Courtesy of the Trustees of the British Museum.*

in the north, Assyria was no longer able to intervene in the west, as Egypt's successful bid for independence now showed. Josiah's reform included repudiation of the cult of Assyrian gods and centralization of the cult according to the prescriptions of Deuteronomy, discovered in 622 (p. 102). He extended these measures even into northern Israel, territory which Assyria could no longer effectively hold. Judah was a free nation now, and Assyria's end came in the closing years of the century. In 612, Nineveh, the Assyrian capital, fell to allied forces of Babylonians and Medes; a couple of years later the remnants of the Assyrian army were driven from Haran, where they had attempted a last stand. Josiah lost his life at Megiddo in 609 attempting to prevent Egypt, now more afraid of Babylon than of Assyria, from bringing the Assyrians aid.

Palestine now lay under Egyptian control. Within a short time, however, at the decisive battle of Carchemish (605), Babylonia drove Egypt from the field; shortly thereafter Judah became a vassal of the Neo-Babylonian (Chaldean) empire. Under the unworthy Jehoiakim (609–598), Josiah's reform was completely undone. At a moment of what he took to be Babylonian weakness, Jehoiakim rebelled and brought retribution in the form of an army led by Nebuchadnezzar (Nabuchodonosor—605–562). By the time it arrived at Jerusalem, however, Jehoiakim was dead, and his son Jehoiachin was king. Nebuchadnezzar sacked the Temple and the city, deported Jehoiachin and thousands of upper-class citizens to Babylon, and installed Zedekiah (597–587) as king—the last Judah was to have.

Zedekiah was a weak ruler, addicted to following the wrong advice. He turned a deaf ear to Jeremiah, a prophet since the days of Josiah, and took the road to destruction. In 589, in concert with Tyre and

Figure 18. *Assyrian siege tactics. Assyrian bowmen stand behind high shields while a battering ram attacks the walls; other soldiers rush defenders by means of a ladder. Three captives have already been impaled on stakes. From an 8th century relief. Courtesy of the Trustees of the British Museum.*

Ammon, with the perennial promise of help from Egypt, Judah again revolted. The Lachish letters (p. 13; *ANET* 322) tell a story of hopeless resistance: Jerusalem and Lachish alone hold out, the signals from Azekah can no longer be seen . . . Jerusalem fell to Nebuchadnezzar in 587; the walls were razed, the Temple and other large buildings were put to the torch. There was a second deportation of leading citizens which left behind only "some of the country's poor" as vinedressers and farmers (2 Kgs 25:12). Many of these later fled to Egypt for fear of reprisals after the assassination of Gedaliah, whom the Babylonians had made governor of Judah (25:22–26). Thus ended the kingdom of Judah. Every human consideration would lead us to expect that the exiles of Judah would be dispersed and lost to history as those of the Northern Kingdom had been. Why this did not happen will be the topic of a later chapter.

THE BOOKS OF SAMUEL

The division of Samuel into two books was first made in the Septuagint; they were originally one book and should be treated as a single composition. They cover the period from the appearance of Samuel (ca. 1070) to near the end of David's life (ca. 961) and can be outlined as follows:

    A. *Samuel's Childhood:* 1 Samuel 1–3
    B. *History of the Ark:* 4–6 (completed in 2 Samuel 6)
    C. *Samuel and Saul:* 7–15

D. *Saul and David:* 1 Samuel 16–2 Samuel 1
E. *David, King of Judah and Israel:* 2 Samuel 2–8
F. *Succession to David's Throne:* 9–20 (completed in 1 Kings 1–2)
G. *Appendices:* 21–24

The book in its present form teaches that David's kingdom is the legitimate successor to the tribal league and that through him God's promises to the Fathers have been fulfilled. Yet even a casual reading of the book reveals parallel narratives, bewilderingly different attitudes towards Saul and the monarchy, and quite different pictures of Samuel. So, for example, there are three traditions of Saul becoming king (p. 124, n. 2); twice he is rejected by Samuel (1 Sam 13:8–15; 15), twice David is introduced to him (16:14–23; 17:55–58), twice David flees from him (19:11–18; 20), twice David spares his life in the wilderness (24; 26). A hostile attitude towards the monarchy is displayed in 1 Samuel 8, a favorable one in 9 (cf. especially v 16); in the former Samuel is a prophet-judge who rules all Israel, and in the latter he is a small-town seer. The reason for all this is the complexity of the sources used in the composition of Samuel.

There is no universally accepted analysis of these sources. The attempt to distribute the bulk of the material between two main sources, one early and promonarchic,[7] the other late and antimonarchic,[8] is an oversimplification; the compilers of Samuel appear to have utilized a number of separate sources. The role of the deuteronomists in the production of Samuel is also uncertain. All admit that they incorporated Samuel into their historical work, but some scholars think they found the book substantially as it is now. Others think that they compiled it from older sources and themselves composed substantial parts of it (especially the sections critical of the monarchy: 1 Samuel 7–8; 10:17–27; 12). The position adopted here is that Samuel is a deuteronomic compilation of older sources, some of which (especially the antimonarchic passages) have been reworked so as to bring out more clearly the deuteronomic point of view. On that hypothesis, the following remarks concerning sources and teachings are made.

1) *Samuel's Childhood* (1 Samuel 1–3) is a separate source, probably composed long after the events; here he is depicted as a prophet known throughout Israel (3:19–4:1). He is likewise shown as a leader with authority over all Israel in 7–8 and 12, but as a Judge (who functions both as a magistrate and as a military leader) rather than a prophet. In 15 he is again depicted as a prophet, rebuking Saul for his sin. These passages probably represent separate sources, but have in common the exaltation of spiritual authority in Israel over kingship.

---

[7]Including 1 Samuel 4–6; 9:1–10:16; 11:1–11; 24 (*or* 26); 25; 27–31; 2 Samuel 2–7; 9–21.

[8]Including 1 Samuel 1–3; 7–8; 10:17–27; 12; 26; (*or* 24); 28; 2 Samuel 1.

2) *The History of the Ark* (4–6; 2 Samuel 6) is a separate, early source; it makes no mention of Samuel. It breathes a primitive sense of wonder and awe for this symbol of the divine presence, yet contains a keen satire on idolatry (cf. 5:3–4). The story shows the rule of David, who brought the Ark to a worthy resting place, to be the legitimate successor to the tribal league.

3) *The section from Samuel's ministry to Nathan's oracle* (1 Samuel 7–2 Samuel 8) is concerned with three matters: the legitimacy of the monarchy for Israel, the rejection of Saul, and the establishment of David's kingdom and line. Here especially, parallel accounts and conflicting attitudes give the clearest evidence of compilation from a variety of sources, some of them fairly extensive. One told of the rise of Saul (1 Sam 9:1–10:16; 13–14), another of the rise of David (much of the material from 1 Samuel 16 on); another was an antimonarchic account of the institution of the kingship (1 Samuel 8; 10:17–27; 12).

The diverse attitudes of the sources reflect Israel's own struggle over the legitimacy of the monarchy. Israel was not supposed to be "as other nations," but the tribal league had failed to cope with the Philistine threat. From the point of historical fact the monarchy had emerged to meet the threat. Was it a valid solution? Some, obviously, had strong reservations, to say the least. There were antecedent theological reasons. In Israel's faith, even in the earliest period, Yahweh was hailed as King,[9] and it was felt that this office should not be communicated to any man.[10] Then, too, in the nations around them, the king was believed to have divine power; in Egypt the king was venerated as a god, while in Mesopotamia he was considered the representative of the gods. Nothing like this could be at home in Israel. The antimonarchical passages also reflect the experience of a later period that Israel's kings had often led her astray. In fact the monarchy could be, and had been, a two-edged thing; the king could be a channel of God's saving acts or an occasion of apostasy. The sources accurately reflect a tension that Israel never resolved. The deuteronomic editors used their sources to grant a grudging recognition to the kingship as a (then) present thing, but also to insist that it must be exercised in a way compatible with Israel's faith.

Thus the stage was set for the clash of prophet and king that was to go on throughout the history of the monarchy. Classical prophetism had not yet emerged, but we get a preview of what is to come in the conflict between Samuel and Saul. Although the picture of Samuel as a prophet has been heightened by later theologizing, his claim to represent prophecy has a basis in his association with the bands of ecstatic prophets (p. 149) that were beginning to appear in premonarchic Israel (1 Sam 10:5–10; 19:20). These ardent Yahwists stirred

---

[9]See *BHI* 149–150.
[10]The earliest passages do not call Saul or David king (*melek*) but ruler or leader (*nagid*); 9:16; 10:1; 13:14.

the people to religious fervor and enabled them to resist the encroachments of enemies without and Canaanite ways within. There is reason to believe that Samuel organized such bands and that he could also speak for them.

Samuel was willing to support Saul as long as he was content to be a political and military leader, but when Saul seemed to grasp at the sacral aspects of kingship, Samuel withdrew his support. The account of Samuel's rejection of Saul in 13:8–15 is puzzling, for Saul's conduct seems irreproachable; in 15, however, he is blamed for setting himself above Israel's tradition of the holy war by relaxing the ban in favor of plunder. In Samuel's interpretation, the king should be subject to God's spokesman, but Saul would not accept this. In rejecting Saul, Samuel meant to depose him, but in this he failed. Saul continued to rule and Samuel withdrew from the scene. Yet Saul's deterioration continued until he was guilty of such irreligious acts as slaying the priests of Nob (22:6–19) and consulting the witch of Endor (28). He was not the man after Yahweh's heart and his line was not established in the kingship.

The account of David's anointing (16:1–3) sets the theme which predominates the rest of this section of Samuel: David is the man after Yahweh's heart (13:13–14; 15:27–29), possessing the fulness of His spirit (16:13), which has departed from Saul (16:14). Step by step, inexorably, the kingdom is transferred from Saul to David. The able and wily David, of course, did much to make himself the logical choice once Saul should no longer be on the scene, but only because God's choice had fallen upon him could he succeed; even Saul is made to acknowledge this while he is king and David a helpless fugitive (24:20). David has the favor of Samuel and prophetic support (22:5) and becomes the protector of Abiathar, the last survivor of the priesthood of the tribal league. Established at last as king of a united Israel, he incorporates the very heart of the tribal league into the new order by bringing the Ark to Jerusalem. Nathan's oracle (2 Samuel 7), finally, assures David that his throne will be secure and will be possessed by his line for ages to come; the covenant thus established and the promise that David and his line were adopted as Yahweh's "son" (v 14) bestow a profound theological significance on the Davidic dynasty (p. 144).

4) *The Throne Succession Narrative* (2 Samuel 9–20; completed in 1 Kings 1–2) is a separate source, written very near the time of the events by someone with intimate knowledge of David's family and court. Its objectivity, charm, and narrative skill have caused many to bestow on its unknown author, five centuries before Herodotus, the title "the father of history." Rowley says, "there is no historical writing of comparable length in any known literature of the world that can stand beside it in age, lucidity and honesty."[11] The author was certainly

---

[11]H. H. Rowley, *The Growth of the Old Testament,* p. 68.

someone from the circle of the royal court. It is suggested that he was commissioned to write the account of how Solomon came to succeed David, even though three sons with prior claims (Amnon, Absalom, and Adonijah) stood before him, and thus to establish the legitimacy of Solomon's succession—an end somewhat obscured by the present dislocation of the conclusion of the story.

The author's intention, however, went far beyond any such commission; without pious comment, simply letting the events speak for themselves, he conveys through the story a moral teaching. It is not an edifying story, for it tells of adultery, murder, incest, and rebellion; it is the story of David's sin and its consequences. David's adultery with Bathsheba and his indirect murder of Uriah, her husband, is told with admirable directness (11); no excuse is offered for him at all. Nathan's confrontation with David, with his parable and the dramatic "You are the man!" (12:1–15), is one of the *OT* masterpieces. David's sin is forgiven (12:13) in that his life is spared in spite of two capital crimes; but his sin, true to the *OT* concept of it, returns, boomerang-fashion, upon the head of the sinner, inexorably working its mischief in him and his family. The death of Bathsheba's child, Amnon's rape of Tamar, his half-sister, Absalom's assassination of Amnon to avenge his sister, his subsequent rebellion, and the other evils that afflict David in his latter years are traced back to his rebellion against Yahweh. Yet, in God's mysterious providence, it is Bathsheba who becomes the mother of Solomon, the one who eventually sits upon David's throne.

The deuteronomists were able to utilize these sources, often with little or no change, because they suited their purpose as they stood. The function of Samuel in their historical work was manifold: the setting up of the monarchy with its inherent tension, its possibility for good or evil, sets the stage for the procedure employed in Kings (see below); the story of Saul demonstrates the tragic results when kingship becomes independent of covenant faith; the transfer of the Ark to Jerusalem is related to the theme of unity of sanctuary (as is the purchase of the Temple site—2 Samuel 24); the Succession History is a vivid illustration of the theme of rewards and punishments; and, though it is not characteristic of deuteronomic teaching, God's saving intentions are advanced through His covenant with David.

THE BOOKS OF KINGS

SOURCES AND COMPOSITION. Like 1–2 Samuel, 1–2 Kings was originally a single book. The period covered is from just before Solomon's accession (961) to the fall of Judah (587), with a final note from King Jehoiachin's 37th year in exile (561—2 Kgs 25:27–30). The problems of composition are less difficult than they were in Samuel. The sources of Kings are more easily identifiable, and its composition may be more confidently attributed to the deuteronomists.

Some of the sources used are explicitly cited: the acts of Solomon (1 Kgs 11:41), the chronicles of the kings of Israel, and the chronicles of the kings of Judah (the latter two expressions may refer to the royal archives). Other sources are not cited but can be inferred. The most important of these were cycles of stories about prophets; some were quite popular, even legendary, in nature (e.g., many of those concerning Elijah and Elisha scattered through 1 Kings 17-2 Kings 13), while others were more objective and sober. The abundance of information on the building of the Temple and the reforms of Hezekiah and Josiah suggests that special sources were employed here, too. Some sources were used with little or no change, but others were reworked to more clearly bring out the desired teaching. There is no reason to doubt, for example, that the prophet Ahijah incited Jeroboam to revolt and then later rejected him, but the deuteronomic diction of his oracles as they now stand (1 Kgs 11:30-39; 14:7-16) reveals the work of the editors. Finally, there are some passages which are pure deuteronomic compositions, such as Solomon's Temple dedication speech (1 Kings 8) and the commentary on the fall of the Northern Kingdom (2 Kgs 17:7-29).

The first edition of Kings was probably completed during the reign of King Josiah. Appearing in the heyday of the deuteronomic reform, it was intended to draw from history a solemn warning of the danger of unfaithfulness and motives for sincere renewal. This edition must have ended in 2 Kings 23, before the concluding words of v 25: "nor could any after him compare with him." During the exile a second edition, adding the events subsequent to the death of Josiah and certain other passages (p. 104, n. 4), was produced. God's threats for violation of the covenant were thus seen to have been fulfilled, and a modest hope was held out for the future. The book, in its final form, exhibits this outline:

A. *Reign of Solomon:* 1 Kings 1-11
B. *Divided Monarchy:* 1 Kings 12-2 Kings 17
C. *Judah Alone:* 2 Kings 18-25

TEACHINGS. The special concerns of the authors of Kings are revealed in those matters to which they give most space, i.e., the building of the Temple and its dedication (1 Kings 5-8), Jeroboam's revolt and the altars he set up (12:1-13:10; 14:1-16), the religious crisis in the north (reflected especially in the stories about Ahab, Jezebel, Elijah, and Jehu scattered from 1 Kings 16 to 2 Kings 11), the fall of the Northern Kingdom (2 Kings 17), the reform of Hezekiah (18-20), the corrupt reign of Manasseh (21), and the reform of Josiah (22-23). All of these have to do with religious purity, with special emphasis on unity of sanctuary.

The building of the Temple was, of course, of capital importance for the deuteronomists; centralization of the cult there, they felt, was the surest way of avoiding pagan contamination (p. 106). Yet Solomon, the builder of the Temple, also introduced a corrupting influence by building shrines for the false gods worshiped by his foreign wives (1 Kgs 11:1-8). The evil implications of Jeroboam's rebellion were seen when he added religious separation to political separation by forbidding his subjects to go to Jerusalem, sending them to the shrines at Dan and Bethel instead. Another foreign wife, Jezebel, was a major factor in the further corruption of the religion of the northern tribes with her strenuous promotion of the cult of the Tyrian Baal. Hezekiah and Josiah carried out reforms aimed at removing pagan cults, eliminating syncretism from Yahwistic worship, and centralizing it in the Temple. These concerns are the same as those found at the beginning of the deuteronomic code, Deuteronomy 12-13.

The inclusion of the prophetic materials was an important ingredient of the deuteronomic teaching. They contain stirring stories of heroic defenders of Yahwism such as Elijah, depict the religious conditions of the times, and, most important, illustrate the power of the word of Yahweh to create weal and woe. The stories about Elijah are a good example. The account of his "duel" with the prophets of Baal on Mt. Carmel (1 Kings 18), one of the most dramatic narratives in the *OT*, tells of an altar of Yahweh fallen into disrepair, of Israelites who, when challenged by Elijah to choose between Yahweh and Baal, refused to give answer. In spite of his victory he goes, almost in despair, to Mt. Horeb to complain to the Lord of altars thrown down, of prophets slain, and of mortal danger to himself (19). Hand in hand with the corruption of covenant loyalty to Yahweh went corruption in those matters which covenant law regulated, as the story of Naboth shows (21). Naboth could refuse to sell his vineyard to King Ahab because Israelite custom regarded the right to family property as sacred, and even Ahab was forced to respect it. But Jezebel, whose baalism did not concern itself with human rights and justice, had no such scruples. The ease with which the judicial murder was arranged with the leading citizens is an index of how little regard was then being paid to covenant law.

Elijah's pronouncement of doom upon Ahab and his line when he hears of the Naboth affair is but one of the many examples which show the power of the word of Yahweh to bring punishment upon those who forsake His covenant and to accomplish the good He has promised. About a dozen times the deuteronomists explicitly note the fulfillment of prophetic oracles (e.g., 1 Kgs 12:15; 15:29; 16:12). The case of Ahab is not wholly typical, for his repentance obtains a mitigation of the sentence, but it has the advantage of showing that the threatened doom can be averted. Even the inclusion of the miracles worked by the prophets have the effect of enhancing their words (1 Kgs 17:24: "Now indeed I know that you are a man of God. . . . The word of the Lord comes truly from your mouth"). By this emphasis on Yahweh's word, a theme already present in the prophetic sources, the authors show that the history of the kingdom followed the course determined by the word of Yahweh when He gave Israel His commandments and threatened destruction for disobedience.

The most characteristic mark the deuteronomists have left on Kings is found in the framework within which the reign of each king (beginning with Rehoboam) is described. The opening formula for each king of Judah tells when he began to reign, his age, the length of his reign, and the name of his mother; then follows a judgment on his reign and an account of his deeds; the closing formula contains a reference to sources of further information, a notice on his death and burial, and the name of his successor. The framework for the kings of Israel differs slightly, omitting the king's age and the mother's name. The account of the king's deeds is mainly concerned with the religious situation, the authors' controlling interest. It seldom dwells on the king's political or military activity; Omri and Jeroboam II, two of Israel's most important monarchs, are dealt with in seven or eight verses each.

The most important part of the framework is the judgment upon the king, where we reach the heart of the deuteronomic teaching. Basically the judgment given depends on whether the king observed the principle of a single sanctuary or not. The kings of the north are all condemned because of what we might call Jeroboam's "original sin," the shrines of Dan and Bethel. Of the kings of Judah, only two receive unqualified praise; they are Hezekiah and Josiah, the two who attempted to centralize the cult. Six others (Asa, Jehoshaphat, Jehoash, Amaziah, Azariah, and Jotham) receive an approval qualified by the note that they did not remove the "high places."[12] The others are all judged unfavorably.

If it seems unfair to judge kings on the basis of an ideal that became law only in the days of Josiah, a number of considerations temper that impression. There can be no doubt, for example, that Jeroboam's desire to provide rival shrines for Jerusalem was a perversion of the religious unity of the covenant people; he acted from motives of political expediency without regard for the disasterous effects that would follow. Then, too, although centralization of worship is most often given as the explicit basis for judgment, it has value as an epitome of religious fidelity rather than as the sole norm. It is not really the basis for the favorable judgment passed on kings who received qualified approval, but only the basis for withholding full approval. The authors also ask whether the king's heart was perfect (1 Kgs 15:3), whether he trusted Yahweh (2 Kgs 18:5), whether he did what was right in His

---

[12]The term, which *per se* designates a particular type of sanctuary, whether Canaanite or Israelite, is used in Kings to designate all shrines other than the Temple, even Yahwistic ones.

sight (2 Kgs 12:2), and whether he kept the commandments (2 Kgs 18:6).

Finally, the authors' concern for centralization of worship was in fact concern for religious purity, and this was the real basis of their judgment. Religious purity, in turn, was not simply a question of what name was given the god to be worshiped or how sacrifice was to be offered, but the very concept of divinity and morality. The pagan cults they rejected included such things as the degrading fertility cult, with its male and female prostitutes, and infant sacrifice—practices imported into the very bosom of the covenant People of Yahweh. The deuteronomists' desire for religious purity was not priestly concern for cultic exactitude, but the thirst of the prophetic spirit for covenant loyalty.

INTERPRETATION OF HISTORY. The deuteronomic corpus is not simply a history but a theology of history. It is an exposition of the inner meaning of historical events as an interplay between the working out of God's plan and human response. By beginning with covenant, covenant law, and blessings and curses, continuing through the fulfillment of God's gracious promises, describing the ungrateful response of the people, and ending with the destruction of the nation, the corpus teaches that the end came because Israel had rejected covenant loy-

Figure 19.
*Assyrian soldiers
take booty and
captives away from
a captured city;
blocks and beams fall
as the city is
demolished. From
a 7th century relief.
Courtesy of the
Trustees of the
British Museum.*

alty. This teaching emerges both from the dispassionate account of what happened and from the comments of the deuteronomists. When they pass judgment on a king, they are passing judgment on the whole people, of whom the king is the embodiment. When the series of judgments is, by and large, unfavorable, when they attribute the fall of Israel and the fall of Judah to the sinfulness of king and people (2 Kgs 17:7–23; 21:10-15), they are claiming to know the meaning of God's activity in the history of the period.

Can this claim be accepted? Would it not be truer to say that Israel and Judah, lying in the path of expanding imperialistic powers, were overwhelmed in a flood they could never have escaped? In answer it may be said that there is nothing unrealistic about recognizing God as the Lord of history whose providential plan includes the play of power politics over the centuries; moreover, Israel's many failings did have something to do with the course of events. If unconscionable oppression had not provoked a disruption that left two weak states instead of one strong one; if Josiah's reform had not come to an untimely end with his death as he attempted to play a role in the power struggle; if Zedekiah had followed Jeremiah's advice in 589; if, finally, Israel had concentrated on being the People of God and all that that entailed, they might have survived as a nation. It requires at least as much revealed knowledge to say what *had* to happen as to explain why what did happen came to pass.

The interpretation of history given by the deuteronomists is not their creation but rests on that of the prophets. They were aware that events had happened "as [the Lord] had foretold through all his servants, the prophets" (2 Kgs 17:13, 23; 21:10; 24:2). The prophets claimed to be God's spokesmen, to have knowledge of God's plan, of His will to bless, of His reaction to sin. They foretold the fall of Israel, the fall of Judah, and the restoration and were vindicated by the events. The deuteronomists have told the story of what happened, but have done it against the background of the prophetic teaching of why it happened. The Jewish Canon classifies these books as The Former Prophets, a designation that reflects an important aspect of their character.

READING SUGGESTIONS

JBC §9-10. *OTRG* #7. *AUOT* 167–97, 234–67, 296–340, 359–64. *BHI* 179–339. *MTES* 132–88. *VAI* 91–177, 312–39. *WBA* 121–82. *WITOT* 157–82.

Conroy, C., *1-2 Samuel, 1-2 Kings, Excursus on Davidic Dynasty & Holy City Zion. OTM,* Vol. 6.

Jones, G. H., *1 and 2 Kings*. 2 vols. Grand Rapids: Eerdmans, 1984.

Maly, E., *The World of David and Solomon*. Englewood Cliffs: Prentice-Hall, Inc., 1966.

Pritchard, J. B., *Solomon & Sheba*. London: Phaidon, 1974.

Rost, L., *The Succession to the Throne of David*. Sheffield: Almond Press, 1982.

Whybray, R.N., *The Succession Narrative*. Naperville, Ill.: Allenson, 1968.

Ackroyd, P. R., "The Succession Narrative (so-called)," *Int* 35 (1981) 383-96.

Albright, W. F., "King Joiachin in Exile," *BAR* 106-12.

Birch, B., "The Choosing of Saul at Mizpah," *CBQ* 37 (1975) 447-57.

Coats, G. W., "Parable, Fable, and Anecdote: Storytelling in the Succession Narrative," *Int* 35 (1981) 368-82.

Garner, G., "Shiloh and Its Destruction," *Buried History* 19 (1983) 23-27.

Kelly, W., "First and Second Samuel: A History of the Rise of the Davidic Monarchy," *TBT* #100 (Feb. 1979) 1885-92.

Levenson, J. D., "The Davidic Covenant and Its Modern Interpreters," *CBQ* 41 (1979) 205-19.

_____, "1 Samuel 25 as Literature and as History," *CBQ* 40 (1978) 11-28.

Lundbom, J. R., "The Lawbook of the Josianic Reform," *CBQ* 38 (1976) 293-302.

McCarter, P. K., Jr., "'Plots, True or False': The Succession Narrative as Court Apologetic," *Int* 35 (1981) 355-67.

McCarthy, D. J., "The Inauguration of Monarchy in Israel (*A Form-Critical Study of 1 Sam 8-12*)," *Int* 27 (1973) 401-12.

Maly, E. H., "God and King in Ancient Israel," *TBT* #100 (Feb. 1979) 1893-1900.

March, W. E., "II Samuel 7:1-17," *Int* 35 (1981) 387-400.

Mendenhall, G. E., "The Monarchy," *Int* 29 (1975) 155-70.

Miller, J. M., "Saul's Rise to Power," *CBQ* 36 (1974) 157-74.

Stern, E., "Israel at the Close of the Period of the Monarchy," *BA* 38 (1975) 26-54.

Ussishkin, D., "King Solomon's Palaces," *BA* 36 (1973) 78-105.

Wright, G. E., "The Temple in Palestine Syria," *BAR* 169-84.

Yadin, Y., "New Light on Solomon's Megiddo," *BAR* 2 240-47.

12

Redemptive Themes
in Deuteronomic History

THE TRIUMPHS and catastrophes related in the deuteronomic corpus played a role in Israel's historically-conditioned and ever-deepening understanding of redemption. Possession of the land was another step in the fulfillment of the promises to Abraham, and the development of new forms to meet new crises showed God's continued care.

On the other hand, the warnings that went with the covenant and their fulfillment in history show that covenant is not a magic, automatic road to blessing and salvation. Covenant implies relationship, and relationship implies response. An Israel that looked for an easy, no-strings-attached salvation found its kingdom in ruins. Yet they survived as a people and could continue to hope. We must now look more closely at one of the principal forms of Israel's hope.

Although the deuteronomists were not overly sympathetic to the monarchy, as we have seen, it is in their work that the fundamental text for royal messianism was preserved; they have, moreover, incorporated the theme into their theology of history. The text in question is 2 Samuel 7; it tells of Nathan's oracle concerning David's dynasty.[1] This passage comes as the climax to the story of David's rise; not only is David's rule confirmed by divine promise, but the vista of continued blessings to David's line stretches out to the distant future. After David had brought the Ark to Jerusalem, he conceived the plan of building a temple to replace the tent which housed it, and sought prophetic approval. Nathan, speaking in God's name, rejects this departure from ancient desert and tribal league tradition: David is not to build a house for Yahweh. Rather, he says, Yahweh will build a house

[1] Ps 89:20–38 gives a longer, poetic form of the oracle which, in spite of some ⸗ sion, probably better preserves the original than 2 Samuel 7.

144

for David. By a play on the word "house," David is promised a dynasty that will continue throughout successive ages. The word translated "heir" (*zera*—see p. 95) in v 12 is collective, though this is difficult to bring out in English translation in the following verses.[2] God promises that David's line will continue to rule (v 16), and that each successive son will rank as God's (adopted) son (v 14).

Although the word does not occur in 2 Samuel 7, this promise amounts to a covenant by which God brings David and his line into a special relationship with Him; v 15 speaks of God's *hesed,* His covenant loyalty, which will never fail. Psalm 89 speaks of covenant four times and *hesed* seven times. God's covenant with David cannot be considered a personal favor to him. David was Israel's king, not a private individual. In virtue of the concept of corporate personality, the king was considered to be the embodiment of the whole nation, not merely a governor or a figurehead. Every blessing that came to him came to the whole nation. Even the designation of David and his line as God's son supposes the previous relationship between God and the people, for Israel had long before been called His son (Exod 4:22–23). Just as before God's relationship with His people had been established through the Sinai covenant, so now it was given new form through the Davidic covenant, which can be said to have subsumed the earlier one. Stable monarchic succession was bringing the tradition of charismatic leaders to an end; the Davidic covenant was a way of assuring that Israel would continue to be governed by God and that the covenant, so essential to Israel's very existence, would take on new meaning in a new situation. Only by some such adaptation of the covenant idea could it continue to be the basis of Israel, now so changed from the days of Sinai and the tribal league.

At Sinai the covenant was made with the people as such, with Moses acting as mediator. In later years, leaders were raised up from the people as they were needed. Now that Israel has become a monarchy, the covenant is made with the king, the head, representative, and embodiment of the people, and through him becomes effective for all the people. Henceforth the covenant relationship of Israel to God is mediated through David and his line; God's covenant blessings flow to the people only through David. As a result, relationship to David determines relationship to covenant salvation. These implications of the Davidic covenant were accepted and elaborated in certain circles, especially in prophetic and priestly schools in Jerusalem. There these ideas were given prominent expression in the cult (as many psalms show), which probably included an annual celebration of the Davidic covenant. Kingship thus took on a new religious meaning within the covenant relations of God and people. The expectation of covenant

---

[2]It is generally agreed that v 13 is a later addition. Whereas the sense of the oracle is "You will not build me a house, but I will build you a house," v 13 is saying "You will not build me a house but your son will."

salvation through David's line is sometimes called "dynastic messianism."

The Davidic covenant theology was not accepted throughout Israel. Particularly in the north, more tenacious of the tribal league traditions, the older ideas continued to hold sway. After the rupture of the kingdom, the northern tribes were dissociated from the Davidic monarch. Quite understandably, Jeroboam's first move was to assure that they would no longer frequent the Temple with its cultic celebration of the Davidic covenant. The north never accepted the principle of dynastic succession; there, prophetic designation and charismatic qualities continued to be the criteria for the selection of a leader, ideally at least, if not always in practice. It is not surprising, then, that the concern of deuteronomic theology, with its roots in northern traditions (p. 102), sought a renewal of the older covenant concepts and had little sympathy for Davidic covenant theology or with kingship in general. Yet their teaching was imparted by recording and interpreting facts of history, and as good historians they recorded what God had done for Israel through David and what He had promised him through Nathan.

But the deuteronomists did more than this. Their attempt to bring about the renewal that would avert disaster ended in failure; in Babylon new chapters were added to their work to show that God's threat of judgment had overtaken the nation. But could this be the end? Had God cast them off forever? Running through Kings are a number of significant references to David; some allude to the promise God had made to him (1 Kgs 9:5; 11:13, 36; 15:4; 2 Kgs 8:19), while others hold him up as the ideal king against whom other kings of Judah are measured (1 Kgs 14:8; 15:3; 2 Kgs 14:3; 22:2). The David pictured in the second series of texts, the David whose heart was entirely with Yahweh, who always did what was pleasing to Him, is not the David of the Succession Narrative. Rather, as von Rad points out, the picture comes from an independent cycle of messianic conceptions which the deuteronomists have incorporated into their theology of history.

It is only against the idealized picture of David and the reminders of the promise that there should never want a son to sit upon the throne of Israel, that the significance of the concluding verses of the whole corpus is seen. In the 37th year of the exile of King Jehoiachin, Evilmerodach (Amel-marduk), king of Babylon, freed Jehoiachin from prison, gave him a seat above the other prisoner-kings, and provided a daily allowance of food for him (2 Kgs 25:27–30). David's line has not been extinguished; the promises of God to him can still be actualized. This was a very modest basis for hope; it was all the deuteronomists, as historians, could report, but to them it was significant.

From the preceding discussion it is clear that David is far more than a type of Christ. We have here another beginning which finds its completion in Jesus. In deuteronomic history a new dimension is added to messianism: David's dynasty has a special role in God's redemptive plan as the channel of blessings to be bestowed. The appearance of royal messianism does not eliminate other messianic themes; it remains one development within God's broad plan to bring blessing and salvation. Yet it is a central one; the one, in fact, which gives us the terms "Messiah" and "messianism." *Mashiah* (Messiah), "anointed one," was a term used to designate the king; "Christ" comes from its Greek equivalent. The final verses of 2 Kings show that David's son can stand as the symbol of hope for a conquered nation, but there is no suggestion of a particular individual to come, the Messiah. For this we must turn to the prophets.

13

Spokesmen for God

(Recommended Scripture reading: 1 Samuel 10; 1 Kings 17–22;
Isaiah 6; Jeremiah 1; Ezekiel 1–2)

AS WE APPROACH the study of the prophets, it would be useful to
recall the traditional three-fold division of the Canon into the Law,
the Prophets, and the Writings (see above, p. 5, and below, p. 270).
The section called "the Prophets" is subdivided into "Former Prophets" (Joshua, Judges, 1–2 Samuel, 1–2 Kings) and "Latter Prophets"
(Isaiah, Jeremiah, Ezekiel, and "the book of the twelve"—i.e., the
twelve so-called minor prophets). The first of these groups was dealt
with as "deuteronomic history," but its inclusion among the prophets
can be justified in that it contains a prophetic interpretation of history
as well as much material about many of Israel's early prophets.[1] Thus
in Samuel and Kings we read about Samuel, Nathan, Ahijah, Elijah,
Elisha, and other prophetic figures, including women such as Deborah
and Huldah. The second of these groups, the "Latter Prophets," is
composed of books we more readily designate prophetic books, those
containing the oracles of the prophets for whom they are named.
These are thus often called the canonical prophets, or (because in
them prophecy reached its high point) the classical prophets, or (less
aptly) the writing prophets.

But however we designate them, Israel's prophets were an extraordinary group. They helped form Israel's faith and preserved her in
time of crisis. Without them Israel's faith would not have survived
and the Bible would not have been written. Their contribution to the
OT goes far beyond the prophetic books, for it is their interpretation
of history that is at the heart of the historical books. The importance
of the prophets can hardly be exaggerated.

---

[1]The principal reason for the designation, however, the tradition that these books
were written by prophets such as Samuel and Jeremiah, would be difficult to defend on
historical-critical grounds.

148

The English word "prophet" derives from the Greek *prophetes,* "one who speaks for another." This is a good description of the classical (canonical) prophets, those who represent the high point of the prophetic movement, for they are, above all, spokesmen for God. The *OT,* however, applies one and the same term (Hebrew *nabi*—etymology uncertain) to men of diverse stamps, including some that we would call false prophets. Absolute distinctions are difficult to make, but the general lines can be traced.

DEVELOPMENT OF PROPHETISM

EARLY PROPHETISM. The earliest historical references to prophetism come from the days of Samuel[2] in the description of the ecstatic group encountered by Saul (1 Sam 10.5-13). After Saul's anointing, Samuel sent him on his way with the promise that he would soon meet a group of prophets equipped with musical instruments; they would be "prophesying," and the Spirit of the Lord would come upon Saul so that he, too, would "prophesy" and would undergo a transforming experience. The activity described as "prophecy" here is ecstatic prayer induced by rhythmic dancing and singing. This is a type of enthusiasm found frequently in religious movements, akin to that of later Mohammedan dervishes. Some non-biblical references (e.g., Wen-Amon's encounter with an ecstatic at Byblos in the 11th century—*ANET* 26) indicate that it was known among the cultures around Israel at this time; the prophets of Baal in 1 Kings 18 are also cultic ecstatics. Prophetic groups appear frequently in Kings, often as sizable communities. During Jezebel's persecution 100 survived by hiding in caves (1 Kgs 18:4); Ahab consulted some 400 prophets before undertaking an important campaign (1 Kings 22); and Elisha was associated with groups of them at Bethel, Jericho, and Gilgal (2 Kings 2-6).[3]

They may well have had cultic functions, for most of the places they were associated with had well-known shrines. The enthusiasm they generated was infectious and others were sometimes caught up by it willy-nilly (1 Sam 10:10; 19:18-24). Although there was nothing necessarily supernatural about such behavior, and though certain aspects of it strike us as odd, this movement was a force for good in

---

[2]Samuel himself is called a seer (*ro'eh*) in the earliest texts (1 Sam 9:6-14), i.e., one who could give information about hidden matters. Divination, so widely practiced in ancient times, was strictly forbidden in Israel (Deut 18:10-14), although the sacred lot (urim and thummim) was tolerated as late as the time of Saul and David (1 Sam 14:41-42; 23:9-12). Oracular responses by priest or seer might also have been given on the basis of dreams, or of real or supposed powers of clairvoyance.

[3]In the north, during the 9th and 8th centuries such groups were called "the sons of the prophets," a term which simply means "members of the prophetic order," "guild prophets."

the Israel of this time in encouraging the people to resist Philistine arms and Canaanite culture. Recent studies emphasize that while such group ecstaticism bears outward resemblance to that of other cultures, its content and purpose was unique in Israel. Just as law, kingship, and covenant, common institutions in the ancient world, became vehicles for God's work in Israel, so it was with these ecstatic groups. Nevertheless, we are a long way from the classical prophetism of later centuries.

These prophetic guilds, as we may call them, transmitted the traditions and techniques of prophecy and so gave stability to the institution. Individuals became members of the prophetic order by entering such a group; no text suggests that a specific, individual call from God was required. Although individuals could expect to be paid for oracular responses (1 Sam 9:8; 1 Kgs 14:2-3; 2 Kgs 8:8-9), the support of a large group must have posed problems; conditions were not always easy (2 Kgs 4:1, 38-39). Those who became attached to the king's court could live on the royal bounty, but this brought with it the temptation to say what the king wanted to hear and to exploit their calling for gain. The prophet who predicted disaster for the king might find himself in prison and on short rations of bread and water (1 Kgs 22:27). There is little doubt that the prophetic guilds lost much of their primitive fervor because of the trend toward professionalism.

In his youth Samuel had been with the priests at Shiloh, but in later life he was associated with the ecstatic prophets; he encouraged their spread and even presided over one of the groups (1 Sam 19:20). Other individuals who appear in the early monarchy, such as Nathan, Ahijah, Elijah, and Elisha, *may* have come from such groups, but we cannot be sure. The fact that Elijah and Elisha exhibit ecstatic behavior at times (1 Kgs 18:46; 2 Kgs 3:15), that Elisha presided over the "sons of the prophets" after Elijah's disappearance (2 Kgs 2:4-6), and that stories about these two were preserved and transmitted in prophetic communities, suggests close relationships, even though the Elijah narratives usually show him as a lone wolf.

Elijah must have become a legend even in his own lifetime; he was a "man of God," filled with power to fight uncompromisingly for Yahwism against every pagan encroachment. Ahab, by whose sufferance Jezebel was able to carry out her baalizing program, considered him the "troubler of Israel" and his own personal enemy (1 Kgs 18:17; 21:20). In the narrative of 1 Kings 17-18, Elijah, in order to prove that it is Yahweh, not Baal, who gives and withholds fertility, confronts Ahab and tells him that there would be no rain or dew until he (Elijah) said the word, and then departs. In spite of Ahab's attempts to find him, he manages to stay hidden and to sustain himself during three and a half years of drought and famine until he voluntarily confronts Ahab again. He has Ahab summon the people and the prophets of Baal and calls down fire from heaven after the prophets of Baal have tried and failed to do so. The prophets of Baal are slaughtered and the drought ends in a thunderstorm. While the story has obviously lost nothing in the telling, at the very least it bears witness to the popular image of Elijah as a man of power and action.

The account of Elijah at Mt. Horeb (19) traces the political policy followed by Elisha back to Elijah and may be correct in doing so. Elijah certainly foretold the overthrow of Ahab's line (21:20-24), though it was Elisha who instigated the revolt of Jehu which accomplished it. Such political action was characteristic of the early prophets. It is in his role of prophet that Samuel attempted to depose Saul (1 Samuel 15); Nathan played an active role in Solomon's succession (1 Kgs 1:11-27); and Ahijah encouraged Jeroboam to lead the ten northern tribes in revolt (11:29-30). Elisha and other prophets are found traveling with the armies of Israel (1 Kgs 20:13-28; 2 Kgs 3:9-20); the king could even call Elisha "Israel's chariots and horsemen." (2 Kgs 13:14), a title bestowed also, perhaps secondarily, on Elijah (2:12). These were men of mighty deeds who did Israel a service, but they do not yet represent prophecy at its best.

CLASSICAL PROPHETISM. In the days of Jeroboam II, Amaziah, priest of the northern sanctuary at Bethel, encountered Amos, a man who was preaching a message unacceptable to the priest, a message of punishment and destruction. Recognizing that Amos was from Judah, he ordered him to return and to earn his living by prophesying there—but not at Bethel! Amos' answer was unequivocal: "I was no prophet, nor have I belonged to a company of prophets; I was a shepherd and a dresser of sycamores. The Lord took me from following the flock, and said to me, Go, prophesy to my people Israel" (Amos 7:12-16). Amos thus rejects the suggestion that he is a professional prophet; he declares that he had no formal connection with the prophetic calling until he received a peremptory summons to carry to Israel a message committed to him by God, on whose authority he is now acting. So inescapable is the duty of prophesying when God calls, that Amos elsewhere likens it to the fear instinctively felt when a lion roars (3:8).

In his consciousness of a vocation to be bearer of Yahweh's word, Amos is typical of the line of great prophets from the middle of the 8th century to postexilic times whose words are preserved in the *OT* prophetic books. Of course any attempt to make an absolute distinction between these men and their predecessors will break down in many details; the great age of Israelite prophecy was the flowering of a plant long maturing. Nathan rebuking David, or Elijah rebuking Ahab, speak in the name of Yahweh and covenant morality as clearly as the later prophets, among whom, moreover, ecstatic behavior is sometimes found. With a sufficiently broad perspective, however, the distinction stands: the mission of the classical prophets is identified with their message in a way that leaves no remainder. They carried the word to kings, but we do not find them taking part in palace intrigues or instigating revolts; Hosea condemns the bloody purge of Ahab's line (Hos 1:4) that Elisha was ultimately responsible for. Prophetic circles preserved extensive traditions about Elijah and Elisha, but little of the material approaches the level of the great literary prophets.

The prophet was called by a power greater than himself to preach a message that was not his own. Jeremiah's vocation (Jer 1:4-19) is an illustration of this. On hearing Yahweh's call to the prophetic ministry, his first reaction was to refuse, alleging his youth as the reason; but God accepts no refusal:

> To whomever I send you, you shall go;
> whatever I command you, you shall speak.

The command is accompanied by a gesture: "Then the Lord extended his hand and touched my mouth, saying, See, I place my words in your mouth!" In spite of God's promise of assistance Jeremiah continued an unwilling prophet, but forsake his vocation he could not. Even if he resolved to speak no more, the word became like a fire in his bones that he could not contain (20:9). The Book of Jonah tells of a prophet who, when sent eastward with a message for Niniveh, at once boards a ship heading west; after storm and fish, a sadder but wiser Jonah finds himself again on the seashore and trudges off to proclaim the message to Niniveh. The story is fictitious, but reveals Israel's experience of the divine initiative which overcomes prophetic reluctance.

The accounts of God placing His word in Jeremiah's mouth and Ezekiel eating a scroll (Ezek 2:8-3:3) are graphic portrayals of the conviction that the prophets were bearers of God's word, but do not, of course, give real explanations of how this word was communicated to them. No more do the declarations of Amos and the other prophets, "The Lord said to me . . ." Behind the vocation narratives lie religious experiences (most clearly expressed in Isaiah 6), akin to those of later mystics, which enabled the prophets to comprehend the divine nature in a way not given to their fellows; visions, auditions, and other sensations seem to have formed part of such encounters, but the basic communication was far deeper than anything that could be perceived through the senses. The prophet's vision of God gave him a basis for judging events; not every "Thus says the Lord . . ." is based on a new communication. Yet the initial experience of God was supplemented by later visions and by revelations of things to come. Prophetic oracles sometimes allude to visions (Amos 7-9; Jer 4:23-28; 25:15-28; Ezek 37:1-14), and there is no reason to think this is simply a literary conceit. Throughout his ministry the prophet was aware of being supported by God's hand, of being His mouthpiece.

In such an encounter the holiness and might of God was perceived in an immediate way, and it was a soul-shattering experience. The prophet came away from his initial contact with the divine a changed man; things no longer looked the same. In the light of his perception of the awesomeness and nearness of God, Israel's naive complacence in her election, her easy satisfaction with external response through sacrifice and cult, her comfortable compromise with paganism, and her facile disregard of God's will revealed in His commandments took on a different tone. Isaiah's first reaction was one of fear and compunction: "Woe is me, I am doomed! For I am a man of unclean lips, living among a people of unclean lips; yet my eyes have seen the King, the Lord of hosts" (6:5). Before this God, Israel was like clay in the potter's hands (Jer 18:1-10), the most powerful nation but an instrument of His policy (Isa 10:5-27). The word the prophets spoke was the word of this mighty God; it had an inherent power to accomplish that for which it was sent[4] and needed no political activity of theirs for its realization.

The prophet's vision of God, coupled with Israel's traditional faith, gave him deep insight into God's moral will and His plan in history. He knew this plan was ultimately one of salvation, but as he shifted his gaze from the holiness of God to the perversity of Israel, awareness of an impending judgment of doom was uppermost in his mind. Sometimes this is presented as almost inevitable because of Israel's sin (as in Amos), sometimes as avoidable through repentance and conversion, sometimes as a necessary purification before salvation could come. This sort of message was seldom what the prophets' contemporaries wanted to hear; it often flatly contradicted popular notions of their times and brought them into conflict with religious and political authority.

TRUE AND FALSE PROPHETS

While Ahab was planning to battle Syria for Ramoth-gilead, 400 court prophets told him he would be victorious; but one other prophet, Micaiah, predicted that he would be killed and his army scattered. In the event, Micaiah proved to be right (1 Kings 22). After the deportation of the first captives of Judah in 597 (p. 132) Jeremiah foretold that their exile would last seventy years and proclaimed that all who remained in the land must become subject to the king of Babylon. Hananiah, another prophet, flatly contradicted him, saying Babylon's power would be broken and all would return within two years (Jeremiah 28). Frequently Jeremiah and other canonical prophets accuse men held to be prophets of leading the people astray (Jer 14:13-16; 23:9-32; 27:12-22; Mic 3:5-11; Ezekiel 13). Although the Hebrew *OT* does not use the term "false prophets,"

[4]In Semitic thought, the word, once uttered, had a dynamic, autonomous power of its own; cf. the blessing of Isaac on Jacob which could not be withdrawn even though it was obtained through deceit (Genesis 27). Yahweh's word was supremely effective (Isa 55:10-11); Jeremiah likens it to a fire and to a hammer that shatters rocks (Jer 23:29).

that is what we would judge such deceivers to be. There was no easy way of drawing the line of distinction, however. A prophet was not false simply because he was a court prophet or professional or ecstatic. Micaiah seems to belong to the same circle as the 400 others; Jeremiah and Hananiah confront each other as men of the same calling. The true prophets do not deny that their adversaries are prophets; they simply say that their message is false. The inner certitude given the true prophets was such that they could not doubt their commission or the truth of their message. The oracles of the canonical prophets indicate clearly enough *their* solution to the problem. Jeremiah told Hananiah bluntly: "the Lord has not sent you." Elsewhere he says:

> Visions of their own fancy they speak,
>   not from the mouth of the Lord (23:16).
> I did not send these prophets,
>   yet they ran;
> I did not speak to them,
>   yet they prophesied (23:21).

They did not share in the deliberations of God's heavenly court, as the true prophets did (23:22).

But what of the man on the street? Whom was he to believe? Deut 18:13–22 declares that an oracle that is not fulfilled is one the Lord did not speak; Jeremiah, in his dispute with Hananiah, gives fulfillment of predictions as a criterion of genuine prophecy (28:9). It was a criterion of limited value, however, for fulfillment was often long in coming, as Jeremiah's contemporaries derisively pointed out (17:15). And even the canonical prophets were left with some predictions unfulfilled.

More helpful, then, is the implication of Deut 13:2–6 that the very content of the prophetic message is an indication of its authenticity, at least in the negative sense that it must accord with Israel's tradition of religious loyalty. The prophet who would lead them away from that preaches rebellion (Heb.: *sarah; NAB:* "apostasy") against the Lord. Note that it is precisely of preaching rebellion (*sarah*) that Jeremiah accuses Hananiah (Jer 23:15–16—and Shemaiah: 29:32). The message of the true prophet was self-authenticating in terms of Israel's covenant faith: Israel's flouting of covenant loyalty cried out for judgment, and that is what he promised. The prophets who promised peace and Yahweh's good will to an apostate nation were deceivers, as the people might be expected to recognize:

> They say to those who despise the words of the Lord,
>   Peace shall be yours (Jer 23:17).

The prophetic mission had always been to call men back to Yahweh, but the false prophets were guilty of "siding with the wicked, so that no one turns from evil" (23:14); "did they but proclaim to my people my words, they would have brought them back from their evil ways and from their wicked deeds" (23:22).

The false prophets were not conscious deceivers, but they were guilty of self-deception, timidity, and wishful thinking. They believed that the thoughts that came to them in their ecstatic trances were from the Lord; yet such self-induced ecstasy was not the same as the sort of religious experience that only God can initiate. Assiduous moral purification also had its part to play in a prophet's grasp of the divine will. When Jeremiah complained bitterly about the difficulties of his prophetic ministry, the divine response was an uncompromising admonition:

> If you repent so that I restore you,
> in my presence you shall stand;
> If you bring forth the precious without the vile,
> you shall be my mouthpiece (15:19).

The false prophets were often lacking in moral courage; Micah accuses them of announcing peace when they were paid, war when they were not (Mic 3:5, 11), and Ezekiel calls them "whitewashers" (Ezek 13:2-16). The pressure to underwrite royal policy must have been great; the false prophets succumbed to it, while the true prophets courageously resisted it. When Micaiah was being led to King Ahab he was admonished: "Look now, the prophets are unanimously predicting good for the king. Let your word be the same as any of theirs; predict good." His answer was that of every genuine prophet: "I shall say whatever the Lord tells me" (1 Kgs 22:13-14).

LITERARY PROPHETS

While only scattered pronouncements of the earlier prophets have been preserved (mainly in Samuel and Kings), extensive collections of the classical prophets are found in the *OT* prophetic books (the Latter Prophets of the Jewish Canon). The first three of these, Isaiah, Jeremiah, and Ezekiel,[5] are designated Major Prophets, while the remaining twelve are called Minor Prophets; the distinction is based mainly on the length of the books. The classical prophets are often called "literary prophets," a term coined when it was thought they were literary authors of the books named for them. The term is still useful for distinguishing them from the earlier prophets, but it is now recognized that the books took shape through the efforts of others who collected and edited their oracles—a process not completed until after the exile.

[5]Daniel, though grouped with the prophetic books in most Christian Bibles, is apocalyptic rather than prophetic literature (p. 252).

The prophet was, first of all, a man who brought God's word to his contemporaries. Sometimes he did this through symbolic actions (Isaiah 20; Jeremiah 19; 27; Ezekiel 4), but more often he did it by preaching. The basic unit of prophetic communication is the oracle; it was usually a brief composition and was most often cast in poetry, a form apt for expressing deeply felt sentiments, for impressing the hearers, and for easy memorization. Because the prophet speaks in the name of God the oracle is often introduced by "Thus says Yahweh" or terminated by "oracle of Yahweh" (*NAB:* "says the Lord"). The oracle may predict doom or good fortune to come; it may warn, threaten, or reproach. The prophet may take over poetic forms used by his contemporaries in civil life when they are suited to the mood he wishes to convey, e.g., the dirge to tell of Israel's fall (Amos 5:1-2) or the taunt-song to mock Assyrian arrogance (Isa 37:22-29).

Not all the prophetic oracles were preserved by any means. Since they were composed for contemporaries and delivered orally, many must have perished. Those that we have were saved by being memorized or written down after delivery. Often this was the work of disciples or prophetic schools over which the prophet presided. Jeremiah dictated many oracles to Baruch, his disciple and secretary, to be written down (Jeremiah 36). Of Isaiah it is said explicitly that he committed teaching to his disciples to be preserved (Isa 8:16). Prophetic schools, such as the disciples of Isaiah, may have endured for generations or even centuries, preserving and continuing the spirit and teaching of their great masters. The similarities of doctrine and formulation of Deutero-Isaiah (Isaiah 40-55—p. 194) and Trito-Isaiah (Isaiah 56-66—p. 211) to the great Isaiah of the 8th century are best explained in this way. An important group of scholars argue that the prophetic teachings were passed on almost solely by oral tradition and that they were committed to writing only after the exile. Though this is far from certain, oral tradition surely played an important role. The poetic form in which most oracles were cast aided memorization and faithful transmission, though sometimes changes and additions were introduced to make the teachings relevant to a new generation.

The grouping of individual oracles into collections may have begun fairly early and was the next step towards the production of the canonical book. The grouping was usually, though not always, on the basis of similarity of content. For example, Jer 23:9-40 is a collection of oracles "concerning the prophets"; Jeremiah 46-51 is a collection of oracles "against the nations"; and Isaiah 2-4 is a collection of oracles "concerning Judah and Jerusalem."

The finished book was the work of an editor who brought together and arranged single oracles, collections of oracles, and autobiographical and biographical material. Biographical material was preserved most often, no doubt, by disciples or in prophetic circles. Autobiographical material goes back to the prophet himself and may include the account of his vocation, visions, and other experiences; a unique example of this category are the "confessions" of Jeremiah (p. 181). It sometimes happened that in a book named for one prophet oracles of others were included; this was a way of expanding the original teaching in accord with the editor's intention, and of preserving anonymous oracles that would otherwise have been lost. Sometimes a principle of arrangement for the collected materials is evident, sometimes not. In Hosea, for example, the autobiographical and biographical materials are arranged at the beginning (ch. 1–3), but the rest of the book consists of oracles in little apparent order. The editors often placed promises of restoration after oracles of doom so that individual sections and whole books would end on a note of hope.

To situate the individual prophets in their historical context, see the chronological chart at the end of the text.

Reading Suggestions

JBC §12. *OTRG* #14, *AUOT* 226 32, 246–58 *MTES* 22–44, 140–49.

Blenkinsopp, J., *A History of Prophecy in Israel.* Philadelphia: Westminster Press, 1983. Pp. 19–79.

Eaton, J. H., *Vision in Worship. The Relationship of Prophecy and Liturgy in the Old Testament.* New York: Seabury Press, 1981.

Lindblom, J., *Prophecy in Ancient Israel.* Philadelphia: Fortress Press, 1965.

McKane, W., *Prophets and Wise Men.* Naperville, Ill.: Allenson, 1965.

von Rad, G., *The Message of the Prophets.* New York: Harper & Row, 1967, pp. 9–101.

Rowley, H. H., "The Nature of Old Testament Prophecy in the Light of Recent Study," *The Servant of the Lord and Other Essays on the Old Testament.* 2nd ed., rev; Oxford: Basil Blackwell, 1965, pp. 95–134.

Vawter, B., *The Conscience of Israel.* New York: Sheed & Ward, 1961, pp. 1–58.

Westermann, C., *Basic Forms of Prophetic Speech.* Philadelphia: Westminster Press, 1967.

Copeland, P. E., "A Guide to the Study of the Prophets," *Themelios* 10 (1984) 4–9.

Craghan, J. F., "Mari and Its Prophets. The Contributions of Mari to the Understanding of Biblical Prophecy," *BTB* 5 (1975) 32–55.

Hernando, E., "The sin of the 'false' prophets." *TD* 27 (1979) 37–40.

Huffmon, H. B., "Prophecy in the Mari Letters," *BAR* 3 199–224.

Wifall, W., "Israel's Prophets. Viziers of the King," *BTB* 10 (1980) 169–75.

14

The Pre-exilic Prophets

(Recommended Scripture reading: Amos 1–9; Hosea 1–6; 9; 11–14;
Isaiah 1–12; 28–30; Micah 1–6; Jeremiah 1–7; 18–24; 26–33)

ISRAEL'S golden age of prophecy was a brief one—only a little more
than two centuries. It opened with Amos in the middle of the 8th century, just a few decades before the collapse of the Northern Kingdom,
and ended near the close of the exile. The prophetic writings from
postexilic times seldom approach the heights of the earlier period.
Here we will discuss, in chronological order, the most important of
the prophets who appeared during the monarchy: Amos, Hosea,
Isaiah, Micah, and Jeremiah.

Amos

THE MAN AND HIS TIMES. Amos stepped boldly into prominence ca. 760
during the latter part of the reign of Jeroboam II (786–746). Israel was
enjoying security for the moment because Syria, her perennial enemy
to the north, had been brought low by Assyria. It was also a time of
peace with Judah. The sister kingdoms had extended their borders
almost to those of David's kingdom and were reaping tolls from the
caravan trade as in the days of Solomon.

Yet socially and religiously the country was sick. Excavations,
especially those in Samaria, reveal an era of wealth and luxury; but the
riches were not for all. Farmers, herdsmen, and others who barely
eked out an existence from the soil had no share in the prosperity. The
fiery words of Amos reveal them as a class oppressed and ground
down by the rich; even ordinary justice was often denied them in a
society where bribery of judges was commonplace. Shrines flourished
and religious feasts were celebrated as never before, but it was an
empty externalism among a people who had forgotten covenant
brotherhood. Pagan practices also flourished; though Jehu had rid the
country of Jezebel's brand of paganism, worship of the local Baal
continued unabated, and even Assyrian deities were imported.

Amos was from Tekoa, a town of Judah about 12 miles south of Jerusalem. His previous occupation as shepherd (1:1; 7:14) does not necessarily indicate he was a poor and simple rustic. The Hebrew term in 1:1 (*noqed*) is used also of Mesha, king of Moab, in 2 Kgs 3:4; moreover, the literary skill and breadth of knowledge evident in his oracles suggest a more sophisticated background. If we are surprised to find Amos, a man of Judah, preaching in the north, the only explanation offered is the irresistible divine summons. He asserts that he had had no connection with prophetic institutions and that he was constituted a prophet[1] when Yahweh "took" him and commanded him to prophesy. Severe and unsentimental, he denounced unsparingly the sins of Israel, especially the crimes of the rich against the poor. Yet he knew how to intercede for a sinful people and hold out whatever hope for the future he could muster. His oracles have great power and even an austere beauty because of their literary quality and depth of religious perception.

THE BOOK. Like other prophetic books, Amos was arranged by an editor long after the oracles were pronounced. The collection falls into three parts:

A. *Judgment against the Nations and Israel: 1–2*
B. *Words and Woes denouncing Israel: 3–6*
C. Visions: 7–9

The first part, though somewhat long for a prophetic oracle, probably formed a single composition from the beginning. The second part consists of collected oracles, many of which begin with "Hear this word" or "Woe to . . ." The third part consists of a series of visions, into which have been interpolated biographical material and oracles; it ends with messianic promises.

Doubts are raised, with good reason, concerning the authenticity of the judgment against Judah in 2:4–5; it weakens the climactic effect of the following verses, raises the number of judgments to eight instead of the expected seven, and is general rather than specific in content. The doxologies of 4:13; 5:8–9; and 9:5–6 are also widely contested. Most scholars deny the concluding verses of ch. 9 to Amos, though some amputate at v 8b, others at v 11, and still others at v 13.[2] There have always been men of learning to defend some of them.

---

[1] Amos' words in 7:14 are often taken to mean that he refused to classify himself as a prophet (*RSV:* "I am no prophet . . ."), but this is probably not the case. The Hebrew text leaves the verb to be supplied, and Rowley argues that it should be in the past tense. This is the interpretation the *NAB* follows ("I was no prophet . . ."). It is to "prophesy" that he is sent (7:15; cf. 3:8), and he surely includes himself among the prophets referred to in 2:12 (cf. 7:16).

[2] The problem of authenticity, here and elsewhere, does not affect the inspired nature of the passage or the truth of the teaching; it is merely a question of whether a disputed

His Message. The critics of the 19th century commonly taught that the prophets were innovators, that they first laid the foundations of Israel's ethical monotheism. Few would defend this position today. Amos, the first of the classical prophets, does not argue as one who is introducing a new idea but as one who would recall Israel to obligations which cannot be questioned. Well-known to his hearers is Israel's election by Yahweh (2:9-11; 3:2; 9:7-8), Judge of all the earth though He is (1:3-2:3). Amos does not explicitly mention the covenant, but it appears to be presupposed in his teachings concerning Israel's election, her obligations, and the judgment to come upon her for her crimes.

The opening oracle concerns Yahweh's judgment on the nations and on Israel (1-2). It is a thoughtfully constructed piece which depends for part of its effect on the element of surprise. We should remember that it was first delivered orally, probably at the Bethel sanctuary before a large audience of well-to-do worshipers—people who sought to please Yahweh by offering sacrifices bought with money unjustly taken from the poor. The crime of hypocrisy added to oppression was often the target of Amos' attack.

The opening judgments against six of the nations around Israel would have won Amos a sympathetic hearing; his audience would willingly hear their enemies criticized and condemned. Amos' prophetic teaching would appear reasonable to them, too, for these nations were worthy of condemnation. And by assenting to his judgment on the nations, as they undoubtedly did, they would be agreeing that the crimes enumerated—crimes of cruelty and inhumanity, sometimes against Israelites—were damnable.

But after these six judgments, in the climactic seventh place,[3] Amos lowers the boom on—Israel! (2:6-16). Accusations follow one another as he indicts Yahweh's people for injustice against the poor, for pagan practices, and for using the proceeds of oppression in hypocritical worship. The charge that "they sell the just man for silver, and the poor man for a pair of sandals" probably refers to the practice of taking a man into slavery (after a previous foreclosure on his property) for a debt he cannot pay. Had they not just heard Philistia and Tyre condemned for their foreign slave trade? How much worse those who had no compassion on their own brothers! Other expressions used here reveal utter contempt for the poor and disregard for their rights on the part of the rich. Elsewhere Amos indicates that the poor were the victims of every sort of injustice, even of judicial bribery (5:7-15; 6:12; 8:4-6). Here he identifies the "poor man" as the "just man."

passage should be attributed to the prophet in whose book it is found or to some other (usually later) composer.

[3]Assuming the judgment on Judah to be a later insertion.

How abominable that these rich oppressors thought to please Yahweh with their sacrifices! Injury is piled on injury. At their sacrificial banquets, Amos says, they drank wine exacted from the poor and reclined on garments taken from them in pledge. The latter reference reflects a provision found in Exod 22:25-26:

> If you take your neighbor's cloak in pledge, you shall return it to him before sunset; for this cloak of his is the only covering he has for his body. What else has he to sleep in? If he cries out to me, I will hear him; for I am compassionate.

This law is in the Covenant Code, an ancient northern collection (p. 89), and so was well known in the Israel of this day. Because worship was thus hypocritically carried out, because it led people to feel upright in spite of their crimes, and because the cult no longer recalled them to covenant obligations, Amos roundly condemns it and forecasts destruction upon the sanctuaries (4:4-5; 5:4-5, 21-27).

Amos was not a social reformer but a prophet announcing a word from Yahweh. Israel's obligation to act with justice and mercy is primarily a religious one. Amos bases it in Yahweh's election of Israel and thus, implicitly, in the covenant, as he recalls the exodus, the conquest, and God's other gracious favors (2:9-11). Israel's rejection of the obligations that grow out of election, furthermore, supplies the reasons for the punishment which he says is soon to fall upon them (2:13-16). Thus he sweeps away the major premise of those who thought that election meant that Yahweh would preserve Israel in all dangers and that she was therefore secure in her wrong-doing. In the first oracle of the following collection Amos again rejects complacency, insisting that Israel's privileged status increases her guilt and punishment: "You alone have I favored more than all the families of the earth; therefore I will punish you for all your crimes" (3:2). Thus Amos introduces, probably at the beginning of his ministry, the threat of destruction. Israel has presumed on election and has not responded in justice to Yahweh, the God of justice who chose her; she will fall before His judgment as the pagan nations will.

It has been suggested, with good reason, that Amos and the prophets who followed him foretold the destruction of the nation because they saw that Israel's repudiation of the covenant had activated the covenant curse. In any case, Amos does not appear to think that destruction can be avoided: Israel has exhausted her opportunities for amendment. In 4:6-12 Amos recounts a series of afflictions sent to lead Israel to repentance, ending each time with the note "yet you returned not to me"; the section concludes: "So now I will deal with you in my own way, O Israel! . . . prepare to meet your God." The three visions of 7:1-8 tend toward the same conclusion: after the first two forewarnings of judgment Amos successfully intercedes,

> Forgive, O Lord God!
> How can Jacob stand?
> He is so small!

But after the third vision God's decree stands: "I will forgive them no longer" (see also 8:1–2). Many passages indicate that Amos expected judgment in the form of military defeat and exile (3:11; 4:2–3; 5:3, 27; 6:7). Some believe he identifies Assyria as the enemy power in 6:14. The instrument of God's policy, however, is a matter of indifference, and it is to be noted that his starting point is not the might of Assyria or any other nation but the wickedness of Israel.

Scathingly he denounces all those things in which men put their confidence. The luxurious houses they had built and the choice vines they would not enjoy (3:15; 5:11). Even their cult centers would do them no good; because they had forsaken the God of justice, their ceremonies were only occasions for greater sins (4:4–5). Israel's election is turned against them as the leaders of "a nation favored from the first" are told that "they shall be the first to go into exile" (6:1–7).

Amos aims another blow at false confidence with his teaching on the "day of the Lord" (5:18–20). Although this oracle is the earliest *OT* reference to the belief, the casual way in which Amos introduces it indicates that it was already well-known. The origin of the belief is obscure. Most likely from Israel's holy war tradition developed the belief that Yahweh would arise to subdue His foes, as in the days of old.[4] Amos does not reject belief in Yahweh's day; what he does reject is the popular expectation that it will be Israel's triumph, too. This is *Yahweh's* day, he says, the day on which His justice will triumph against all His enemies; for Israel it will be "darkness and not light."

Does Amos leave any room for hope? There have been those who deny that he does. Yet if his message were wholly negative, there would be little point to his prophetic ministry. It does seem, however, that any hope Amos holds out lies only beyond disaster. Although exhortations like "Seek the Lord, that you may live" (5:6; cf. 5:4, 14) imply the possibility of escape, other passages suggest that Amos expected benefits only for a surviving remnant:[5]

> Hate evil and love good,
>   and let justice prevail at the gate;
> Then it may be that the Lord, the God of hosts,
>   will have pity on the remnant of Joseph (5:15).

[4]This position has been cogently argued by von Rad; see, e.g., *The Message of the Prophets,* 97–99.

[5]The remnant concept, first mentioned in Amos, became an important theme in later prophets. A remnant surviving disaster is sometimes thought to be implied in 5:1–3 and in 3:12. Since there are good reasons for accepting the authenticity of 9:8b–10, it would seem that Amos expected the preservation of a *just* remnant.

Amos knows that punishment can have a medicinal as well as destructive aspect (4:6–11), and so a glimmer of hope can be seen beyond judgment. Yet even this remains a "perhaps," and he offers little description of what the restoration would be like. If 9:11–12 be accepted as authentic, he expected—like a good Judean—restoration through David's dynasty. Amos was sent to shake up the complacent during the prosperous days of Jeroboam; others would come later to sketch in confident colors the salvation which God would prepare beyond tragedy.

HOSEA

HISTORICAL BACKGROUND. Hosea's prophetic ministry began a couple of decades later than Amos', towards the end of Jeroboam II's reign, and ended sometime before the fall of Samaria (721). These were uncertain, violent, tumultuous times as dynasty succeeded dynasty through murder and revolution (p. 130). Much of the unrest was caused by party rivalry. As the threat posed by Assyria's expansion became clear, some leaders thought Israel's safety lay in allying herself with Egypt, the only Near Eastern power able to challenge Assyria, and the anti-Assyrian coalition, while others urged submission as the only way of escaping destruction. Kings were set up for their policy on this question and then assassinated for the same reason. Israel's first king had been anointed to deliver her from military threat; now her kings, forgetting where the nation's true strength lay, seemed bent on rushing her to destruction. The violence of the times and disgust with the monarchy are apparent in many of Hosea's oracles (5:13; 7:3–11; 8:4; 10:9; 13:10–11).

Hosea prophesied in the Northern Kingdom and seems to have been a subject of that kingdom. Little is known of him beyond what ch. 1–3 tell us of his marriage and its significance as a call to prophecy—information whose interpretation is widely disputed. His oracles show him to have been sensitive and emotional, able to move from pity to wrath to forgiveness within the compass of a few lines. Some of the crudest and some of the tenderest, most touching passages of the OT come from him. While lessening not one whit the criticisms and demands of Amos, he adds the note of Yahweh's compassion and unfailing love.

THE BOOK. The material of Hosea is divided into two main parts:

    A. *Hosea's Marriage*: 1–3
    B. *Collected Oracles*: 4–14

The first part consists of biographical material (1), autobiographical material (3), and an oracle that exploits the theme of Hosea's marriage (2). Of this material, it is probable that 1:7; 2:1–3, 23–25 are additions by a later hand. The *NAB* has transferred 2:1–3 to the end of ch. 3 and 2:8–9 after 2:15 where they probably belong.[6]

The rest of the book consists of oracles from various periods of Hosea's ministry arranged with little apparent order. Many of them gain significance in coming, as they do, after the account of Hosea's marriage, so that the book as a whole demonstrates some attempt at arrangement.

HOSEA'S MARRIAGE AND HIS TEACHING. Amos, as we have seen, does not explicitly mention the covenant, even though it is implied in many of his words. The covenant concept is much more clearly present in Hosea's teaching; it is referred to directly in 6:7 and 8:1 (passages whose authenticity is disputed by some), and on it rests most of the teaching drawn from his marriage. Almost every element in the marriage narrative of 1–3 is disputed. The following interpretation, though far from agreed upon,[7] seems to accord best with the data of the book and to be the most likely of those proposed. Hosea married Gomer, a woman he deeply loved and greatly esteemed. In the event, she proved to be a shamelessly unfaithful wife and may even have become a sacred prostitute in the fertility cult. Hosea's first reaction was to repudiate her in jealousy and anger (cf. 2:4, which constitutes a primitive divorce formula).

Yet, in spite of all, he found that he still loved her and was unable to give her up forever. In his attempt to bring her back to himself as a faithful wife he had first to redeem her "for fifteen silver pieces and a homer and a lethec of barley" (3:2).[8] He then set her a time of probation: "many days you shall wait for me; you shall not play the harlot or belong to any man; I in turn will wait for you" (3:3). The final outcome for Hosea as far as Gomer is concerned is not revealed, but in these experiences of his personal life, he gained an insight into the boundless persevering love of Yahweh for Israel, His faithless covenant partner. He saw in his marriage, real though it was, an allegory of the divine love seeking Israel and willing to forgive in spite of infidelities, if only she would return in contrition, sincerity, and purity. This awareness constituted Hosea's call to the prophetic ministry, which could then be formulated: "The Lord said to Hosea: Go, take a harlot wife . . ." (1:2).

Israel's greatest crime, as reflected in Hosea's teaching, was religious infidelity, especially that of Baal worship and the fertility cult. It isn't clear that this always took the form of open apostasy; it

---

[6]The *NAB* chapter and verse numbering follows the Hebrew, and differs from that of the *RSV* and some other translations.

[7]For a different view, see reference to the article of Rowley at the end of the chapter.

[8]This "redemption" may have been required because Gomer had sold herself into slavery for debts or because she had dedicated herself to a shrine for cultic prostitution.

may also have consisted in fertility rites conducted at legitimate shrines as a form of Yahweh worship. At any rate, Israel's apostasy through this sort of religious perversion forms the background for the matchless ch. 2, the heart of Hosea's unique contribution to prophecy.[9] Behind this oracle lie Hosea's persevering efforts to turn Gomer's heart back to him, mingling harshness with tenderness as he strove to have her again loyal, pure, and faithful.

But the words are presented here as Yahweh's, as He tells of Israel's sin and His reaction. She has gone after lovers who, she says, give her bread and water, wool and flax, oil and wine (v 7). That is, Israel attributes to Baal the fertility that she enjoys. Yahweh, the true giver of these gifts, will snatch them back and afflict her with all manner of evil (vv 10-14).

> I will punish her for the days of the Baals,
> tor whom she burnt incense
> While she decked herself out with her rings and her jewels,
> and, in going after her lovers,
> forgot me, says the Lord (v 15).

Yet even these afflictions are strategems to turn her back to Himself:

> If she runs after her lovers she shall not overtake them;
> if she looks for them she shall not find them.
> Then she shall say,
> "I will go back to my first husband,
> for it was better with me then than now" (v 9).

With deepening tenderness He speaks of leading her into the desert, the place of honeymoon after the exodus, the time of her youthful fidelity; there she shall learn again to respond to Him in love (vv 16-19). From this grows the promise of an ideal restoration (v 20) and the assurance:

> I will espouse you to me forever:
> I will espouse you in right and justice,
> in love and in mercy;
> I will espouse you in fidelity,
> and you shall know the Lord (vv 21-22).

These last lines reveal the miracle of divine love: Yahweh will have Israel return to Him, but Israel cleansed of her apostasy, backsliding, and adultery—Israel chaste and faithful again. It is the strength and persistence of love which will accomplish this. Terms like those used in the above passage—right, justice, love, mercy, fidelity, and knowledge of God—sum up the qualities Israel needs to have but now

---

[9]The theme of Israel as Yahweh's bride is taken up by later prophets and is continued in the *NT*, where the Church is pictured as the bride of Christ, now cleansed of every stain (cf., e.g., Eph 5:21-33; Rev 21:2, 9-11).

sadly lacks. Hosea, in truth, denounces the Israel of his day as violently as Amos does. In 4:1 he complains: "There is no fidelity, no mercy, no knowledge of God in the land." The word translated "mercy" here (and translated "love" in 2:21) is *hesed,* a term which suggests fidelity, affection, and covenant loyalty (p. 83); Yahweh's *hesed* is unfailing, and Israel's should be like His.

"Knowledge of God" comes close to summing up the totality of Israel's obligation. "Knowledge" in Semitic thought designates not so much an intellectual acquisition as a mode of life and behavior. "To know" a person indicates a concrete and intimate relationship. Yahweh "knows" Israel in bestowing blessings or punishments,[10] while Israel "knows" Yahweh when she responds by loving obedience. Her shallowness is manifested in that she claims to know Him, whereas in fact she does not (8:1-2). Her *hesed* vanishes like a morning mist (6:4); she thinks she can substitute sacrifices for *hesed* and knowledge of God (6:6). When the priests conducted liturgical celebrations of the covenant, they should have instructed Israel in the obligations of election, not only its privileges. Since they did not, Hosea has a special polemic against them (4:4-14).

Like Amos, Hosea condemns injustice, but he shows greater concern about Israel's paganizing practices and religious aberrations. Hosea 2 concentrated on Israel's addiction to the fertility cults; other passages, such as 9:1-2, are equally explicit. The frequent accusations of "harlotry" could, *per se,* refer to any brand of religious apostasy but suit the fertility cult best. Israel's liturgy, corrupt as it is through pagan practices and insincerity, does not please Yahweh and cannot save Israel; the multiplication of altars and sacrifices will not avert His anger (8:11-13). Hosea rails at the bull shrines set up by Jeroboam I at Dan and Bethel (p. 129), and even dares to distort "Bethel" (house of God) into "Beth-Aven" (house of iniquity; e.g., 4:15; 5:8). His remarks seem to equate worship at these Yahwistic shrines with common idolatry (8:4-6; 13:2).

Hosea, like Amos, sees punishment ahead in the form of defeat and exile (2:13-15; 3:4; 5:8-9; 7:12; 13:2-15). Both Assyria and Egypt are named as the land of exile—Assyria because by then it posed a clear threat, and Egypt because it was traditionally the land of Israel's bondage (9:3-6; 11:5-7). More clearly than Amos, however, Hosea saw that beyond destruction lay restoration; the persevering love of Yahweh would somehow triumph over human perversity to bring Israel back to Himself. This is manifest in the allegory of Hosea's marriage (2:16-22; 3:5) and in other passages, some of them the most moving ever written (11:8-11; 14:2-9). That the Northern Kingdom as such was never restored does not destroy the validity of Hosea's expectation. He was thinking of Yahweh's covenant partner, not a

---

[10]Cf. Amos 3:2; literally: "You only have I known"; the *NAB* uses "favored" to bring out the sense.

political entity. The community restored after the exile consisted mainly of elements of Judah with only remnants from the north; but they called themselves "Israel," and rightly so.

A word should be said about the emotional and passionate nature of God as He is depicted by Hosea. We are told, indeed, that God is impassible, that no change, such as that involved in passion, can be predicated of the divine nature. This is perhaps true, but it is a negative assertion which, standing by itself, would be misleading. God is concerned and involved, and to present Him with passions of love, anger, and jealousy is one way of asserting this—perhaps the only way. Undoubtedly such anthropomorphisms are misleading to a degree, but not nearly so much as picturing God as a Stoic. Paradoxically, it is just after Yahweh has said "My heart is overwhelmed, my pity is stirred. I will not give vent to my blazing anger, I will not destroy Ephraim again" that He adds, "for I am God and not man" (11:8-9). For Hosea it is precisely *because* Yahweh is God that He manifests the love and forgiveness of His *hesed*.

ISAIAH

THE BOOK. The assertion that prophetic books are collections of collections (p. 156) is true in a special manner of the one named for Isaiah. This book reached completion only in postexilic times and some sections of it come from the exile and later. The oracles of Isaiah, along with later materials, are found in ch. 1-39; ch. 40-55 come from an anonymous prophet of the exile, usually referred to as Deutero-Isaiah (p. 194); ch. 56-66 are a postexilic collection, designated Trito-Isaiah (p. 211). Since the later materials are attributable to disciples of Isaiah and members of the prophetic circle which continued to flourish long after his time, the whole collection can justly be designated as Isaianic.

At present we are concerned only with ch. 1-39. This material can be broken down into the following collections:

A. *Oracles concerning Judah and Jerusalem:* 1-12
B. *Oracles against pagan nations:* 13-23
C. *The apocalypse of Isaiah:* 24-27
D. *Later oracles of Isaiah:* 28-33
E. *The vindication of Zion:* 34-35
F. *Historical appendix:* 36-39

Ch. 1-12 and 28-33 are the two principle collections of Isaiah's oracles. The first stems mainly from his early ministry, around the time of the Syro-Ephraimitic War (735); the second comes mainly from a later period, the time of Isaiah's unsuccessful attempt to dissuade Hezekiah from revolting against Assyria (705-701). Ch. 1-12 contain a number of smaller collections, the most important of which is the "book of testimony" (6:1–9:6), which consists of the prophet's vocation narrative (6), Isaiah's "memoirs" (7–8—an account of the events around 735, possibly put together either by Isaiah himself or one of his disciples), and a concluding oracle of promise (8:23–9:6). Ch. 13–23 contain oracles of Isaiah as well as later material, while 24–27 and 34–35 derive wholly from later authors. Ch. 36–39 correspond in great part to 2 Kgs 18:13–20:19 (from which, however, Hezekiah's thanksgiving hymn of Isa 38:9–20 has been omitted). In all probability this material was put together by Isaiah's followers and was utilized in both literary complexes, first in Kings and then in the Isaiah collection.

THE MAN AND HIS TIMES. Isaiah's ministry began ca. 742 ("the year King Uzziah died"—6:1) and continued until sometime in the reign of Hezekiah (715–687—1:1); none of his oracles can be surely dated after 701, and his ministry may have ended around that time. He prophesied in the Kingdom of Judah, mainly, it would seem, in Jerusalem. Little is known of his background, though his easy access to Judah's kings suggests to some that he came from an aristocratic family.

Isaiah's period was an important one for the kingdoms of Judah and Israel. It was a time of crisis occasioned by Assyria's determined westward expansion and plans for world empire. It witnessed the fratricidal Syro-Ephraimitic War in the days of Ahaz—a conflict resolved by the intervention of Assyria and at the cost of vassalage for Judah and devastation for Israel (p. 130). It saw the final collapse of the Northern Kingdom in 721 and Judah's own near-destruction at the hands of Sennacherib in 701 after Hezekiah revolted against Assyria.

HIS TEACHING. Isaiah's message is characterized by an overwhelming sense of Yahweh's holiness; by His conviction that the course of events was controlled by Yahweh's plan, conceived in wisdom and executed with irresistible power; and by the demand for faith that necessarily sprang from this conviction.

Isaiah's awareness of Yahweh's unspeakable holiness was rooted in his call to the prophetic ministry (6). In vision the prophet saw the Lord enthroned in kingly glory in the Jerusalem Temple. To the awesome sight was added the cry of the Seraphim, heavenly ministers of the deity: "holy, holy, holy is the Lord of hosts! All the earth is filled with his glory!" Isaiah's favorite title for God is "the Holy One of Israel," a title seldom found elsewhere in the *OT* except in Deutero-Isaiah. Holiness is the divine quality *par excellence,* that which sets God apart from man and marks Him as the "wholly other," elevated and transcendent. Holiness in *OT* thought, then, does not designate primarily moral perfection as it does for us. Moral perfection is included, however, and Isaiah's first reaction to the vision of the Holy One was an awareness of his own and his people's sinfulness. It is from Yahweh's holiness, too, that His moral demands spring.

Figure 20. *"He will give a signal to a far-off nation, and whistle to them from the ends of the earth; speedily and promptly will they come. . . . Their arrows are sharp, and all their bows are bent. The hoofs of their horses seem like flint. . . ." (Isa 5:26, 28). This picture of an Assyrian king (Asshurbanipal hunting with his servants) seems almost like an illustration of Isaiah's words. From a 7th century relief. Courtesy of the Trustees of the British Museum.*

Yet this holy God had associated Himself with a people through election and dwelt in their midst in the Temple. This was a dangerous situation for a foolish, sinful, and unthinking nation, as Isaiah saw Judah to be. He himself was purified (signified by the purging of his lips) to make him worthy to be the bearer of God's word (6:7); but to the many his message was to be simply an occasion for closing their eyes, stopping their ears, and hardening their hearts, with the result that the destruction which might otherwise have been averted would come upon them (6:9–12).

Granted this conception of a mighty and holy God, it follows that the course of events lies in His hands. The world He created and governs will be directed according to the plan He has formed and to the end He has determined, not according to the will or by the power of man. Isaiah's magnificent description of the day of the Lord in 2:10–21 leaves no place for human pride to stand before this God:

> Human pride will be abased,
> the arrogance of men will be brought low,
> And the Lord alone will be exalted on that day (2:17).

God has a purpose to carry out and the men of Judah are frequently rebuked for failing to perceive it (5:12, 18–19; 28:14–21; 30:1; 31:1). The power of Assyria and the other nations cannot hinder Yahweh's purpose; rather, they are His unwitting instruments. He whistles and they come bounding like a dog (5:26–29); they are an axe or a rod with which He strikes (10:5–15). When He is finished with them, they too will be chastened (10:24–27). Election means that Israel and Judah have a special place in God's plan; it will bring salvation or judgment depending on whether faith prevails or not.

Isaiah was not content to give mere lip service to God's purpose in history and His power to carry it out. These were the concrete realities which should determine the behavior of the individual and the policy of the nation; all eggs must be put in the one basket labeled "faith." Faith for Isaiah and the *OT* was not an assent of the intellect to a revealed truth, but a choice of the will committing oneself to God without reservation. The most significant *OT* terms for faith are derived from the verb *aman* (to be firm or solid) and suggest firmness, solidity, trustworthiness, and truthfulness. The causative form of the verb (*he'emin*) means to commit one's trust to that which is firm and sure; in the case at hand, the firmness derives from the guarantee of God. *Emeth* and *emunah,* nouns derived from *aman,* signify truth and faithfulness respectively; along with *hesed* they are frequent attributes of God in the prophetic writings and the Psalms. Isaiah also uses other terms and images, such as "to lean on" (10:20) and "to wait for" (8:17).

Belief in God's purpose and might implied that Judah's safety and well-being lay in God's hand alone. Thus Isaiah, at various times, condemned as equally pointless appeal for Assyria's help, rebellion against her control, and covenants with Egypt. In all political crises he challenged the king to have faith in Yahweh and condemned as lack of faith any other course. In 735 Syria and Israel invaded Judah in an attempt to force Ahaz to join the anti-Assyrian coalition (p. 130; Isaiah 7); part of their plan was to depose Ahaz and to set up a king of their own choosing. Ahaz, on his part, was weighing the extreme course of submitting to Assyria and asking their help. At this juncture, when "the heart of the king and the heart of the people trembled, as the trees of the forest tremble in the wind" (7:2), Isaiah challenged Ahaz to have faith: "Take care you remain tranquil and do not fear; let not your courage fail. . . . Thus says the Lord: This shall not stand, it shall not be" (7:4–7). In spite of the promises that the might of Syria and Israel would soon vanish (7:16; 8:1–4), Ahaz did turn to Assyria, and this lack of faith eliminated him in Isaiah's eyes from all consideration as an instrument of Yahweh's saving grace.[11] Ahaz's policy could only bring disaster; a people that rejected the quiet compelling power of Yahweh would be submerged by the might of Assyria (8:5–7).

---

[11]Ahaz's appeal was not needed, for Assyria would have moved to crush the rebellion in any case. Ahaz's submission to Assyria included religious innovations intended to give recognition to Assyria's gods (2 Kgs 16:10–16).

At a later time, when, at the death of Sargon II of Assyria (705), Hezekiah determined to put his trust in Egypt's help and rebel against Assyria (p. 131), Isaiah likewise condemned the plan and tried to deter the king (28:14-22; 30:1-17; 31:1-3; 39). It was better, he insisted, to await the liberation Yahweh would bring in His own good time:

> For thus says the Lord God,
>   the Holy one of Israel:
> By waiting and calm you shall be saved,
>   in quiet and in trust your strength lies (30:15).

He called the alliance with Egypt a "covenant with death" (28:14-18) and foretold disaster. His words were verified in 701 when Sennacherib, Sargon's successor, came to compel submission; the land was devastated and only Jerusalem was left intact.[12] After the debacle Isaiah reminded the people of their frenetic efforts at fortification and added: "But you did not look to the city's maker, nor did you consider him who built it long ago" (22:8-11).

Neither early nor late in his ministry, then, did Isaiah find the requisite faith. Men went their own way, hatching their own plans, forgetful of the Holy One in their midst who had called them into being and whose will would ultimately prevail. Faith was not the only quality Judah lacked. Like the prophets who preceded him, Isaiah complains in Yahweh's name of injustice, immorality, and idolatry. The Song of the Vineyard (5:1-7) tells of the care God had lavished on the Chosen People to no avail:

> He looked for judgment, but see, bloodshed!
>   for justice, but hark, the outcry!

Isaiah proclaims the judgment to come; the vineyard is to be trampled and made a ruin.

Yet God's purpose and plan of salvation, Isaiah knew, would not be thwarted even by human wickedness. Though almost universal destruction should come, God would preserve, purify, and convert a remnant—a holy seed from which a people could be formed anew. That the remnant theme was of some importance to Isaiah is indicated by the fact that he gave his older son the symbolic name Shear-Jashub (7:3), which means "a remnant will return" (i.e., turn back to God, be converted). The name contains both a threat and a promise: the survival of a mere remnant implies overwhelming destruction; but at least that much could be promised—the people would not perish utterly.

---

[12]Surprising as it may be, it seems that on the occasion of some campaign of Sennacherib, Isaiah encouraged Hezekiah to resist and foretold that Jerusalem would be spared (36-37; 2 Kgs 18:3-19:37). Since Isaiah condemned Hezekiah's rebellion against Assyria in 705 and foretold it would bring disaster, support is given for the theory of a second campaign of Sennacherib at a later date (p. 131, n. 6).

The remnant theme held a positive hope for the future. The punishment to come would be Yahweh's judgment on a sinful nation, but it
would also effect the purification of those who survived (1:25). The
purified remnant would be converted to Yahweh in faith; in this holy
people God's plan of election would be continued and completed.
God's might alone could accomplish this:

> For out of Jerusalem shall come a remnant,
>   and from Mount Zion, survivors.
>
> The zeal of the Lord of hosts shall do this (37:32).
> On that day
> The remnant of Israel,[13]
>   the survivors of the house of Jacob,
>   will no more lean upon him who struck them;
> But they will lean upon the Lord,
>   the Holy One of Israel, in truth.
> A remnant will return, the remnant of Jacob,
>   to the mighty God (10:20–21).

Since faith is the very basis of the new edifice God will build, Isaiah
sees that the foundations are already being laid:

> See, I am laying a stone in Zion,
>   a stone that has been tested,
> A precious cornerstone as a sure foundation;
>   he who puts his faith in it shall not be shaken (28:16).

The foundation stone of the future community is already a reality in
the faith of Isaiah and his followers, signs and portents of things to
come: "For I will trust in the Lord, who is hiding his face from the
house of Jacob; yes, I will wait for him. Look at me and the children
whom the Lord has given me: we are signs and portents in Israel from
the Lord of hosts who dwells on Mount Zion" (8:17-19).

Another line of hope for Isaiah sprang from the promises God had
made to David and his line. The theology of the Davidic covenant
flourished in cultic and prophetic circles in Jerusalem (p. 146); from
such circles came the royal psalms (e.g., Psalms 2; 20; 21; 45; 72; 89;
110; 132). These compositions repeat and develop the dynastic oracle
of Nathan: David's dynasty is to endure forever and each successor of
David is counted as Yahweh's son; through David's line God's
kingdom will be realized over all the earth—a kingdom of justice,
right, and peace. Each historical king could be described in the most
idealistic terms because he was the embodiment of the dynasty and of
the hopes connected with it. Isaiah's oracles show that his thought was

---

[13]Though "Israel" designated the northern Kingdom during the period of the divided
monarchy, the more basic reference of the term was to the People of God's covenant as
such; in this sense Isaiah often calls Yahweh "the Holy One of Israel." After the fall of
Samaria, "Israel" often designates Judah, the surviving part of the covenant people.

strongly influenced by this theology. Here, as in all cases, historical events helped shape his message.

During the crisis of 735 the position of King Ahaz was very precarious; one of the invaders' objectives was to place an outsider on his throne (7:6). Isaiah promised delivery from the immediate threat, demanding that Ahaz put his trust in Yahweh alone and adding the threat: "Unless your faith is firm you shall not be firm" (7:9). The indications are that the royal advisers, "the wise" against whom Isaiah waged a running battle throughout his ministry (cf. 5:18-21; 29:14), were urging recourse to Assyria. To counter their influence Isaiah offered the king any sign he might choose as a proof that the word he spoke truly came from the Lord. When Ahaz refused even to ask for a sign, Isaiah gave him the sign of Immanuel (7:10-17). The sign is a favorable one in that it spoke of the birth of a child whose name (Immanuel—"God with us") signified God's favor, on the most likely interpretation a new heir to the throne of David, and of speedy deliverance from the threat of Aram and Israel. The sign was two-edged in that it also indicated that Ahaz's short-sighted policy would bring on the Assyrian flood, and Immanuel would grow to maturity living on "curds and honey," the food available in a devastated land.

Isaiah seemed to have expected great things of this new son of David, who, through the purifying trials Isaiah had foreseen (1:24-26), would learn "to reject evil and choose good," and in this sense would be the very antithesis of Ahaz. What Isaiah expected God to accomplish through this son of David can be gathered from 8:23-9:6, an oracle possibly composed around this same time. It refers to deliverance from foreign oppression and the establishment of a vast and eternal kingdom characterized by judgment and justice—"The zeal of the Lord of hosts will do this!"

If the Immanuel for whom Isaiah held out such great hopes was Hezekiah, who was in fact Ahaz's son and successor, he fell far short of the prophet's hopes (in spite of the good he accomplished and the high praise of 2 Kgs 18:3). These oracles remained, however, as signposts of something still to come. Toward the end of his long career, after many disappointing experiences with Judah's kings, Isaiah seems to have deferred his hope to the more distant future. In 11:1-9,[14] an oracle probably delivered after the rout of 701, he speaks of an ideal king to come who shall be the recipient of Yahweh's spirit and who shall exhibit all the qualities of a perfect king. For Isaiah it is no longer the dynasty as such which shall be the bearer of salvation, but a new David whom God will raise up. His reign is pictured

---

[14]Many authors deny this oracle to Isaiah because it seems to suppose a time when Judah's historical kingship has ceased and needs to be reestablished (11:1). A better explanation is that Isaiah considers the dynasty to be morally defunct and that therefore the ideal ruler is pictured not so much as a branch of the withered family tree as a new growth from the root—in truth, a new David!

idyllically as a return to the conditions of paradise (11:6-9) and so depicts the complete fulfillment of God's redemptive purpose. It was not historical circumstance, least of all Judah's kings, that led Isaiah to this picture of final salvation, but his faith in the power and zeal of Yahweh of hosts.

Isaiah expressed his hopes not only in terms of a future son of David but also in terms of Jerusalem, Yahweh's holy city. The oracle in 2:2-4, of all nations flowing to Zion to receive *torah* (instruction) from Yahweh, learning to live in peace, and beating their swords into plowshares, is one of the most beautiful in all prophetic literature.[15] If we compare this passage with 30:8-14, in which Yahweh's rebellious "children" reject His *torah* and so come to ruin, we see that, for Isaiah, the difference between the present evil situation and the future blessed one is dependent on a different response to Yahweh's *torah*. The change, we have to suppose, Isaiah would relate to the "zeal of Yahweh of hosts," who alone has power to heal the perversity of the human heart. We are close to the beginnings of a theology of grace.

MICAH

THE MAN AND HIS TIMES. Micah was a contemporary of Isaiah and so his prophecy has the same political background. His ministry may not have been as long as the inscription of his book (1:1) suggests, though on the evidence of his oracles it began before 721 (Samaria still stands in 1:6) and continued at least until 701 (1:8-16 seems to refer to Sennacherib's campaign in Judah). Micah's teachings exhibit similarities to those of Isaiah, by whom he may have been influenced. Their social backgrounds, however, were quite different. Unlike the cosmopolitan Isaiah, Micah was from a small village, Moresheth-gath, in the Shephelah of Judah. His background was like that of Amos, whose teaching his own often resembles. Like Amos he was concerned for the hard lot of the poor and vigorously condemned the rich who oppressed them. He complains, like Amos, of the rich seizing the property of the poor, of pledges, and of bribes (2:2, 10; 3:11). Although he probably prophesied in Judah only, some of his words are addressed to the north.

THE BOOK. The editor of Micah's oracles was not concerned with chronological order but alternated threat and promise. A series of doom-oracles (1-3) is followed by a collection of promises of restoration (4-5); a third collection, consisting mainly of admonitions and threats (6:1-7:6) softened by further promises (7:7-20), completes the book.

---

[15]There are no compelling arguments for denying this oracle to Isaiah, as some scholars do; it accords well with many elements of his teaching as found elsewhere in his book.

Although the genuine words of Micah may have been expanded by later additions, there is little in the book that could not have come from this eighth century prophet. Critics of an earlier period denied to Micah the oracles of restoration and the messianic promises, but their similarity to like pronouncements of Isaiah is an argument for their authenticity.

HIS TEACHING. We can pause for only a few of the high points of Micah's message. Near the beginning of his book (1:2-9) and again near the end (6:1-8) he provides us with examples of what has often been called the covenant lawsuit: Yahweh expostulates with His People, accuses them, calls them to account for their breaches of the covenant.[16] The pattern may have a liturgical background; we may recall especially the covenant renewal ceremonies that were an important aspect of the Yahweh cult. The second is the clearer example of the two. In this passage the mountains, hills, and foundations of the earth are called to witness that, "the Lord has a plea against his people, and he enters into trial with Israel" (6:1-2). It is not Israel's transgressions that are recounted, however, but the saving deeds of Yahweh (vv 3-5). The purpose is to recall to the people their debt of gratitude and obligation of obedience. No defense is possible and none is presented; they ask, rather, what would be an adequate offering of reparation. Could sacrifices of calves and rams please Him? Would He be appeased with streams of oil or even a first-born son? (vv 6-7). It is the prophet who answers:

> You have been told, O man, what is good,
>   and what the Lord requires of you:
> Only to do the right and to love goodness (*hesed*),
>   and to walk humbly with your God (v 8).

This verse is rightly considered an epitome of prophetic teaching. Yet it is no novel doctrine, no new demand, but what Israel's conscience imposed from the moment the covenant was enacted.

A small town man, Micah was shocked by the wickedness of the big cities:

> What is the crime of Jacob?
>   Is it not Samaria?
> And what is the sin of the house of Judah?
>   Is it not Jerusalem? (1:5).

For all of Isaiah's pronouncements of doom, he never predicted the destruction of Jerusalem. Many in Judah thought that the election of Mount Zion was as sure as that of David and that Jersalem was inviolable; some scholars think Isaiah shared this view. Micah, at any rate, did not. He rejected the idea of those who said,

---

[16]See also Deuteronomy 32; Isa 1:2-20; 3:13-15; Jer 2:4-13. But note the reservations of R. E. Clements, *Prophecy and Tradition* (Atlanta: John Knox Press, 1975), 17-20.

> "Is not the Lord in the midst of us?
> No evil can come upon us!" (3:11).

He boldly predicted Jerusalem's downfall:

> Therefore because of you,
>   Zion shall be plowed like a field,
>   and Jerusalem reduced to rubble,
> And the mount of the temple
>   to a forest ridge (3:12).

More than a hundred years later this prophecy was remembered and cited in defense of Jeremiah when his life was endangered for having made a similar prediction (Jer 26:7–10); the account suggests that Micah's prophecy made a deep impression even in his own day.

Micah shared with Isaiah the assurance that Yahweh would deliver His People, after the judgment to come, through a scion of the line of David. As with Isaiah (Isa 11:1), disgust with Judah's line of kings led Micah to look back to the very origins of David for the source from which the one awaited would come. In the oracle of 4:14–15a,[17] probably given during Sennacherib's siege in 701, he pictures Jerusalem fortified but surrounded, her king overcome and insulted (4:14). In contrast he thinks of the lowly home of David's clan:

> But you, Bethlehem-Ephrathah,
>   too small to be among the clans of Judah,
> From you shall come forth for me
>   one who is to be ruler in Israel;
> Whose origin is from of old,
>   from ancient times (5:1).

Micah attributes to him the powerful but loving care of the shepherd that David was (5:3). Unlike Hezekiah, whose political machinations brought war and destruction, "he shall be peace" (5:4a). To the extent that this picture differs from that of Isaiah's messianic king, it complements it.

The authenticity of 5:2 is disputed; it is an enigmatic verse whether we attribute it to Micah or not. "She who is to give birth" may refer to the mother of Immanuel of Isaiah's prophecy (Isa 7:14), spoken some 35 years earlier, or both oracles may rest on a common background of thought that we can only guess at. Another possible explanation may be that Micah is thinking of a personification of the people: Israel will soon be in travail (cf. 4:10) with the punishment that shall fall upon her, but this purifying punishment is the prelude to a restoration and the condition for the coming of the ideal king.

---

[17]Chapter and verse numbers follow the Hebrew text and *NAB*; the passage is 5:1–5a in *RSV*.

JEREMIAH

HIS TIMES. Jeremiah was born ca. 645 in the village of Anathoth, a few miles north of Jerusalem, during the paganizing reign of Manasseh (687–642). He was called to be a prophet in 627, the thirteenth year of Josiah (640–609). His prophetic activity continued until sometime after the fall of Jerusalem in 587. This long period was a momentous one for Judah. Josiah's reform had begun in 628 (2 Chr 34:3), a year before Jeremiah's call. Though Judah was still nominally a vassal of Assyria, the overlord had grown too weak to assert control. In 612 Niniveh fell, and in 609 Josiah was killed at Megiddo trying to prevent Egyptian help from reaching the remnants of the Assyrian army.

For a brief time Egypt held sway over Judah, but Babylonia's decisive victory at Carchemish (605) broke Egypt's power; soon Judah, now under Jehoiakim (609–598), was a vassal of Babylonia. Under Jehoiakim the reform quickly lapsed. Judah's political situation, too, deteriorated as he almost immediately began intriguing at the rebellion that brought retribution he didn't live to see—the sack of Jerusalem in 597 and the deportation of Jehoiachin and the cream of the citizenry. Zedekiah (597–587), listening to foolish council, followed a similar course and provoked the final catastrophe of 587.

Jeremiah's ministry continued for a period in Judah under Gedaliah, the governor appointed by the Babylonians, and then in Egypt, where he was forced to accompany those who fled Judah after Gedaliah's assassination.

THE BOOK. Commentators frequently distinguish three types of material in the Jeremiah collection: poetic oracles composed by the prophet himself; biographical prose, regularly attributed to Baruch, Jeremiah's friend and secretary; and prose discourses that preserve the words of Jeremiah as remembered and repeated by the circle of his friends and followers. Others have argued that the prose materials are the work of the deuteronomists, whose interest was not biographical but rather concerned the function of God's word through the prophet, its fulfillment, human reaction to it, obedience to the law, results of disobedience, etc.—interests which mirror those of the narratives of the deuteronomic history. This approach does not question the historical truth of the events related nor deny that the prose discourses rest on genuine words of Jeremiah; and the essential role of Baruch as source of the detailed knowledge of the life of Jeremiah they presuppose is maintained. (See especially E. W. Nicholson in chapter-end bibliography.)

The variety of the materials and the haphazard order of their arrangement make this a difficult book to study, but the following division may serve as a starting point:

   A. *Mostly condemnations of sin and threats of punishment:* 1–25
   B. *Biographical narratives:* 26–29
   C. *"The Book of Consolation":* 30–33
   D. *Further biographical narratives:* 34–45
   E. *Oracles against the nations:* 46–51
   F. *Historical appendix:* 52

Jeremiah 36 records that in 605 Jeremiah dictated to Baruch the oracles he had delivered from the beginning of his ministry in 627 until that time. The scroll thus composed was read successively to the people, the princes, and King Jehoiakim. Though the king destroyed the scroll, Jeremiah and Baruch produced another, expanded, edition. It is likely that this scroll was the beginning of the Jeremiah collection. To the oracles from 627 to 605 have been added later ones, many prose discourses, and Jeremiah's "confessions" (p. 181).

The narratives of 26–29 and 34–45 describe events from 609 on, though not in chronological order. Ch. 30–33 contain promises of restoration from various periods of Jeremiah's ministry. The historical appendix (52), taken mainly from 2 Kgs 24:18–25:30, aptly demonstrates the fulfillment of the prophet's predictions.

HIS LIFE AND TEACHING. Jeremiah's teachings are best understood against the background of his own life and the people and events that shaped his message. This would be true of the teaching of any of the prophets, but only in the case of Jeremiah do we have the wealth of biographical detail necessary to attempt to do this with reasonable confidence.

Jeremiah's call came to him early in life and found him reluctant to accept (1:6). Try to imagine an inexperienced small town youth of about college age who is told:

> This day I set you
>   over nations and over kingdoms,
> To root up and to tear down,
>   to destroy and to demolish,
>   to build and to plant (1:10).

That all this was to be accomplished without any political means whatever is testimony to the power of Yahweh's word. The timid youth is told that Yahweh Himself will supply what is wanting:

> For it is I this day
>   who have made you a fortified city,
> A pillar of iron, a wall of brass,
>   against the whole land:
> Against Judah's kings and princes,
>   against its priests and people (1:18).

In spite of such assurances, Jeremiah remained a reluctant prophet;

understandably so, for he foresaw the opposition his mission would stir up.

The fact that Jeremiah came from a priestly family of Anathoth suggests the possibility of descent from Abiathar, the priest exiled to Anathoth by Solomon (1 Kgs 2:26–27), and through him from Eli, the guardian of the Ark while it was at Shiloh (1 Samuel 1–4). Certain emphases in his teaching seem to reflect the influence of northern traditions; specifically, he is more concerned with the Mosaic covenant and God's gracious acts in Israel's early history than with the theology of David's election that was at home in Jerusalem circles. He was also strongly influenced by the northern prophet Hosea.

Jeremiah's early oracles,[18] those given before Josiah's reform was well under way, are largely devoted to condemnation of pagan practices and forebodings of judgment to come. Like Hosea he pictures Yahweh's people as a bride who, though faithful at first, turns harlot through the fertility cult, idolatry, and other pagan practices:

> I remember the devotion of your youth,
>   how you loved me as a bride,
> Following me in the desert,
>   in a land unsown (2:2).
> Long ago you broke your yoke,
>   you tore off your bonds.
> "I will not serve," you said.
> On every high hill, under every green tree,
>   you gave yourself to harlotry (2:20).

Other nations do not forsake their gods, false though they are, but Israel has forsaken Yahweh; she has turned from the source of living water to hew out useless cisterns (2:11–13). Their behavior in the valley of ben-Hinnom (where idolatry and infant sacrifice were practiced) is likened to that of a she-camel in heat, rushing hither and yon in shameless search for satisfaction (2:23–25). Only in moments of danger do they remember their God (2:27–28).

Rebel Israel, already divorced by Yahweh (a reference to the fall of the Northern Kingdom) for her sins, seems almost just compared to Judah, and Jeremiah addresses a fervent invitation to return:

> Return, rebel Israel, says the Lord,
>   I will not remain angry with you;
> For I am merciful, says the Lord,
>   I will not continue my wrath forever.
> Only know your guilt:
>   how you rebelled against the Lord, our God
> How you ran hither and yon to strangers . . . (3:6–13).[19]

[18]Jeremiah's utterances are often difficult to date. Jeremiah 2–3 is composed mainly of oracles from the earliest period of his career.

[19]Other oracles of consolation directed to northern Israel during this period of Jeremiah's career are 31:2–6, 15–22.

In the longing of his heart Jeremiah hears words of sincere repentance:

> "Here we are, we now come to you
>   because you are the Lord, our God.
> Deceptive indeed are the hills,
>   the thronging mountains;
> In the Lord, our God, alone
>   is the salvation of Israel.
>
> . . . .
> Let us lie down in our shame,
>   let our disgrace cover us,
>   for we have sinned against the Lord our God . . ." (3:22-25).

But the repentance existed only in the prophet's hopes.

Josiah's reform, begun in 628, entered a climactic phase in 622 with the finding of the deuteronomic law code (2 Kgs 22-23; p. 102). Jeremiah undoubtedly approved the reform, for its central aim, the rooting out of pagan vices, coincided with that of his own preaching. The deuteronomic spirit, too, based in northern prophetic and priestly traditions, was congenial to his own. While Josiah was extending his control and the reform even to northern Israel, Jeremiah was inviting the people there to return to Yahweh. The official reform had a strongly nationalistic tinge, however, for it also aimed at throwing off Assyrian domination. Carried out by the authority of the king as it was, it could easily accomplish such ends as the removal of pagan cult objects and the smashing of local altars (2 Kgs 23:4-20), but it could not enter the heart or convert the spirit. If Jeremiah became disillusioned with the reform, as it seems he did, it was because it did not effect the sincere return he saw was needed.

Jeremiah's oracles from the period after the reform show that he found no true repentance, no lasting conversion. His disillusionment may date from as early as the latter years of Josiah; the situation is all too clear from the very beginning of Jehoiakim's reign. One of the best examples is Jeremiah's Temple address (7:1-15; cf. 26), delivered shortly after 609. The picture he paints is not a pretty one: apostasy through idolatry and Baal worship added to the crimes of murder, adultery, theft, perjury, and oppression of fellow Israelites; yet withal there was the naive assurance that no evil would befall them because they were Yahweh's people and He was in their midst (7:4; cf. 5:12). By such reasoning they would make Yahweh a protector of their criminal ways, His Temple a den of thieves (7:10-14). The deuteronomic reform with its emphasis on the Temple had heightened the popular belief in its inviolability. Jeremiah rejects that belief and declares that the Temple will fall just as the earlier Yahweh shrine at Shiloh had (7:12-14; p. 124).

The judgment passed on the populace is quite pessimistic: "Roam the streets of Jerusalem . . . to find even one who lives uprightly and seeks to be faithful and I will pardon her!'' (5:1). Corruption is found among high and low (5:4-9); idolatry is a family affair (7:16-20). By now Jeremiah has little hope that any true conversion will be forthcoming; as likely that the leopard will change its spots as that this people, hardened in sin, will do good (13:23)!

Because of such convictions the prophet speaks with ever more assurance of the blow which is to fall, a blow which would sweep away the nation and its cherished institutions—the inevitable judgment for past sins and the necessary condition for future restoration. Assembling officials of Jerusalem before one of its gates, he smashed a pottery flask, saying: "Thus says the Lord of hosts: Thus will I smash this people and this city, as one smashes a clay pot so that it cannot be repaired" (19:1-13). Because of the power a symbolic action of this sort was believed to have, Jeremiah was setting in motion Yahweh's word of destruction!

As the conflict of world powers progressed, the agent of that destruction began to emerge more clearly. Several of Jeremiah's oracles give warning of the "foe from the north" (1:12-16; 4:6; 6:1, 22). If any of these date from his early ministry they may indicate no nation in particular; almost any enemy except Egypt came from that direction. But from the moment of Babylonian victory in 605, Jeremiah had no doubts. In that year he had Baruch read the scroll of his earlier oracles in the Temple court, vainly hoping that in the light of this newly emerging threat they would make some impression (36).

Castigation of popular vices, promises of invasion, and threats against the Temple and city brought upon Jeremiah the hatred of king and people alike. After his Temple address he narrowly escaped death (26) and after the incident of the flask he was beaten and put in the stocks (20:1-6). Jehoiakim would undoubtedly have put him and Baruch to death after hearing the contents of the scroll if he could have found them (36:25-26); he did execute another prophet, Uriah, for prophesying similar things (26:20-24).

Jeremiah's prophetic calling, unwanted by him from the first, became a veritable Golgotha under Jehoiakim. Without wife (16:1-4), almost without human companionship (15:17; 16:5-9), excluded from the Temple (36:5), taunted and mocked by the people (17:15; 20:7), Jeremiah had the further trial of seeing his admonitions go unheeded and having to pronounce destructive judgment upon the people he loved. Because of the courage and constancy with which he fulfilled his mission, he must indeed have seemed "a pillar of iron, a wall of brass, against the whole land" (1:18), but inwardly he rebelled and would gladly have laid down his commission.

This hidden struggle is shown to us in his "confessions,"[20] poems which reveal his inmost thoughts and sentiments. In them he laments

[20] 11:18-12:6; 15:10-21; 17:14-18; 18:18-23; 20:7-13, 14-18. It is likely that all of these date from Jehoiakim's reign.

his hard lot, accuses God of having seduced him (20:7) and of deserting him in his hour of need (15:18); he lashes out at his persecutors and prays God to take vengeance upon them; he even determines to preach God's message no more (20:9). In spite of such words Jeremiah never abandoned his post and, at times at least, realized that "the Lord is with me, like a mighty champion" (20:11). The sublime commandment to love one's enemies had not yet been taught, and Jeremiah in this respect did not rise above the level of his times. Nevertheless, it is clear that he interceded ceaselessly for his people, strove to avert catastrophe from them, and joyfully promised restoration after the blow had fallen. Though despised in his own day, later tradition rightly recognized him as one who greatly loved his people and prayed for them and for the holy city (2 Macc 15:14).

Jehoiakim's last act was the rebellion that brought Babylonian power to the gates of Jerusalem. The final ten years of Judah's existence as a kingdom were lived under the shadow of that power. Jeremiah was not persecuted by Zedekiah as he had been by Jehoiakim, but the word of Yahweh for the new political situation was, if anything, more unpopular than before. Nebuchadnezzar had taken to Babylonia Jehoiachin, king for three months, the queen mother, the elite of the populace, and many of the Temple furnishings. A heavy blow had fallen on Judah and Jeremiah's predictions had begun to be vindicated. The long-awaited conversion might now have been expected, but none was forthcoming; the crucible of adversity which ought to have purged Judah's dross had left it like unrefined silver (6:29–30). Those who had already gone into exile Jeremiah compared to good figs because, having now been chastened, they were ready to return to God "with their whole heart" and ripe for favors He would bestow on them. The survivors in Judah, however, were figs too rotten to be eaten and were fit only for the further punishment of "sword, famine, and pestilence, until they have disappeared from the land" (24).

The easy victory of Babylonian arms in 597 should have served as a pointed warning of the folly of further intrigues, but Judah's populace was in no mood to receive warnings. Within four years the ambassadors of Edom, Moab, Ammon, Tyre, and Sidon were in Jerusalem plotting a new rebellion (27:2–3). Nationalistic prophets were promising an end of the oppressor's power and the return of Jehoiachin, the exiles, and the Temple furnishings within two years (28:1–11; 29:20–32). If ever a message was dictated by wishful thinking, this was it! In the face of this naive optimism, Jeremiah preached Yahweh's word: He it was who had given the conquered lands into Nebuchadnezzar's power, and all were to submit; whoever would not submit his neck to the king of Babylon would perish (27:4–22). To illustrate the point Jeremiah went about wearing an ox-yoke on his neck. It was in these circumstances that he had his dramatic conflict with the prophet Hananiah (28). To the exiles Jeremiah sent a letter telling them to settle down, raise families, and pray for the welfare of the land of their captivity; Yahweh looked upon them with favor and would restore them, but only after "seventy years" (29). In fact, he was telling them, only in the next generation or so would the restoration take place.

For reasons not clearly apparent the rebellion did not materialize at this time. But in 589 Zedekiah gave in to the nationalistic party and provoked the Babylonian assault which culminated in the tragedy of 587—a tragedy Jeremiah's counsel would have averted. During the long siege the prophet's message to king and people remained what it had been all along: Yahweh Himself has set His face against this city; submit that you may live (21:1–10; 34:1–7; 38:1–4). Final proof of the people's perfidy was given when the Babylonians temporarily lifted the siege to give battle to an approaching Egyptian army. Shortly before, the people of Jerusalem had proclaimed emancipation for their slaves (a belated observance of the provision in Deut 15:12–18) and confirmed it by oath; but when the siege was lifted, they forced their slaves back into service (34:8–16). Jeremiah promptly predicted that the Egyptian army would be defeated and the siege resumed (34:17–22; 37:1–10). Indeed, he said, even if Judah should rout their attackers, the wounded survivors would rise up and destroy the city with fire (37:10).

To Jeremiah such teachings were the word of Yahweh, but to the princes and generals they spelled sedition. The prophet was cast into a miry cistern and left to die, but was later released from the cistern and imprisoned in the court of the guard until the fall of the city (38:1–28). Unable to avert the disaster, rejected by his people, Jeremiah must have judged himself a failure. Only after the smoke of battle had cleared would his people realize that he had been a true prophet, that the word of Yahweh had been with him from the first.

But his mission had been not only "to destroy and to demolish" but also "to build and to plant" (1:10). Consistent with his belief that only when the old institutions had been swept away and false hopes dashed could a new beginning be made, Jeremiah directed his promises of restoration to those who had already experienced Yahweh's purifying judgment. We have spoken of the fervent invitations offered to northern Israel during his early ministry and the promise of restoration sent to the exiles after 597. It was only by a slight anticipation, then, that Yahweh's word of consolation came to him during the height of the siege, while he was in prison; all human hope was gone, the city was as good as fallen (32).

In these circumstances a relative, Hanamel, came to Jeremiah with the offer: "Buy for yourself my field in Anathoth, since you, as nearest relative, have the first right of purchase." Hanamel was calling upon Jeremiah to fulfill the obligation of the next of kin to redeem land that must be sold so that it would not pass out of the family (Lev 25:25). With the country already in the hands of the Babylonians, real estate hardly seemed a favorable investment, but moved by Yahweh's impulse, he bought the field, going through all the customary legal steps. But when Hanamel had departed, he expostulated with Yahweh, asking, in effect: "Why, in this hopeless situation, did you have me do that?" God's response indicates that the purchase was a symbolic act to show that life would one day be resumed in the ravaged land:

> Is anything impossible to me? . . . I will bring them back to this place and settle them in safety. They shall be my people, and I will be their God. One heart and one way I will give them, that they may fear me always. . . . I will make with them an eternal covenant, never to cease doing good to them. . . . I will replant them firmly in this land, with all my heart and soul. . . . Fields shall again be bought in this land, which you call a desert, without man or beast, handed over to the Chaldeans. Fields shall be bought with money, deeds written and sealed . . . when I change their lot, says the Lord (32:27-44; cf. 33:1-13).

Though the symbolic act of land purchase is the occasion for this oracle, Jeremiah's vision of the restoration is not simply a return to "business as usual"; such a view would be unworthy of the great prophet and inconsistent with the tenor of the concerns manifested throughout his teaching. Here he speaks of God bestowing a heart "that they may fear me always" and making an eternal covenant. Of the exiles of 597, too, he had said: "I will give them a heart with which to understand that I am the Lord" (24:7).

"Heart" is one of the characteristic concerns of Jeremiah's religious thought; it occurs again in 31:31-34, the "new covenant" passage, justly considered a high point of prophetic teaching. The Sinai covenant has been nullified by heinous apostasy, but, such is God's mercy and the enduring quality of His election, a new one is forthwith promised. The central provision remains the same: "I will be their God, and they shall be my people." But the new covenant will be characterized by an immediacy not known before, for God's law will be written in their hearts, not on tablets of stone; all shall "know" Yahweh (p. 166) so that there will be no need for others to mediate God's word to them, as priests and prophets had done in the past. Jeremiah expected more than simply a return to Judah's former state; he expected, rather, a new act of God which would in truth effect the end He had in calling Israel.

Not the least of Jeremiah's importance is that he enabled his people to survive the destruction of their state. This he did not only by holding out hope for the future but also by explaining, in terms of Israel's faith, *why* the tragedy had overtaken them—something the popular theology of the time had said couldn't happen. Though unheeded in his own time (even by the remnant who dragged him to Egypt—44), his teachings stirred repentance and hope among the exiles in Babylonia.

READING SUGGESTIONS

JBC §14-19. *PBS* #25-28. *OTRG* #15-16. *AUOT* 270-94, 300-31, 343-48, 367-96. *BHI* 259-63, 286-96, 331-39. *MTES* Ch. 9-10, *passim*. *WITOT* 183-97, 208-21, 232-38, 241-47, 252-55.

Anderson, B. W., *The Eighth Century Prophets*. Philadelphia: Fortress Press, 1978.

Blenkinsopp, J., *A History of Prophecy in Israel, pp. 80-176*.

Boadt, L., *Jeremiah 1-25*. *OTM*, Vol. 9.

_____, *Jeremiah 26-52, Habakkuk, Zephaniah, Nahum*. *OTM*, Vol. 10.

Bright, J., *Jeremiah*. *AB* 21; Garden City, N.Y.: Doubleday & Company, Inc., 1965.

Clements, R. E., *Isaiah 1-39*. Grand Rapids, Mich.: Eerdmans Publishing Co., 1980.

Hillers, D., *Micah*. Philadelphia: Fortress Press, 1984.

Jensen, J., *Isaiah 1-39*. *OTM*, Vol. 8.

Kaiser, O., *Isaiah 1-12*. Philadelphia: Westminster Press, 1983.

Koch, K., *The Prophets. Volume One: The Assyrian Age*. Philadelphia: Fortress Press, 1982.

Nicholson, E. W., *Preaching to the Exiles: A Study in the Prose Tradition in the Book of Jeremiah*. Oxford: Basil Blackwell, 1970.

Sakenfeld, K. D., *Faithfulness in Action*. Philadelphia: Fortress Press, 1985.

Vawter, B., *The Conscience of Israel*, pp. 61-289.

_____, *Amos, Hosea, Micah, Excursus on Classical Prophecy*. *OTM*, Vol. 7.

Wolff, H. W., *Joel and Amos*. Philadelphia: Fortress Press, 1977.

_____, *Confrontations with Prophets*. Philadelphia: Fortress Press, 1983.

_____, *Micah the Prophet*. Philadelphia: Fortress Press, 1981.

Behler, G. M., "Jeremiah's vocation crisis," *TD* 18 (1970) 114-21.

Bright, J., "A Prophet's Lament and Its Answer (*Jeremiah 15:10-21*)," *Int* 28 (1974) 59-74.

Craghan, J. F., "Traditions and Techniques in the Prophet Amos," *TBT* #60 (Apr. 1972) 782-86.

Doohan, H., "Contrast in Prophetic Leadership: Isaiah and Jeremiah," *BTB* 13 (1983) 39-43.

Eichrodt, W., "The Holy One in Your Midst," *Int* 15 (1961) 259-73.

Hayes, H. H., "The Tradition of Zion's Invulnerability," *JBL* 82 (1963) 419-29.

Jensen, J., "The Age of Immanuel," *CBQ* 41 (1979) 220-39.

_____, "Weal and Woe in Isaiah: Consistency and Continuity," *CBQ* 43 (1981) 167-87.

Lind, M. C., "Hosea 5:8-6:6," *Int* 38 (1984) 398-403.

Nickels, P., "An Eternal Witness — Isaiah 1-39," *TBT* #92 (Nov. 1977) 1343-49.

Peifer, C. J., "Isaiah: Man of Jerusalem," *TBT* #92 (Nov. 1977) 1350-57.

Rowley, H. H., "The Marriage of Hosea," *Men of God* London: Thomas Nelson and Sons, Ltd., pp. 66-97.

Sklba, R., "Dishonesty: A Jeremian View of Sin," *TBT* #63 (Dec. 1972) 966-73.

Tucker, G. M., "Prophetic Authenticity (*A Form-Critical Study of Amos 7:10-17*)," *Int* 27 (1973) 423-34.

Vanden Busch, R., "Jeremiah: A Spiritual Metamorphosis," *BTB* 10 (1980) 17-24.

15

The Exilic Prophets

(Recommended Scripture Reading: Ezekiel 1-6; 8-11; 16; 18; 21; 34; 36-37; 47; Isaiah 40-55)

JUDAH'S poignant grief over the fall of Jerusalem is enshrined for all ages in the five poems that make up Lamentations. The opening lines set the mood:

> How lonely is she now,
>   the once crowded city!
> Widowed is she
>   who was mistress over nations (Lam 1:1).

Leaving behind the smoking ruins, the exiles of 587 began the long march to Babylonia to join those who had gone there ten years earlier.

The policy of uprooting large numbers of subject peoples was intended to prevent unrest and rebellion in the conquered territories. To this end the victors removed precisely those elements that gave shape and direction to a people—the influential nobles, religious and civil officials, the artisans, etc. There was good reason, then, for the exiles of Judah, though their total number was small (perhaps less than 20,000), to consider themselves the only surviving "Israel" (see p. 172, n. 13). Archeological evidence shows that most of the towns and villages of Judah had been razed and the land largely depopulated; "sword, famine, and pestilence" had taken a more severe toll than deportation. Though Yahwistic worship continued in Palestine, it was probably of a highly syncretistic sort; the survivors in Palestine exercised little direct influence on *OT* religion.[1] Israel's precious traditions survived mainly among the exiles; to Babylonia they brought them, engraved on their hearts and in their memories or written on the scrolls they carried.

---

[1]The validity of the claim of the exiles to be the true "Israel," over against those who remained in the land, is one of the themes E. W. Nicholson (*Preaching to the Exiles,* esp. pp. 107-111, 116-35) finds in the prose sections of Jeremiah.

GOD'S PEOPLE IN EXILE. Life was not too difficult for those who were taken to Babylonia. They had a good measure of freedom; they formed their own communities, obtained property, and practiced trades. The principal danger they faced was a crisis of faith. The temptation to abandon faith in Yahweh arose both from the events of the past and their present circumstances. In the popular mind Yahweh's election of Jerusalem and the Davidic dynasty had meant that the city and the monarchy couldn't fall. Had Yahweh been powerless to avert it? What they saw of Babylonian culture only posed the question more acutely. Nothing they had heard in Palestine had prepared them for the wealth and grandeur of the cities and temples they now saw—the magnificent gates and towers, the awesome religious processions. They recognized that the Temple and city they had gloried in were small and poor by comparison. And after all, had not the gods of Babylon overcome Yahweh when their minions conquered His people?

How many succumbed to such temptations we shall never know. The exiles of the Northern Kingdom, in an analogous situation in Assyria, had disappeared without leaving a trace; humanly speaking, the same fate should have overtaken those of Judah. One reason the exiles of Judah survived was that the conservative Jerusalem priesthood maintained a purer form of Yahwism than the custodians of the north's scattered shrines ever had; more important, however, was the influence of the prophets. The Northern Kingdom had gone under in spite of the efforts of Amos and Hosea, the first of the classical prophets. Although Judah, too, fell in her turn, she had had a century and a half to meditate on the words of Amos and Hosea and to receive their message anew from an impressive line of successors; Jeremiah, the most recent of these, had presided at the nation's last agony. Here in Babylonia there should be no doubt that they were true prophets and that their unpopular message had been Yahweh's word. They had foretold what would happen and had given an interpretation of events, before they came to pass, that accorded with Israel's traditional faith. The fulfillment of their prophecies showed, more clearly than ever, that Yahweh was Lord of history.

This realization alone could have led to despair. They had sinned, they had abandoned the covenant, and Yahweh had handed them over to their enemies. All this was true, but nevertheless He had not cast them off. Beyond disaster was the hope the prophets held out—there was a future for them in which God's redemptive purpose in history would be accomplished. Even in Babylonia great prophets continued to appear; Ezekiel and the one we call Deutero-Isaiah were the most noteworthy, but there were others as well.

It was probably during the exile that synagogue meetings began. With no Temple at which to offer sacrifice and celebrate the customary feasts, they met together out-of-doors or in private homes to hear the words of the prophets or other parts of Israel's sacred heritage repeated and discussed. The exile was a time of intense literary activity, as the prophetic oracles and ancient religious traditions were collected and edited. The pentateuchal sources, the deuteronomic history, the prophetic collections, and almost every part of the *OT* show signs of exilic reworking.

The exiles found a new devotion to their laws and their own peculiar practices, especially circumcision and the Sabbath. Such practices set them off from their neighbors and gave them a stronger sense of identity and cohesion than they had had before. Some traits characteristic of the new Judaism appear already in the teachings of Ezekiel, often called the father of Judaism. It is to him we must now turn.

EZEKIEL

THE MAN. Ezekiel's call to prophecy came to him in 593 in Babylonia, where he lived as an exile, one of those deported in 597. The last of his dated oracles (29:17) is from 571, and his ministry may have ended around that time. Ezekiel's character, as revealed in his oracles, displays an unusual mixture of diverse traits. He combines the ecstatic behavior of the early prophets with the profound teaching of the classical ones; a priest, he manifests a devotion to cult that is new to prophetism; and the somewhat bizarre nature of his visions and the symbolism employed by him make him a forerunner of the later apocalyptic writers.

Ezekiel is perhaps the least attractive of the prophets. His threats of punishment betray no compassion for his people, and his promises of restoration seem to be made almost reluctantly. "Insensibility made man" one commentator called him. Such a judgment is unjust, however. The prophet who was commanded to "groan in silence" but manifest no grief at the death of his wife, "the delight of his eyes" (24:15-17), exalted the justice and transcendence of God by submerging his own emotions. Only one who loved his people keenly could have accomplished the good this great man did.

THE BOOK. The Ezekiel collection manifests a much more consistent and orderly plan than we find in the other prophetic books, as may be seen in the following outline:

A. *Judgment on Judah and Jerusalem:* 1-24
   1. Ezekiel's call: 1-3
   2. Guilt and punishment of Judah and Jerusalem: 4-24
B. *Judgment on the nations:* 25-32
C. *Restoration of Israel:* 33-48
   1. Promises of restoration: 33-39
   2. Idyllic vision of restored Israel: 40-48

The first and third sections (A and C) correspond to two phases of Ezekiel's prophetic task, that of warning the exiles of Jerusalem's doom while the city stood, that of consoling and encouraging them after it had fallen. The location of the oracles against the nations (B) between the punishment and restoration of the Chosen People is deliberate and meaningful: it presents one aspect of the place of the Gentiles in God's plan. God's people are indeed the first to feel His wrath precisely because election brings them under His special providence and makes their sin more grave (Amos 3:2; 6:1-7). But the pagan nations, though used as instruments of God's judgment, shall also be punished for their crimes (Isaiah 10; 13-23; Jeremiah 46-51). Rather than a conclusion to the first section (A), however, the oracles against the nations form an introduction to the third section (C): the first phase of the establishment of God's kingdom will be the vindication of His justice throughout the earth; only then comes the restoration of Israel.

A closer inspection of the book reveals that its origin and history is not as simple as the broad outline might suggest. Doublets, displacement in the order of oracles, and expansions of Ezekiel's words indicate that the process of collection was complicated and that the hands of others, probably the prophet's disciples, have been at work. Since the condemnatory oracles in 4-24 are directed against those dwelling in Judah, not against the exiles, some critics have claimed that Ezekiel's call to prophecy came to him in Judah, that only the later part of his ministry was exercised in Babylonia, and that his detailed visions of events in Jerusalem (cf. 8-11) are really accounts of things he witnessed in person. According to this hypothesis, the present arrangement of the Ezekiel material gives a misleading impression. It seems more probable, however, that the book accurately reflects the general lines of his ministry. The materials of 4-24, in spite of their diversity (oracles, symbolic acts, visions, allegories), make eminently good sense in terms of a ministry to exiles who need to be told that Jerusalem must fall and why.[2]

HIS TEACHINGS. Jeremiah called the exiles of 597 "good figs" and proclaimed God's good will toward them (Jeremiah 24; 29). To Ezekiel they were a rebellious people, "stubborn of brow and obstinate in heart" (2:3-8; 3:4-9). But the very narrative in which these characterizations are found contains more than a germ of hope. There in Babylonia the glory of Yahweh had appeared to Ezekiel, transported thither on a throne-chariot propelled by spirit and cherubim (1:1-3:15). True, this was only a brief visit whose object was to constitute Ezekiel a prophet and watchman (3:17-21) for the peo-

[2]For a thorough discussion of all such introductory questions, see W. Zimmerli, *Ezekiel 1*. tr. R. E. Clements (Philadelphia: Fortress Press, 1979), pp. 1-77.

ple, yet it showed Yahweh's concern for the captives and that His power extended to the land of their captors. In contrast, His glory would soon abandon the Temple and city profaned by the sins of those dwelling there, transported by the same awesome vehicle (10; 11:22–23).[3]

The early part of Ezekiel's ministry, from 593 to 587, was dedicated to preparing his fellow exiles for the fall of Jerusalem. As long as the capital stood, their understanding of Yahweh's election of Jerusalem and of David led them to expect that He would intervene miraculously to crush the Babylonians, deliver the city, and restore Jehoiachin to the throne and themselves to their land. As we have already seen, there were not wanting prophets even among the exiles to fan such hopes (Jeremiah 29). Ezekiel inveighs against these prophets of peace (Ezekiel 13) and relentlessly crushes the false hope that Jerusalem would be spared. His insistence all the while that Yahweh Himself was fighting against the city proclaimed its destruction to be a sign of His power, not of His weakness.

Ezekiel employed a wide range of methods to communicate to the exiles the certainty of Jerusalem's destruction; all of them bear the stamp of his unusual personality. At one time he drew the plan of the city upon a clay tablet and went through all the steps of laying siege against it (4); at another he acted out the part of an exile going into captivity (12). To make clear the justice of God's judgment, he recounted to the exiles his vision of the abominations perpetrated in the very Temple precincts (8–11). There in Babylonia he uttered oracles against the "high places" of paganized worship in Judah (6) and pronounced a ringing indictment of Jerusalem (22). His vivid imagination described the sword which Yahweh had sharpened and polished cleaving right and left (21:1–21). He described the king of Babylon on his way to conquest hesitating at a fork in the road: would he take the road to Ammon or to Jerusalem? To Jerusalem, of course! (21:23–28).

Ezekiel makes frequent use of allegory, often to underline the sinfulness and worthlessness of Israel. Two of his allegories draw on Hosea's image of Israel as Yahweh's spouse (16; 23); the second of these uses Jeremiah's variation on the theme, depicting Israel and Judah as sisters espoused to Yahweh. In Ezekiel's treatment, however, the warm tenderness of Hosea and Jeremiah is not found; their insistence on the endurance of Yahweh's *hesed* and His willingness to forgive the spouse He still loves disappears. Instead Ezekiel emphasizes the wanton lewdness of Israel, depicted as a nymphomaniac soliciting every passer-by, and the punishment that will overtake the adulteress—death (e.g., 16:35–43). Hosea and Jeremiah thought of the exodus period as a honeymoon, the period of Israel's bridal fidelity.

---

[3]Note that the *NAB* has rearranged the materials of ch. 8–11 in an attempt to restore the original order; some verses in ch. 1 have also been rearranged.

For Ezekiel, however, Israel's fidelity never was—her adultery began before she left Egypt. His long review of Israel's history of apostasy in ch. 20 makes the same assertion in plainer terms.

This hard, uncompromising teaching was intended to justify the doom that had fallen and was still to fall upon the nation: Israel, unfaithful from the beginning, unfaithful to the end, was reaping the fruit of her apostasy. Ezekiel also cut off all occasion of self-pity for the exiles. "Fathers have eaten green grapes," they were fond of saying, "thus their children's teeth are on edge" (18:2). By this proverb the exiles claimed that they were being punished for the crimes of earlier generations. Ezekiel's reply was a repeated insistence on personal responsibility. Punishment for sin does not pass from generation to generation; the innocent son of a wicked man will not suffer for his father's sins. In great detail Ezekiel runs through various possible cases of innocence and guilt, of turning from good to evil and from evil to good (18; 33:10–20). The wicked land will not be saved by the presence of a few good men; their virtue will deliver only themselves (14:12–23). In the vision of punishment for the abominations in Jerusalem, those innocent of idolatry are spared; not until the angelic scribe has marked a tau on the foreheads of the faithful do the avenging angels strike (9:1–11).

Ezekiel's rigid, unfeeling insistence on Israel's sin and the demands of justice has the effect of exalting the holiness and transcendence of God—an important teaching for a people who were tempted to doubt His power or question His justice. God's power and transcendence are likewise emphasized by the frequent use (about 90 times) of the title "son of man" for Ezekiel himself—a title which, in its use here, underlines the prophet's mere human state before the majesty of Yahweh.[4]

Much of this strikes us as gloomy and pessimistic, but it had the advantage of providing a foundation for the positive side of Ezekiel's ministry as well as for the negative. With the arrival of news that Jerusalem had fallen (33:21–22), his task becomes one of consolation—a task he performs in his own dour, inimitable way. The promises of blessing and restoration are all the more firm because they are spoken in the name of Ezekiel's holy and transcendent God.

Ezekiel's restoration material, like the rest of the book, exhibits a rich variety of forms: oracle (36), allegory (34), vision (37:1–14), and symbolic act (37:15–28). The prophecies against Gog (38–39) approach developed apocalyptic (p. 253), and the utopian description of the restored Israel (40–48) is in a class by itself.

The prophet's vision of the dry bones (37:1–14), perhaps the best-known part of his book, provides an answer to the exiles' complaint, "Our bones are dried up, our hope is lost, and we are cut off" (37:11). In vision he sees dry and scattered bones, as remote from life as

---

[4]On "son of man" see also p. 256.

anything can be. But at God's word they are articulated bone to bone and covered with flesh and skin; by the power of the spirit, the breath of life, "they came alive and stood upright, a vast army" (37:10). So also can the power of God create good from a hopeless situation—in the case of the exiles a virtual resurrection from the dead: "O my people! I will put my spirit in you that you may live, and I will settle you upon your land; thus you shall know that I am the Lord. I have promised, and I will do it, says the Lord" (37:14).

The restoration, for Ezekiel as for the other prophets, was far more than simply a return to Palestine. Replacing the wicked, selfish rulers of Israel's disastrous past, Yahweh Himself will become shepherd of His sheep (34). He will gather them together and bring them to their own land (34:11-16), and make a "covenant of peace" with them (34:25-31). He will cleanse them of all their impurities by the sprinkling of clean water and will give them a new heart and a new spirit so that they will live by His law; they shall be His people and He will be their God (36:24-32; cf. 37:23-28). They shall be safe from the most formidable enemies, for Yahweh Himself will be their protector (38-39).[5] The notice, so characteristic of Ezekiel, "not for your sakes do I act, house of Israel, but for the sake of my holy name" (36:22), completely lacks the warm affectionate tone of Jeremiah, but it puts the promises on the surest possible footing—that which is demanded by Yahweh's holiness cannot fail to be.

The description of the restored Israel in 40-48 may be described as utopian vision. A genuine ecstatic vision may have been the starting point, but it has been greatly expanded by Ezekiel and others. Although some details of the picture are unrealistic, "utopian" is not used here in a pejorative sense. In the new Israel Ezekiel pictures, the abuses and evils of the past are eliminated, and measures to guarantee they will not reappear are incorporated. The importance he attributes to cultic matters in these measures reveals the contact he undoubtedly had with the circles which produced the Priestly Code. The government is theocratic rather than strictly monarchic. In other places Ezekiel looks forward to the exercise of Yahweh's kingship through a new David (34:23-24; 37:24-25; cf. 17:22-24); here, however, a succession of rulers is expected and legislation is provided to curb their selfish tendencies (45:8-9; 46:16-18).

Just as Yahweh's glory had earlier abandoned the sanctuary defiled by idolatry and infidelity, so now Ezekiel sees His glorious throne-chariot return and enter the new Temple (43:1-9). Yahweh is the source of life and well-being to His people, and the prophet sees a stream that springs forth from the threshold of the Temple and grows into a mighty river; it flows to the south, producing paradisiac abun-

---

[5]Though reworked and expanded, 38-39 probably go back to Ezekiel in substance. Whether an invasion by a specific foe is envisioned or the final apocalyptic struggle (p. 255) is disputed.

dance and fertility in the land, and makes the waters of the Dead Sea fresh (47:1–12).

The final paradox of Ezekiel's utopian vision is the capital of the restored Israel. Though centrally located it is not in the territory of any of the tribes; twelve gates, each named for one of the tribes, indicates that it pertains equally to all. It is no longer called Jerusalem, an old Canaanite name, but *Yahweh-shammah*—Yahweh is here! (48:35).

Ezekiel's idyllic conception of what the restoration would bring, when seen against his pessimistic view of Israel's previous history, is an impressive testimony to his faith in the creative power of God. Having explained how completely worthless the Chosen People had been throughout their history and how perfectly merited was the destruction of their nation, he goes on to tell of the great things God would do for them for the sake of His holy name—He would give them a new spirit and a new heart, and would enable them to serve Him in their own land again. Again we have material for a theology of grace.

DEUTERO-ISAIAH

THE MAN AND HIS TIMES. Virtually nothing is known about the great prophet who composed the oracles of Isaiah 40–55; even the title Deutero-Isaiah (Second Isaiah) is a term of convenience, for his name is unknown. The influence of Isaiah on his teaching and terminology makes it likely that he belonged to a circle that preserved and extended the teaching of the great 8th century prophet. Deutero-Isaiah prophesied during the closing years of the exile, probably from ca. 550 to 538. His mission was to raise the spirits of his fellow-countrymen with the message that deliverance was in sight, to help them overcome the temptations of Babylonian religion, and to illumine a new facet of God's redemptive work.

Babylonia's only serious rival at the beginning of the exilic period were the Medes; Babylonia's allies during the conquest of Assyria, they now held vast territories to the east and to the north. Babylonia therefore gladly encouraged Cyrus, vassal-king of Anshan in Persia, when he revolted in 556 against his Median overlords. Too late they discovered their mistake! By 550 he had taken Ecbatana, capital of the Medes, and made himself master of the empire. When he crossed the Halys to defeat Croesus, king of Lydia, in 543 and so annexed Asia Minor, Babylonia's days were clearly numbered. Cyrus was much more lenient to conquered peoples than the Semitic rulers of the Near East had been; rather than to terrorize, he wanted to be welcomed as a liberator and to conciliate his subjects.

By 539 Cyrus began his invasion of Babylonia. Within a short time the defending army was crushed at Opis on the Tigris, and the Persians took Babylon without a struggle. Not long after the fall of the capital the Babylonian lands to the border of Egypt were incorporated into the Persian empire. Cyrus' triumphant progress is reflected in many oracles of Deutero-Isaiah.

HIS MESSAGE. The earlier prophets had looked forward to the restoration as to a distant dawn of hope that would surely follow the black night of Israel's humiliation. It was Deutero-Isaiah's joy to be able to proclaim that punishment was at an end and restoration imminent. His commission is characterized in the opening lines of these chapters:

> Comfort, give comfort to my people,
> says your God.
> Speak tenderly to Jerusalem, and proclaim to her
> that her service is at an end,
> her guilt is expiated;
> Indeed, she has received from the hand of the Lord
> double for all her sins (40:1-2).

With fine poetic skill the prophet pictures a triumphant return, with God Himself leading the procession, along a highway to be constructed through the desert:

> A voice cries out:
> In the desert prepare the way of the Lord!
> Make straight in the wasteland a highway for our God!
> Every valley shall be filled in,
> every mountain and hill shall be made low;
> The rugged land shall be made a plain,
> the rough country a broad valley (40:3-4).

As in the days of the exodus, water springs up in the wilderness (43:18-21; 48:20-21; 49:8-13). This is, in fact, a new and greater exodus, a new redemptive act which is to be recalled and celebrated rather than the old one:

> Remember not the events of the past,
> the things of long ago consider not;
> See, I am doing something new! (43:18-19).

In one magnificent passage the prophet combines creation, exodus, and restoration almost as a single act of the redemptive power of God (51:9-11; see p. 51, n. 5).

The occasion for these words of assurance was the irresistible advance of Cyrus. The prophet did not see in his successes merely a fortunate circumstance that might incidentally benefit the Jews. Rather he saw Cyrus as one raised up by Yahweh precisely to release His people in fulfillment of the ancient prophecies. Like the prophets of old, Deutero-Isaiah saw foreign powers as instruments of Yahweh's will; but Cyrus, as liberator and benefactor, is given a far more sympathetic treatment than Nebuchadnezzar! Cyrus is called champion of justice, Yahweh's shepherd, and His anointed one; it is Yahweh who has commissioned the Persian and delivered lands and nations to him (41:1-4; 44:28-45:7). All of this is "for the sake of Jacob, my servant, of Israel my chosen one," that Cyrus may "say of Jerusalem, 'Let her be rebuilt' and of the Temple, 'Let its foundations be laid' " (44:28). To Cyrus Yahweh says, "you know me not" (45:5), but to Israel:

> I give Egypt as your ransom,
> Ethiopia and Seba in return for you.
> Because you are precious in my eyes
> and glorious, and because I love you.
> I give men in return for you
> and peoples in exchange for your life (43:3-4).

The restoration is described in idyllic fashion, in terms more poetic and attractive than those of Ezekiel. Desolate Jerusalem shall be made like Eden (51:3), she shall be enlarged to accommodate the multitude of those returning (54:1-3). Hosea's marriage imagery is utilized as Jerusalem is addressed in tenderest terms:

> The Lord calls you back,
> like a wife forsaken and grieved in spirit,
> A wife married in youth and then cast off,
> says your God.
> For a brief moment I abandoned you,
> but with great tenderness I will take you back.
> In an outburst of wrath, for a moment
> I hid my face from you;
> But with enduring love I take pity on you,
> says the Lord, your redeemer (54:6-8).

Paradise themes, such as the reference to Eden and to precious stones for the construction of the streets and walls of the new Jerusalem (54:11-12; cf. Ezek 28:13-14), are reminders of the theological import of the holy city; it is God's dwelling place on earth and the one focus of salvation.

Our prophet is, in fact, aware that God's concern extends beyond the Jews, and that He calls all men to look to Him for redemption. This is already implicit in the many passages which speak of all men recognizing the work of Yahweh in Israel's restoration (40:5; 41:1, 20; 45:6, 14-17). Israel's restoration is but one instance of Yahweh's lordship of all creation and history, a theme that pervades Deutero-Isaiah from end to end. Yahweh's relationship to the nations rests on His universal lordship, and Israel is the means of revealing Himself to them.

God's lordship of all men, for salvation as well as for judgment, is a logical consequence of the strict monotheism the prophet preaches—a monotheism that rejects pagan gods as simply nonexistent in a way that is not met earlier in the *OT*. Statements like "I am the first and I am the last; there is no God but me'' (44:6) are common; the challenge of Babylonian religion helped make explicit something that was present in Israel's faith from the beginning. Deutero-Isaiah frequently refers to the predictions of the earier prophets, now being so evidently fulfilled, as a proof that Yahweh rules history and as an occasion for heaping scorn on the pagan gods.[6] In 41:21-24 Yahweh summons the pagan gods to present their case, challenging them to prove themselves:

> Foretell the things that shall come afterward,
>   that we may know that you are gods!
> Do something, good or evil,
>   that will put us in awe and fear.
> Why, you are nothing and your work is nought!

In another text, addressed to ''fugitives from among the gentiles,'' an indictment of idolatry is followed by the invitation:

> Turn to me and be safe,
>   all you ends of the earth,
>   for I am God, there is no other!

and Yahweh swears by Himself:

> To me every knee shall bend;
>   by me every tongue shall swear, saying,
>   ''Only in the Lord are just deeds and power . . .'' (45:20-24).

Gentile peoples are invited to sing praise to Him (42:10-12).

Seldom if ever before[7] have the Gentiles been so explicitly accorded a share in Yahweh's saving plan. This contribution alone would be sufficient to rank Deutero-Isaiah high among the great prophets. The universalism of God's plan in no way diminishes the import of Israel's election, for it is only through Israel that the Gentiles can know and turn to God. The consequence is that Israel has a mission to the nations. This is implicit in Yahweh's command that Israel bear witness before the nations to what He has foretold and brought to pass; the pagan gods cannot produce witnesses that they have ever done this, but Yahweh can (43:9-13; 44:8). It becomes explicit in 55:3-5:

[6] E.g., 41:21-24; 42:9; 43:9-13; 44:6-8; 45:20-22; 46:8-10; 48:4-7. The important point is not that Yahweh *knows* the future but that He brings to pass what He foretells through His prophets; cf. 46:11.

[7] See, however, Isa 2:2-4 and the parallel Mic 4:1-4, which I would attribute to Isaiah (p. 174, n. 15). The matchless Isa 19:18-25 is to be judged a late composition. The position of those scholars who reject any universalism in Deutero-Isaiah seems to me to be incorrect. The ''fugitives from among the gentiles'' of 45:20 may well be Jewish remnants, but v 22 speaks of ''all the ends of the earth'' turning to Yahweh and v 23 of ''every knee'' bowing to Him (and see 42:10-12). Moreover, the Servant of the Lord has a mission to the nations as well as to Israel, being made ''a light to the nations, that my salvation may reach to the ends of the earth'' (49:6).

> I will renew with you the everlasting covenant,
>   the benefits assured to David.
> As I made him a witness to the peoples,
>   a leader and commander of nations,
> So shall you summon a nation you knew not,
>   and nations that knew you not shall run to you,
> Because of the Lord, your God,
>   the Holy One of Israel, who has glorified you.

Israel's mission to the nations comes prominently to the fore again in the so-called Servant of the Lord songs (42:1–4; 49:1–6; 50:4–9; 52:13–53:12).[8] In spite of the debates which continue to rage concerning many aspects of these passages and their precise interpretation, they are of immense importance and mark the high-point of prophetic thought.

These four poems delineate the figure of the Servant and describe his mission and its accomplishment. He is Yahweh's chosen one, the recipient of His spirit; through a ministry characterized by gentleness he will bring justice and instruction to all the earth (first song). The Servant experiences frustration, but Yahweh strengthens him and defines his task; it would be "too little" for the Servant to have a mission to Israel alone: "I will make you a light to the nations, that my salvation may reach to the ends of the earth" (second song). The Servant meets opposition; he is struck and spit upon, yet he remains confident in the knowledge of God's sustaining help (third song). The climax of the Servant's mission is reached in the fourth song. Kings and others stand in awe at the sight of what he has suffered. He was rejected, despised, unjustly condemned, and put to death; his afflictions seemed to mark him as one smitten by God, and even in burial he was reckoned among the wicked. But—now the onlookers realize—he was innocent; his suffering was for the sins of others which Yahweh laid upon him. His life was freely given as a sin-offering and wins pardon for others. The triumph of his mission the Servant now enjoys, seemingly raised again to life; he sees "the light in fulness of days" and receives his "portion among the great."

Who is the Servant thus described as laying down his life in innocent suffering so that the sins of others may be pardoned? The question here concerns the prophet's intention, not historical fulfillment. Whom did Deutero-Isaiah have in mind?

Countless interpretations have been put forward and it would be impossible to discuss them all. The oft-made suggestion that the prophet spoke of some historical individual (e.g., Moses, Jeremiah, Jehoiachin, or Deutero-Isaiah himself) founders on the fact that in Isaiah 40–55 Israel is frequently called Yahweh's "servant" (e.g., 41:8–9; 44:1–2, 21) and that in the second song the Servant is called

---

[8]Some scholars extend the first song to 42:7, the second to 49:9, and the third to 50:11. The additional lines may well be expansions or commentaries on the original songs.

"Israel" (49:3).[9] That the prophet should attribute to Israel a mission to the world accords well with what was said above.

At first glance, then, the Servant of the songs would seem to be a personification of a collectivity, i.e., of Israel. Many do hold this and see in the death and resurrection of the Servant in the fourth song a reference to the destruction of the nation and its restoration. But there are serious objections to this interpretation, too. Israel outside the songs is not depicted as steadfast in faith, obedience, and service. Quite the contrary! Israel is rebellious and insincere (43:22–28; 48:1–9) and even as servant is blind and deaf (42:19). Deutero-Isaiah could depict Israel as innocent, suffering in exile for the sins of the nations, only by rejecting the judgment of the earlier prophets, something his constant reference to fulfillment of prophecy suggests he didn't do (and cf. 42:24–25). Moreoever, since the Servant has a mission to Israel (49:5–6), he cannot be simply identified with the people. Finally, the concrete details of the description of the Servant in the fourth song seem to suit an actual person better than a collectivity.

The indications that point both to an individual and to a collectivity suggest that we are dealing with the concept of corporate personality. Ancient Semitic thought could consider a collectivity (e.g., family, tribe, nation, race) to be totally embodied in an individual (e.g., a patriarch, prophet, priest, or king) who functioned as its representative. Thus certain stories told of Jacob are also stories about the people Israel (p. 69); Israelite traits are those already found in the ancestors (Hos 12:3–7). In a sense Jacob *is* Israel and Israel *is* Jacob. The concept obviously permits a certain fluidity that is foreign to modern thought, an unmarked transition from the individual to the collectivity and back again.

In Hebrew thought, then, there is no necessary conflict between "individual" and "collectivity," and that fact gives us the key to the mystery of the Servant: he is an individual who, as Israel's representative and embodiment, fulfills Israel's mission through his innocent suffering. The Servant *is* Israel, but Israel as embodied in a single representative person.

C. R. North and H. H. Rowley, scholars who have contributed important studies on the Servant, believe there was a development in the prophet's thought. At first he simply considers historical Israel as the Servant who would fulfill the mission entrusted to it by Yahweh; but a fuller realization of Israel's need for purification, the difficulties of the mission, and the suffering it will entail, leads him to expect a future individual, supremely God's Servant, by whom Israel's mission will be accomplished. The *NT* and Christian thought has, not surpris-

---

[9]Some proponents of "historical individual" theories attempt to evade these objections by asserting that the songs are compositions by someone other than Deutero-Isaiah which have been interpolated into Isaiah 40–55, and that "Israel" in 49:3 is a gloss. Such assertions seem to be made in the interests of the theory, however, and the weight of evidence is against them.

ingly, seen this expectation fulfilled in the work of Jesus of Nazareth.
As G. W. Anderson remarks: "in spite of all uncertainties of interpretation, the anticipation in the fourth Song of the Passion of Christ
is one of the miracles of Old Testament literature."[10]

[10]*A Critical Introduction to the Old Testament* (London: Gerald Duckworth & Co.,
1959), p. 118.

READING SUGGESTIONS

JBC §21-22. *PBS* #30-32. *OTRG* #20. *AUOT* 399-422, 437-72. *BHI*
343-60. *WITOT* 197-205, 222-30.

Blenkinsopp, J., *A History of Prophecy in Israel*, pp. 177-224.
Clifford, R., *Fair Spoken and Persuading: An Interpretation of Second
Isaiah*. New York: Paulist Press, 1984.
Cody, A., *Ezekiel. OTM*, Vol. 11.
Koch, K., *The Prophets; Volume Two: The Babylonian and Persian
Periods*. Philadelphia: Fortress Press, 1984.
McKenzie, J. L., *Second Isaiah. AB* 20; Garden City, N.Y.: Doubleday &
Company, Inc. 1968.
North, C. R., *The Suffering Servant in Deutero-Isaiah*. 2nd ed.; Lon-
don: Oxford University Press, 1956.
Robinson, H. W., *Corporate Personality in Ancient Israel*. Philadelphia:
Fortress Press, 1980.
Rowley, H. H., *The Servant of the Lord*. pp. 3-93.
Scullion, J., *Isaiah 40-66. OTM*, Vol. 12.
Zimmerli, W., *Ezekiel 1*, tr. R. E. Clements. Philadelphia: Fortress Press,
1979.

Farmer, W. R., "The Geography of Ezekiel's River of Life," *BAR* 284-89.
Fishbane, M., "Sin and Judgment in the Prophecies of Ezekiel," *Int* 38
(1984) 131-50.
Freedman, D. N., "Son of Man, Can These Bones Live? (*The Exile*),"
Int 29 (1975) 171-86.
Greenberg, M., "The Design and Themes of Ezekiel's Restoration,"
Int 38 (1984) 181-208.
Lind, M. C., "Monotheism, Power and Justice: A Study in Isaiah 40-
55," *CBQ* 46 (1984) 432-46.
Wilson, R. C., "Prophecy in Crisis: The Call of Ezekiel," *Int* 38 (1984)
117-30.

16

Redemptive Themes
in the Prophets

THE DELIVERANCE from Egypt, as we have seen, formed the beginning of Israel's understanding of redemption (p. 96). Later historical experiences, especially as interpreted by the prophets and the deuteronomic writers, deepened Israel's understanding of the ethical dimension of redemption by revealing that obedience was a necessary condition for her continued relationship with God. The prophets further advanced Israel's understanding of the meaning of redemption in their teaching on the messianic restoration. We must now attempt a synthesis of their thought in this area.

In spite of individual differences and emphases, the prophets we have studied exhibit a similar pattern of ideas. Yahweh, the Lord of history, chose Israel and entered into covenant with her. Israel was unfaithful to her covenant obligations and merited the judgment that did in fact come upon her when she was exiled from her land. But the story was not to end there. The fact that God had long ago chosen and called Israel indicated a purpose, a plan, and it was inconceivable that it could be frustrated by human sin. There were also the enduring quality of God's elective love and the promises He had made to David. Beyond disaster all the prophets saw hope for the future, though in various forms and with different degrees of clarity.

The prophetic formulations of the future hope are bewildering in their variety and profusion. Hosea sees a new exodus and a return to the conditions of paradise. Isaiah's expectations are closely tied to a faithful remnant and to the reign of an ideal king, while Jeremiah thinks of a new covenant. Ezekiel has elements taken from previous prophets and adds his picture of the ideal theocracy of the future. Deutero-Isaiah uses the ''new exodus'' theme, speaks of the glory of the restored Jerusalem, extends God's plan to all nations, and sees it climaxed by the atoning work of the Servant.

In every case the restoration is pictured as something far more than a return to the *status quo ante*—something more than a return to their land and the old institutions. The prophets were thinking of the establishment of a new order in which the abuses and evils of the old order would be unthinkable. Their different approaches present different aspects of what redemption would involve; they are all valid insights even though it would be inadvisable or even impossible to try to combine all the details into one perfectly consistent picture.

The future redemption, as the prophets understood it, would eliminate the pernicious effects of human sin and sin itself and would bestow all those blessings which should flow from God's covenant with Israel. The Yahwist's story of the Garden and the Fall seems not to have been widely known until near the end of the *OT* period, for it is seldom if ever directly referred to before then. But parallel concepts of an early age of bliss and innocence were current, and the prophets use them to describe the new age. Hosea speaks of a covenant with animal nature and an end of war (Hos 2:20); Isaiah's description of the reign of the messianic king also includes a return to the conditions of paradise (Isa 11:6-9). Behind such descriptions is the conviction that sin will be eliminated in the new order and that God will again bestow the blessings that went with original innocence. Hosea's paradisiac description comes after the promise of a return to the desert where Israel will learn to respond in fidelity, and Isaiah's coincides with a kingly reign characterized by justice and faithfulness.

The expectation of blessings to come through God's covenant with David underwent considerable evolution; Nathan's oracle was subjected to reinterpretation even before the fall of the monarchy. In the covenant with its promise of an eternal dynasty and implications of covenant blessings through David's line, the prophets saw the outlines of a kingdom of justice, truth, and peace.[1] The historical kings had not been the channel of blessing they should have been, and both Isaiah and Micah, probably as early as the days of Hezekiah, look for an individual who will possess the qualities of David and in whom the dynastic promises will be realized.

Jeremiah was not deeply influenced by the theology of Jerusalem circles and his most characteristic restoration oracles make no reference to a Davidic king. Yet, even though he predicts the end of the monarchy (Jer 22:20-30), he expects it to be reestablished by a new David under whom Judah and Israel will know salvation and security (Jer 23:5-6; 30:8-9). Ezekiel also predicts, in allegory and oracle, the downfall of the Davidic dynasty and its restoration (Ezek 17:22-23; 21:32); twice he includes "David" as shepherd and prince over a restored Israel (34:23-24; 37:24-25). That such promises are given by Jeremiah and Ezekiel, prophets who otherwise exhibit no enthusiasm for the monarchy, attests to the strong influence the dynastic oracle

---

[1]Isa 11:1-9; Jer 23:5-6; Ezek 34:23-24; 37:24-25; Mic 5:1-4.

exercised on prophetic thought. Even though hope must be deferred, it is not abandoned.

The justification for the reinterpretation the oracle underwent lies in the prophets' confidence in the power of Yahweh's word to accomplish His purpose in history despite all obstacles, coupled with their progressively deeper insight into God's nature and His plan. His intention could not ultimately be the creation of a privileged political power; the reign of the Davidic king, His son by adoption, must be as broad as creation and must rest on those virtues required by Yahweh.

Hosea, Jeremiah, and Ezekiel hark back to the older Sinai tradition of election when they make a new or renewed covenant the basis of the new order.[2] Deutero-Isaiah attains a sort of synthesis by extending David's covenant to the whole people: "I will renew with you the everlasting covenant, the benefits assured to David"; by this means Israel will be made the leader and rallying point of the nations turning to Yahweh (Isa 55:3–5).

Deutero-Isaiah's Servant is in many respects a parallel concept to the Davidic Messiah. Both are corporate personalities who can represent the whole people before God; both are associated with the establishment of God's justice and his reign over all men; each stands as head of the people of the new order.[3] But in that the Servant is the very instrument of God's redemptive work, in that this work consists primarily in deliverance from sin, and in that this is accomplished through suffering, the Servant concept differs notably from that of the Davidic Messiah. It is no doubt significant that Deutero-Isaiah does not mention the Davidic king; for him the Servant theme is a different, profounder approach to redemption.

It is hardly surprising that the *OT* presents no satisfactory synthesis of the two figures. Later Jewish speculation was not notably successful, either. One famous Aramaic paraphrase (Targum) of Isaiah 53 identifies the Servant as the Messiah, but so far perverts the teaching of the song as to relieve the Servant of the burden of death and sin-bearing; 53:8 becomes, in part: "for he will remove the dominion of the Gentiles from the land of Israel, and transfer to them the sins my people have committed." Jewish literature knows of a Messiah who will die in the final apocalyptic struggle, but he is the "Messiah son of Joseph," distinguished from the "Messiah son of David." Jewish interpretation generally sees the Servant as a purely collective figure—Israel or some segment of it.

Nothing is more logical than the prophetic expectation of a reunited Israel,[4] though at first glance it seems the most patently unfulfilled

---

[2]Hos 2:16–22; Jer 31:31–34; Ezek 34:25; 37:26.

[3]For the Davidic king this is obvious; for the Servant it is implied in Isa 53:10, 12.

[4]Ezek 37:15–22; Hos 2:2; Jer 3:18; 31:2–6. N.B. In this and the following notes, no attempt is made to distinguish later oracles from the authentic words of the prophets in whose books they are found. See p. 160, n. 2.

and unfulfillable of the *OT* prophecies. The separation of Israel from Judah was, of course, a terrible thing; almost two hundred years afterwards Isaiah cited the schism as an example of the worst imaginable sort of calamity (Isa 7:17). It arose from oppression, occasioned a deep religious rift, and weakened the two parts so that neither could stand in security. The new order, in which the ills of the past are to be remedied, would of necessity include a healing of this age old separation, or so the prophets said. Large numbers of Israelites continued to live in the northern territory after the fall of Samaria, and as long as Judah stood there was always the possibility of unification. Hezekiah's and Josiah's reforms did have some success among them, but this would hardly have satisfied the prophets' expectation of reunion. With the fall of Judah, such hopes seemed impossible of fulfillment.

Yet the prophetic hope grew far beyond its original limits; not only was there to be a gathering together and a return of the dispersed exiles of the north (Jer 31:15-22) and of the south (Ezek 34:11-13) and a reunion under one head, but the nations, too, were to be gathered into unity with Israel in one faith under Yahweh.[5] Thus the question of the unity of the new order was raised to a broader and higher plane. When Israel, now represented by the survivors of Judah and the remnants of the northern tribes that had joined them before 587, emerged from the exile, she was and remained a unified faith and people. This unity was maintained, however, only by rejecting the Samaritans, descendants of the somewhat mixed population of the northern territories, though they claimed to be worshipers of Yahweh (Ezra 4:1-3), and by a rigid policy against marriage with foreigners (Ezra 9-10; Neh 13:23-30). The perfect establishment of unity was not yet; it would be achieved only when unity in one faith could include all—Jews, Samaritans, and Gentiles.

We have, then, a number of themes which express prophetic expectations of the new order: expiation of and deliverance from sin and its effects, a new heart, the gift of God's spirit, a new exodus event, a new and eternal covenant, a kingdom of justice and peace in which the Gentiles share, and a return to the conditions of paradise. Taken together they spell the perfect establishment of God's kingdom, a new order of salvation and redemption. Though the prophets express themselves in figures and symbols, it would be a mistake to translate these into purely abstract, spiritual realities and so strip their message of its concrete aspects. The many who today equate salvation simply with "going to heaven" are out of touch with biblical thought and suppose that only the soul, not the total human person, is worth saving. The prophets saw mankind in its concrete reality and knew that it was here that redemption had to be realized; unless the disorders within the individual, the disorders of society, the disorders between

[5]Isa 2:2-4; 19:18-25; 45:20-23; 56:6-8; 66:18-21; Jer 16:19-21; Zech 8:20-23; 14:16-19.

nations, were set right, redemption would be incomplete—and God's work cannot be less than complete. Ultimately *complete* redemption would call for personal immortality through bodily resurrection; this stage of belief was reached only late in the *OT* period, but it is perfectly consonant with prophetic thought: what God could do for the nation (cf. Ezek 37:1–14; Isa 26:19) He can also do for the individual.

The return of the Jews from the exile brought only a very partial fulfillment of these expectations. The people survived, Israel was restored to her own land, Jerusalem and the Temple were rebuilt—with much toil and no precious stones! The new order expected by the prophets was not in evidence (cf. Zech 1:7–17). Had they been wrong? The disappointments of the restored community were occasioned by what is often called the prophets' lack of temporal perspective. The promises of earlier prophets (e.g., Hosea and Isaiah), though they envisioned salvation beyond tragedy, had not been tied to this particular historical situation. But Jeremiah, Ezekiel, and Deutero-Isaiah, in foretelling restoration from the Babylonian captivity, expected that the new order would be inaugurated then. The error lay not in the expectation of a new order but in the assumption that its inauguration was tied to the return from exile.

Only with the passage of time did it become evident that this separation of the elements of prophetic promise could and should be made. Hope was deferred, but it was not abandoned; from these "small beginnings" great things would still come (Zech 4:10; Hag 2:3–9). The "when" of all this continued to be a troublesome question, especially in times of persecution. For example, Daniel 9 is an attempt to reinterpret Jeremiah's "seventy years" (Dan 9:2) during the persecution of Antiochus IV (175–163). The author expects the establishment of God's kingdom to coincide with the end of the persecution: "transgression will stop and sin will end, guilt will be expiated, everlasting justice will be introduced, vision and prophecy ratified, and a most holy will be anointed . . ." (9:24). Again hope had to be deferred.

When Jesus appeared proclaiming the advent of God's kingdom, then, those He addressed knew of what He spoke. Here was the greatest of the prophets proclaiming and bringing fulfillment of prophecy. In His work and person the *NT* writers see a wonderful convergence of all the *OT* themes of redemption.

Jesus Himself was very reserved about the title "Messiah"; the image of a triumphant king ruling over Israel and subjecting the nations to his dominion à la Psalm 2, for example, did not correspond well with His conception of His mission. The only time He could be said (on a critical reading of the gospels) to have claimed messianic dignity was on Palm Sunday, when He acted out Zechariah's prophecy of a humble savior:

> Rejoice heartily, O daughter Zion,
>   shout for joy, O daughter Jerusalem!
> See, your king shall come to you;

> a just savior is he,
> Meek, and riding on an ass,
> on a colt, the foal of an ass (Zech 9:9).

Jesus preferred to explain His mission in terms of Deutero-Isaiah's Servant. He believed His passion had been foretold in the *OT* (Mark 9:11; 14:21), and the gospel pattern of rejection, suffering, death, and resurrection (Mark 8:31; 9:29–30; 10:32–34) corresponds closely to the fourth Servant song. Like the Servant, His life was to be given as a ransom for many (Mark 10:45) and He was to be reckoned with the wicked (Luke 22:37).

The completion of Jesus' mission as Servant brought with it the Servant's triumph. In His resurrection and exaltation to God's right hand the *NT* writers see the bestowal of the kingly dignity He had not grasped at during His ministry (e.g., Acts 2:30–36; Heb 10:12–13).[6]

His inauguration of the kingdom of God brings with it the new age, but again, the course of events reveals the need to distinguish successive stages. Through His death and resurrection atonement and pardon are granted, and through the law of love and the gift of the Spirit the means of transforming human life and human society are bestowed—means all too imperfectly utilized. The perfect establishment of God's reign, however, according to Christian belief, awaits the return of Christ on the Day of the Lord.

[6]On Jesus' use of the title Son of Man, see p. 256, n. 6.

READING SUGGESTIONS

Gray, J., *The Biblical Doctrine of the Reign of God.* Edinburgh: T. & T. Clark, 1979.

Klausner, J., *The Messianic Idea in Israel.,* tr. W. F. Stinespring, New York: Macmillan, 1955.

Mowinckel, S., *He That Cometh*, tr. G. W. Anderson. Oxford: Basil Blackwell, 1959.

Vawter, B., *The Conscience of Israel*, pp. 289-95.

Grassi, J., "The Transforming Power of Biblical Heart Imagery," *Review for Religious* 43 (1984) 714-23.

Hoffnung, A., "Redemption in the Bible," *Dor le Dor* 10 (1982) 229-33.

King, P. J., "Hosea's Message of Hope," *BTB* 12 (1982) 91-95.

Lemke, W. E., "Life in the Present and Hope in the Future," *Int* 38 (1984) 165-80.

McKenzie, J. L., "Royal Messianism," *Myths and Realities*, 203-231.

Noth, M., "God, King and Nation in the Old Testament," *The Laws of the Pentateuch and Other Essays*, pp. 145-78.

Potter, H. D., "The New Covenant in Jeremiah xxxi 31-34," *Vetus Testamentum* 33 (1983) 347-57.

Vawter, B., "The God of the Hebrew Scriptures," *BTB* 12 (1982) 3-7.

17

The Restoration

(Recommended Scripture reading: Ezra 1; 3-7; Nehemiah 1-2; 4-5; 8; 13; Haggai 1-2; Zechariah 1-3; 6; Isaiah 56; 58-64)

IN 538, within a year of his conquest of Babylon, Cyrus gave the Jews permission to return to their homeland. The Bible preserves two documents issued by Cyrus which record the details. The first (Ezra 1:2-4) was a proclamation to be published among the exiles and was written, therefore, in Hebrew. It gave permission to return and to rebuild the Temple and provided that those who remained behind could contribute to the work. The second (Ezra 6:3-5) was an archival memorandum in Aramaic, the official language of the Persian empire. It provided that the cost of rebuilding the Temple be paid from the royal treasury and prescribed its dimensions. The provisions of both documents accord well with Cyrus' policies as known from non-biblical sources. In one cylinder text, for example, Cyrus attributes his victory to the gods of Babylon and tells of how he restored the worship, images, and shrines not only of them but also of the gods of many other regions (*ANET* 315-316).

Not all of the exiles chose to return to Palestine. Even those who had been teen-agers in 587 were now in their sixties; the younger ones had never seen or at least would hardly remember the land of their fathers. Many had found so comfortable and prosperous an existence in Babylonia that they were loath to leave; if they felt they were taking the line of least resistance, their contributions undoubtedly eased the pangs of conscience. The diaspora, here, in Egypt,[1] and elsewhere, had become a permanent feature of Judaism.

Those who did return did not all set out in 538. The return was

---

[1]Especially noteworthy was the large Jewish colony established at Elephantine in Egypt during the 7th and 6th century. Much is known of the colony thanks to the recovery of many papyri from the Persian period. The Jews there had a temple of their own and seem to have practiced a syncretistic form of Yahwism.

made in successive waves.[2] The first group seems to have been quite small; it was led by Sheshbazzar, "prince of Judah" (probably one of the sons of Jehoiachin), who functioned as governor over them when they reached Palestine. What disillusionment and disappointments met them in the land of hope! The radiant promises of the prophets hardly prepared them for the ruined cities and the poverty-stricken land they found. The land had never been completely depopulated, it is true, but the ones who had stayed on probably did not welcome with open arms those now returning to reclaim family property; and their syncretistic brand of Yahwism must have shocked the more orthodox faith of the returnees. Further difficulties arose from the hostility displayed by neighboring peoples.

The biblical accounts for the period are rather complicated and possibly disarranged, so it is difficult to reconstruct the period with certainty. We can be sure the altar of holocausts was rebuilt almost at once and the official cult resumed. Shortly later the foundations for the new Temple were laid. But after this vigorous start the work began to languish. The need to raise food and build houses for themselves, coupled with drought, poor crops, disappointment, and indifference, was certainly part of the reason (Hag 1:2–11). The account in Ezra 4:1–5, however, stresses opposition from the Samaritans. They asked to join the work on the Temple on the plea that they, too, worshiped Yahweh; but they became openly hostile when rudely rebuffed. Zerubbabel, grandson of Jehoiachin, succeeded Sheshbazzar as governor of Judah sometime between 538 and 522; Joshua, the high priest, appears along with him in the earliest references.

The Work of Haggai and Zechariah; Trito-Isaiah

The failure of the new community to rebuild the Temple was a serious set-back to their religious life. For one thing, the old inhabitants of the land practised a cult that included many pagan elements, and those newly returned, without a focus for their stricter Yahwistic faith, were subjected to the old temptations of the nature cults (Isa 57:3–13; 65:1–7). For another, many of the messianic promises of the prophets were tied to the Temple; without it, languishing hopes could not burn brightly again. But now two prophets appeared; at the moment of their appearance the world situation seemed to augur better things for the Jews.

When Cyrus died in 530, his son Cambyses became king. Under him, in 525, Egypt was added to the Persian empire. On the road

---

[2]The Bible mentions four separate groups led by the following men: Sheshbazzar (ca. 538); Zerubbabel (sometime before 522); Ezra (458); and Nehemiah (445).

home from Egypt in 522, he received word that a usurper had seized his throne. Cambyses, for reasons unknown, took his own life; thereupon Darius, an officer of royal blood, proclaimed himself king. Darius put down the usurper but then had to face rebellions throughout his vast territories. The period of 522-520 was one of turmoil, one in which it seemed likely the empire would fall.

It was toward the end of this period that the prophet Haggai appears; his oracles, precisely dated, fall within a four-month period in 520. He chides the Jews for busying themselves about their own affairs while neglecting the Temple, urging that this neglect was the cause of their problems (Hag 1:1-12). Nothing could be more indicative of the change in prophecy since the days of the monarchy. In pre-exilic times the prophets with one voice had criticized the people's naive trust in the externals of religion, seeming to condemn the cult itself because of the empty dispositions with which it was offered. But now the cult was essential if the people were to survive as a religious community, and the prophets rallied to the cause. Moved by Haggai's exhortation, Zerubbabel, Joshua, and the people set to work. It had been eighteen years since the return of the first group of exiles but the work on the Temple had not progressed beyond the foundations. Even when completed the new Temple would be but a modest structure compared to the grand one raised by Solomon, but Haggai promised that its future glory would be greater (2:1-9). The situation in the Persian empire undoubtedly encouraged him to think that the time was near when Yahweh would shake the heavens, the earth, and the nations (2:6-7, 21-22).

The prophet Zechariah, too, helped promote the building of the Temple. He appears slightly later than Haggai, their dated oracles overlapping by a month. Not all of the collection named for Zechariah comes from this 6th century prophet; his authentic oracles are found in Zechariah 1-8, while Zechariah 9-14 come from an anonymous 4th century prophet usually referred to as Deutero-Zechariah. Zechariah contrasts with the rather prosaic Haggai, for his revelations came to him in strange and mysterious visions that approach developed apocalyptic (p. 253). Early in his ministry it must have been evident that Darius had mastered his enemies, for the first of the visions reflects the disappointment that the upheavals had passed without ushering in the new order; but the prophet adds words of comfort, promising God's mercy and blessing for Jerusalem (1:7-17). He promises that Zerubbabel will complete the Temple and that the "day of small beginnings" is a herald of a glorious future (1:16; 4:9-10). The Temple was completed and solemnly dedicated in 515 (Ezra 6:14-18).

Both Haggai and Zechariah seem to have expected the Davidic dynasty to be restored in Zerubbabel, the heir-apparent to David's throne. On the day of Yahweh's intervention, says Haggai, He will make Zerubbabel, His chosen one, like a signet ring (Hag 2:20-23)—a reference to Jer 22:24, where the downfall of the dynasty was foretold under the image of a signet ring (Jehoiachin) being plucked off. Zechariah seems actually to have crowned Zerubbabel and to have addressed him by the messianic title "Shoot"[3] (Zech 6:9–15; cf. 3:8; Isa 4:2; Jer 23:5; 33:15). But, although a descendant of David was again ruling a remnant of Israel in their own land, there was no restoration of the monarchy. The trouble was, of course, that the new Israel was a small part of a mighty empire and they enjoyed only the degree of independence their overlords saw fit to grant them; their leaders ruled only by the sufferance of the king of Persia—and no leave had been given to restore the monarchy.

It has been conjectured that Zerubbabel was deposed from his governorship or even executed for what might have seemed an act of rebellion to the Persians; this is possible but is far from certain. At any rate, Zerubbabel disappears from the scene shortly after the events related. Henceforth the internal affairs of the Jews are governed by Joshua and his successors in the high priesthood, while the political affairs were looked after by a governor appointed by the Persian court. The expectations attached to Zerubbabel by Haggai and Zechariah reveal the constancy of the Davidic hope but show little sign of the reinterpretation and deepened understanding of it already found in earlier prophets.

It is probably to the decades after 538 that most of the material in Isaiah 56–66 is to be dated. This collection, exhibiting many contacts with Deutero-Isaiah, is designated Trito-Isaiah (or Third Isaiah). These chapters appear to be of mixed authorship, probably by disciples of Deutero-Isaiah; some of the oracles may be from Deutero-Isaiah himself, now back in Palestine.

The collection reflects the difficulties and disappointments as well as the firm hopes of the postexilic community. The sins of the people are exposed and rebuked (57:3–13; 58; 59:1–15; 65:1–7) and are cited as the reason for the delay of the expected salvation (59:1–2). Nevertheless fervent prayers are to be offered to God until His word has been fulfilled:

> O you who are to remind the Lord,
>   take no rest
> And give no rest to him,
>   until he re-establishes Jerusalem
> And makes of it
>   the pride of the earth (62:7).

But promises of Jerusalem's future glory, like those of Deutero-Isaiah, also form an important part of these chapters (60; 62; 66:7–16).

---

[3]The name of Joshua the high priest now stands in Zech 6:9–15, but virtually all critics agree that the account originally told of the crowning of Zerubbabel. The later substitution of Joshua in the text reflects the prominence in fact obtained by the high priesthood during the postexilic period.

The postexilic emphasis on the Law is reflected in Trito-Isaiah in diverse ways. For example, in the universalistic oracle of 56:1-8 the inclusion of foreigners in the community is conditioned on their keeping of the Sabbath and other covenant observances. Yet ritualism is not an end in itself; fasts and other practices are of no avail unless they are accompanied by obedience to the deeper demands of justice and charity (58).

Trito-Isaiah includes passages that in beauty and profundity rival Deutero-Isaiah. For example, there are the consoling promises to Jerusalem in 60-62, so like some passages in Isaiah 40-55. The haunting beauty and moving eloquence of the psalm of lamentation in 63:7-64:11 has seldom been surpassed. The oracle concerning a "new heavens and a new earth" that Yahweh will create (65:17-25) emphasizes the completeness of the scope of His redemptive work, but at the same time puts it outside history into the eschatological age (p. 254).

EZRA AND NEHEMIAH;
THE WORK OF THE CHRONICLER

Two very important figures in the postexilic community, from around the middle of the 5th century and later, are Ezra and Nehemiah. Our principal source of information on their careers are the *OT* books named for them; but because of the problems these books present, it will be necessary to go into the broader literary complex of which they are a part.

Ezra and Nehemiah form the concluding section of an extensive historical work begun in 1-2 Chronicles; the author is designated, for convenience, as the Chronicler. The whole complex (1-2 Chronicles-Ezra-Nehemiah) is comparable to the deuteronomic corpus, though the scopes and purposes of the two differ considerably. The Chronicler's history might be said to go back to creation, for it begins with Adam; but the period from Adam to the beginning of Israel's monarchy is covered almost exclusively by genealogies, special emphasis being given to the lineages of David and of the Levites (1 Chronicles 1-8). Detailed coverage begins only with the accession of David, and from this point the narrative closely parallels Samuel and Kings except for certain changes that advance the Chronicler's particular ends (see below). The narrative of Chronicles extends to the fall of Jerusalem (2 Chronicles 36). No new details of the exile are given, but the history of the postexilic community is taken up in Ezra-Nehemiah. Here the Chronicler utilized, in addition to other sources, autobiographical memoirs written by Ezra and Nehemiah; however, since the division of this section of the work into two books (Ezra and Nehemiah) is late and artificial, their contents do not simply reflect the careers of these two men.

Ezra 1–6 tells of the decree of Cyrus, the return of the first group from exile, and the history of the new community until after the dedication of the Temple in 515. Hereafter the narrative of Ezra-Nehemiah is concerned with the work of Ezra and Nehemiah, and it is here that serious chronological problems have been raised. The narrative introduces first Ezra and his work (Ezra 7–10), then Nehemiah (Nehemiah 1–7), then returns to Ezra (Nehemiah 8–10), then goes back to Nehemiah (Neh 12:27–13:31). Moreover, on occasion the two of them are mentioned together (cf. Neh 8:9; 12:26, 36). Nevertheless, the Nehemiah memoirs seem not to have been part of the Chronicler's original work and many have argued that their present location in the text, coming only after the introduction of Ezra, gives a false impression. There is no doubt that Nehemiah's first mission, commencing in the twentieth year of Artaxerxes I (464–423), began in 445 B.C. Since Ezra is introduced earlier, in the seventh year of Artaxerxes, he would appear to have come to Palestine in 458, thirteen years before Nehemiah. However, because much of Ezra's work seems to suppose the successful conclusion of the reforms attributed to Nehemiah, it has often been urged that Ezra must be dated either to the thirty-seventh year of Artaxerxes I (supposing there is a scribal error in the text), i.e., in 428, or to the seventh year of Artaxerxes II (404–360), i.e., in 398.[4] More recently, however, F. M. Cross, utilizing material from a variety of sources, has argued convincingly that the traditional order, first Ezra and then Nehemiah, and the date for Ezra's coming most obviously suggested by the biblical texts, the seventh year of Artaxerxes I (458), is in fact correct.[5] Based on this position, the following reconstruction of events can be given.

Ezra, characterized as "a scribe, well-versed in the law of Moses" (Ezra 7:6), was commissioned by the Persian king to regularize Jewish religious observance in Palestine in accordance with the law he brought with him; ample powers were given for implementing this commission (Ezra 7). Surprising as it may seem, Persian kings did concern themselves with the religious affairs of subject peoples as the "Passover Papyrus" of Elephantine demonstrates (*ANET* 491). No doubt regulation of such affairs contributed to peace within the empire. What exactly was "the law of Moses" that Ezra brought with him cannot be stated with certainty, though it was probably the Pentateuch in a form close to that in which we now have it.

On the Feast of Booths (Tabernacles), about two months after his arrival, Ezra assembled the Jewish community and expounded to them the law of Moses. The people were moved to tears by the reading of the law; they gathered branches and palms from the country-side, constructed shelters from them, and celebrated the week-long festival in the manner the Law prescribed (Nehemiah 8).

---

[4]For a fuller discussion of the problem and of the case for a date of 428 for Ezra, see *BHI*, 392–403.

[5]F. M. Cross, "A Reconstruction of the Judean Restoration," *JBL* 94 (1975) 4–18.

Ezra then turned his attention to the danger which had arisen from the introduction of foreign elements into the restored people. We have seen that the returned exiles had rejected the claims of the Samaritans to share their religion; the Jewish community consisted only of the exiles and those who embraced their strict form of Yahwism (Ezra 6:21). Now contamination threatened from another direction, for Jews were marrying foreigners. No doubt Ezra felt that the offspring of such unions, forbidden by Deut 7:1-4, would be unlikely to maintain strict Jewish faith, and that Jewish national identity was at stake. By manifestations of his own distress and by public acts of penance, Ezra moved the leaders of the people to solemnly promise to put away foreign wives and their children (Ezra 9-10). We can but imagine the heartbreak on both sides this drastic step must have entailed.

After a ceremony of atonement (Nehemiah 9), the people solemnly renewed the covenant, swearing "to follow the law of God which was given through Moses the servant of God, and to observe carefully all the commandments of the Lord" (Neh 10:29). In addition to this general declaration, they bound themselves to avoid marriage with foreigners, observe the Sabbath, support the Temple, and pay the tithe, among other things (Neh 10:31-39).

Later Jewish tradition regarded Ezra as a sort of second Moses, the one who decisively influenced the faith and practice of the restored Israel. Ezra certainly did determine the direction taken by the restored community. The forms of the past, whether tribal league or monarchy, could not be revived; a new one had to be found if Israel was to survive. That new form Ezra gave it, making religious law and observance the basis of Jewish life to a degree it had never been before. Although there were dangers inherent in this emphasis on the Law—concerned largely with externals and fostering an exclusive spirit—it is doubtful whether without it Judaism could have withstood the stresses to which it was then subject.

Nehemiah's mission began as follows. Although a Jew, he held a high position in the Persian court; it was there that in 445 he was distressed by a report of the sad plight of the Jewish community in Palestine (Nehemiah 1). The full report probably told of the opposition and harassment from neighboring peoples, of the Jews' attempt to rebuild Jerusalem's walls as a measure of self-defense, and of the successful intervention of the Samaritan officials, with Persian approval, by force of arms (Ezra 4:7-23). It may also have told of religious apathy in the restored community such as that reflected in the prophecy of Malachi.

Nehemiah obtained authorization from the king to go to Palestine to rebuild Jerusalem (Neh 2:1-8). His first task was to restore the city walls, and this he proceeded to do in spite of threats and harassment; opposition continued to come from the local officials of Samaria, Ammon, and other territories (Sanballat, Tobiah, and Geshem are named—Neh 2:10, 19)—even though some of them appear to have been Yahwists. An index of their hostility is seen in the fact that the Jews had to take elaborate defensive measures throughout the work of rebuilding (Nehemiah 4). Even after the walls had been rebuilt, Jerusalem was so badly underpopulated that Nehemiah induced the Jews to cast lots to choose one person in every ten to live in the city (Neh 11:1-2). Another of Nehemiah's reform measures was to persuade rich Jews to remit to the poor crushing debts that made life impossible for them (Nehemiah 5).

In 432 Nehemiah returned to his post at the Persian court, but after a time he was back in Judah to continue his reform work (Nch 13:6-31). Among other things, he enforced observance of the Sabbath and, like Ezra, exerted himself against mixed marriages, apparently a recurrent problem. Thus to some extent Ezra and Nehemiah directed their activities to some of the same ends, even though they exercised independent ministries and their methods were quite different. On the matter of foreign wives, for example, Ezra rent his garments, prayed, and wept (Ezra 9:1-10:1), while Nehemiah cursed and assaulted the offenders (Neh 13:23-27). Each, in his own way, helped the Jews of the restoration community acquire a sense of identity: Ezra, through his emphasis on the law, helped them see themselves as the ideal Israel encamped at the foot of Mt. Sinai, obedient to the Lord and heirs to the Holy Land; Nehemiah, by rebuilding and repopulating Jerusalem, gave them again one of the great symbols of Israel's past, one connected with its greatness both politically and religiously.

THE CHRONICLER'S TEACHING. As we have already seen, 1-2 Chronicles and Ezra–Nehemiah are parts of a single historical work. Jewish tradition names Ezra as its author, but, although his memoirs became part of the final work, the complete explanation is more complicated. For a long period many scholars placed its composition between 400-300 B.C., but Cross now provides what is probably a better founded explanation. We will say more of this toward the end of the discussion.

In fashioning the Ezra-Nehemiah complex, the Chronicler incorporated a number of documents contemporary with the events and so preserved valuable historical sources. In addition, he provided almost the only direct information we have on the restoration. 1-2 Chronicles is less valuable as an historical work. For the most part this composition tells of events already covered in Samuel and Kings, often reproducing their text word for word; when it does depart from the text of these older books, its own version is suspect. There was a time when all such departures were attributed to the Chronicler's imagination. Now it has been demonstrated that he sometimes provides reliable information not elsewhere preserved. Each case must be evaluated on its own merits. Though the Chronicler never names his sources when he quotes Samuel or Kings, he does cite other sources under a bewildering variety of titles (cf., e.g., 1 Chr 9:1; 29:29; 2 Chr

9:29; 12:15)—all of which *may* refer to different sections of a single, popular historical composition.

When the Chronicler follows Samuel or Kings, we are able to see how he uses his sources. He sometimes transcribes them verbatim, sometimes omits long sections, sometimes freely rewrites.[6] This would be a scandalous procedure if he were aiming simply to write history, but he is not; after all, the story of the monarchy had already been told in the books he used. His concern is centered, rather, in the community of his own time. The history of Israel's monarchy interests him because it is relevant to this community in its present existence and its hopes for the future, and he tells the story in a way that makes the relevance clear.

His special concerns are revealed by the space he devotes to David (1 Chronicles 11–29). For the Chronicler, the ideal Israel is a theocratic community worshiping Yahweh in the Temple through liturgy faultlessly performed, ruled by a king who is truly Yahweh's vicar. The origin of this community he sees in the reign of David, who is presented as founder not only of the monarchy and Israel's greatness, but also of the Temple and its worship. As in 2 Samuel, David conceives the plan of building a Temple and obtains the site on which it was eventually built (1 Chronicles 17; 21:1–22:1); but Chronicles also pictures him gathering the materials which will be needed (22:2–19) and organizing its personnel from the priests to the gatekeepers (23–26). Before his death David solemnly commissions Solomon to build the Temple (28–29). How different from David's "last will and testament" in 1 Kgs 2:1–9!

Nevertheless, there is justification for making David the founder of the Temple liturgy. His reputation as a singer and composer of psalms was undoubtedly deserved and accords well with the historical narratives (1 Sam 16:14–23; 2 Sam 1:17–27; 3:33–34). He did in fact bring the Ark to Jerusalem with great solemnity and established a shrine for it on the site of the future Temple. Many elements of the liturgy there established were undoubtedly taken into that of the Temple when it had been built. Idealization and exaggeration, yes; pure imagination, no! The new community, restorer of the Temple and its liturgy, is the legitimate successor of the Davidic monarchy and heir to its blessings and promises.

With the realization of this there can still be hope for better days to come. David is idealized not only as founder of the theocratic community, but also because he was founder of the messianic dynasty. To this end everything that would reflect discredit on him is omitted—his career as an outlaw, his struggle for the kingship, his adultery with Bathsheba, his family troubles, etc. Nathan's oracle, with its promise

---

[6]The rewritings and additions are often in the interest of a rigid doctrine of retribution. Thus, e.g., Joash led an exemplary life, yet died by assassination according to 2 Kings 12; the account in 2 Chronicles 24, however, tells of apostasy by Joash that makes his violent end appear merited.

that the throne of David's son would be established forever (1 Chr 17:11-14), is repeated, but certain slight modifications indicate that it has abiding significance as a messianic text. The general reference to David's offspring now becomes individualized as "one of your sons"; the immediate reference would be to Solomon, but the promise goes far beyond anything fulfilled in him. There is now no suggestion of sinful behavior that would bring punishment as in 2 Sam 7:14, and the house and kingdom in which David's son is to be established is called God's rather than David's. God's promises remained sure and the future would see them fulfilled. The splendors of David were, in the Chronicler's thought, more than a memory of the past, more than a legitimation of the postexilic community. They were a pledge for the future to a community that remained open to God's continued work among them.

Cross's reconstruction, referred to above (see n. 5), postulates that the Chronicler's work as we now have it went through three stages of development. The earliest would have consisted of most of what is now 1-2 Chronicles, with its emphasis on the Davidic dynasty and the Temple; this first edition would have been composed between the laying of the foundation of the second Temple (520) and its completion (515) and would have been intended "to give urgency and meaning to the tasks at hand," namely, the restoration of Davidic rule (see above on Haggai and Zechariah) and the restoration of the Temple and its cult. The second stage would have been about half a century later with the addition of the account of Ezra's work; the expectation of a renewal of the dynasty is no longer in evidence, but is replaced by emphasis on the Law. Finally, toward 400 B.C. a final editor inserted Nehemiah's memoirs and added the genealogies of 1 Chronicles 1-9 to give us the extensive amalgam we now call the Chronicler's history.

READING SUGGESTIONS

JBC §23-24. *PBS* #33. *OTRG* #21. *AUOT* 471-501. *BHI* 360-403. *WBA* 202-211. *WITOT* 205-208, 267-72, 275-77, 317-28.

Ackroyd, P. R., *Exile and Restoration.* Philadelphia: Westminster Press, 1968.

Blenkinsopp, J., *A History of Prophecy in Israel*, pp. 225-80.

Kaiser, W. C., *Malachi: God's Unchanging Love.* Grand Rapids: Baker Book House, 1984.

Kodell, J., *Haggai, Malachi, Obadiah, Baruch, Joel, Lamentations, Zechariah. OTM*, Vol. 14.

Mangan, C., *Ezra, Nehemiah, 1-2 Chronicles. OTM*, Vol. 13.

Myers, J. M., *The World of the Restoration.* Englewood Cliffs, N.J.: Prentice-Hall, Inc., 1968.

Ackroyd, P. R., "The History of Israel in the Exilic and Post-exilic Periods," *ATI* 328-50.

Bossman, D., "Ezra's Marriage Reform: Israel Redefined," *BTB* 9 (1979) 32-38.

Collins, J. J., "The Message of Malachi," *TBT* 22, 4 (July, 1984) 209-215.

Cross, F. M. "A Reconstruction of the Judean Restoration," *JBL* 94 (1975) 4-18; reprinted in *Int* 29 (1975) 187-204.

Goldingay, J., "The Chronicler as a Theologian," *BTB* 5 (1975) 99-126.

Hoppe, L. J., "The School of Isaiah," *TBT* 23,2 (Mar., 1985) 85-89.

Kraeling, E. G., "New Light on the Elephantine Colony," *BAR* 128-44.

Newsome, J. D., Jr., "Toward a New Understanding of the Chronicler and His Purpose," *JBL* 94 (1975) 201-17.

Petersen, D. L., "Zechariah's Visions: A Theological Perspective," *Vetus Testamentum* 34 (1984) 195-206.

Polan, G. J., "Salvation in the Midst of Struggle," *TBT* 23, 2 (Mar., 1985) 90-97.

Vawter, B., "Postexilic Prayer and Hope," *CBQ* 37 (1975) 460-70.

18

The Songs of Israel

THE FORMATION of a people, as we have had occasion to note, is not an incidental byproduct of God's redemptive work in history but the indispensible goal of that work. So also the liturgy of the people is not an incidental, dispensible byproduct but an essential activity. Redemptive history involves a dialogue between covenant partners, a dialogue that proceeds through call and response. In the liturgy God's people, gathered in community, offer their response of praise, adoration, and thanksgiving, express contrition for failures, and make known their needs in petition. An adequate response, of course, must be a total response and must engage every member of the community in his or her whole being and in every phase of his or her life. For this reason the response of the liturgy is but a beginning, an earnest of what is to be rendered to God by each in his work, social contacts, etc. Beginnings, however, are not to be despised. Liturgy consists of words and symbols, it is true, but words and symbols which express—or even help create—dispositions of the heart. Response which ended there would be sterile, indeed; that this sometimes happens is the fault of shallow human nature and is not a necessary result of external worship. Without the community liturgy, few could make even the beginning of a response.

That Israel's full response to God's saving acts was far from perfect is the admission of her own literature; with a frankness without parallel among other peoples she tells of constant infidelity to her God. Not that the nations were innocent! While they still worshiped idols and sought only the blessings that nature can give, Israel, through election and grace, was learning the just demands of the one God—and her own weakness. Though the prophets eloquently tell us that Israel's response fell short of God's demands, the Psalms reveal religious dispositions that are profound and beautiful—Israel's response of adoration and gratitude for God's love and benefits. These inspired songs were composed as vehicles of worship for God's people and possess a beauty and simplicity that have not dulled even after thousands of years of use. No other compositions have replaced them and none are likely to.

HEBREW POETRY

Many parts of the *OT,* including some we have studied, are poetic compositions; e.g., most of the prophetic oracles and some passages in the historical books. The wisdom books (Chapter 19) are mainly verse compositions, some (especially Job) of high poetic quality. A proper appreciation of the Psalms and these other *OT* compositions requires some understanding of the Hebrew verse form in which they are written.

Unlike much modern verse, Hebrew verse is not characterized by rhyme or regular meter,[1] but by rhythmic beat and parallelism. The basic unit is the verse or line, which usually consists of two, though sometimes three or even four, stichs (also called cola);[2] a stich may contain from two to four stressed syllables. The commonest verse form is two stichs of three accents each (3/3). The 3/3 rhythm can be approximated in the English translation of, e.g., Ps 3:2:

> O Lórd,   how-mány-are   my-ádversaries!
> Mány   rise-úp   agaínst-me!

The second most common pattern is a stich of three accents followed by one of two (3/2). Many other combinations also occur. Ideally the same verse form would be used throughout a given poetic piece, but Hebrew composition is quite fluid in this, and the pattern is often varied.

Though the rhythm of stressed syllables is apparent only in the Hebrew original, parallelism can be seen in any good translation, since it is essentially a thought echo or "thought rhyme." The commonest and most characteristic form is a verse of two stichs, the second of which repeats the thought of the first in different words; this is called synonymous parallelism. The second member may match the first one

---

[1] Regular meter requires a fixed pattern of long and short syllables; according to the more common view, Hebrew poetry counts only stressed syllables.

[2] The verse—as basic unit of poetry—will not always coincide with the verse numbering in modern Bibles; the verse limits are ascertained, rather, by sense and structure. In Bibles whose text format is arranged to indicate the versification of poetic sections, each stich (colon) is usually printed as a separate line.

very closely, word for word, or it may correspond only in general meaning:

> Because he clings to me, I will deliver him;
>   I will set him on high because he acknowledges my name (91:14).

> What is man that you should be mindful of him?
>   or the son of man that you should care for him? (8:5).

> He judges the world with justice;
>   he governs the people with equity (9:9).

Sometimes the two members present the same idea in contrasting ways; this is called antithetic parallelism:

> False scales are an abomination to the Lord,
>   but a full weight is his delight (Prov 11:1).

> The virtue of the upright saves them,
>   but the faithless are caught in their own intrigue (Prov 11:6).

Sometimes the second member simply balances the first by completing its thought; e.g.:

> Praised be the Lord, I exclaim,
>   and I am safe from my enemies (Ps 18:4).

This is called synthetic parallelism, though in fact the parallelism is in the form rather than the thought. In synthetic parallelism the second member sometimes partially repeats and further expands the statement of the first member; or the statement may be simply echoed in the second and carried forward in a third. This procedure may advance two or three steps, "staircase" fashion; e.g.:

> Lift up, O gates, your lintels;
>   reach up, you ancient portals,
>   that the king of glory may come in! (24:7).

Other compositional structures are also found. The very lack of hard and fast rules makes Hebrew poetry exceedingly rich and varied. But these examples will have to suffice.

A word must be said about the color and vividness of Hebrew poetic imagery. The Israelite's boundless trust in God, his concrete way of conceiving things, and his powerful imagination allows him to use images and figures that astound us. In Psalm 18, for example, Yahweh is a fire-breathing warrior who flies on the storm clouds to rescue His suppliant. In Psalm 23 He is a shepherd tricked out with rod and staff. Other examples could be drawn from almost any psalm.

Figure 21. *Egyptian harpist. From a 14th century relief. Courtesy of the Rijksmuseum van Oudheden, Leiden, The Netherlands.*

CULT AND CLASSIFICATION

The Psalter is a collection of 150 religious lyrics composed for use as prayer. As a compilation the Psalter had a long, complex history and was completed only in postexilic times, though the majority of the Psalms are from earlier periods. Not all of Israel's sacred songs, by any means, found their way into this collection. Many similar compositions are preserved here and there in other *OT* books; e.g., the Song of Miriam (Exod 15:1–18) and the Song of Deborah (Judges 5).[3] Though some of the Psalms were composed for private prayer, most of them were intended for public liturgical worship. The modern service of Vespers or Evensong would be much too tame as an illustration of the *OT* liturgical use of psalms. Israel's worship included such exuberant behavior as joyful shouts, hand clapping, dancing, and prostrations; musical instruments were often of the noisier kind, such as trumpet, horn, timbrel, and cymbals (Psalms 95; 98; 149; 150).

Psalms were sung during the offering of sacrifice in the Temple

---

[3]See also Deuteronomy 32; Isa 38:9–20; 42:10–17; Habakkuk 3; Jonah 2:2–10; Sir 51:1–12.

worship (2 Chr 29:27-30; 1 Macc 4:54-59; cf. Jer 33:11). They were sung, too, in solemn procession (Exod 15:20-21; 2 Sam 6:5). Psalm 68 reflects the stages of a procession and even describes some of those participating:

> The singers lead, the minstrels follow,
> in their midst the maidens play on timbrels (v 26).

A ritual dialogue between priest guardians of the Temple gate and the leader of a procession is probably preserved in Ps 118:19-26; v 27 is rubric for the group as it enters the Temple precincts:

> Join in procession with leafy boughs
> up to the horns of the altar.

How dear these festivals were to Israel's heart is seen in the words of one who laments his distance from the Temple:

> Those times I recall
> now that I pour out my soul within me.
> When I went with the throng
> and led them in procession to the house of God,
> Amid loud cries of joy and thanksgiving,
> with the multitude keeping festival (42:5).

Even while predicting the fall of Judah Jeremiah looked forward to the restoration of the cult:

> In this place . . . there shall yet be heard . . . the sound of those who bring thank offerings to the house of the Lord, singing,
> "Give thanks to the Lord of hosts, for the Lord is good;
> his mercy endures forever" (Jer 33:10-11).

Not all psalms were appropriate for all occasions, of course. There were times for praise, times for petition, times for thanksgiving; sometimes the community as a whole addressed God, sometimes an individual with those who shared his joy or distress. By analysing individual psalms it is possible to determine the sort of occasions for which they were composed and used. Although his conclusions have been modified in some important respects by later studies, Gunkel's form critical studies (p. 9) set the fashion in this field.

Gunkel was able to classify most of the Psalms according to a limited number of literary types. Psalms of each type exhibit similar patterns and characteristics because the form a prayer took in a given situation was relatively fixed by the power of custom; when the psalmists composed they normally followed conventional patterns. The form exhibited by a particular psalm is, therefore, determined by the life situation (*Sitz im Leben*) which called it into being. While Gunkel held that psalm types arose in the early liturgy, he thought that the psalms of our Psalter were, for the most part, later, private compositions which preserve the liturgical patterns through force of custom. Sigmund Mowinckel, through a more consistent application of the same principles, has convincingly maintained that most of our present psalms are liturgical, not private, compositions. Gunkel distinguished five main types: Hymns (Psalms of Praise), Communal Laments, Royal Psalms, Individual Laments, and Individual Thanksgiving Psalms; he distinguished several lesser types, of which the Communal Thanksgiving Psalms, Pilgrimage Psalms, and Wisdom Psalms are of special interest. It would be a mistake to expect a rigid adherence to pattern; the Semitic spirit is far too free to be so confined. Many psalms exhibit a mixture of forms, while others defy all attempts at classification.

While the whole psalm must be regarded in assigning it to a category, the opening line is usually a good clue to its type, just as the salutation of a letter often typifies it. Just as letters beginning "Dear Sirs," "Dear Mom," "Dear John," or "Dearly Beloved" will be of different sorts, so also will be psalms beginning: "Hearken to my words, O Lord"; "I will give thanks to you, O Lord, with all my heart"; "Praise, you servants of the Lord, praise the name of the Lord." The following pages will explain the characteristics of each type, while the chart at the end of the chapter will classify individual psalms according to type.

HYMNS (PSALMS OF PRAISE). A typical song of this class has three parts: invitation, body, and conclusion. The *invitation* is an exhortation to praise or bless God; it may be addressed to Israel, the nations, nature, the psalmist himself ("Bless the Lord, O my soul"—103:1), etc. The invitation may be extended for several verses; Psalm 150 consists of nothing else. The *body* of the song develops the motives or reasons for praising God. These are sometimes His mighty deeds in Israel's history (103; 105; 114; 135; 136), sometimes His goodness in creation and nature (8; 29; 33), sometimes His gracious attributes, such as majesty, holiness, or mercy (33:4–5; 65:4; 96:4–6; 136; 145). No motive is given more frequently than Yahweh's *hesed*; the phrase "for his mercy endures forever" recurs throughout the Psalter like a refrain. Nothing is too trivial; even God's goodness in giving food "to the young ravens when they cry to him" is noted (147:9). The *conclusion* has no fixed form; it sometimes simply repeats the invitation.

Two groups of songs in this category merit special attention. The first is composed of the so-called Songs of Zion.[4] These psalms praise God for the privileges bestowed on Jerusalem—its choice as His dwelling, its strength, etc. In spite of the keen awareness of Israel's election, a strongly universalistic note is sometimes present (87). The second

[4] 46; 48; 76; 87; 132.

group is composed of the so-called Enthronement Psalms,[5] compositions which exalt Yahweh's kingship over all the earth and speak of His coming in judgment. Debate rages over the life situation of the psalms in this group. Gunkel considered them late compositions celebrating the kingship of Yahweh as an event to come in the final age; as such they draw on the teaching of the canonical prophets. Mowinckel sees them rather as rooted in a special feast of Yahweh's kingship celebrated from early monarchic times.

Mowinckel argues that, on the cultic principle, these psalms must have a life situation in Israel's liturgy. He points to the expressions in them which parallel elements in Israel's coronation ceremony.[6] He also argues from the New Year festival celebrated in the religions of the Fertile Crescent—the major celebration of the annual cycle. As observed in Babylonia and elsewhere, this festival was a cultic reenactment of the creation myth in which the chief god overcame the chaos monster, performed the work of creation, and was enthroned (p. 50). Though the *OT* legislation does not mention a feast of Yahweh's kingship, Mowinckel believes it was celebrated in monarchic times during the Feast of Booths (Tabernacles); he finds confirmation in Zech 14:16: "All who are left of the nations that came against Jerusalem shall come up year after year to worship the King, the Lord of hosts, and to celebrate the feasts of Booths."

The Enthronement Psalms celebrate Yahweh's creative victory and His acts in Israel's history. In Israel's liturgy, Yahweh's enthronement would not mean that He had ever ceased to be King, but it would be a way of rendering vivid and actual for the worshipers one of the central facts of salvation. In this view the prophetic teaching on Yahweh's kingship and role as universal judge, especially as seen in Deutero-Isaiah, would be derived from these psalms and not vice versa. Closely connected with the celebration of Yahweh's kingship and His saving deeds would be a renewal of the covenant in the particular form of a renewal of the Davidic kingship.

This much oversimplified exposition of Mowinckel's theory will have to suffice. While his thesis cannot be said to be proved and while few accept every element of his detailed reconstruction, scholarly opinion seems to be ever more favorable to its general lines.[7]

LAMENTS (PSALMS OF SUPPLICATION). Experience teaches that we are more apt to turn to God when we need help than at any other time; the fact that Individual Laments are the most numerous category in the Psalter (see chart for listing) suggests that in this matter the ancient Israelites were not notably different.

[5]47; 93; 95–99. Some scholars would add a great many more.
[6]E.g., the shout "Yahweh is king!", trumpet blasts, procession, and assent to the throne; cf. 2 Sam 15:10; 1 Kgs 1:32–48; 2 Kgs 9:13.
[7]Cf., e.g., W. L. Moran, "Enthronement Feast" in *NCE*.

It is usually possible to distinguish in an Individual Lament the following parts: invocation, complaint, supplication, motive for being heard, and expression of confidence. The *invocation* addresses God directly and often contains an urgent appeal for help. The Semite is not noted for his patience, and in these compositions the psalmist often calls very insistently to be heard, even reproaching God for being slow to help: "Why, O Lord, do you stand aloof? Why do you hide in time of distress?" (10:1); "My God, my God, why have you forsaken me . . .?" (22:2). In the *complaint* (lament) the psalmist makes known his needs. Most often his distress is occasioned by the hostility of enemies or by a serious illness. The description may be long and vivid but is often in stereotyped terms that tell us little about his actual situation: his enemies rise up in great numbers, they surround and attack him like bulls or lions or dogs, etc. Sometimes the psalmist seems to be the defendant in a legal process. The prophetic books and the case of Naboth (1 Kings 21) shows us that sometimes the just man, especially if he was poor, could expect scant justice; so the psalmist turns to God for his vindication.

The account of Hezekiah's illness, of his prayer, and of his tears (Isa 38:1-3; 2 Kgs 20:1-3) illustrates the distress occasioned by sickness and the threat of death that we see reflected in many psalms. The sufferer depicts his situation in the darkest colors, sometimes picturing himself already at the gates of the nether world. Part of the distress occasioned by illness sprang from the conviction that it came directly from God and was a sign of His displeasure for sins committed; cf. 38:2-3:

> O Lord, in your anger punish me not,
>   in your wrath chastise me not;
> For your arrows have sunk deep in me,
>   and your hand has come down upon me.

Even though the belief in a one-to-one relationship between sin and temporal affliction was an oversimplification, such psalms are valuable for the vivid awareness of sin and the punishment it merits expressed in them. It is not surprising that six of the seven Penitential Psalms[8] belong to this group.

The *motive* alleged for being heard may be God's goodness, the psalmist's trust in Him (25:20), the sacrifice or psalms of thanksgiving he vows (54:8; 69:31-32), or even the concern God should have to preserve a worshiper He would otherwise be deprived of (88:10-13).

The *confidence* of being heard is often a striking feature of these psalms. A good example is Psalm 22, in which the mood abruptly changes in v 23 to a confidence which is maintained to the end. See also 6:9-11; 7:11-18; 27:6; etc. This new assurance may spring from

[8]6; 32 (a Thanksgiving Psalm); 38; 51; 102; 130; 143.

the psalmist's general certitude that God hears the just man who calls upon Him. But there is also the possibility that in some cases it is occasioned by a favorable response from a priest or prophet connected with the sanctuary in which the prayer is offered; one such response may be preserved in 12:6. Sometimes the note of confidence so dominates the psalm that its character of supplication disappears; prayers of this sort are called Psalms of Confidence.[9]

Communal Laments[10] differ from Individual Laments in that they are offered on behalf of the whole community for deliverance from a common peril, but the pattern of composition is similar. Usually they can be distinguished by whether the speaker is "I" or "we," but it is not always so simple. The "I" who speaks is sometimes a figure who speaks in the name of all. This is clearly the case, e.g., in Psalm 89, where the suppliant is the king and the afflictions described affect the whole nation. The fact that "I" can occasionally alternate with "we" in a Communal Lament (44:5, 7, 16; 74:12; 123:1) also suggests the possibility that some "I-Laments" are really communal, e.g., Psalm 77. But to assert that a great many of the Psalms are of this type, as some authors do, is to go beyond the evidence.

Lamentations 5 is one example of a Communal Lament outside the Psalter. It was composed shortly after the fall of Jerusalem in 587 and illustrates one possible life-setting for psalms of this type—national humiliation at the hands of foreign enemies. Many of those in the Psalter are from the same occasion or from lesser military defeats. Other calamities, such as drought or locust plague, could also be the cause of public assembly and lamentation (1 Kgs 8:35-36; Joel 1-2).

PSALMS OF THANKSGIVING. Aside from a few Communal Thanksgiving Psalms (e.g., 67; 107; 124), songs of this class express the gratitude of an individual for deliverance from affliction or for petitions granted.[11] They have been called "the other side of the coin" to Psalms of Supplication; in the one case the psalmist petitions for a favor, in the other he gives thanks for favors granted. After Hezekiah's cure, for example, he wrote a psalm of thanksgiving (Isaiah 38). Sometimes a psalm was composed in fulfillment of a vow, as we have seen. Psalm and sacrifice (thank-offering) normally went together; it would be a festive affair with friends and the poor invited to the sacrificial banquet (66:13-17; and cf. 22:23-27).

The *introduction* of these psalms announces the theme of thanksgiving in terms that often resemble the Hymns, though the verbs are usually indicative rather than imperative. In the *body* of the psalm the specific grounds for gratitude are set forth: I was in such-and-such a predicament, I called upon Yahweh, and He delivered me.

[9] 4; 11; 16; 23; 27:1-6; 62; 131.
[10] 44; 74; 79; 80; 83; 85; 89; 106; 123; 125; 137.
[11] 18; 30; 32; 41; 92; 116; 118; 138.

The psalmist often describes his former distress so vividly that, surprisingly, this section may closely resemble the central part of a Lament, the same images and phrases recurring.

ROYAL PSALMS. The compositions in this group[12] are singled out on the basis of content rather than form: they tell about the king or are spoken by the king. On the basis of literary type, in fact, some of them fall into other categories, such as Lament (89) or Thanksgiving (21). Earlier critics dated many of these psalms late in the postexilic period because of their messianic features. Now, however, conceding the liturgical background for the psalms, scholars generally date them to the monarchy; only during the period Israel had a king can a plausible life-setting be found for them. The specific occasion for some of them (e.g., 2; 110) must have been either the coronation of a new king or an annual festival that included the renewal of the kingship such as that proposed by Mowinckel (see above). Psalm 45 was composed for a royal wedding.

The "messianic" features are present not because these compositions primarily intend to delineate an ideal king to come, but because they reflect the place the Davidic dynasty, embodied in each successive king, held in Israel's theological thought. The king is called God's son (2:7; 89:27–28) and has claim to a kingdom of vast extent (2:8; 72:8–11; 89:26), over which he rules by God's own authority (2:7; 45:7–8; 89:21–22; 110:1–2); the dynasty is an eternal one (45:7; 89:4–5, 29–38; 132:11–12). These prerogatives are easily traceable to Nathan's oracle (2 Samuel 7—p. 145), quoted or paraphrased in some of the psalms (2;89; 132); so there is no need to seek a basis for them in Mesopotamian ideas of kingship.

Nevertheless, these psalms are not therefore emptied of messianic import. The prophetic and priestly circles in Jerusalem that preserved Nathan's oracle and celebrated it in the Temple liturgy also developed and made explicit something implicit in the oracle—God's intention of bestowing the blessings of salvation through David's line. The descriptions in the psalms are not drawn from the historical kings of whom they spoke; they derive ultimately from an ideal picture of what God intended the dynasty to be and to accomplish. When the dynasty failed the psalms remained an expression of hopes still to be fulfilled by the one in whom the dynasty would be restored.

WISDOM PSALMS. The poems in this group[13] are characterized by the same preoccupations and teachings found in Israel's wisdom literature (Chapter 19). For example, Psalm 1 and Psalm 112 contrast the happy lot of the virtuous and the sad lot of the wicked; others (37; 49; 73)

---

[12]2; 18; 20; 21; 45; 72; 89; 101; 110; 132.
[13]1; 37; 49; 73; 78; 91; 111; 112; 119; 127; 128; 133.

are, like Ecclesiastes and Job, concerned with the problem of God's justice posed by the prosperity of the wicked and the sufferings of the just. The psalmist sometimes repeats wisdom sayings (111:10) or he may employ the terminology of the sages:

> My mouth shall speak wisdom;
> prudence shall be the utterance of my heart.
> My ear is intent upon a proverb;
> I will set forth my riddle to the music of the harp (49:4–5).

Several of these psalms (37; 111; 112; 119) are acrostic compositions in which the lines or strophes begin with successive letters of the Hebrew alphabet.

The classification of psalms in the following chart necessarily involves some oversimplification. The term "mixed" could have been used much more frequently, for many of the Psalms display characteristics of more than one type; it is used here only when no type is clearly predominant. Furthermore, scholars disagree among themselves on the correct classification of a number of psalms.

Ps	Classification	Ps	Classification	Ps	Classification
1	Wisdom	25	Ind. Lam.	48	Song of Zion
2	Royal	26	Ind. Lam.	49	Wisdom
3	Ind. Lam.	27	Ind. Lam.	50	
4	Ind. Lam.	28	Ind. Lam.	51	Ind. Lam.
5	Ind. Lam.	29	Hymn	52	Ind. Lam.
6	Ind. Lam.	30	Ind. Thank.	53	
7	Ind. Lam.	31	Ind. Lam.	54	Ind. Lam.
8	Hymn	32	Ind. Thank.	55	Ind. Lam.
9 ⎱	Ind. Thank.	33	Hymn	56	Ind. Lam.
10 ⎰	plus Lam.	34	Ind. Thank.	57	Ind. Lam.
11	Confidence	35	Ind. Lam.	58	Com. Lam.
12	Ind. Lam.	36	Mixed	59	Ind. Lam.
13	Ind. Lam.	37	Wisdom	60	Com. Lam.
14	Com. Lam.	38	Ind. Lam.	61	Ind. Lam.
15		39	Ind. Lam.	62	Confidence
16	Confidence	40	Mixed	63	Ind. Lam.
17	Ind. Lam.	41	Ind. Thank.	64	Ind. Lam.
18	Thank.; Royal	42 ⎱	Ind. Lam.	65	Hymn
19	Hymn	43 ⎰		66	Mixed
20	Royal	44	Com. Lam.	67	Com. Thank.
21	Thank.; Royal	45	Royal	68	Hymn
22	Ind. Lam.	46	Song of Zion	69	Ind. Lam.
23	Confidence	47	Enthronement	70	Ind. Lam.
24			Hymn	71	Ind. Lam.

Ps	Classification	Ps	Classification	Ps	Classification
72	Royal	98	Enthronement	127	Wisdom
73	Wisdom		Hymn	128	Wisdom
74	Com. Lam.	99	Enthronement	129	Com. Thank.
75			Hymn	130	Ind. Lam.
76	Song of Zion	100	Hymn	131	Confidence
77	Com. Lam.	101	Royal	132	Royal; Zion
	I-form	102	Ind. Lam.	133	Wisdom
78	Wisdom	103	Hymn	134	
79	Com. Lam.	104	Hymn	135	Hymn
80	Com. Lam.	105	Hymn	136	Hymn
81		106	Com. Lam.	137	Com. Lam.
82		107	Com. Thank.	138	Ind. Thank.
83	Com. Lam.	108		139	
84	Pilgrimage	109	Ind. Lam.	140	Ind. Lam.
85	Com. Lam.	110	Royal	141	Ind. Lam.
86	Ind. Lam.	111	Wisdom	142	Ind. Lam.
87	Song of Zion	112	Wisdom	143	Ind. Lam.
88	Ind. Lam.	113	Hymn	144	Mixed
89	Lam.; Royal	114	Hymn	145	Hymn
90	Com. Lam.	115		146	Hymn
91	Wisdom	116	Ind. Thank.	147	Hymn
92	Ind. Thank.	117	Hymn	148	Hymn
93	Enthronement	118	Ind. Thank.	149	Hymn
	Hymn	119	Wisdom	150	Hymn
94	Ind. Lam.	120	Ind. Lam.		
95	Enthronement	121			
	Hymn	122	Pilgrimage		
96	Enthronement	123	Com. Lam.		
	Hymn	124	Com. Thank.		
97	Enthronement	125	Com. Lam.		
	Hymn	126	Com. Lam.		

Key: Com. = Communal; Ind. = Individual; Thank. = Thanksgiving; Lam. = Lament.

READING SUGGESTIONS

JBC § 13; 35. *PBS* #43–46. *AUOT* 502–27. *MTES* 265–85. *WITOT* 278–87.

Anderson, B. W., *Out of the Depths. The Psalms Speak for Us Today.* Philadelphia: Westminster Press, 1983.

Bright, J., *Jeremiah*, pp. CXXV-CXXXVIII.

Keel, O., *The Symbolism of the Biblical World: Ancient Near Eastern Iconography and the Book of Psalms*, tr. T. J. Hallett, New York: Seabury Press, 1978.

Murphy, R. E., *The Psalms, Job*. Philadelphia: Fortress Press, 1977, pp. 11-57.

Stuhlmueller, C., *Psalms. OTM*, Vols. 21-22.

Coddaire, L., and L. Weil, "The Use of the Psalter in Worship," *Worship* 52 (1978) 342-48.

Freedman, D. N., "Pottery, Poetry, and Prophecy: An Essay on Biblical Poetry," *JBL* 96 (1977) 5-26.

Gerstenberger, E. S., "Enemies and Evildoers in the Psalms: A Challenge to Christian Preaching," *Horizons in Biblical Theology* 4/5 (1982-83) 61-77.

Hunt, I., "Recent Psalm Study," *Worship* 47 (1973) 80-92; 49 (1975) 202-14, 283-94; 51 (1977) 127-44; 52 (1978) 245-58.

Mays, J. L., "Psalm 29," *Int* 39 (1985) 60-64.

Miller, P. D., "Enthroned on the Praises of Israel: *The Praise of God in Old Testament Theology*," *Int* 39 (1985) 5-19.

Old, H. O., "The Psalms of Praise in the Worship of the New Testament Church," *Int* 39 (1985) 20-33.

Sellers, O. R., "Musical Instruments of Israel," *BAR* 81-94.

Stuhlmueller, C., "Psalm 22: The Deaf and Silent God of Mysticism and Liturgy," *BTB* 12 (1982) 86-90.

Westermann, C., "The Role of the Lament in the Theology of the Old Testament," *Int* 28 (1974) 20-38.

19

God's Wisdom in Israel

IN WHAT might be termed "an ancient whodunnit," Solomon is said to have disposed of an apparently insoluble riddle: how to ascertain the truth when the only witnesses gave contradictory versions of what happened (1 Kgs 3:16-28). This tale about two women claiming the same baby was a popular one in ancient literature and was told of more than one eminent man; its use in Kings was to glorify the wisdom for which Solomon was so famous: "When all Israel heard the judgment the king had given, they were in awe of him, because they saw that the king had in him the wisdom of God for giving judgment" (1 Kgs 3:28). Elsewhere it is said that Solomon's wisdom surpassed that of the sages of the East, that he composed 3000 proverbs, and that he could discourse about plants from the cedar of Lebanon to the lowly hyssop, about animals, birds, reptiles, and fish (5:9-14; *RSV:* 5:29-34); the Queen of Sheba came from the East to hear his wisdom (10:1-13). Further evidence of Solomon's reputation for wisdom is the ascription to him of several of Israel's wisdom writings (cf. Prov. 1:1; Eccl 1:1; Cant 1:1; Wis 9:7-8, 12) even though they are, in the opinion of modern scholars, postexilic compilations and though one of them (Wisdom) was written in Greek.

THE WISDOM MOVEMENT

The association of wisdom with Solomon, however, rests on a firm foundation, for he was its first and principal patron in Israel. Egypt and Mesopotamia had wisdom traditions before Israel became a nation and the literature in which it is embodied indicates the royal court with its scribal schools and highly trained officials as its point of

Figure 22. *Egyptian scribes at work. From a 24th century relief. Courtesy of the Künsthistorische Museum, Vienna, Austria.*

origin.[1] In patterning his own court and administration after the great capitals, Solomon brought Israel into a tradition of wisdom international in scope.

The wisdom of the ancient Near Eastern court circles arose from experience and reflection on experience and was characteristically practical and empirical; it was concerned in large measure with formulating and passing on advice gained from experience and observation. This advice often tended toward the practical end of helping the young scribe or courtier succeed through being prudent, and it could deal with matters such as conduct at banquets, care in lending money, behavior toward women, toward superiors, etc. Often enough the advice was cast in the form of admonitions and presented as the instructions of a father (frequently a king) to his son. For example, the vizier Ptah-hotep instructs his son:

> If thou art one of those sitting at the table of one greater than thyself, take what he may give, when it is set before thy nose. . . . Let thy face be cast down until he addresses thee, and thou shouldst speak (only) when he addresses thee. Laugh after he laughs, and it will be pleasing to his heart . . . (*ANET* 412).

Even on the practical level there is something more than a Dale Carnegie approach to success here. Egyptian thought contrasts the "passionate man" and the "silent man." The former is unwise and a failure because, overcome by his impulses, he is led to act imprudently; the latter is wise and a success because, being master of himself, he remains master of every situation in which he finds himself. This approach to discipline was obviously a help toward a well-ordered life.

[1]For extensive samples of this literature, see *ANET* 405–40.

Since the wisdom schools nurtured future leaders and rulers (in all probability they trained the sons of nobles as well as future scribes), they aimed at instilling the highest moral and ethical principles, especially with reference to honesty in speech, in giving judgment, and in commercial dealings, and often exhibited a touching concern for the helpless members of society, widows, orphans, and the needy (cf. *ANET* 413, 422, 423, 424). Many of the finest provisions of Israel's law exhibit the same sort of concern (e.g., Exod 22:20–22, 24–26; 23:1–2, 4–9; Lev 19:9–10, 13–16) and may ultimately have stemmed from wisdom ethic. The prophets often supposed this sort of ethic and recent studies have shown the influence of the wisdom tradition on Amos, Isaiah, and other prophets. One Mesopotamian composition even recommends doing good to one's enemies (*ANET* 426), and we are cautioned that in giving precepts Jesus may often have been more in the line of the wisdom teacher than in that of the legislator.

In addition to concerning itself with formulating rules of conduct, Mesopotamian and Egyptian wisdom speculated concerning problems of life, death, suffering, justice, etc. (cf. *ANET* 405–407, 434–40), problems which reappear in Israel's literature, particularly in Ecclesiastes, Job, and some of the psalms.

Israel was aware that wisdom did not begin with her. The fact is acknowledged when Solomon's wisdom is exalted by comparing it with that of the sages of the East. Names of eastern sages appear in Israel's literature: Ahikar,[2] Amen-em-ope,[3] Agur (Prov 30:1), and Lemuel (Prov 31:1); and the setting of Job is in Edom, a land renowned for wisdom.

Israel's wisdom literature has much the same character as that of Egypt and Mesopotamia, especially in the earlier texts. The great *OT* themes of covenant, election, and redemption are virtually absent. But the leaven of Yahwistic faith operated here, too, as a transforming influence. The story of Solomon's judgment takes on a special significance because it follows upon the account of the dream in which Yahweh granted his request for an understanding mind (1 Kgs 3:4–15); the judgment, further, is said to demonstrate the divine wisdom he possessed (v 28). Wisdom is here not simply a result of observation, experience, or human cleverness, but a gift bestowed by God enabling one to walk in higher ways. This is a theme developed at length in Israel's later writings. In Job 28, for example, wisdom is said to be hidden with God, inaccessible to human investigation, yet able to be appropriated by the individual through a godly life:

[2]Cf. Tob 1:21; 2:10; 11:18; 14:10; the "Words of Ahiqar" are found in *ANET* 427–30.

[3]Cf. the *NAB* rendering of Prov 22:19, based on a conjectural reading of the Hebrew. That Prov 22:17–24:22 is dependent on "The Instruction of Amen-em-opet" (*ANET* 421–25) is admitted by virtually all scholars.

And to man he said:
>   Behold, the fear of the Lord is wisdom;
>   and avoiding evil is understanding (v 28).

One of the latest books, Sirach, identifies wisdom with the Law (see below).

THE GNOMIC COLLECTIONS

(Recommended Scripture reading: Proverbs 1–3; 8–10; 31;
Sirach 1–3; 24–26; 44–50)

We are all familiar with "wise sayings" traditional in our own culture. They are normally brief in formulation, concrete in expression, but wide in application. "Look before you leap," "Don't put all your eggs in one basket," and "Don't cross your bridges before you come to them" are familiar examples. Such terse, pithy sayings are called gnomes, aphorisms, apothegms, or proverbs. Israel, too, formulated her traditional wisdom in brief, pithy sayings, though those preserved in her wisdom literature usually exhibit the parallelism characteristic of Hebrew verse (p. 220). The Hebrew term for a saying of this type, *mashal,* is somewhat broader in meaning than the English "proverb." *Mashal* suggests a comparison and can designate a parable, an allegory, a riddle, an example, etc. Thus while the Hebrew name for the Book of Proverbs (*mishle shelomoh:* "proverbs of Solomon") is derived from the collection of short sayings beginning at Prov 10:1, it is broad enough to include the other forms in this book. And indeed, although we may characterize Proverbs and Sirach as "gnomic collections," we meet a variety of forms here. One of the most important of them is the "instruction," a wisdom form that is attested as early as the third millennium B.C. in both Egypt and Mesopotamia. The typical *OT* proverb consists of two stichs in parallelism, the verb in the indicative; it doesn't command or exhort, but it contains a value judgment that has implications for behavior. The "instruction" is far more complex. It usually begins with a call to attention in the imperative addressed to the child/pupil by the parent/teacher; it contains exhortations (also in the imperative) as well as motivations for carrying them out. Some examples of the instruction form in Proverbs are 1:8–19; 2:1–22; 3:1–12; and 23:15–28.

Seven books in the Catholic Canon are traditionally designated as wisdom books: Job, Psalms, Proverbs, Ecclesiastes (Qoheleth), Canticle of Canticles, Wisdom, and Sirach (Ecclesiasticus). Strictly speaking, however, Canticle of Canticles and most of Psalms do not fit into this category. Of the remaining books, Proverbs and Sirach are composed, for the most part, of collections of maxims. Taken together, these two give an insight into the development of the concept of wisdom in Israel.

THE BOOK OF PROVERBS. Proverbs is not a unified composition but rather an anthology of wisdom literature. The collected sayings which form the bulk of it are mainly from monarchic times, though the completed book is postexilic. No topical outline is possible; the following division indicates the collections which can be discerned:

A. *Introduction:* 1-9
B. *First Solomonic Collection:* 10:1-22:16
C. *Sayings of the Wise:* 22:17-24:22
D. *Other Sayings of the Wise:* 24:23-34
E. *Second Solomonic Collection:* 25:1-29:27
F. *The Words of Agur:* 30:1-14
G. *Numerical Proverbs:* 30:15-33
H. *The Words of Lemuel:* 31:1-9
I. *Alphabetic Acrostic praising the Worthy Wife:* 31:10-31

The heart of the book are the two Solomonic collections (B and E). Although it is impossible to date the individual sayings precisely, there is no reason to doubt that many of them go back to monarchic times. Preservation was no problem, for part of the training of scribal students consisted of copying out lists of maxims; the scribes, moreover, appear as a fairly conservative group. The terse form and practical nature of early wisdom is evident in these chapters. The value of many of them as norms for virtuous living is equally evident, as well as their religious motivation (e.g., 11:1, 20; 12:22; 13:13; 14:31). Wisdom is identified with virtue and folly with vice. These sayings are pervaded with a hardy trust that virtue brings reward and that wickedness brings disaster (10:2, 3, 6, 7; 11:4, 11; etc.). This conviction springs ultimately from faith rather than from experience, and some later writings (Job and Ecclesiastes) will insist that experience, too, be taken into account. It is possible to point to features in the other collections that differentiate them from the Solomonic ones, but generally the same attitudes and teachings are found in them.

The one responsible for the completed book was more than a collector or an editor, for it was probably he who composed ch. 1-9, a long Introduction intended to set the tone of the book and give meaning to the collections which follow. Unlike the latter, the Introduction consists mainly of long, sustained developments. The basic theme is stated at the outset: "The fear of the Lord is the beginning of wisdom" (1:7); the same thought is repeated near the end (9:10).

The Introduction contains exhortations to prudence and care (3:1-12; 4:10-27) and lengthy warnings about the evils of adultery and the wiles of the adulteress (5:1-23; 6:20-7:27). But most characteristic of this section are the praises of wisdom (1:20-2:22; 3:13-20; 4:1-9;

8:1–9:6). In some of these wisdom is personified and herself addresses warnings and exhortations. She is depicted as a prophet crying out in public places, urging men to forsake folly and warning them of bitter consequences if they do not (1:20–33). The glory of the prophets was to be bearers of God's word, but Wisdom is, herself, of inestimable value—worth more than silver or gold, a veritable tree of life to those who possess her (3:13–18). The prophets stood in God's council, but Wisdom, created before His other works, was with Him and assisted Him when He made the world (8:22–31). Yet Wisdom's delight is to be with the sons of men. Her will is to honor and ennoble them and to fill them with the good things of the banquet she has prepared for them (9:1–6, 10–12). Folly, too, is personified, but as a harlot waiting to mislead the simple (9:13–18).

In these chapters, then, the author depicts wisdom as a divine quality, the fruits of which can be communicated to mankind. It is of inestimable value, worth all the effort one makes to acquire it. By it one is freed from danger and led to the highest good in life. It is against this background, this understanding of wisdom, that the author wants us to read the collections of proverbs he has gathered.

THE WISDOM OF SIRACH (ECCLESIASTICUS). The conservatism of what may be called the right wing of the wisdom tradition is well illustrated in Sirach. Although written in the first quarter of the 2nd century B.C., some of its sayings read in translation like strays from the Solomonic collections: cf., for example:

> Water quenches a flaming fire,
> and alms atone for sins (3:29).[4]
> Sow not in the furrows of injustice,
> lest you harvest it sevenfold (7:3).

Until recent times the Hebrew verse forms of couplets like these could be reconstructed only by scholarly guesswork, for Sirach, one of the deuterocanonical books, was preserved only in the Greek of the LXX and in other translations. But beginning in 1896 documents have been recovered containing about two-thirds of the Hebrew text of Sirach. The NAB translation follows the Hebrew text where it is available.

The author was Jesus ben Sira (Greek form: Sirach), a Jerusalem sage who imparted the fruit of his deep reflection on the Scriptures and on life to those who came to the school he conducted. He eventually committed his teachings to writing, probably ca. 190–180 B.C.; his grandson brought the book to Egypt and there translated it into Greek sometime after 132 B.C.

[4]Verse numbers in some translations may differ slightly from those of the NAB given here.

It would be no more possible to give a topical outline of Sirach than of the older collections in Proverbs; the same variety of subjects and lack of systematic arrangement characterizes both. But while Sirach does contain many short sayings, the typical unit is longer and presents a more elaborate development of thought. Furthermore, the materials are usually grouped according to content in a way they were not in Proverbs. But we find the same sort of reflections on wisdom, wealth, friends, speech, women, parents, childcare, and anger. The advice of ben Sira is as useful today as it was when he formulated it. His words, like those of all the wisdom writers, are best read slowly, in short sections, with ample time for reflection.

Like the writer of the prologue of Proverbs, ben Sira personifies wisdom and never tires of praising her (1:1-8; 6:18-31; 24:1-22; 39:1-11). She is God's creature and His gift to men (1:7-8), yet is acquired only through a demanding discipline (6:18-31). New, however, is ben Sira's teaching that Wisdom's special abode is among the Chosen People and in the Jerusalem Temple (24:8-12) and his identification of her with the Law (24:22). New also is ben Sira's "praise of the fathers," i.e., the passage 44:1-50:21 which glorifies illustrious men from the patriarch Enoch to the high priest Simon II and recapitulates Israel's history. In this late stage, then, election, Law, covenant, cult, and saving history do find a place, albeit a modest one, in wisdom literature.

There is little echo in ben Sira of the problem which so exercised the authors of Job and Ecclesiastes (see below), that of retribution and the suffering of the righteous. He seems to share the confident optimism of Proverbs, almost as though Job had never been written; cf., e.g.:

> He who fears the Lord will have a happy end;
> even on the day of his death he will be blessed (1:11).

He does urge resignation in the face of death as something which inevitably overtakes all (41:1-4). The inequities of life, he seems to think, can all be adjusted at the moment of death:

> The day of prosperity makes one forget adversity;
> the day of adversity makes one forget prosperity.
> For it is easy with the Lord on the day of death
> to repay man according to his deeds.
> A moment of affliction brings forgetfulness of past delights;
> when a man dies, his life is revealed.
> Call no man happy before his death,
> for by how he ends, a man is known (11:25-28).

To this important problem of retribution we must now turn our attention.

The Problem Books

Recommended Scripture reading: Ecclesiastes 1–4; 12;
Job 1–14; 29–31; 38–42).

The pagans of Canaan and Mesopotamia regarded their gods as
sometimes capricious and irresponsible and yet do not seem to have
been greatly troubled thereby. Remember, for example, that in the
Mesopotamian version of the flood story the gods brought on the
destruction for no apparent reason. Israel, however, could never con-
ceive of Yahweh as anything less than perfectly just; as Israel retold
the flood story, corruption and rebellion of all mankind supplied the
motivation for destruction. Yahweh's law commanded that the mer-
chant use just weights and just measure, that the judge administer
justice without regarding the person of any man. Such demands
reflected the justice of Yahweh Himself. Deuteronomy and the
deuteronomic history simply exploited an indisputable principle in
proposing the motives of rewards and punishments. During the exile,
Ezekiel applied the same teaching to the individual level and insisted
on personal accountability (p. 192), though he was by no means introducing an idea new in Israel.

There was no concept of a satisfactory life after death in Israel
throughout most of her history (p. 52). Sheol, the abode of the dead,
was "the land of darkness and of gloom, the black, disordered land
where darkness is the only light" (Job 10:21–22). Moreover it was the
destination of good and bad alike, for there was no distinction among
the dead. It follows, then, that God's just retribution must take place
in this life—no other possibility lay open; the just should prosper and
the wicked suffer. This is, in fact, the theme of many of the wisdom
sayings, as we have seen, and it is asserted in many of the Psalms;
Psalm 1 is a classic example.

The trouble was that experience contradicted these facile formulations of the human situation. As early as Jeremiah, at least, the difficulty was felt:

> You would be in the right, O Lord,
>   if I should dispute with you;
>   even so, I must discuss the case with you.
> Why does the way of the godless prosper,
>   why live all the treacherous in contentment? (Jer 12:1).

The plaint is not prompted by a narrow envy which begrudges the
prosperity of others but by a deeper consideration; it seemed to
Jeremiah and others that God's justice was compromised when the
wicked went unpunished. More pressing was the case of the innocent
man who suffered. Jeremiah was a prime example.

Some of the Wisdom Psalms attempt to deal with the problem, but without notable success (Psalms 37; 49; 73). The author of Psalm 37 commends confidence in God and insists that the prosperity of the wicked soon vanishes and that "those who wait for the Lord shall possess the land"; as an act of faith it is magnificent, but it does not describe the world of experience. Psalm 73 poses the problem more acutely but can only answer that the wicked face a bitter end (vv 17-20). Yet the crisis of faith through which the psalmist passed (vv 1-3, 13-14) led him to the profounder realization that the just man enjoyed unrivaled blessedness in a fellowship with God that nothing could destroy or diminish (vv 23-28).

ECCLESIASTES. The author of this book was a most unusual sage who wrote during the 4th or 3rd century B.C. His name is not given, though the Hebrew text refers to him as Qoheleth, a title which apparently designates his role as leader of an assembly or master of a school; "Ecclesiastes" is an attempted equivalent in Greek. Ecclesiastes was written later than Job, but because it poses the problem without offering a solution and would, in any case, seem anticlimactic after Job, it seems better to discuss it first.

Qoheleth's intention is not to investigate the problem of retribution but to reflect on the meaning of life and the value of its various aspects. The beginning and end of his consideration is: "Vanity of vanities! All things are vanity!" (1:2; 12:8). The fact that neither a person's virtue nor his wisdom guarantees success or happiness, leads him to this conclusion, so retribution looms large in his thought.

Qoheleth takes his stand squarely on experience; he does not repeat the tired cliches of the past except to rub their faces in the mud of life as known through observation. He constantly asks what is the profit or advantage of this or that aspect of human existence. In modern terminology we would say he is asking what there is of ultimate value that makes life worthwhile. In fact his searching leads him to rather negative conclusions. Life is unsatisfying, nor is any improvement of the present situation expected since change is only apparent and illusory: there is nothing new under the sun (1:4-11). An important consideration for him is that death intervenes as a limiting factor on any value that otherwise might make life meaningful. Thus even wisdom, though better than folly, is only of limited worth; when all is done, the wise man meets the same end as the fool (1:12-18; 2:13-17). Pleasures do not bring lasting satisfaction (2:1-12); riches are a cause of worry and may be easily lost (5:9-16).

Man must endure evils over which he has no control. Whether they be occasioned by the wicked or by chance circumstances, they lead Qoheleth to reflect that the will of God is inscrutable. He would doubtless have conceded that the traditional view on retribution was eminently reasonable, but he didn't see it operative in fact: "there are just men treated as though they had done evil and wicked men treated as though they had done justly" (8:14); "Love from hatred man cannot tell; both appear equally vain, in that there is the same lot for all, for the just and the wicked . . ." (9:1-2); "I have seen all manner of things in my vain days: a just man perishing in his justice, and a wicked one surviving in his wickedness" (7:15). Qoheleth always maintains a reverent attitude and never questions the goodness, wisdom, or justice of God; but he asserts that man cannot understand the meaning of God's work (3:11; 8:17).

All in all, his reflections are very humbling; man is no better off than a beast, nor will he have any advantage in death (3:18-20). Yet man has the consolation of reasonable enjoyment in his fleeting life; this is a gift of God, and Qoheleth counsels taking advantage of it with gratitude (2:24-26; 3:12-13, 22; 5:18-19; 8:15; 9:7-10).

The inclusion of this unusual book in the Canon has often occasioned surprise; it doesn't seem edifying and doesn't say the things we are accustomed to expect. At any rate, its inclusion proves that God is not served by pious platitudes that contradict reason or experience and that the Church sees nothing irreligious or irreverent in a bold critique of cherished formulations—even when little positive contribution is made.

Qoheleth was a pessimist. Yet his candid appraisal of life and his failure to find in it anything of ultimate value can be taken as the basis of an argument for the need of an after-life. Such an argument supposes that God intended man's existence to be meaningful—but this is a reasonable supposition.

THE BOOK OF JOB. Though both Job and Ecclesiastes investigate the question of retribution and both reject traditional solutions, they are profoundly different in spirit. Qoheleth was a philosopher, the author of Job a poet; Qoheleth discussed with detachment (cf. Eccl 5:7), the author of Job was fiercely involved. They were undoubtedly poles apart in temperament, but it is also probable that one had not suffered and the other had. Qoheleth left behind occasional jottings, while the author of Job achieved one of the literary masterpieces of all time. Job was probably composed ca. 500 B.C. or earlier.

For his hero the author seems to have taken a non-Israelite legendary figure renowned for his virtue (cf. Ezek 14:14, 20). There may even have been an Israelite story about him. The prose prologue and epilogue of Job contain the essential elements of a tale of a man tested by suffering and then restored; it may have been an earlier piece which the author of Job utilized as a framework within which to compose the poetic section—the bulk of the book and the part which presents his profoundest teaching. The book as it now stands may be outlined as follows:

Elihu's speeches are probably an interpolation; aside from his not being mentioned elsewhere in the book, his wordy exposition comes just where Yahweh's response to Job's plea (31:35–37) is expected. The poem on wisdom (28), too, disturbs the structure and is probably a later addition.

The drama is begun in the prologue. Here the reader learns, something that neither Job or his three friends know, that Job's afflictions are permitted by God as a test. The Satan,[5] an angel whose job is to spy out men's failings and accuse them before God, has suggested that Job's virtue is not disinterested and that he would turn against God if afflictions were substituted for the blessings he enjoyed.

Job's three friends are introduced as proponents of the traditional notion of retribution; they push it even to conclusions that the reader sees to be false. The first two cycles of speeches consist of six discourses apiece: each friend speaks and is answered by Job; the third cycle proceeds in the same fashion but, probably because the text has been disarranged, has no speech by the third friend, Zophar. The friends assert not only that the just prosper and the wicked perish; they also say, indirectly at first and then more boldly, that Job must have sinned because of what he suffers (4:7–11; 11:1–6, 13–19; 22:5–11). Job should acknowledge his guilt and repent, they urge, and God will restore him.

Job maintains his innocence throughout and rejects the validity of their arguments. The wicked *do* survive; they live in prosperity and die in peace (21:7–17); the proverbs of the traditional view fall before experience (21:17–18). The arguments of the friends are "ashy maxims" (13:12); they cannot please God by distorting the truth in His defense (13:7–11). There is not a consistent and logical development in the long debate, though new facets of the problem are illumined from time to time.

Job's debate with his friends is really secondary to his quarrel with God. The contentions of the friends Job can refute to his own satisfaction, at least; what he can't fathom is God's treatment of him. Job

---

[5]Only later does "Satan" become a proper name and refer to a malevolent being who tempts man to sin; cf. 1 Chr 21:1 and p. 95.

seems to have been rejected, condemned, crushed by God, though all the while he is aware of his own innocence. This inexplicable behavior of God afflicts Job more than his sufferings and the accusations of his friends; often a reply to one of the three turns into an address to God. Job would like to take his case directly to Him, but there is no way of doing this (23). Job's reputation for patience rests on the initial submission depicted in the prologue (1:22-23; 2:10); but the Job of the dialogue is angry and bitter. At times he accuses God in almost blasphemous terms of being cruel, arbitrary, even unjust. God unceasingly watches for sin in him and mercilessly attacks him (7:17-21); almighty as He is, no one can contend with Him, though He slay the innocent and laugh at their despair (9:11-23); God it is who causes rulers to judge falsely and Himself treats Job unjustly (9:24; 19:6).

Yet in spite of such outbursts Job longs for God's friendship and approval. Job reminds God of the care with which He formed him in the womb and of His former favors (10:8-12). He longs for a hearing, to have a definite charge so that he can refute it (13:15-23; 16:18-21; 23:1-7). At one point, at least, Job's trust leads him to certitude of final justice; asking that his words be imperishably preserved for the day they will be proved true (19:23-24), he proclaims:

> But as for me, I know that my Vindicator lives,
>   and that he will at last stand forth upon the dust
> Whom I myself shall see, and not another—
>   and from my flesh I shall see God;
>   my inmost being is consumed with longing (19:25-26).

In his peroration Job contrasts his former happy state (29) with his present affliction (30) and swears a series of oaths that he is innocent of specific sins, invoking sanctions upon himself (31:1-34). He begs for an explicit indictment and concludes: "This is my final plea; let the Almighty answer me!" (31:37). Job's answer comes (after the speeches of Elihu) as Yahweh speaks to him from a storm—a common feature of *OT* theophanies (cf. Exod 19:16). God challenges Job to answer a series of questions concerning the works of creation and the wonders of nature; with none too gentle irony, He interjects: "You know, because you were born before them, and the number of your years is great!" (38:21). Can Job, He asks in effect, perform such works? Can he control the forces behind them? Can he understand the mysteries they contain? No answer is possible and Job offers his submission (40:3-5), but the Lord continues. Now He chides Job with the question: "Would you condemn me that you may be justified?" (40:8). If Job has failed, it was in defending his own righteousness to the point of impugning that of God. Job has been inconsistent, too, as Murphy points out, for he denies the traditional theory yet demands that God hold to it and treat him according to his merits. The Lord goes on to ask Job if he can, like the Almighty, topple the proud with a glance or hold in check the fearsome monsters, Behemoth and Leviathan. Job's second submission follows (42:1-6).

The two-fold restoration to Job of his former blessings seems an ironic twist, for it accords perfectly with the view of retribution that the book as a whole refutes. Yet, according to the old prose story, Job's sufferings were the Satan's test to see if Job could remain faithful in adversity, so it was necessary that the test be ended and Job restored. The principal teaching, however, lies elsewhere. Job had, in fact, declared himself satisfied before the restoration of his goods:

> I have dealt with great things that I do not understand;
> things too wonderful for me, which I cannot know.
> I had heard of you by word of mouth,
> but now my eye has seen you.
> Therefore I disown what I have said,
> and repent in dust and ashes (42:3–6).

Job speaks thus not because God has ruthlessly overwhelmed him, but because God, by appearing and speaking to him, has ended Job's sense of estrangement; God has answered him, God is still with him. This is, to be sure, no solution to the problem of innocent suffering and divine justice, but a number of points have been made. The traditional view of retribution is seen to be simplistic and sometimes false; God's wisdom in governing the world and man is seen to be beyond man's comprehension, but is not, for that, to be denied; Job has shown that man can serve God without hope of reward—the Satan loses his wager, for Job never disowns God.

LIFE BEYOND DEATH:
A FINAL ANSWER

(*Recommended Scripture reading:* 2 Maccabees 7; Wisdom 1–6)

The foregoing discussion shows how wide of the mark is the not infrequent assertion that biblical religion was created or invented by man's longing for a blessed immortality. Faith in an after-life did finally emerge, but only very late in the *OT* period, after Israel's faith was formed in all its essential lines. Indeed, it may be said that there is an heroic aspect to *OT* faith in that it accepted Yahweh's unlimited demands, simply because He is God, without the expectation of eternal reward or punishment.

It was not the desire for immortality that created Israel's belief in God; rather, the conviction of an after-life arose from her conception of God as He revealed Himself to her. It may be said that Ecclesiastes and Job, beyond their authors' intention, lead to the persuasion that only a life beyond death can make human existence intelligible in the plan of the wise and good God Israel knew; this is especially true of Job, with its concern for fellowship with God. In a sense it is postulated also by the conclusion of Psalm 73 (see p. 240).

When faith in an after-life did come, it was within the context of the problem of divine retribution, posed now in its severest form. Toward the middle of the 2nd century B.C., during the persecution of Antiochus IV (p. 251), many Jews suffered the ultimate penalty of death for their religious faithfulness; others escaped death through apostasy. Could the reward for faithfulness be the loss of every hope? Was the man who abandoned God finally better off than the one who didn't? Some, at least, did not think so. The author of Daniel, writing during this persecution, says:

> Many of those who sleep
>   in the dust of the earth shall awake;
> Some shall live forever,
>   others shall be an everlasting horror and disgrace (Dan 12:2).

The account in 2 Maccabees 7 of the mother and seven sons martyred under Antiochus IV, though doubtless exaggerated and embellished, also testifies to belief in a bodily resurrection at this period. Just as the mysterious origin of life in the womb is effected by God's power, so it will be with the mystery of birth to new life after death (vv 22 23). See also 2 Macc 6:26; 12:43-46; 14:46.

The fact that belief in a future life arose in response to the problem of retribution does not reduce it to the level of human logic or invalidate it as revelation. It is a conclusion of faith from the nature of God as revealed to Israel. That the belief should arise in this context shows that revelation is progressive in nature and historically conditioned; it appears as a response to need, not as a whisper detached from time and place.

Given the Hebrew conception of man (p. 52), it is understandable that a future life should be thought of primarily in terms of a resurrection of the body. Yet this aspect of biblical faith should not be considered primitive and materialistic, something inferior to the more spiritual Greek concept of the immortality of the soul. God's redemptive work touches man precisely as man. The OT belief in the resurrection of the body is a resounding affirmation of *human* values, an affirmation that God does not despise the work of His hands. It is a paradox that many moderns glorify physical pleasure and beauty even beyond the limits imposed by modesty, prudence, and reason, yet judge the body unworthy of a share in eternal life. Or perhaps this is no paradox.

THE BOOK OF WISDOM. Further response to the problem of retribution is given in Wisdom, a book composed in Greek by a Jew of the Diaspora, probably at Alexandria, in the 1st century B.C. The author, solidly based in Jewish faith though also influenced by Greek philosophy, wishes to set before his fellow Jews in Egypt the true way of wisdom and so to fortify them against the blandishments of the pagan wisdom so highly esteemed in this culture.

Without going into the hotly debated question of the outline of Wisdom, it seems best for our purposes to give this three-part division (adapted from Addison Wright):

A. *Wisdom and human destiny:* 1:1–6:21
B. *The nature of wisdom and means of acquiring it:* 6:22–11:1
C. *God's wisdom displayed in Israel's history:* 11:2–19:22

In the first of these sections the author's main concern is retribution. With dramatic effect he describes the thoughts and plans of wicked men—their conviction that this life is all, their determination to live as they please without regard for right or wrong, and their decision to maliciously slay the just man because his very life is a rebuke to them (2:1–20). Their way of thinking is folly, however, for all that is said and done is seen and judged by God (1:6–12). Their oppression of the just is pointless for "the souls of the just are in the hand of God," and though their passing is counted destruction by the foolish, they are in peace and their hope of immortality is not in vain (3:1–9). But the wicked, apparently at a "last judgment," shall see the just vindicated and their own folly and malice condemned (3:10–12; 4:18–5:14).

What is new here is that the author does not explicitly tie his teaching on a future life to bodily resurrection as Daniel and 2 Maccabees had done. This does not mean he rejected the idea; more likely he thought it would not appeal to those imbued with Greek philosophy (cf. St. Paul's problem with the Corinthians—1 Corinthians 15). He himself shows the influence of Greek thought, though his argumentation is basically biblical and his starting point is the creation and Fall narrative of Genesis 1–3. God's creation was wholesome and man was formed to be imperishable (1:13–14; 2:23); death was not one of His creatures but entered through the malice of unjust men, the very ones who experience it (1:16; 2:24). Here it must be noted that "death" is a pregnant concept, as it often is in Scripture. Since "death" is experienced by the wicked alone, the author is not thinking simply of physical death (which the just also undergo); he thinks of a spiritual death through sin which causes physical death, when it comes, to stretch into eternal death. This God never planned for mankind, and the just do not experience it. In the light of man's eternal destiny other earthly afflictions undergo a new scrutiny, too. Even barrenness and early death, considered grave afflictions in earlier *OT* books, are seen to be occasions of blessings for the innocent (3:13–4:15).

The third section (11:2–19:22) is a review and interpretation of the biblical account of the ten plagues of Egypt and the exodus. The author draws from these events lessons concerning God's dealings with man. Israel, here highly idealized, is shown to be the recipient of divine favors because of election, innocence, and God's plan; but much attention is also devoted to God's motives in sending afflictions upon the Egyptians. A series of contrasts shows how the very sort of things that punished sinful Egypt benefited just Israel (e.g., 11:6–14; 18:5–19:22). Yet Egypt's afflictions were tempered by mercy (11:17–12:2) and were intended to teach the folly of idolatry, for punishment came from the very things they worshiped as gods (11:15–16). The relevance of this polemic and apologia to the author's situation in the very land of which he wrote is obvious.

These chapters are usually classified as midrash, a term often used rather loosely by Christian writers but now somewhat more precisely defined.[6] The word (derived from the Hebrew verb *darash,* to seek, seek out, search, examine, etc.) means an investigation of a Scripture text to learn its hidden meanings and apply them to new situations; thus the term can be applied to a certain type of Scriptural investigation. In Jewish usage midrash usually designates the end product of this process, a specific body of literary works (the Midrashim), i.e., collected commentaries or interpretations of Scripture texts of the type described. Midrashic interpretation which gives rules of conduct is called halakah (from *halak,* to go, walk, conduct oneself), while other types are called haggadah.[7] Midrash can also be used to designate a literary form under which can be classified any composition characterized by the distinctive features described.

Wisdom 11:2—19:22 (except for the digression on idolatry in 13–15) falls into this category. Further examples of midrash in the Bible are the expositions of Jeremiah's prophecy of 70 years in Dan 9:1-2, 21-27, and the treatment of Psalm 95, Ps 110:4, and Genesis 14 in Heb 3:7—4:13; 6:19—7:28. Much of the Sermon on the Mount (Matthew 5-7) is halakic midrash on *OT* legislative texts.

[6]See A. Wright, *The Literary Genre Midrash* (Staten Island: Alba House, 1967).

[7]Haggadah also came to be used in a broader sense to cover a variety of free compositions, sometimes of a fanciful nature, which were not commentary and therefore not really midrash. In this broader sense it is sometimes used to designate didactic fiction like Esther and Tobit.

READING SUGGESTIONS

JBC §28-34. *PBS* #35-39. *OTRG* #22; 24. *AUOT* 528-62. *MTES* 211-64. *WITOT* 287-99, 307-310, 407-412.

Bergant, D., *Job & Ecclesiastes. OTM,* Vol. 18.

——————, *What Are They Saying About Wisdom Literature?* New York: Paulist Press, 1984.

Cox, D., *Introduction to Sapiential Books & Proverbs. OTM,* Vol. 17.

Crenshaw, J. L., *Old Testament Wisdom: An Introduction.* Atlanta: John Knox Press, 1981.

MacKenzie, R. A. F., *Sirach. OTM*, Vol. 19.

Murphy, R. E., *The Forms of the Old Testament Literature. Vol. XIII. Wisdom Literature: Job, Proverbs, Ruth, Canticles, Ecclesiastes, Esther.* Grand Rapids: Eerdmans, 1981.

_____, *The Psalms, Job*, pp. 61-89.

Reese, J., *Wisdom of Solomon/Song of Songs. OTM*, Vol. 20.

Rowley, H. H., *The Book of Job.* Grand Rapids: Eerdmans, 1981.

Winston, D., *The Wisdom of Solomon.* AB 43; Garden City: Doubleday & Company, Inc., 1979.

Wright, A. G., *The Literary Genre Midrash.* Staten Island: Alba House, 1967; cf. *CBQ* 28 (1966) 105-38, 417-57.

Bergant, D., "What's the Point of It All?" *TBT* 22,2 (Mar., 1984) 75-78 (on Qoheleth).

Crenshaw, J. L., "The Problem of Theodicy in Sirach: On Human Bondage," *JBL* 94 (1975) 47-64.

Di Lella, A., "An Existential Interpretation of Job," *BTB* 15 (1985) 49-55.

Emerton, J. A., "Wisdom," *ATI* 214-37.

Fischer, J. A., "Ethics and Wisdom," *CBQ* 40 (1978) 293-310.

Habel, N. C., "Of Things Beyond Me: Wisdom in the Book of Job," *Currents in Theology and Mission* 10 (1983) 142-54.

MacKenzie, R. A. F., "The Transformation of Job," *BTB* 9 (1979) 51-57.

Malchow, B. V., "Wisdom's Contribution to Dialogue," *BTB* 13 (1983) 111-15.

Murphy, R. E., "The Theological Contribution of Israel's Wisdom Literature," *Listening: Journal of Religion and Culture* 19 (1984) 30-40.

Sawicki, M., "What Did Job See?" *TBT* #91 (Oct. 1977) 1304-10.

Scobie, C. H. H., "The Place of Wisdom in Biblical Theology," *BTB* 14 (1984) 43-48.

Southwick, J. S., "Job: An Example for Every Age," *Encounter* 45 (1984) 373-91.

Vawter, B., "Intimations of Immortality in the Old Testament," *JBL* 91 (1972) 158-71.

Viviano, P. A., "The Book of Ecclesiastes: A Literary Approach," *TBT* 22,2 (Mar., 1984) 79-84.

20

The Fourth Beast
and the Son of Man

(Recommended Scripture reading: 1 Maccabees 1–4;
2 Maccabees 3; 10; Daniel 1–3; 7; 9–12.)

LITTLE is known of the Jews in Palestine after the time of Ezra and Nehemiah until we find them groaning under foreign oppression toward the middle of the 2nd century B.C. Important events had taken place on the stage of world history in the meantime, but they appear to have had little immediate impact on Yahweh's community. The Persian Empire, in spite of setbacks in Egypt and Greece, continued to maintain a façade of fearful might almost to the eve of its dissolution. But in 334 B.C. Alexander the Great crossed the Hellespont and so began the adventure that brought the Persian Empire, and much more besides, under his heel.

In addition to conducting brilliant military campaigns, Alexander planned how best to organize his new territories. His dream was an empire united and ennobled by the advantages Greek civilization offered. He gave some substance to his dream by founding around 70 colonies and organizing them as Greek cities. In this and other ways powerful impetus was given the wave of Hellenization which spread through the Near East. The translation of the Hebrew Scriptures into Greek to produce the LXX and the composition of Wisdom in Greek, both in Egypt, bear witness to the new influence.

THE STRUGGLE WITH GREEK CULTURE

When Alexander died without an heir in 323, his generals divided up his empire and then fought among themselves for larger portions. One of these, Ptolemy by name, having seized control of Egypt and made Alexandria his capital, established his claim over Palestine. During the century Palestine was ruled by the Ptolemies, Greek ways began to be known there, though the Jews continued to enjoy relative peace and liberty. But this situation was not to last. Seleucus, another of Alexander's generals, received Babylonia as his portion after Alexander's death and then extended his rule to Syria and Asia Minor. He founded Antioch as royal capital and it became a center of Hellenistic influence for all Syria. He and his successors laid claim to Palestine, too, but it was not until 198, when the Seleucid king Antiochus III (223–187) shattered the forces of Ptolemy V, that the claim could be enforced.

In spite of his successes elsewhere, Antiochus III lost out when he clashed with the might of Rome, now beginning to assert itself in Asia. Henceforth the Seleucids would live under the fear of Roman intervention and this fear would add urgency to the desire to unify their territories along the lines begun by Alexander. Under Antiochus IV (175–163) this policy was pressed so far as to cause the Jews to rise in rebellion.

PERSECUTION AND THE MACCABEAN REVOLT. We are relatively well informed concerning the events of this period, thanks to the Books of Maccabees. They are named for Judas Maccabeus[1] and his brothers Jonathan and Simon, leaders of the Jewish resistance. These two deuterocanonical books are independent works, not divisions of a continuous composition as 1–2 Samuel or 1–2 Kings are. Many of the same events are related in both, though 1 Maccabees is broader in scope, covering the period from the accession of Antiochus IV (175) to the death of Simon Maccabeus (134); 2 Maccabees ends with a crucial victory won by Judas in 165.

Though both books intend to relate religious history, their approaches differ notably. The author of 2 Maccabees places much emphasis on the marvelous, relating many miracles and striking, visible manifestations of God's intervention to bring victory to His people (e.g., 3:24–28; 10:29–30); he clearly wishes to edify and impress. He does not vouch for the historicity of every detail (2:27) but presents his composition as an abridgement of a five volume work by one Jason of Cyrene (2:23). The author of 1 Maccabees also wishes to edify and is no less convinced of God's hand in the events he relates; he is satisfied, however, that this emerges for the eye of faith from a straightforward account somewhat in the manner of David's court historian. The basic agreement of these independent works on the events they relate testifies to their fundamental accuracy.

Affairs in Palestine did not go as smoothly under the Seleucids as they had under the Ptolemies. Already the Jews themselves were dividing into two camps over the creeping Hellenization of the land; some embraced it gladly while others considered it a threat to their ancestral religion. When Antiochus IV ascended the throne, he gladly encouraged the former group and even sold the Jewish high

---

[1] "Maccabeus" is a nickname which probably means "hammer." It was applied first to Judas and then to the brothers who succeeded him.

priesthood to whomever offered the largest sum and promised fullest cooperation.

Between the efforts of Antiochus, high priests who were his creatures, and the Jewish party eager to adopt Greek ways, there was enough to alarm faithful Jews. Ancient cultures were far less compartmentalized than ours and the changes introduced were bound to have an impact detrimental to faith. Even the gymnasium now established in Jerusalem represented far more than Greek sports; Jews who joined found themselves shamed for their circumcision (and attempted to disguise it—1 Macc 1:14–15), shared in the worship of Greek gods of sport, and owed allegiance to a king who claimed divine honors. In more directly religious affairs the Hellenizing tendency would be to identify Yahweh with Zeus; while this was not a direct repudiation of Israel's God, it was as grave a distortion of Israel's concept of divinity as the earlier attempts to identify Him with Baal.

The resistance of loyal Jews to the new ways led Antiochus to sterner measures. In his desire to make his whole kingdom "one people," he forbade Jewish practices and imposed pagan ones (1 Macc 1:41–63). The regular Temple sacrifices were proscribed as well as circumcision, observance of the Sabbath, and possession of sacred books. Jews were forced to eat foods forbidden by their Law and to sacrifice at pagan altars set up throughout the land. Disobedience in any of these cases was punishable by death, and many died rather than submit. The crowning affront was the desecration of the Temple in 167 with the erection of the "abomination of desolation," i.e., an altar to (and possibly an image of) Zeus Olympios, on the altar of holocausts.

Jewish resentment had by now risen to fever pitch. The spark that kindled it into open revolt was supplied by Mattathias, father of Judas Maccabeus and his four brothers and priest of the village of Modein. He killed the king's official who came there to induce the Jews to offer pagan sacrifice, then fled into the hills with his sons and other loyal Jews (1 Macc 2:1–28). This courageous band of desperate men waged guerrilla warfare against the Seleucid forces and the renegade Jews who sided with them. When Mattathias died, military leadership of the group passed to Judas, a vigorous and able warrior. Under his guidance the rebel band, now substantially augmented as more and more Jews flocked to their banners, was able to defeat first the Syrian forces stationed in Palestine and then the larger armies sent to still the rebellion. Since Antiochus was engaged in Parthia with the bulk of his military force, these victories left Judas free to seize control of Jerusalem and purify and rededicate the Temple (1 Macc 4:36–61; 2 Macc 10:1–9). This was done in 164, just three years after it had been desecrated. The Jewish feast of Hanukkah celebrates the rededication.

This, however, was not the end of the struggle. Antiochus died in 163 during the Parthian campaign and Lysias, a general Antiochus had named regent in his absence and who had led one of the Syrian expeditions against Judas, usurped his throne. When Judas beseiged the citadel the Syrians had erected in Jerusalem, Lysias hastened to its relief. The Jews fared badly this time, but news of a rival to his throne led Lysias to make peace on favorable terms, granting religious freedom to the Jews.

The details of later events need not detain us. Judas continued to fight for greater autonomy and in 160 was killed in battle. He was succeeded by his brother Jonathan, a man who joined diplomatic skills to military prowess. He was able to play off rival claimants to the Seleucid throne against one another and to obtain privileges and concessions in return for his support. Under him the Jews won a good measure of political independence; he himself obtained appointment as high priest. Treacherously slain in 142, he was succeeded by his brother Simon. Simon, too, was appointed high priest and was given the title ethnarch besides (1 Macc 14:47; 15:2), offices which were passed on to his descendants.

Thus was founded the Hasmonean[2] dynasty which continued in power until 40 B.C. The nobility of purpose with which this family began was not maintained. Pious Jews were shocked to see their high priests engaged in bloody intrigues and driven on by lust for power. Soon those very elements which had supported the Maccabean revolt were in opposition to the dynasty. Beginning with Aristobulus I (104–103) the Hasmoneans called themselves kings, a policy which further increased opposition. The rule of this line came to an end in 40 B.C. when Rome, having incorporated Syria and its territories into the empire in 63 B.C., made Herod, son of the governor of Idumea, king of the Jews. This inglorious end of the line that began so nobly was an ironic twist of fate, for it was John Hyrcanus, son of Simon Maccabeus, who had conquered Idumea and forcibly imposed Judaism on its citizens.

THE BOOK OF DANIEL

Although the Book of Daniel presents itself as an account of the adventures, dreams, and revelations of Daniel, a Jewish lad in the Babylonian Exile in the 6th century, the true background of its composition is Palestine during the persecution of Antiochus IV. Thus while historical references to the period of the exile are vague and often inaccurate, those to the Seleucid period (still in the future according to the literary artifice employed by the author) are detailed and precise. This is seen most clearly in Daniel 11, where the kings "of the south" are Ptolemies, the kings "of the north" are Seleucids, and the "despicable person" of vv 21–45 is Antiochus IV. The desecration of the Temple had already taken place at the time of writing (9:26–27;

---

[2]Named for a forefather of Mattathias.

11:31), but not its rededication. The time of composition can therefore be placed in the period 167-164 B.C.

The location of Daniel among the Major Prophets in the Christian Canon is somewhat misleading, for the book is not a prophecy; on its relationship to prophecy, see below. In the Jewish Canon it is placed among the Writings. The hero of the book may be taken from a legendary figure (as in the case of Job), possibly the Daniel known from Ugaritic literature; but the adventures described in 1-6 are fictional rather than historical. Daniel 7-12 consists of apocalyptic visions, a matter we will discuss below. The book may be divided as follows:

> A. *Adventures of Daniel and his companions at court:* 1-6
> B. *Apocalyptic revelations:* 7-12
> C. *Deuterocanonical additions:* 13-14

CHAPTERS 1-6. The six episodes at the royal court related in 1-6 may be classified as didactic fiction (as also the tales in 13-14). Some of these stories are earlier compositions[3] which the author has utilized. All of them depict Daniel and his companions as models of steadfast Jewish faith, persevering in spite of the dangers and blandishments of the pagan court. The Jews of 167 B.C. would have had no trouble in seeing the parallel with their own situation, for the stories were composed or adapted to encourage them to a like perseverance. Just as the Jews and their faith had outlasted the mighty Babylonian Empire, long gone when these stories were written, so could they outlast the Syrians.

There is an obvious pertinence to the later situation in Daniel's refusal to eat unclean food (1) or to omit his religious practices and pay divine honor to the king (6). The same is true of his companions' refusal, even under pain of death, to worship the image set up by the king (3). That they are divinely preserved through all these dangers teaches that God delivers and does not forsake His faithful ones. Above this motif, however, is the determination to remain steadfast whatever the cost: "But even if [God] will not [deliver us], know, O king, that we will not serve your god or worship the golden statue you have set up" (3:18). Other episodes exalt the divinely revealed wisdom of the Jews at the expense of pagan wise men (2) or suggest that the king has overreached himself in sacrilegious wickedness and faces speedy retribution (5).

APOCALYPTIC. Before turning to Daniel 7-12, we must say something about the literary form of this section. The Book of Revelation is sometimes called the Apocalypse of St. John; it received this strange name because it presents itself as an *apokalypsis* (revelation—Rev

---

[3]See L. Hartman, "The Great Tree and Nabuchodonosor's Madness," in *The Bible in Current Catholic Thought,* ed. J. L. McKenzie (New York: Herder and Herder, 1962), pp. 75-82.

1:1); it is one of the chief examples of a type of literature which flourished between 200 B.C. and 100 A.D., and the whole genre is named apocalyptic.

Apocalyptic has often been called the child of prophecy, an apt designation. Both the prophet and the apocalyptist exhort to faithfulness, see God as Lord of history, foretell the future, describe visions, and expect imminent judgment. But apocalyptic is a literature which arises in time of trouble and persecution, and its end is to give hope to men who face death for their faith. Whereas the prophet addressed himself to sinful men and warned them to repent, the apocalyptist speaks to the faithful and urges them to persevere. Amos warned a complacent people that the Day of Yahweh meant judgment upon them, but in apocalyptic the coming judgment brings deliverance from persecution and reward for fidelity. The prophets generally considered the pagan nations instruments of God's wrath against a sinful people, whereas the apocalyptist sees a pagan nation wrongfully and wickedly persecuting an innocent people until God intervenes to deliver. The apocalyptist sees the world divided into two camps; he wishes to give hope and strength to the good but has little hope that the wicked will be converted.

Apocalyptic is usually pseudonymous; the author consigns his teaching in the guise of revelations made to some ancient worthy. The reason for this is debated. At the very least it hid the identity of the writer; since he was counseling resistance to the ruling power, this was no small advantage. It is unlikely that his contemporary Jews would have been led astray by the artifice as later generations have been.

One of the striking features of apocalyptic is its use of fantastic visions and bizarre imagery. This device is already found in the later prophets who were forerunners of apocalyptic, especially Ezekiel, Zechariah, and Joel (Ezekiel 38–39; Zech 1:7–6:8; Joel 2:2–11; 4:1–21). The angel-interpreter that appears already in Zechariah becomes a standard feature of later compositions. The visions of full-blown apocalyptic, unlike most of those described in prophetic books, are probably in the main literary conventions rather than true visions. The details of such visions draw heavily on earlier Scripture, a factor which would make their veiled teaching intelligible to a Jew but not to a pagan persecutor who happened to read the book. The details and their meaning tended to become stereotyped, almost like a code message that could be deciphered bit by bit by those who had the key. For example, an animal usually represents a pagan empire, a horn stands for a king (or is sometimes a symbol of power), while three and a half years designates the period of tribulation.

Special attention should be given the apocalyptic view of history. Through the device of an ancient hero the author places himself in some past era (in Daniel, e.g., in the period of the exile), but his real interest lies with the events of his own time—the immediate past, present, and future—concerning which he speaks in great detail, though in a veiled fashion. The apocalyptist views history, beheld especially in the succession of world empires, as unrolling under the provident eye of God; when the predetermined moment comes, God will intervene to bring these kingdoms to an end and establish the messianic kingdom. This begins a new era beyond human history, the final age (Greek: *eschaton*). Thus apocalyptic is strongly eschatological in its orientation. A final terrible struggle between the forces of good and evil is foreseen as the prelude to the establishment of God's kingdom. The apocalyptist knows that God does not abandon those who trust in Him, and he foresees a saving intervention—and *soon*! The deliverance comes by divine help, not human means; the author advocates fidelity and hope, not rebellion.

The apocalyptist sees the tribulation of his times as the final struggle and deliverance as the first step in the final act of redemption. In a similar fashion the prophets had expected the establishment of the new order of messianic redemption to coincide with the restoration after the exile.

Many of the characteristics just described can be seen to be verified not only in Daniel, Revelation, and the non-canonical apocalypses (e.g., 2 Esdras and the Book of Enoch), but also in Ezekiel 38-39, Jesus' discourse on the end in Mark 13, and St. Paul's warning in 2 Thess 2:1-12.

CHAPTERS 7-12. Of the four visions in Daniel 7-12, the one in ch. 7 is undoubtedly the masterpiece; it is, moreover, an outstanding example of the method and message of apocalyptic. We must devote a little attention to it.

The four fearsome beasts represent four great world empires: Babylonian, Median, Persian, and Greek.[4] That they rise from the sea suggests that they are hostile, chaotic forces opposed to God (see p. 51, n. 5). Special attention is given to the fourth beast (the Greeks); its terrifying appearance and destructive behavior bring to mind the persecution endured by the author and his contemporaries. The "little horn" that speaks arrogantly (v 8) is a contemptuous reference to Antiochus IV.

But now comes the judgment, and attention flashes to heaven (vv 9-12). God mounts His throne and the punishment decreed for wickedness is administered. The fourth beast, the persecutor of the saints, perishes at once. The milder treatment accorded the other three perhaps reflects the prophetic teachings that the Gentiles, too, have a part in God's plan.

---

[4]The succession of kingdoms is not wholly accurate historically. The Medes were allies of the Babylonians in overthrowing Assyria and their kingdom was contemporary with Babylonia's; both were gobbled up by Persian conquest. The same succession is found in the king's dream in 2:31-45, a passage which alludes to the fragmentation of Alexander's kingdom but otherwise presents basically the same teaching as ch. 7.

The negative, destructive phase of the final drama was necessitated by the perverse opposition of the anti-God forces (labeled Antichrist in the *NT),* but now the way is clear for the positive phase, the establishment of the messianic kingdom (vv 13-14). This is represented by the investiture of "one like a son of man"—a poetic way of saying "a human figure." Just as the pagan kingdoms were aptly symbolized by monstrous beasts, so God's kingdom is aptly symbolized by a man on whom are conferred "dominion, glory, and kingship." The Son of Man, then, stands primarily for a collectivity,[5] though an individual to exercise, under God, the kingship bestowed is not excluded. The text does not speak of the Davidic Messiah; the bestowal of kingship from above, rather than the restoration of the Davidic dynasty, is an alternate approach to God's redemptive act.[6]

In 7:25 the author indicates that the time is short—three and a half years! In the third vision, in ch. 9, he returns to the question of time. He poses the problem of why Jeremiah's prediction of restoration (i.e., in the sense of messianic redemption) after 70 years had not been fulfilled (v 2) and answers with a midrashic interpretation (p. 247). He meditates on the curses attached to non-observance of the Law (vv 11-13) and, probably influenced by Lev 26:18 (which speaks of seven-fold chastisement for sins), arrives at 70 *weeks* of years, i.e., 490 years, as the period of punishment (v 24). He then distributes the first 69 "weeks" over the periods from Jeremiah to his own time. His interest centers on the final "week," the period of persecution. It begins with the slaying of an anointed one (v 26—probably a reference to the high priest Onias III, murdered ca. 170 B.C.; cf. 2 Macc 4:33-34). It reaches its mid-point with the abolition of the daily sacrifices and the desecration of the Temple (v 27; 167 B.C.). Since these events had already taken place when the author wrote, he is saying that only half a "week" is left until the persecutors are destroyed and "everlasting justice will be introduced" (v 24).

God did indeed deliver those who trusted in Him, not through a judgment hurtling down from heaven but through the Maccabean leaders, whom He raised up as He had the Judges of old. Their hardy "praise the Lord and pass the ammunition" approach was not what the author of Daniel expected, nor did their victory usher in the messianic kingdom with all its blessings. The rule of the Hasmoneans who followed them was, in fact, often marked by violence and corruption. The author of Daniel was right in his discernment of the pattern of redemption in God's activity and in predicting deliverance; he shared

---

[5]The interpretation in vv 18 and 27 simply substitutes "the holy people of the Most High" for the Son of Man.

[6]Later writings take over and develop the Son of Man figure. In the apocryphal Book of Enoch, for example, the Son of Man appears as a preexistent heavenly being who will appear on earth for judgment in the last days. Jesus used the title Son of Man to refer both to His lowly condition as Servant and to His power and future glory.

the prophets' lack of temporal perspective in expecting that the end of *this* crisis would bring final redemption.

The inspired message of Daniel is one of hope and steadfastness. However long God's kingdom might be in coming, hope would not, could not be abandoned. The *OT* period thus ends on a note of expectation, of hope firmly held but deferred yet again. Less than two centuries after the composition of Daniel there would be a vigorous new community in Palestine that believed Israel's hope had been fulfilled, that the last age had been inaugurated. They would trace the origin of their belief to a Prophet who had appeared to urge repentance and to announce the glad tidings that God's kingdom was bursting in upon them—a Prophet who in His suffering and triumph was like the Servant, and who promised to return like the Son of Man. They would believe that in Him God's promise to Abraham concerning "all the nations of the earth" had been fulfilled, that in Him God had spoken His perfect Word to Israel. But the *OT* tells of expectation, not fulfillment, so here our study must end.

READING SUGGESTIONS

JBC §20; 26-27. *PBS* #34. *OTRG* #13. *AUOT* 569-91. *BHI* 407-29, 461-67. *WITOT* 313-17.

Collins, J. J., *1-2 Maccabees, Daniel, Excursus on Apocalyptic Movement. OTM*, Vol. 16.
_____, *Daniel with an Introduction to Apocalyptic Literature.* Grand Rapids: Eerdmans, 1984.
_____, *Between Athens and Jerusalem. Jewish Identity in the Hellenistic Diaspora.* New York: Crossroad Press, 1983.
Hartman, L. F., and A. Di Lella, *The Book of Daniel. AB* 23; Garden City, N.Y.: Doubleday & Company, Inc., 1978.
McNamara, M., *Intertestamental Literature. OTM*, Vol. 23.
Rowland, C., *The Open Heaven: A Study of Apocalyptic in Judaism and Early Christianity.* New York: Crossroad Press, 1982.
Russell, D. S., *Daniel.* Philadelphia: Westminster Press, 1981.

Bushinski, L., "Daniel: Midrash and Apocalyptic," *TBT* 21,4 (July, 1983) 227-33.
Collins, J. J., "Apocalyptic Eschatology as the Transcendence of Death," *CBQ* 36 (1974) 21-43.
_____, "The Court Tales in Daniel and the Development of Apocalyptic," *JBL* 94 (1975) 218-34.
_____, "The Intertestamental Literature," *Listening: Journal of Religion and Culture* 19 (1984) 41-52.

Di Lella, A., "The One in Human Likeness and the Holy Ones of the Most High in Daniel 7," *CBQ* 39 (1977) 1-19.

Gammie, J. G., "On the Intentions and Sources of Daniel i-vi," *Vetus Testamentum* 31 (1981) 282-92.

Hanson, P. D., "Old Testament Apocalyptic Reexamined," *Int* 25 (1971) 454-79.

Koch, K., "Is Daniel Also Among the Prophets?" *Int* 39 (1985) 117-30.

Lindberger, J. M., "Daniel 12:1-4," *Int* 39 (1985) 181-86.

Nicholson, E. W., "Apocalyptic," *ATI* 189-213.

Towner, W. S., "The Preacher in the Lion's Den," *Int* 39 (1985) 157-69.

Viviano, P. A., "The Book of Daniel: Prediction or Encouragement?" *TBT* 21,4 (July, 1983) 221-26.

Walker, W. O., Jr., "Daniel 7:13-14," *Int* 39 (1985).

APPENDIX I

The Word of God in Words of Men

Revelation, Inspiration, Inerrancy, Canon

The Bible may be approached as a merely human work, as in fact it is by many. Even on this level its value is great and the rewards of studying it inestimable. The Book of Job is one of the world's greatest literary classics; the moral earnestness of the prophets presents us with high ideals of religion and social justice; and from an historical and cultural point of view, we would be hard put to point to anything which has had so profound an impact on our western world—on our social and political institutions, on our literature and art, and on our ideals. For the believer the importance of the Bible is greater still, for it is accepted as the word of God. This acceptance is not always easy in today's world, characterized, as it is, by empiricism. The empiricist will tend to equate the world of experience, circumscribed as that may be, with total reality and to reject the existence of anything outside of it. This stance, which is perhaps an inevitable by-product of our scientific age, may go so far as to insinuate that only what can be verified empirically is true or that statements which cannot be proved scientifically are meaningless. It is a stance which can rob us of ideals and higher aspirations, items which are in short supply even in the best of circumstances.

The human spirit, in the broad sweep of history, contradicts empiricism. It has always been the imponderables, things which cannot be weighed, measured, or precisely defined, that people consider worth dying for—things like love, honor, truth, freedom, and human rights. If a man is willing to die for something, he is convinced that it exists, that it is more important than himself, and even, perhaps, that it has ultimate value. The biblical authors believed that ultimate values were rooted in God, a personal being who revealed Himself to mankind. They believed that the Creator of the universe and its laws

259

was able to operate within it, that the Creator of the human heart was able to speak to it.

REVELATION

To speak of God revealing Himself to us is to enter a complicated and disputed area; obviously it is not a matter of a whisper in someone's ear. Revelation comes in a manner consistent with human nature. Man is a bodily creature situated in profound unity and continuity with the rest of material creation, from which, in fact, he has emerged as the climax of a long process of evolution. Consonant with the sacramental and incarnational character of redemption, revelation often comes in concrete and observable phenomena. Salvation history consists of a series of historical events, some of them scientifically ascertainable, which have a meaning within God's plan—a plan which they advance and accomplish. But the events are revelatory only to the extent that their meaning within God's plan is made clear. In the traditional "salvation history" approach (as typified, e.g., in O. Cullmann) the interpretation of events is supplied mainly from a series of great figures raised up to be spokesmen for God—Moses and the prophets in the *OT,* Jesus and the apostles in the *NT.* "Event plus interpretation" is the heart of this understanding of revelation. Ultimately the prophet's knowledge of the meaning of the event rests on a religious experience in which he comes to know God's nature and will; these he attempts to mediate to the people in human concepts. Other approaches are possible. W. Pannenberg, for example, insists that revelation in history is *indirect* (and he distinguishes it from the *direct* revelation of a theophany) but that the event carries its meaning within itself and does not have to be superadded to it through an interpretation from outside. Perceiving the meaning of the event, however, involves seeing it within the context of the meaning it had for those who experienced it and within the history of its transmission through new generations, as it takes on ever new significance. Moreover, Pannenberg's horizon is not simply the history of Israel and the Church but universal history. God is revealed in history, but history seen in its totality.

Revelation accords with the human condition in its progressive character. Few today would hold to a naive belief in a primitive revelation by which the first man would have known all there was to know about God. The knowledge of God and of His plan has come slowly and gradually. Even this gradual ascent could not have been made except through God's light; but it was light given in measure to the darkness and the capacity of the viewer, so as to illumine and not to blind. We can assert that biblical revelation and redemptive history begin with the call of Abraham and yet insist that a long period of preparation preceded that call; Abraham had to have some notion of a personal God who could call him to an undivided allegiance. A long development also had to follow this call before God's plan began to emerge—a development in which superstition had to be sorted out from religion and God's moral demands made known.

The perfecting of the understanding of God's plan continued throughout redemptive history and reached its final stage with the coming of Christ. In this final stage was made clear what Israel had perceived dimly all along, that God's purpose was to give His human creatures the only gift worthy of an infinitely good God, namely, Himself.

The belief that God has spoken to man was not limited to Israel; it is a belief that has been widely held in all ages. Men have always been convinced that God's will cannot be known unless He Himself reveals it and that, because God is concerned with His human creatures, He does reveal it. Needless to say, the fact of the wide diffusion of such belief founds no argument either for or against the truth of the belief.

Nevertheless, Israel's claim that God has spoken to her is unique in many ways; that claim is confirmed by the character of her faith and history in a way that makes its acceptance reasonable. Israel's concept of God cannot be explained as a product of the pagan beliefs of her neighbors; cultures more ancient, more noble, more intellectual than hers never approached it early or late. Israel's literature, even though produced by men widely separated in time and place, contains a consistent interpretation of the meaning of the broad aspects of her history; to Israel this was no mystery, for she saw these authors as spokesmen for the One who gave her history its meaning. And in the emergence of Christianity the deepest aspirations and hopes stirred up in the *OT* find satisfaction.

If these things are viewed as signs of God's activity in Israel's history, as steps in a coherent plan, then we have an explanation consistent with the facts. If this explanation is rejected, then the phenomenon of Israel and its issue in Christianity—the most remarkable forces ever to appear in human history—must remain an enigma.

The acceptance of this explanation accords with reason, then, even though it goes beyond what objective evidence imposes as a conclusion. Indeed, if it did not go beyond an evidential conclusion, this acceptance would be logic or science, but not faith; faith is the only basis on which revelation can be accepted.

The rationalist, of course, will reject this. If he did not, he would cease to be a rationalist. Yet his rejection is not as scientific and objective as he would have us think, for it is based on assumptions and hypotheses that are not susceptible of scientific proof. Detachment, too, is ruled out, for to admit that God has revealed Himself is to realize that man is invited to surrender himself to God. Who can be utterly detached in deciding a question whose answer spells personal involvement?

INSPIRATION

The final issue of God's revelation in Israel is, as pointed out in Chapter 1, redemption and a worshiping community. The record of the deeds by which God brought these things to pass is contained in the inspired literature of the Old and New Testaments. The concept of inspiration must be examined in some detail.

BELIEF IN INSPIRATION. Israel was convinced that she possessed the word of God in writing. It is hardly possible to say precisely how or when this conviction first originated. Its beginnings stretch at least as far back as the discovery of the "book of the law of the Lord" in the days of King Josiah (2 Kings 22-23). The behavior of Josiah and his followers shows that they considered the book authoritative for them; the reason was undoubtedly the authority of the name of Moses, to whom God had spoken (Exod 33:11). There was, in fact, a still earlier conviction that God had caused Moses to record certain events and laws (Exod 17:14; 24:3-4; 34:27), and so it may be supposed that written texts existed and were attributed to Moses and ultimately to God's authority. We also find references to prophets writing down the word of the Lord which they had received (Isa 30:8; Jer 30:2; Hab 2:2). Such writings had a special claim to be considered sacred and to be regarded as the word of God. By the end of the *OT* period the Jews believed they possessed sacred books written in words of absolute truth. These were books which they retained, even when to do so might mean death at the hands of persecutors (Dan 9:2; 1 Macc 1:59-60; 12:9). By the time the preface to Sirach was written, the three-fold division of the Jewish Canon (see p. 270) had already emerged. Jesus, His disciples, and the ones responsible for the *NT* in general show their full acceptance of the sacred, authoritative character of the *OT*. The words of the "Law and the Prophets" must be fulfilled; it was God or the Spirit who spoke through the *OT* writers; the Scriptures "cannot be broken."[1] Very soon the early Church accorded to the gospels and the other apostolic writings a dignity equal to that of the books of the *OT*. It would seem that St. Paul's epistles were recognized as Scripture by the time of the writing of 2 Peter (2 Pet 3:16).

In the early Church, then, there existed the firm belief that the Scriptures had been inspired by God. There was at that time, however,

---

[1]Matt 5:17-18; Luke 24:26-27, 44; Mark 7:10, 13; 12:36; Acts 4:25; 28:25; 2 Pet 2:21; 2 Tim 3:15-16.

little attempt to define or explain more fully the nature of inspiration. The Council of Constantinople (381 A.D.) declared that the Holy Spirit had "spoken through the Prophets," and the Council of Florence (1441) acknowledged that the same God was "author of both the Old and New Testaments since the saints of both had spoken by the inspiration of the same Holy Spirit." The Council of Trent (1546) and the First Vatican Council (1870) also spoke of God as the author of the Bible, as did Vatican II (1965). The early Church Fathers had used similar expressions; the usual assertions are that God inspired the Scriptures, that they were written at the dictation of the Holy Spirit, that He used the human authors as a musician uses a musical instrument, that God spoke through them, and so forth.

ROLE OF GOD AND ROLE OF MAN. Such words express the conviction that ultimately Scripture is the word of God. Less clearly expressed is the role of the human author; see, for example, the words of St. Gregory the Great quoted above (p. 7). Yet even a cursory examination of the Bible shows to what an extent the human element has entered into its composition. We speak of the Prophecy of Isaiah, the Wisdom of Sirach, the Gospel according to Mark, the Epistles of St. Paul, and so forth, because we understand that the men named are either the literary authors of the books in question or are in some way responsible for them. The authors of the biblical books often show themselves aware of the labor they expended, mention the sources they utilized, and often betray no consciousness of being inspired in their work.[2] Specialized study of the individual books reveals the individual character of the human contributor: the literary genius of Isaiah is not the same as Jeremiah's; the theological doctrine of Jeremiah differs from Ezekiel's; Amos and Hosea were worlds apart in temperament. Since these and other men have so clearly left their "fingerprints" on the books of the Bible, it is apparent that they contributed, too, and were not simply uncomprehending secretaries. Any acceptable theory of inspiration, therefore, must take account both of the assertion of faith that the Bible is the word of God and of the conclusion of reason and observation (which faith has never sought to deny) that it is also a human composition. In short, such a theory should explain how one book can be the work of both God and man.

THEORY OF INSTRUMENTAL CAUSALITY. The explanation that was long considered the most acceptable is that based on the analogy of instrumental causality. St. Thomas's name is often linked to it because he used this analogy to explain the effectiveness of the Sacraments, applied it to the concept of prophetic inspiration, and spoke of

---

[2]Luke 1:1–4; 2 Macc 2:25–33 (from this passage comes our expression "sweat and midnight oil"—a vivid description of the labor that went into the composition of 2 Maccabees); 15:38–40.

biblical writers as instrumental authors. The detailed application of the analogy of instrumental causality to the problem of the literary inspiration of the Bible is the work of more recent authors, especially M.-J. Lagrange and Pierre Benoit.

This theory takes as its starting point the distinction between principal and instrumental causality. An instrument has a certain inherent power to produce the effect or accomplish the action it was designed for: a saw can cut through a log, a knife can carve the surface of wood, a brush can spread paint. An instrument, however, can do what it was designed to do only when it is applied, that is, put into operation or moved, by the user (the principal cause). An instrument is an extension of the one who wields it, and he uses it because his hand or finger could not work so well, or even at all, without it. Nails are driven more easily with hammers than with fists; fingerpainting has yet to produce a Mona Lisa. The instrumental cause, when moved by the principal cause, is said to be elevated in that it produces an effect of an order higher than its own causality. A paint brush is apt only for spreading paint, but in the hands of a capable artist it can produce a landscape of matchless beauty.

The effect produced by the principal cause moving an instrumental cause must be attributed to both causes, though in different ways, according to the level of causality proper to each. The painting must be attributed to both the artist and the brush, but in different ways. The brush strokes in a painting are the effect of the brush; but they are at the same time so much the effect of the artist and so characteristic of him that an expert can distinguish an original by a known master from a forgery on the basis of the brush strokes alone.

In an analogous way, the theory goes on to say, the Bible is the product of both God and man because God uses man as His instrument; each is totally the cause of the Bible, but on different levels of causality. God may be called the principal author, man the instrumental author. Man, elevated and moved by God, produces an effect he could not produce alone—a book which is the word of God.

This is an analogy, of course, and should not be understood mechanically. An instrument is used in a manner that accords with its nature; we don't drive nails with paint brushes. If it is said that God uses man as an instrument, it is to be understood that all those faculties proper to a human being—even to *this* human being—are brought into play. Thus God, in applying His human instrument to the task of composing a book, is said to utilize him as a creature having a free will and an intellect, as a man with a particular vocabulary, as a product of a particular tradition, and as a member of a particular age and culture. The writer's free will remains intact, even though God moves him to will to write. Precisely how it is that God can move man to want to do something without infringing his free will is a mystery; but this is true of every act that is performed under the influence of divine grace, and is not peculiar to the problem of inspiration.

Man's intellect, according to this theory, is affected by the grace of inspiration. The speculative judgment grasps the truth that God wants taught. The practical judgment decides how best to communicate it or to accomplish whatever is the end of the book to be written; this may be to exhort to good, console in time of affliction, draw others to love God, and so forth. The decision will involve the choice of the literary form to be used, and other similar matters.

Because the final stage will involve formulating the teaching in words and sentences, the theory proposes that even here man is not left on his own, but is moved, elevated, and applied to the task by God, so that even the choice of words is not withdrawn from the divine influence. This is what is meant by the term "verbal inspiration," at least as used by Catholic authors. It should be noted that this involves a quite different concept than "verbal dictation," an understanding of inspiration that would reduce the role of the human author to little more than stenography. (Non-Catholic authors sometimes use "verbal inspiration" to refer to what is here called "verbal dictation," but it would be preferable to keep the concepts distinct by use of separate terms.)

SOCIAL CHARACTER OF INSPIRATION. Many modern scholars feel that the theory of instrumental causality is no longer adequate to explain the inspiration of the Bible in all the complexity of its origins as we now understand them, even though it is admitted that no systematic and comprehensive explanation has been provided to take its place. It has been pointed out that although the concept of the Bible as "God's word" is scriptural, that of "God as author" is not. (On this and much more, see reference to Vawter in bibliography at the end of this appendix.) It is objected that only very improperly can God be considered the *literary* author of the Bible and that the analogy of instrumentality, when pressed in all its logic, leaves the human author not much more than a secretary. Again, the emphasis on God as literary author neglects the fact that fixation in writing may often be incidental to a far more important development in stages of oral tradition. A problem with "verbal inspiration" is raised on the grounds that content and literary conventions often did more to determine the words used than the author's choice.

But difficulties are experienced most especially because of all that literary analysis has taught us about the origins of the biblical books. The theory, as originally conceived, seemed to suppose that each book of the Bible had a single author and was produced within a limited period of time, as modern books usually are. In fact, the essential teaching of many portions of the *OT* reached a more or less completed stage long before being finally fixed in the books we now have. The

Pentateuch can serve as an example. It is now generally conceded that the bulk of the Pentateuch comes from four strands or traditions which reached final form in different places and at various times. No authors' names can be assigned to the traditions; they seem to be the product of traditionary circles rather than of individuals. The ones responsible for the traditions, moreover, drew on earlier sources—stories, family histories, poetic pieces, cult legends, etc.; these, in turn, may already have had a long history of transmission behind them. Some of the sources go back to the Hebrew Patriarchs (first half of the second millennium B.C.), while the finished Pentateuch probably dates from the 5th century B.C. Much of the material was passed on orally for a long time before it was put into writing; during both oral and written stages the material underwent many alterations in order to incorporate new insights into the work of God in Israel. Thus over a period of more than a thousand years countless persons played their parts in shaping the contents of the Pentateuch until it became the reflection of Israel's faith that it now is.

Much of this may have been accomplished while the material was passed on in oral form and therefore before we can speak properly of *literary* inspiration. Was it only when this material began to be written down that inspiration was present? Obviously not! Should it, then, be explained by the distribution of the grace of inspiration to each one who contributed to the final product? John L. McKenzie considers this explanation somewhat mechanical and contrived.

Karl Rahner had already proposed to understand inspiration in the *NT* as a grace which resides primarily in the primitive Church itself rather than in the individual authors (see below on Canon); these authors wrote simply as representatives of the Church. McKenzie points out that the unifying trait of the biblical literature is the recital of the saving deeds of God and the profession of faith of Israel. This recital and profession is shaped by the People of God rather than by the individual writers. What they record is the faith of the community, of which they are the (for the most part) anonymous spokesmen. McKenzie, therefore, wishes to regard the charism we call inspiration as residing in the community, and the biblical writers as spokesmen who record the faith elaborated in and by the community under the guidance of God. This is a valid approach, though we need also to emphasize the role of Israel's leaders—Moses, the prophets, and other—in forming Israel's faith, often against the opposition of the people as a whole.

Inerrancy

It has been traditional in Catholic (and most Protestant) circles to hold that the inerrancy of the Bible is a necessary consequence of its inspired character: if the Bible is the word of God, it is necessarily without error. This has never been defined as a dogma of faith, though it has appeared in various formulations in Church documents. There is universal agreement among scholars who employ the historical-critical approach to Scripture that one ought not attempt to extend inerrancy to matters of science nor to matters of history that do not relate directly to what the biblical author is intending to teach.[3] This conclusion is based on the biblical data themselves. In the first chapter of Genesis, for example, the animals are created before mankind, whereas in the second chapter they come after the first man. There is an obvious discrepancy here, but it is equally obvious that the author or editor who put these two accounts together did not consider that important nor contrary to the truth he was intent on teaching, that, namely, which relates to God's activity as creator, His relationship to mankind, and the place of mankind in creation (expressed in different but complementary fashion in the two accounts). The Bible supposes a geocentric universe, and the notorious condemnation of Galileo was occasioned by the belief that the heliocentric theory therefore had to be false.

Many other examples of this sort could be given, and so it is clear that some qualification has to be introduced into the concept of inerrancy. This has led some to question the appropriateness of the term "inerrancy" itself, a term which they say has "died the death of a thousand qualifications." It is of interest to note that the term was not used by Vatican II in its dogmatic constitution on divine revelation, "Dei Verbum." This omission is perhaps of special significance in view of the fact that the council fathers, in the course of the several drafts through which this constitution went, turned from the more traditional expressions ("the entire Sacred Scripture is absolutely immune from error," "divine inspiration by its very nature excludes and rejects every error in every field, religious or profane") to the more modest assertion that Scripture teaches "without error that truth which God wanted put into the sacred writings for the sake of our salvation." This formulation takes into account the purpose for which God inspired the Scriptures ("for the sake of our salvation"), limits the guarantee against error to it, and offers a much more defensible position than the originally proposed assertion that the Bible is free from error "in every field, religious or profane."

Nevertheless, this assurance of truth is of great importance, for the Bible has always been authoritative and normative for the Church in those things which are taught "for the sake of our salvation." It should be recognized, however, that the discernment of the

---

[3]For a different view, expressed by some evangelical groups, see the summary of "The Chicago Statement on Biblical Inerrancy" in *OTA* 2 (1979) #287. For an exposition and critique of this approach, see P. Achtemeier, *The Inspiration of Scripture: Problems and Proposals* (Philadelphia: Westminster Press, 1980), pp. 50-75.

authoritative and normative teaching of the Bible is no easy task. Lohfink, in an important discussion of biblical inerrancy (see in bibliography at end of appendix), asks whether this special authority is to be predicated of each individual book of the Bible, of each individual author, or only of the Bible as a whole, and then argues that the third position alone is defensible. We can add that although the key to many difficulties lies in ascertaining "what the author intended to teach," this does not always provide a final solution. Israelite hostility to pagans may often be motivated by zeal for true religion, but when Deuteronomy enjoins the extermination of the Amalekites (25:17-19—an injunction Samuel sends Saul to carry out in 1 Sam 15:1-3), the reason given is that the Amalekites harassed Israel's rear guard during the journey from Egypt. Elsewhere in the Bible such vindictiveness of spirit is condemned. When Jesus says, "You have heard the commandment, 'You shall . . . hate your enemy' " (Matt 5:43), He is not citing any *OT* text but simply giving the intent of a passage such as Deut 25:17-19. The corrective is given in His words, "My command to you is: Love your enemies and pray for your persecutors" (Matt 5:44), and in many other passages in both the *OT* and the *NT*.

Problems relating to biblical truth in the particular areas of science, history, and morality require a brief discussion.

THE BIBLE AND SCIENCE. The first effect of advances in science seemed to be a blow at biblical truth and authority. For this reason, the early reactions of believers sometimes took the form of a rejection of scientific findings (as in the condemnation of Galileo or the hostility towards the theory of evolution), on the one hand, or of concordism (the attempt to show that the Bible says the same thing as science), on the other. However, it was soon seen that both these positions were untenable, and the answer was found in a more nuanced understanding of biblical truth. The biblical authors, as we now realize, were children of their own times and shared the prescientific world view of their contemporaries. Many of their statements are incorrect from a scientific point of view.

To admit this is not to reject the authority of the Bible, for such inaccuracies were no part of what the biblical authors intended to teach "for the sake of our salvation." God could have prevented such misstatements only by giving a countless series of revelations; this was not done because it was not necessary for the ends for which God inspired the Bible.

While it would be wrong to limit biblical truth simply to "matters of faith and morals," it is clear that science is not what the biblical authors were concerned about. How surprised we would be if the Bible began with the periodic table of elements! Such information is not unimportant, but to give it in the Bible would not advance the cause of salvation history. The Biblical authors frequently betray the naive

prescientific conceptions of their day; it is one of the tasks of interpretation to seek beneath these conceptions what is being taught "for
the sake of our salvation."

THE BIBLE AND HISTORY. What has been said of science cannot be applied without qualification to history. While it is not the end of the
Bible to teach science, the same is not true of history. The Bible is
called salvation history because its message rests on concrete events; if
the account of those events had no basis in reality, the message of the
Bible would be without foundation, without reality. It can and must
be asserted, however, that history as an exact scientific discipline is
not to be found in the Bible. This topic will be more fully discussed in
Appendix II.

PROGRESSIVE MORAL DEVELOPMENT. A final word should be said
concerning certain imperfections in the *OT* that appear obvious in the
light of more advanced morality. I am not referring here to the serious
failing of great *OT* figures. In recounting such things the Bible is simply being truthful and realistic; the wonder of God's work is seen
more fully when we recognize that it has been accomplished through
the fragile clay of human nature. We are concerned, rather, with cases
in which biblical authors take for granted that God approves of things
which our conscience tells us must be condemned. The *OT* writers
even present them as commands in the mouth of God. For example,
God is said to command Abraham to offer his son Isaac in sacrifice or
to command the Israelites to wipe out their enemies.[4]

Bishop Butler reminds us that all revelation of God to man is

> a divine self-disclosure within human experience, and therefore subject to the limita-
> tions of the human recipient. . . . If it is a revelation directed towards action, it will
> take form and shape in the conscience of the recipient and will be to some extent
> limited by his existing moral stature. . . .

Yet even this faulty apprehension of the will of God is conscience and
its dictates are to be followed as the voice of God.[5] In the story of
Abraham referred to above, it is clear that God did not intend him to
take the life of his son; that Abraham thought, in the first instance,
that He did (and this is all that need be understood by the
"command") can be explained as a case of faulty conscience. But the
author was not asking whether Abraham's conscience was faulty or
informed; the point of the narrative is Abraham's sublime obedience
to what he understood the will of God to be.

As for the other example, the Israelites were rightly convinced that
God abhorred the abominable pagan practices of the Canaanites, that

[4]Genesis 22; Deut 7:1-2; 25:17-19; Josh 6:16-21; 8:2; 1 Sam 15:1-3.
[5]B. C. Butler, *The Church and the Bible* (Baltimore-London: Helicon Press, 1960), p.
71.

such practices merited punishment, and that they were to preserve themselves from them. In these circumstances, their consciences condoned or even dictated the destruction of such men. The dictates of conscience in this case concerned the extirpation of evil; it did not include (as we now see it should have) a long series of other considerations. Even those who violated the ban (and were condemned for it!) acted through cupidity, not kindness (Josh 7:1; 1 Sam 15:10-20). What was said above concerning the progressive nature of revelation is pertinent here.

Difficulties concerning biblical truth will sometimes be laid to rest through a more accurate determination of the author's end; this can often be obtained through study of the literary form—a matter dealt with below (see p. 284).

THE CANON OF SCRIPTURE

The word "Canon," when used of the Scriptures, designates the collection of books which the Church accepts as inspired. Since no scientific or other merely human investigation can determine whether or not a particular writing was produced through divine inspiration, this can be known only on the authority of God made known through the teaching authority of His Church. From this assertion arise two questions. First, the historical question: which books have been recognized as canonical by the Church and when were they so proclaimed? Second, the theological question: how can the inspired character of these books be recognized by the Church?

THE HISTORICAL QUESTION. Although the Church issued no binding decision on the Canon before the Council of Trent (1546), the 72 books named then had long been universally recognized as canonical. The authoritative pronouncement of Trent had the character of a reaffirmation in the face of the doubts raised by the Reformation concerning some of these books. The official consensus within the Church that Trent reaffirmed had not been arrived at easily, however, and it will be necessary to investigate the steps by which it was reached. Our only concern will be the *OT* Canon. (On the *NT* Canon, see *JBC* §67:48-86.)

The Jewish Canon may be taken as a starting point. I will not attempt to review the stages of the process by which this collection was formed and attained recognition—a process in many ways still obscure. It may be regarded as certain that the Jewish Canon was definitively fixed before the end of the 1st century A.D., though it is likely that the process was practically complete as much as two centuries earlier. The three great parts of the Jewish Canon—the Law, the Prophets, and the Writings—were accepted as authoritative and became relatively fixed in that order: the Law (i.e., the Pentateuch:

Genesis, Exodus, Leviticus, Numbers, and Deuteronomy) during the 4th century B.C.; the Former Prophets (Joshua, Judges, 1-2 Samuel, 1-2 Kings) and the Latter Prophets (Isaiah, Jeremiah, Ezekiel, and the Twelve Minor Prophets) around 200 B.C.; and the Writings (Ruth, Psalms, Job, Proverbs, Ecclesiastes, Canticle of Canticles, Lamentations, Daniel, Esther, Ezra, Nehemiah, 1-2 Chronicles) possibly as early as 100 B.C. These are the books accepted as inspired by believing Jews.

Jewish belief and practice, however, does not automatically settle the problem of the *OT* Canon for Christians. The early Church accepted as canonical all the books listed above; it also accepted, not without debate, seven other Jewish writings (Tobit, Judith, Wisdom, Sirach, Baruch, 1-2 Maccabees) as well as additions to Daniel (3:24-90; 13; 14) and to Esther. During the 16th century the term "deuterocanonical" was coined to designate scriptural books whose canonicity had at some time been disputed. The *OT* deuterocanonical books are the seven just listed with the parts of Daniel and Esther; the *NT* deuterocanonical books are Hebrews, James, 2 Peter, 2-3 John, Jude, and Revelation. To clarify the origin and authority of the *OT* deuterocanonical books we must consider the collection in which they are found, the Septuagint.

After the conquests of Alexander the Great, Greek became the common language in much of the Near East, even in the large Jewish colonies which had grown up outside of Palestine,[6] in Egypt and elsewhere. Because Hebrew, in which most of the Jewish Scriptures had been written, was no longer familiar to these Jews, a Greek translation of their sacred books was needed. Around the middle of the 3rd century B.C. the Pentateuch was translated, and at various times the other books of the *OT* also found their way into Greek. Much of this work was done at Alexandria. The collection of the Greek translations of the Jewish Scriptures was called the Septuagint (LXX). This title was given because of an imaginative and tendentious tale that attributed the translation of the Pentateuch to 72 Jewish scholars who, working independently, produced 72 identical versions. The LXX became the Bible of the Jews of the Greek-speaking world. It included some writings that were never part of the Hebrew collection—the seven books already named, and a few others. Some had originally been written in Hebrew (Sirach, 1 Maccabees, Tobit, Judith), while others had been composed in Greek (Wisdom, 2 Maccabees).

It is difficult to know exactly what authority was attributed to the deuterocanonical books by the Greek-speaking Jews. The term "Alexandrian Canon," sometimes applied to the Septuagint collection, is misleading if it is taken to mean that the Jews of the Diaspora

---

[6] The term Diaspora (also Dispersion) is often used to designate, collectively, the Jews living outside of Palestine.

recognized as sacred and authoritative books which the Palestinian Jews did not. These books are never cited by Jews with the technical formula "It is written . . ." Nevertheless, they were widely known and highly esteemed. Sirach was frequently quoted by the rabbis, and fragments of Sirach and Tobit have been found at Qumran. Passages from some of them (Sirach, Wisdom, 2 Maccabees) are alluded to by *NT* writers.

The early Church adopted the Septuagint as its (*OT*) Bible. In so doing it was following the lead given by the apostles and other *NT* writers; not only did they borrow from deuterocanonical books, but they usually employed the Septuagint in giving quotations from the *OT*. St. Paul's early missionary activity was carried out among Greek-speaking Jews; the Bible they knew and which he used in preaching to them was the Septuagint. The early Christian writers generally cited the deuterocanonical books as Scripture and listed them among the books of the Canon.

There were, however, some dissenting voices, especially in the East; among these were Melito of Sardis, Athanasius, Cyril of Jerusalem, and Jerome. The Council of Laodicea in Phrygia (362 A.D.?) listed only the books of the Hebrew Bible as canonical. St. Jerome was the first to call these books "Apocrypha"—a term intended to suggest a mysterious origin, not a spurious character. Nevertheless, in saying that he included these books in his Vulgate translation because of the orders of the bishops (*Prologus in Tobiam*), he shows that his position is not the official one. That there should have been hesitations concerning the Canon is not surprising, for the Church had made no authoritative declaration on the matter.

Such doubts found little place in the West. In agreement with St. Augustine, the Councils of Hippo (393) and Carthage (397 and 419) listed the deuterocanonical books in the Canon. These were local councils, so their decisions were not binding for the universal Church; but they did help settle the matter. Before the end of the 7th century the Council in Trullo (692) adopted for the East the Canon as listed by Carthage. The Council of Florence published the same Canon in 1441. As noted above, the Council of Trent settled the matter for Catholics with a final, binding decision.

THE THEOLOGICAL QUESTION. The Church, in admitting a book into the Canon, declares it to be inspired. It is legitimate to ask how the Church comes to know that a particular book is inspired. This, however, is not an easy question to answer. Various solutions have been proposed. In the past some authors regarded prophetic or apostolic origin as an indication of the inspired character of a writing; others postulated a revelation of all the inspired books before the close of public revelation at the end of the apostolic age. But both explanations present serious difficulties. Before the first could be considered acceptable, it would have to be demonstrated that every work produced by a prophet or an apostle is necessarily inspired; then it would be necessary to demonstrate that each book of the Canon had such an origin. In fact, it would be difficult to establish either of these propositions. The theory of an explicit revelation of the list of inspired books also presents difficulties, for it is contradicted by the long hesitations of so many important teachers over a long period of time. If *they* didn't know of such a revelation, who did? how did it finally come to light?

These two theories, then, appear to be very imperfect explanations of how the Church recognized the inspired nature of a given book, and few today would care to defend either of them. Yet no other solution has been widely adopted. It would seem that the answer should be sought along the lines suggested by Rahner, whose theory of inspiration was mentioned above. Rahner, while leaving an open question the actual mechanism of inspiration, holds that God becomes the author of Scripture (analogously, of course, as in any acceptable theory) by calling into being the apostolic Church;[7] and in so doing, He wills and (mediately) produces the *NT* Scriptures, one of the constitutive elements of the Church. The recognition of the inspired character of the Scriptures can come only through revelation, he holds, but this needn't be in the form of a definitive list. Rather, the revelation is given by the fact that the writing in question emerges as a genuine self-expression of the primitive Church; this occurred before the end of the apostolic age, during which the *NT* writings were produced. The rational and explicit acknowledgment that a certain writing is inspired, may come only after a time and after discussion, when the Church recognizes that it accords with her nature and constitutes part of her very being, so to speak. Primarily, Rahner's explanation regards the *NT*; he thinks that it can be extended to the *OT*, however, in that these earlier writings form the Church's prehistory and were willed and inspired by God to that very end.

Much remains obscure, yet it should not be difficult to grant that the Church, in which the Holy Spirit resides and through which He acts, is enabled to recognize the writings which are the work of the Spirit and to proclaim them as such. The role of the Spirit in the process by which the Church recognizes and acknowledges the Scriptures must not be neglected. As Synave-Benoit say: "The fact is that between the stage of human inquiry and that of dogmatic promulgation there intervenes the action of the Holy Spirit which guarantees the defined truth against all error."[8] It is important to note that the Church does determine the Canon on her own authority and does not

[7] "Apostolic Church" is not a wholly satisfactory translation of Rahner's *Urkirche*; "embryonic Church" might be more accurate, since he seems to envision a stage from which the Church passes to mature stature by a process of development.

[8] P. Synave and P. Benoit, *Prophecy and Inspiration*, tr. A. Dulles and T. Sheridan (New York: Desclee Company, 1961), p. 87.

receive it from any other body. Thus, even concerning the Canon of the *OT,* Jewish practice alone is not the basis for her faith. She neither restricted herself to the books found in the Hebrew Bible, nor accepted all those of the Septuagint, for there are certain writings normally included in the Septuagint collection which have never been received as canonical by the Church.[9]

PROTESTANTS AND THE DEUTEROCANONICAL BOOKS. For the *NT,* Protestants accept all the books that Catholics do; but for the *OT,* they reject the deuterocanonical books and restrict themselves to the Hebrew Canon.

Historically the rejection of these books by Protestants goes back to Luther; he denied their inspiration, but considered them useful reading and so included them in an appendix to the Bible. He followed St. Jerome's lead in calling them Apocrypha, a term regularly used for them by Protestants.[10] The practice of giving these books in an appendix was widely followed for a time, but from the 17th century on they were often dropped completely. In modern times this trend has been reversed. The Chicago Bible[11] is named *"The Complete Bible"* because "it has been truly said that no one can have the complete Bible . . . without the Apocrypha. From the earliest Christian times . . . they belonged to the Bible; . . . historically and culturally they are still an integral part of the Bible" (p. v.). The Revised Standard Version (*RSV*) is available with the Apocrypha as well as without, as is *Today's English Version,* the translation of The American Bible Society.

It can be seen, then, that the Apocrypha have a somewhat privileged position among Protestants. If they are considered non-canonical, at least they are distinguished from books which were never part of either the Hebrew Bible or the Septuagint.[12] Some Protestant authors are willing to go farther than this. Sigmund Mowinckel, for example, writes as follows:

> Instead of discussing whether something is to be cut out of the Canon . . . there may be more point in asking whether the Protestant churches have not made a mistake in gradually cutting the ties between the so-called "canonical" and the so-called "apocryphal" writings of the Old Testament; for the Apocrypha belonged to Paul's Bible, and the early Church's Greek Septuagint, and there are many indications that they were authoritative writings in the circles in which Jesus grew up and

[9]1 Esdras (3 Esdras), the Prayer of Manasseh, and the Psalms of Solomon, at least.

[10]It is to be noted that the term "Apocrypha," as used by Protestants, includes all the writings of the LXX collection not found in the Hebrew Bible, including those mentioned in the previous note. The term is, therefore, slightly more inclusive than "deuterocanonical" applied to the *OT.*

[11]*The Complete Bible: An American Translation,* translated by J. M. P. Smith, E. J. Goodspeed, *et al.* (Chicago: University of Chicago Press, 1939).

[12]Certain early non-canonical writings which imitate the style of Scripture are called Pseudepigrapha by Protestants; Catholics designate such books as "apocryphal."

by which, humanly speaking, his mind was formed. The Roman Catholic Church, therefore, has maintained that the Apocrypha, too, are inspired writings.[13]

H. H. Rowley concedes that "with the Protestant Churches, rejection [of the Apocrypha] has never been universal and absolute,"[14] while C. H. Dodd asks, "Who would not give the Book of Esther for Ecclesiasticus?"[15] It is to be hoped that still greater accord in this matter may be reached by Protestants and Catholics.

[13]*The Old Testament as the Word of God*, tr. R. B. Bjornard (New York-Nashville: Abingdon Press, 1959), pp. 112–13.

[14]*The Growth of the Old Testament*, p. 172.

[15]*The Authority of the Bible* (rev. ed.: New York-Evanston: Harper & Row, Publishers, 1962), p. 155.

READING SUGGESTIONS

JBC §66-67. "Bible, II (Inspiration)" and "Bible, III (Canon)" in *NCE. MTES* 1-44

Achtemeier, P. J., *The Inspiration of Scripture: Problems and Proposals*. Philadelphia: Westminster Press, 1980.

Barr, J., *Fundamentalism*. Philadelphia: Westminster Press, 1978.

_____, *Holy Scripture. Canon, Authority, Criticism*. Philadelphia: Westminster Press, 1982.

Greenspahn, F. E., ed., *Scripture in the Jewish and Christian Traditions: Authority, Interpretation, Relevance*. Nashville: Abingdon Press, 1982.

Moran, G., *Theology of Revelation*. New York: Herder and Herder, 1966.

Rahner, K., *Inspiration in the Bible*, tr. C. H. Henkey, New York: Herder and Herder, 1961.

Vawter, B., *Biblical Inspiration*. Philadelphia: Westminster Press, 1972.

Brown, R. E., "'And the Lord Said'? Biblical Reflections on Scripture as the Word of God," *Theological Studies* 42 (1981) 3-19.

_____, "The Meaning of the Bible," *TD* 28 (1980) 305-20.

Burtness, J. H., ed., "The Bible as Scripture," *Word & World* 1 (1981) 99-188.

Lohfink, N., "The Inerrancy and the Unity of Scripture," *TD* 13 (1965) 185-92.

McKenzie, J. L., "The Social Character of Inspiration," *Myths and Realities*, pp. 59-69.

Stevenson, D. E., "How a Writing Becomes Scripture," *Lexington Theological Quarterly* 17 (1982) 59-66.

Vogels, W., "Inspiration in a Linguistic Mode," *BTB* 15 (1985) 87-93.

Appendix II

Interpretation of Scripture:
The Church and The Individual

IF YOU have ever struggled with one of T. S. Eliot's less pellucid compositions, you know that literature can be difficult to interpret. Even as a purely human composition the Bible would present problems because it was produced in a culture remote from ours in time, space, language, and thought patterns. Quite apart from these considerations, the Bible presents unique difficulties because it is a unique book: the word of God in words of men. Because its message is expressed in human words, it is subject to the same methods of interpretation that apply to all human literature; but because it is also the word of God, it contains a depth of meaning that such methods alone can never plumb. Here we can at least say a few words about the roles of the Church and of individuals in the interpretation of Scripture.

Role of the Church

The people and the book which come into being in the course of redemptive history cannot be considered as separate and mutually independent effects. The book is the product of the people and the expression of its faith.[1] The Bible is and remains the possession of the Church; it is in the Church that it is cherished, preserved, and handed on.

[1] The Christian sees no basic discontinuity between Israel of the *OT* and the Christian Church. The distinction between the two testaments is that of promise and fulfillment; the continuity is provided by the unity of God's plan. The continuity of the people is also assured through the faithful remnant; see p. 171 and J. P. Comiskey, "A Remnant Will Return," *TBT* #18 (Apr. 1965) 1210-15.

The Bible is the unique and inimitable crystallization of the faith of the People of God, for the biblical authors, acting as witnesses to the faith of the community, wrote under the influence of the Holy Spirit. Nevertheless, the written word can never exhaust the breadth and the depth of the fulness of the experience of the People of God. The total experience of God by His people is the context, so to speak, in which the Bible was written, and it continues to be the context of the Bible's transmission and interpretation. This is, in part at least, what Catholics mean by tradition. We will not enter here the question of whether the content of tradition is broader than that of the Bible or not, i.e., whether or not there is revelation in tradition which is separate from and additional to that contained in the Bible (see G. Moran in "Reading suggestions"). While Vatican II left this an open question, the weight of scholarly opinion has moved in the direction of the negative answer.

Tradition, in any case, is not static but is as alive as the Church herself. Tradition comes to contain the collective wisdom of all the ages of the Church in understanding and explaining Scripture. Undoubtedly some ages have contributed more than others, but the patristic age must be given the place of eminence. In the earliest centuries of the Church, God's providence raised up the "Church Fathers," men specially renowned for scholarship, but even more for holiness, whose insights into the sense of Scripture the Church will never cease to study and ponder. The age of the great scholastics and the present age of scientific investigation have made their contributions, too. Thus even though the Church's interpretation of Scripture will normally come from the organs of the Magisterium, such interpretation is not the "invention" of a member of the hierarchy or even of the hierarchy collectively; it is the product of the whole people from the tradition of the past (apostolic, patristic, and scholastic), the investigations of modern Scripture scholars,[2] and the devout reflection of the faithful of all ages.

Tradition is a living, growing thing, and in this regard it cannot be separated from the abiding presence of the Holy Spirit in the Church. It was by the advent of the Spirit upon the little group in Jerusalem at Pentecost that the Church was founded; the Church has since spread far and wide because of the presence of the Spirit which continues to animate and direct her. The presence of the Spirit, "who spoke through the prophets" and who inspired the Scriptures, is what guarantees continual growth in understanding the Scriptures, the re-

---

[2]Cf. the words of Jean Levie: "Between historical, rigorously scientific exegesis and the ecclesiastical exegesis, any cleavage would be illegitimate and contrary to the very principles of the Church. The Church needs the work of its exegetes, historians, and philologists. She cannot do without their exertions or ignore their conclusions. She perfects their work, but in completing it, she fully accepts it." J. Levie, *The Bible, Word of God in Words of Men,* tr. S. H. Treman (New York: J. P. Kenedy & Sons, 1961), p. 301 n.

jection of explanations contrary to the true sense of Scripture, and the authenticity of explanations she makes her own.

From this, we might think it a simple matter to establish the "Catholic" interpretation of any given passage of Scripture, but such a conclusion would be false. There is no official Catholic commentary; nor, in the nature of things, could there ever been, if for no other reason than that such a commentary would fix in static pose something which must always be in dynamic growth. Neither is it always possible to arrive at a "Catholic" interpretation simply by investigating the position held by Catholic authors; counting noses would, in many cases, result merely in establishing the broad range of opinion which can exist in the Church even on important texts.

How, then, does the Church exercise the office of interpreting the Bible? No simple response is possible; even a partial answer will have to point in many directions. First, it may be said, the Church provides a framework within which the general sense of salvation history becomes clear, e.g., as in the ancient creeds. Occasionally the Church rejects as untenable, interpretations put forward by individuals; or she may define the meaning of a text, as when the Council of Trent declared John 3:5 to refer to Baptism. These cases are rare, however, and even such definitions do not exhaust the meaning of the text.

Less directly, the Church exercises her office of interpretation by encouraging and directing the efforts of her exegetes and biblical scholars. The steps taken in this field in the last 80 or 90 years have contributed greatly to the biblical renewal in the Church. In 1893 Leo XIII issued the encyclical *Providentissimus Deus*;[3] conservative and cautious in tone, this document was intended to further biblical studies in the light of sound principles and methods. The same Pope, in 1902, set up the Pontifical Biblical Commission to encourage and direct biblical studies. In 1909 Pius X established the Pontifical Biblical Institute to promote biblical studies and to train biblical scholars. A second great encyclical on biblical studies, *Spiritus Paraclitus*,[4] was issued by Benedict XV in 1920, and a third, *Divino Afflante Spiritu (DAS)*,[5] by Pius XII in 1943.

The last-named document, often termed the Magna Charta of Scripture studies, was to some extent a defense of the use of scientific methods in Bible study against the attacks of those who feared that rationalism had invaded Catholic Scripture scholarship. The Pope speaks at length of the importance of establishing the literal sense of Scripture. The genuine "spiritual" (typical) sense is also to be set forth, according to the encyclical, but flights of eloquent fancy are discouraged. In establishing the literal sense the Scripture scholar is to use all those means which are used in the study of profane writings. Special attention is given to the matter of literary forms. The Pope

³*RSS* 1–29.
⁴*RSS* 43–79.
⁵*RSS* 80–107.

refers to the difficulties which still remain and exhorts scholars to persevere in the quest for solutions. Pius XII did not "invent" the norms of interpretation here proposed, of course. But the encyclical fully approved the use of the scientific method and so defended the scholars who had already adopted it, encouraged others to do so, and disarmed critics who had been leveling charges of rationalism. On the other hand, by insisting on an exposition of Scripture "which is above all . . . theological" and on the proper use of the typical sense, patristic writings, and the analogy of faith, the Pope insured that Catholic scholarship would not deteriorate into learned irrelevance.

About twenty years later came the Pontifical Biblical Commission's instruction "On the Historical Truth of the Gospels" (1964), which distinguishes three stages in the formation of the gospels: the words and events of Jesus' public ministry; the period of the earliest apostolic preaching; and the literary activity of the evangelists. The document recognizes selection and development from the first stage that corresponds to the purposes and goals of the second and third stages. Although the instruction is directly concerned with the formation of the gospels, the development it traces has its counterpart in many areas of the *OT*. Vatican II also had its contribution to biblical studies, as we have already seen.

INDIVIDUAL INTERPRETATION

After Pius XII had described and approved the methods appropriate for arriving at a proper understanding of Scripture, he pointed out that "there are but few texts whose sense has been defined by the authority of the Church, nor are those more numerous about which the teaching of the Holy Fathers is unanimous" (*DAS,* par. 47). Since this is so, a vast field lies open for individual interpretation. I avoid the term "private interpretation" for it would suggest that the individual seeks the meaning of the Bible in seclusion, as it were, from all those helps and hints that the living Christian tradition can give. To recognize that the Bible was produced within the People of God as an expression of its faith, and that it is preserved and transmitted and interpreted within that people, is to recognize also that the faith of the community is the context in which Scripture should be interpreted. Interpretation of the Bible within the context of traditional belief, then, has regard for what is called "the analogy of faith," i.e., the internal harmony of revelation as a whole; we are persuaded that no interpretation which contradicts the truths of faith represents the mind of the author.

This interpretation, then, is not "private," even though it is exercised by the individual. It is to be noted that even the published teachings of a Catholic scholar remain as "individual," in this sense, as the understanding of a beginning student, though the scholar speaks from a broader background and fuller information. Until the student has begun to master the Semitic languages, ancient history, the findings of archeology, etc., however, he will be well-advised to look to the specialist for guidance. On any level of interpretation some knowledge of the senses of Scripture and literary forms is indispensable.

SENSES OF SCRIPTURE. *DAS* directed that "the interpreters bear in mind that their foremost and greatest endeavor should be to discern and define clearly that sense of the biblical words which is called literal" (par. 23; *RSS* 92). The literal sense has been traditionally defined as that meaning which the author intends to convey by his words. The literal sense of a passage does not always leap to the eye at the first reading. Some passages are obscure and ambiguous, and scholars need to have recourse to an exact knowledge of the original language, the literary form, the author's total background and method before arriving at an interpretation—which even then may have to remain tentative. But all these efforts are bent to answering the question, "What was the author intending to say?"; to answer that question is to find the literal sense.[6]

Our terminology has become traditional, but it is not wholly apt. "Literal" suggests a close adherence to the very letter in a wooden and mechanical way, when in fact that is not what is meant. When Jesus said that the wrong-doer is to be forgiven "seventy times seven" times, He was insisting on patient, unlimited mercy, not merely advocating 490 acts of forgiveness. Sometimes the author speaks in parable or metaphor: God is a rock of refuge, He raises up those who have fallen, the just find protection under the shadow of His wings. The literal sense is not that God is a rock or has wings, but that He aids those in need. The literal sense of Jesus' allegory of the vine (John 15) is that, in the realm of the spirit, the Christian's whole life and well-being depends on union with Jesus. This correct meaning is often called the transferred or figurative sense, but it is nevertheless the literal sense, if by that term we mean "what the author intended to say." In more recent times it has been proposed to extend the concept of the "literal sense." See the discussion below on the "fuller sense."

The problem of the *typical sense* (sometimes called the spiritual or mystical sense) is a bit thornier. Our belief in typology[7] is based on God's power so to order things that persons, events, institutions, etc., in one stage of salvation history prefigure and prepare for persons,

---

[6]Cf. the strong words of Charlier: "The deeper understanding given by the Spirit is proportional to the amount of human energy a man is prepared to put into the study of the letter. The deeper the critical study of the Bible, the deeper will be the appreciation of its thought. Without some effort, there can be no spiritual profit." C. Charlier, *The Christian Approach to the Bible*, tr. H. Richards and B. Peters (Westminster, Md.: The Newman Press, 1958), p. 266.

[7]The word comes from the Greek *typos* in its derived meaning of model or pattern.

events, institutions, etc., in a later and more definitive stage. As *DAS* stated it: "For what was said and done in the Old Testament was ordained and disposed by God with such consummate wisdom, that things past prefigure in a spiritual way those that were to come under the new dispensation of grace" (par. 26; *RSS* 93–94). Typology is based on the inner consistency of God's redemptive activity in history and on the progressive nature of His redemptive plan. Redemptive history is realized in successive acts, but the inner consistency and progressive nature of God's plan operate to produce similarities in the pattern of saving events. The meaning of the later event becomes clearer in the light of the earlier event; and the significance already contained in the earlier event becomes clearer in the light of its completion in the later one.

A good example is the exodus theme. In itself the exodus was a deliverance from bondage to an oppressive political power; but it contained the germ of God's redemptive plan and pointed forward to more wonderful deliveries from more terrible oppressions. This is seen already in the *OT,* for the prophets describe the restoration from the exile as a new exodus (e.g., Isa 43:16–21)—a restoration which is to include all the elements of messianic redemption (new covenant, gift of the spirit, forgiveness of sins, and so forth; cf. Jer 31:31–34; Ezek 36:24–32). Yet the true messianic restoration had to await the coming of Christ, whose redemptive work could be described as a new exodus of redemption from sin and death and the conferral of gifts as yet undreamed of.

The exodus includes a whole complex of types which find their corresponding fulfillments (antitypes) in Christian redemption. The paschal lamb, whose blood delivered the Israelites from the destroyer, points to the true Lamb by whose blood we are saved; the sacrificial blood of the Sinai covenant points to a new sacrifice, ratified in the sacrificial blood of Christ; the manna which was the divinely provided food of the Covenant People on their pilgrimage through the desert to the Promised Land prefigures the Eucharist; the passage through the Red Sea finds a completion in Baptism, by which a new deliverance is effected.

The identification of types, to be legitimate, must not be arbitrary. The similarity between type and antitype must consist in the essences of the things compared, not simply in details, and should express the consistency of God's activity in distinct stages of salvation history. Since typology rests, by definition, on God's intention, our knowledge of it will ordinarily come from Scripture (usually the *NT* giving meaning to the events of the *OT*), but the teachings of the Fathers and the Magisterium, as well as the practice of the liturgy, will also give direction.[8]

---

[8]*DAS* urges interpreters to seek out and expound the typical sense "provided it is clearly intended by God. For God alone could have known this spiritual meaning and have revealed it to us" (par. 26).

Typology, then, consists primarily in the relationship, intended by God, between type and antitype. We can speak of a typical sense in those passages in which types are described. The human author describes the type in terms of the meaning it has for him, and this is the literal sense. The typical sense is the meaning the text is seen to have after the appearance of the antitype and the revelation of the relationship between the two.

Some authors postulate also a *fuller sense* (or *sensus plenior*). Although those who propose it do not always agree on how it is to be explained and classified, it may be defined as that deeper, more complete meaning which a Scripture text takes on for us in the light of later revelation, a meaning intended by God the principal author, but not clearly intended by the human author. Some examples will clarify what is intended. In the *OT* there is frequent mention of the "spirit of the Lord." The term often signifies a force or power from God which enables a man to accomplish what he could not do by his own power. But because it is described as distinct from the One who sends it, because to it are attributed guidance, revelation, prophecy (Num 11:17; Ezek 8:3; Zech 7:12) and the work of sanctification (Ezek 11:19; 36:27), and because it is sometimes described in personal terms (Isa 63:10), it so wonderfully anticipates the *NT* revelation of the Holy Spirit and His work that it is tempting to see Him alluded to even in the *OT* texts. Indeed, the *NT* writers sometimes do this (cf. Joel 3:1–4 with Acts 2:1–21). Again, the Davidic King, vehicle of the messianic promises, is sometimes designated as God's son (2 Sam 7:14; Ps 2:7). The reference in the *OT* was to adoptive sonship, but when, in the *NT,* the Messiah is revealed as God's Son in the fullest sense, a new meaning is seen in the *OT* texts. In Isa 7:14 the symbolic name Immanuel (God with us) is given a Davidic King yet to appear. The prophet knew nothing of the mystery of the Incarnation, but thought of one who would be the vehicle of the saving power of God; yet when the Incarnation is revealed, the words take on a new significance for us.

It will be seen that the fuller sense resembles the typical sense. Some authors do classify it with the typical sense, placing both typical and fuller sense in the general category of spiritual or secondary sense. Others hold that the human author must have at least a vague knowledge of the fuller sense and so classify it under the literal sense. (It should be obvious that if the fuller sense did not go beyond the *clear* consciousness of the human author, it would simply coincide with the literal sense.)

The fuller sense must be close to the literal meaning, so that the words are not used in an entirely different sense, and it must be a development of what was literally said in the text. Further, as in the case of the typical sense, there must be some authoritative basis for stating that there is a deeper sense in a given passage. Leo XIII seems to have had something like the fuller sense in mind when he wrote in *Providentissimus Deus:* "There is sometimes in such passages a fullness and a hidden depth of meaning which the letter hardly expresses and which the laws of interpretation hardly warrant."[9]

The authors who deny the existence of the fuller sense do so in part because the theory seems to them to neglect hard-won insights into the incarnational nature of inspiration and the role of the human author. If God really produces an inspired book through the instrumentality of the human author so that the entire book is the product of both God and man, how is it possible to speak of a meaning that would be intended by God but not intended (at least not clearly) by the human author? If the Bible is the word of God in words of men, how can there be a sense of the text that the "men" did not intend?[10] The concept of communication, too, demands that the meaning of the text is that which the writer intended, not just any meaning that the words will lend themselves to. These authors do not, of course, deny the deeper meaning that the *OT* takes on for the Christian in the light of *NT* revelation, but they explain it differently: they maintain that the message intended by God and expressed in human words at a given stage in redemptive history takes on added dimension when it is seen within a larger context through progress in revelation and the unfolding of God's plan. The fuller meaning would thus be seen in the conjunction and comparison of texts, rather than contained in the earlier text taken by itself. Since the fuller sense is obviously closely bound up with an explanation of inspiration based on the analogy of instrumental causality, those who reject the latter will also look askance at the theory of the fuller sense, at least in its classical formulation. Thus Vawter has suggested that a more sophisticated concept of the fuller sense may be defended by an appeal to linguistic analysis: "Language has a force and meaning of its own, so that there is an interaction of the user and the used. Even if he would an author could not exclude from language the fullness of meaning that it possesses and has acquired from its own dynamism, when he makes use of it" (*Biblical Inspiration*, p. 116). Sandra Schneiders argues that the believing interpreter interacts with the text to find a meaning that is in fact in the text, even though it goes beyond the intention of the author; this is part of its *literal* sense. (See article listed at end of Appendix II.)

Both schools of thought seem agreed that their differences are in the realm of theory rather than of practice and that their approaches to exegesis and biblical theology are not notably different. In any case, whether we speak of a "fuller sense" or a "fuller understanding," these studies underline the progressive nature of revelation, the homogeneity of its development, and the unity of the two testaments.

---

[9]*RSS* 14.

[10]The same problem does not arise for the typical sense, at least not so acutely, for in typology the special meaning intended by God but not perceived by the human author is primarily in the "thing" itself, only in a derived or secondary manner in the text.

LITERARY FORMS. "I have been assured by a very knowing American of my acquaintance in London," wrote Jonathan Swift, "that a young healthy child well nursed is at a year old a most delicious, nourishing, and wholesome food, whether stewed, roasted, baked, or boiled; and I make no doubt that it will equally serve in a fricassee or a ragout." Whether we conclude that Swift wrote *A Modest Proposal* from cannibalistic or from humanitarian interest will depend on our identification of the literary form he employed—an identification not correctly made, it is said, by some of his scandalized contemporaries. The example illustrates a point: unless we take into account the literary form employed by the author, we are in danger of mistaking his meaning.

Literary form (genre) may be defined as the method and style of expression adopted by an author as apt for achieving the end for which he writes.[11] In some cases poetry achieves his end better than prose, apocalyptic (p. 253) better than history. We are all familiar with a number of literary forms, though we may never have consciously classified them. The broadest division of literature, into prose and poetry, is partly on the basis of form, and the phrase "poetic license" reminds us that flights of fancy are more usual in poetry than in prose. A list of literary forms we are familiar with would include such items as news report, news analysis, editorial, detective novel, historical novel, history manual, epic poem, satire, science fiction, political speech, war bulletin, shaggy-dog story, love letter, and comic strip. All of them are potential vehicles of truth; obviously some are more apt than others. Each has its own rules and diction; eyes and lips are described differently in love letters than in anatomy textbooks. Some literary forms are tied to a particular time and culture, while others are timeless and universal. In the Bible we find some forms unknown in our society and others that are familiar to us.

The closer attention now given to literary form has had a salutary effect on Scripture studies. Once it seemed taken for granted that the Bible in all its parts ought to combine the exactness of a scientific history with the precision of a dogma manual, and this raised unnecessary difficulties for biblical inerrancy. *DAS* insists on identification of literary form as an essential technique of interpretation: "the interpreter must...determine what modes of writing, so to speak, the authors of that ancient period would be likely to use, and in fact did use" (par. 35; *RSS* 97). Only by investigation can these be established: "What those exactly were the commentator cannot determine as it were in advance, but only after a careful examination of the ancient literature of the East"

---

[11] Although *literary* form would seem necessarily to imply writing, too much emphasis should not be placed on this aspect; many compositions (e.g., political speeches, epic poems) are used for both oral and written communication. Many pieces of great "literature" had a long oral tradition before being committed to writing, e.g., Homer's *Iliad*. This is true of most of the Bible.

(par. 36; *RSS* 97-98). The criterion of what may be admitted is exceedingly broad: "For of the modes of expression which, among ancient peoples, and especially those of the East, human language used to express its thought, none is excluded from the Sacred Books, provided the way of speaking adopted in no wise contradicts the holiness and truth of God" (par. 37; *RSS* 98).

It would be impossible to give a complete or even truly adequate division of the literary forms employed in the Bible; even the broad division into prose and poetry is of limited help because Hebrew poetry differs so much from that of western cultures (p. 220) and because Hebrew prose often exhibits poetic characteristics. The frequently-made division of the *OT* Canon into historical, prophetic, and wisdom books is a rough reflection of literary form, but the classifications are so broad as to be misleading. Only at the expense of calling fiction "history" and grouping together such diversely structured compositions as Job, Canticle of Canticles, and Proverbs, can it be used. We can, indeed, attempt to classify individual books on the basis of literary form. Thus, under "historical" (when the designation is properly understood) we can easily place 1-2 Samuel, 1-2 Kings, Ezra, Nehemiah, 1 Maccabees, and, less easily, Exodus, Numbers, Joshua, Judges, and 2 Maccabees; under "prophetic" we can place Isaiah, Jeremiah, Ezekiel, and most of the Minor Prophets; we can call Tobit, Esther, and Judith "edifying fiction." Job is a didactic poem in dialogue form, while some other Wisdom books are collections of maxims (Proverbs, Sirach). Daniel is largely apocalyptic in form.

Yet even this distribution oversimplifies, for the materials found within some of these books are quite diverse. Many of the prophetic books, for example, contain biographical and historical material in addition to prophetic oracles; even the prophetic oracles can be classified into a number of types. A proper discussion of literary form, therefore, must go beyond the mere classification of individual books.

It is the merit of Form Criticism (p. 8) that it recognized the need to isolate smaller unities within the books and to classify them according to literary form. The range of these literary unities is almost as broad as the human spirit itself. In addition to forms already mentioned, we find parable, allegory, family legend, myth, etiology,[12] war chant, dirge, legislative collection, love song, genealogy, and midrash (p. 247). Some of these are cast in verse form, but examples of most of them can be found in books predominantly prose. The longer compositions this book normally concerns itself with are more intelligible when we recognize the earlier pieces their author has incorporated into them.

---

[12]An etiology is a story intended to explain how something came to be or reached its present state.

Some of the forms mentioned need no explanation; others are treated in the appropriate places. Here we take up the question of historical narrative, a form which bulks large both in extent and importance.

The designation of certain *OT* books as "historical" is necessary, but it can also lead to misunderstanding. The term evokes the concept of a scientific discipline which was unknown until fairly recent times—something which isn't found in the Bible at all. It is necessary, nevertheless, for much of the Bible does deal with a real people and with the concrete events by which their story became redemptive history for all of mankind. The authors of Israel did intend to tell the story of the past, but they told it for the sake of what it revealed of God's work, not simply for its own sake. The name given in the Hebrew Canon to an important group of books (Joshua, Judges, Samuel, and Kings), "The Former Prophets," is significant, for it suggests that the events recounted in them already bear the prophetic interpretation of history. The interpretation is contained in the very way the story is told, rather than being added as commentary. A scientifically objective report was not what these authors were aiming at.

Some narratives come closer to the modern idea of history than others. The degree of historical accuracy in a given writing will depend in large measure on two factors: the author's intention and the sources at his disposal. For example, the author of Joshua had only fragmentary accounts of various phases of the invasion, and his reconstruction of the action was highly theological. On the other hand, much of 2 Samuel is a contemporary account of the affairs of David; the author's deep faith saw God's design so clearly in the events themselves that little embellishment was felt necessary.

During the relatively stable period of the monarchy the sources were far more adequate from an historical point of view than from any period before or most periods after. In practice there was great latitude in all periods with regard to the materials utilized. Not only were contemporary accounts and royal archives used when they were available, but tribal legends, hero stories, cult legends, and other sources were also used. Many were popular in nature and had a long history of oral transmission.

The incorporation of such sources into an inspired work makes them neither better nor worse as historical records. On the one hand we have learned to esteem more highly than before the accuracy of oral tradition in the ancient Near East. In cultures where this was almost the only method of preserving the story of the past, the group memory was far more tenacious than we might imagine. The patriarchal narratives in Genesis, for example, reflect customs of a society long dead by the time they were first written down, details whose significance the Israelites no longer understood, but which they still transmitted as part of the tradition. On the other hand, the very process of oral transmission was selective and formative: only significant, meaningful items were preserved, and even these were recast so as to underline what was considered significant. Thus, to resume the example given above, the stories Israel remembered about the Patriarchs took on new meaning for them in the light of the exodus and the conquest, and this is made clear in the very telling of the stories.

Even when the sources approach the quality required by modern history, the intention of the biblical authors will still be notably different; the biblical books are confessional documents written to celebrate God's gracious deeds.

In practice it is necessary to appraise each passage on its own merits, asking what sources the author used and what his intention was. On the basis of the answers to these questions, some narratives are given special classifications, such as "primeval history" for Genesis 1-11 and "epic history" for Exodus and Joshua. The characteristics of these narratives are discussed where these sections are treated.

To concentrate solely on determining the degree of factual accuracy, however, would be a misplacement of emphasis. Modern history deals only with secondary causes that can be seen at work and recorded; we may try to determine God's plan in the events, but this is only guesswork. The scriptural authors, on the other hand, dealt with secondary causes only to the extent that they saw revealed in them God's saving activity. If we rule out revelation, the Bible is robbed of all but an academic interest, for the interpretation of the biblical authors then becomes nothing more than speculation. Israel's story is unique in its insistence on the hand of God and His saving will in her history. Israel might have exalted herself for the mighty deeds performed within her; instead she recognized that it was God who acted and that her own response had always been inadequate. "Not to us, O Lord, not to us but to your name give glory" (Ps 115:1); so was Israel wont to express her sense of wonder, gratitude, and humility at the work God wrought in her.

READING SUGGESTIONS

JBC §71. *Divino Afflante Spiritu, RSS* 80-107. "Bible, VI (Exegesis)," "Bible, VII (Papal Teaching)" in *NCE. MTES* 60-71, 295-308.

Amerding, C. E., *The Old Testament and Criticism.* Grand Rapids: Eerdmans, 1983.

Boys, M. C., *Biblical Interpretation in Religious Education: A Study of the Kerygmatic Era* (Birmingham: Religious Education Press, 1980).

Brown, R. E., *The Critical Meaning of the Bible. How a Modern Reading of the Bible Challenges Christians, the Church, and the Churches.* New York: Paulist Press, 1981.

Cumming, J., and Burns, P., eds., *The Bible Now. Its Meaning and Use for Christians Today.* New York: Seabury Press, 1981.

Goldingay, J., *Approaches to Old Testament Interpretation*. Downers Grove, Ill.: InterVarsity Press, 1981.

Moran, G., *Scripture and Tradition*. New York: Herder and Herder, 1963.

Reventlow, H. G., *The Authority of the Bible and the Rise of the Modern World*. Philadelphia Press, 1985.

Vawter, B. , *Biblical Inspiration*, pp. 113-31.

Anderson, B. W., "Tradition and Scripture in the Community of Faith," *JBL* 100 (1981) 5-21.

Barr, J., "The Old Testament and the New Crisis of Biblical Authority," *Int* 25 (1971) 24-40.

Malina, B. J., "The Social Sciences and Biblical Interpretation," *Int* 36 (1982) 229-42.

Montague, G. T., "The Process of Interpreting the Bible," *BTB* 20 (1982) 38-44.

Sakenfeld, K. D., "Old Testament Perspectives: Methodological Issues," *Journal for the Study of the Old Testament* 22 (1982) 13-20.

Schneiders, S. M., "Faith, Hermeneutics, and the Literal Sense of Scripture," *Theological Studies* 39 (1978) 719-36.

_____, "From Exegesis to Hermeneutics: The Problem of the Contemporary Meaning of Scripture," *Horizons* 8 (1981) 23-39.

Stendahl, K., "The Bible as a Classic and the Bible as Holy Scripture," *JBL* 103; (1984) 3-10.

Vawter, B., "The Fuller Sense: Some Considerations," *CBQ* 26 (1964) 85-96.

CHRONOLOGICAL CHART

	Prophets	Events of Israel's History	Other Relevant Events
2000 B.C.			Amorite migrations in Mesopotamia and Syria beginning ca. 2000
1900 B.C.			
1800 B.C.		Call of Abraham ca. 1850 (?)	Hyksos invade Egypt beginning 1720
1700 B.C.		Jacob migrates to Egypt	
1600 B.C.			
1500 B.C.			Hyksos expelled from Egypt
1400 B.C.			Amarna Period 1376–1350
1300 B.C.		Exodus ca. 1280	Ramses II 1290–1224 (Egypt) Kingdoms of Edom and Moab founded Egyptian-Hittite "eternal treaty" 1270
		Invasion of Canaan ca. 1240	

Note: A question mark (?) signifies that the chronology of the item is seriously disputed.

Date	Prophets	Events of Israel's History	Other Relevant Events
1200 B.C.		*PERIOD OF THE JUDGES* →	Merneptah's stele ca. 1220
			First wave of Sea Peoples engage Egypt
			Hittite Empire falls
			Philistines established in Palestine
1100 B.C.	*EARLY PROPHETS*		
	Samuel		
		Samuel *MONARCHY*	
	Earliest ecstatic groups	Saul 1020–1000	
1000 B.C.		David 1000–961	
	Nathan		
	Gad	Solomon 961–922	

290

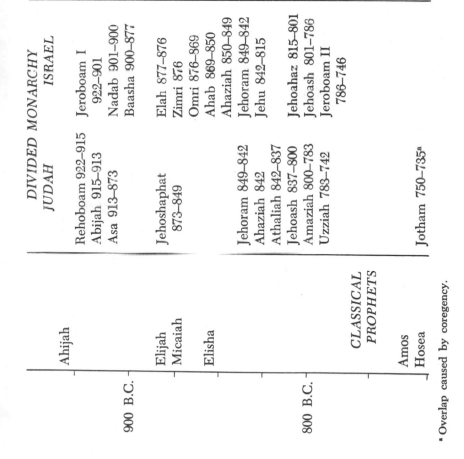

DIVIDED MONARCHY

JUDAH	ISRAEL
Rehoboam 922–915	Jeroboam I 922–901
Abijah 915–913	Nadab 901–900
Asa 913–873	Baasha 900–877
Jehoshaphat 873–849	Elah 877–876
	Zimri 876
	Omri 876–869
	Ahab 869–850
	Ahaziah 850–849
Jehoram 849–842	Jehoram 849–842
Ahaziah 842	Jehu 842–815
Athaliah 842–837	
Jehoash 837–800	Jehoahaz 815–801
Amaziah 800–783	Jehoash 801–786
Uzziah 783–742	Jeroboam II 786–746
Jotham 750–735[a]	

CLASSICAL PROPHETS

Ahijah

Elijah
Micaiah

Elisha

Amos
Hosea

900 B.C.

800 B.C.

[a] Overlap caused by coregency.

291

Prophets	Events of Israel's History	Other Relevant Events
Isaiah Micah	Ahaz 735–715 Hezekiah 715–687	Assyrian expansion under Tiglath-pileser III (745–727) Assyria crushes anti-Assyrian league and strips Northern Kingdom of territories 734–732
	Zechariah 746–745 Shallum 745 Menahem 745–738 Pekahiah 738–737 Pekah 737–732 Hoshea 732–724 Fall of Samaria and exile of Israel 721	
		Assyria ravages Judah; Jerusalem spared 701
Zephaniah Jeremiah Nahum	Manasseh 687–642 Amon 642–640 Josiah 640–609	Babylonia throws off Assyrian rule 626 Fall of Nineveh 612
Habakkuk (?)	Jehoahaz 609 Jehoiakim 609–598	
Ezekiel	Jehoiachin 597 Zedekiah 597–587 Fall of Jerusalem and beginning of Exile 587	
Obadiah (?)		
Deutero-Isaiah	Return from Exile 538	Rise of Cyrus begins 556 Fall of Babylon 539
Haggai Zechariah		

700 B.C.

600 B.C.

292

Date	Biblical writings	Events	
500 B.C.	Trito-Isaiah (?)	New Temple dedicated 515	
	Malachi	Ezra's mission 458	
		Nehemiah's first mission 445	
		Nehemiah's second mission 432	
400 B.C.	Joel (?)		
	Deutero-Zechariah (?)		Alexander conquers Near East 334–323
300 B.C.			
200 B.C.		Palestine passes under Syrian dominion 198	Antiochus IV 175–163
		Persecution of Antiochus IV	
		Maccabean uprising 166	
100 B.C.		Syro-Palestine incorporated into Roman Empire 63	

INDEX

A. GENERAL*

*Author references do not include works cited by abbreviation and page number alone at the beginning of "Reading Suggestions" lists.

295

B. Brief Selection
of Scripture References

NEW TESTAMENT MESSAGE

A Biblical-Theological Commentary

Editors: Wilfrid Harrington, O.P. & Donald Senior, C.P.

"This series outstrips anything else available at its level, converting what the preface calls 'an avalanche of Biblical scholarship' into understandable and relevant textual commentary... This new series sets something of a standard among the compact commentaries designed for a general audience. Certainly no other is so complete and up-to date."

Erasmus Hort, *The Bible Book*